Lecture Notes in Computer Science 8830

Commenced Publication in 1973
Founding and Former Series Editors:
Gerhard Goos, Juris Hartmanis, and Jan van Leeuwen

T0212952

Georgios Paltoglou   Fernando Loizides
Preben Hansen (Eds.)

Professional Search in the Modern World

COST Action IC1002
on Multilingual and Multifaceted
Interactive Information Access

 Springer

Volume Editors

Georgios Paltoglou
University of Wolverhampton
Faculty of Science and Engineering
School of Mathematics and Computer Science
Wolverhampton, UK
E-mail: g.paltoglou@wlv.ac.uk

Fernando Loizides
Cyprus University of Technology
Department of Multimedia and Graphic Arts
Limassol, Cyprus
E-mail: fernando.loizides@cut.ac.cy

Preben Hansen
Stockholm University
Department of Computer and Systems Sciences
Kista, Sweden
E-mail: preben@dsv.su.se

ISSN 0302-9743   e-ISSN 1611-3349
ISBN 978-3-319-12510-7   e-ISBN 978-3-319-12511-4
DOI 10.1007/978-3-319-12511-4
Springer Cham Heidelberg New York Dordrecht London
Library of Congress Control Number: 2014952663

LNCS Sublibrary: SL 3 – Information Systems and Application, incl. Internet/Web
and HCI

Neither the COST Office nor any person acting on its behalf is responsible for the use which might be
made of the information contained in this publication. The COST Office is not responsible for the external
websites referred to in this publication.

Typesetting: Camera-ready by author, data conversion by Scientific Publishing Services, Chennai, India

Printed on acid-free paper

Springer is part of Springer Science+Business Media (www.springer.com)

COST - European Cooperation in Science and Technology is an intergovernmental framework aimed at facilitating the collaboration and networking of scientists and researchers at European level. It was established in 1971 by 19 member countries and currently includes 35 member countries across Europe, and Israel as a cooperating state.

COST funds pan-European, bottom-up networks of scientists and researchers across all science and technology fields. These networks, called 'COST Actions', promote international coordination of nationally-funded research.

By fostering the networking of researchers at an international level, COST enables break-through scientific developments leading to new concepts and products, thereby contributing to strengthening Europe's research and innovation capacities.

COST's mission focuses in particular on:

- Building capacity by connecting high quality scientific communities throughout Europe and worldwide;
- Providing networking opportunities for early career investigators;
- Increasing the impact of research on policy makers, regulatory bodies and national decision makers as well as the private sector.

Through its inclusiveness, COST supports the integration of research communities, leverages national research investments and addresses issues of global relevance.

Every year thousands of European scientists benefit from being involved in COST Actions, allowing the pooling of national research funding to achieve common goals.

As a precursor of advanced multidisciplinary research, COST anticipates and complements the activities of EU Framework Programmes, constituting a "bridge" towards the scientific communities of emerging countries. In particular, COST Actions are also open to participation by non-European scientists coming from neighbour countries (for example Albania, Algeria, Armenia, Azerbaijan, Belarus, Egypt, Georgia, Jordan, Lebanon, Libya, Moldova, Montenegro, Morocco, the Palestinian Authority, Russia, Syria, Tunisia and Ukraine) and from a number of international partner countries.

COST's budget for networking activities has traditionally been provided by successive EU RTD Framework Programmes. COST is currently executed by the European Science Foundation (ESF) through the COST Office on a mandate by the European Commission, and the framework is governed by a Committee of Senior Officials (CSO) representing all its 35 member countries.

More information about COST is available at www.cost.eu.

 ESF Provides the COST Office through an EC contract

 COST is supported by the EU RTD Framework Programme

Preface

The effectiveness and speed of current search engine technology that enables search engines to respond to millions of user queries on a continuous basis is one of the greatest successes in computing. Despite their success, the next decade presents even greater challenges as the number of Web users, and subsequently the volume of requests they have to satisfy, continues to increase and new technologies, such as mobile devices, social web, etc., become even more dominant. These will result in creating a digital environment where search technology must be able to filter, extract, integrate, deliver, and present multilingual and multimodal information to an even wider global audience using a variety of means and devices. Subsequently, multilingual and multifaceted interactive information access research will be a key part of the next generation of search engine systems.

The objective of this book is to discuss and review recent outstanding research in all such related aspects, with a particular interest in professional and enterprise search. It aims to present in a unified way material that has been published fragmentedly in journals and conferences in a diverse set of research areas, including information retrieval (IR), natural language processing (NLP), and human computer interaction (HCI), to mention but a few. It was prepared as the final publication of the COST Action IC1002 on Multilingual and Multifaceted Interactive Information Access (MUMIA) whose objective is to launch an initiative to coordinate the collaboration between these disciplines that will play a key part in the conception and development of the next generation of search technology.

The contributions were collected by initially distributing a call for extended chapter abstracts to the COST consortium (which includes 80+ participants[1] from all over the world) with a deadline of August 2013. These were reviewed for their quality and relevance to the action's general aims and objectives by the book editors, and the authors of selected submissions were asked to provide fully anonymized, full chapters by the end of January 2014. The submissions underwent a two-phase, double-blind peer-review process: After the initial full chapter submission and evaluation by reviewers, authors were given a month to reply, amend their contributions, and submit their updated drafts. These were re-evaluated by the reviewers, who were asked to make a binary decision on whether the contribution should be accepted in the final volume. Finally, at the end of this process, 12 chapters were accepted for publication.

---

[1] http://www.mumia-network.eu/index.php/the-action/participants
This publication is supported by COST.

The book editors wish to thank the reviewers for their rigorous work and invaluable assistance in producing the volume. We are also very grateful to the authors for entrusting their excellent work to us and for their patience in preparing the chapters of the book.

August 2014

Georgios Paltoglou
Fernando Loizides
Preben Hansen

Table of Contents

Patent Search

An Introduction to Professional Search

John I. Tait

johntait.net Ltd.

Today, in the early 21st century, for most people, if one talks about "search" people tend to automatically think of the use of modern internet search engines like Google, Bing!, Baidu or Yandex. Further people think of either general members of the public, or people whose primary job function is not search, undertaking the searches. However, for most of the history of information retrieval, searching has been done by professional information specialists, whose training and skills were and are focussed on locating and retrieving information for and on behalf of others. This volume is focussed on recent research, principally undertaken in the context of the EU-funded COST network MUMIA, reviewing new, mainly technological, research intended to address the needs of professional searchers.

Professional search is defined by the fact that the searchers are undertaking the searches on a professional, paid, basis, as opposed to of their own volition on a voluntary basis out of personal interest. Typically, professional searchers are provided with a brief of some sort ("Find enforceable Indian patents relating to the use of nor epinephrine reuptake inhibitors in the treatment of depression") together with a budget in time or money.

This has two main consequences for the professional searchers methods of working. First, it generates various potential additional sources of error: they may misunderstand the brief, for example because of a lack of technical or legal expertise; or they may not properly understand the notions of relevance for retrieved documents which may be required by their clients; or as here, the brief does not select the collections to be searched or the search mechanisms to be used.

Second, the notion of a budget limits the amount of time which may be spent in query formulation and in results review. All searches are time limited in practice: no one has an infinite amount of time to search for a piece of information. However, in practice amateur searches are on the one hand quite flexible in the amount of time which may be used for query formulation, and on the other hand almost always very short (minutes): perhaps one or two reformulated queries and the review of a couple of screen fulls of snippet results (if that). In contrast, professional searchers may undertake many iterations of query reformulation, may review hundreds of search results, and may, for example, undertake subsidiary searching in an attempt to overcome the vocabulary mismatch problem [1]. Commonly, professional searchers are working to protocols embodying best practice for searching and managing information in their particular area. These may include such things as taxonomies of search types, record keeping to demonstrate due diligence, good practice on assessing relevance and so on (see for example [2]).

This book is organised in the three major sections: introductory material focussed principally on frameworks to facilitate research on professional search;

G. Paltoglou et al. (Eds.): Professional Search in the Modern World, LNCS 8830, pp. 1–5, 2014.
© Springer International Publishing Switzerland 2014

then reports of recent research broadly applicable to a wide range of professional research contexts; and finally a focus on some specific issues around Intellectual Property and Patent Search. Within that it is possible to draw out some specific themes: the growth in the use of Natural Language Processing and Text Extraction generate formal knowledge structure; the adoption of social media to improve the search experience; and the use machine learning to improve document classification and enhance search. In the course of the three sections this book covers three primary area of professional search: medicine; marketing; and Intellectual Property search. Intellectual Property search, and specifically Patent Search, is a major areas of professional search, and is extremely technologically and economically important. A recent study by [3] has shown that in some areas as much as 90% of all technical knowledge is contained in patents: much more than in the academic literature. Further, the global value of patents has been estimate to exceed US$10 trillion in 2009 [4].

The first section, on Frameworks Models and Theory opens with a chapter by Preben Hansen, Anni Järvelin, Jussi Karlgren, and Gunnar Eriksson in which they present a new empirical framework for professional search. This is an important step forward. Empirical work on the effectiveness of professional search has been held back, amongst other things, by the more general problems of the study of interactive search, which have bedevilled the TREC interactive track for example [5]. These problems are especially acute in the professional context where there may be many interaction cycles and long search sessions. Hansen and colleagues propose an easy to use system which aims to better match metrical evaluation with users success criteria.

This is followed by a systematic review of the existing knowledge of the behaviour of professional searchers by Evgenia Vassilakaki, Emmanouel Garoufallou, Frances Johnson and R.J. Hartley. They identify a split between qualitative user-centred studies, and quantitative and system-centred studies and attempt to bring the overall picture together in a way which will assist future developers of search systems for professional users.

Osipov and his colleagues look at search from some important groups of users not considered elsewhere: not only scientific researchers and clinical practitioners, but also, for example, venture capital organisations who need to be confident that they are funding original and protectable R&D. The authors identify a need to develop a new range of technologies to bring together the vast diversity of material in an accessible form, and the need to bring together research published in regional languages into what I would call a global scientific and technical knowledge base. Next Morgan Harvey and Fabio Crestani discuss how social media and other forms of context may be leveraged to improve search.

Lupu, Salampasis and Hanbury set out the position that professional search needs are to too diverse to be satisfied by a single system. They propose a five dimensional model which can be used to analyse requirements for a specific domain, and then apply it in two example domains (clinical and patent search) to show how it can be used to put together effective domain specific search systems.

Second, the section on Tools, Applications and Practice begins with a paper from a group of authors from the University of Duisburg-Essen and the Vienna Technical University which describes ezDL - a flexible interactive search system which allows different information resources to be brought together in a single search framework. A common demand from professional searchers is for a system which allows them to bring together multiple sources and then to search them in flexible way which reflects their complex search behaviours, the need which formed the background to the preceding Lupu, Hanbury and Salampasis chapter. ezDL is such a flexible integrating system which has been demonstrated on a number of application areas. In particular, the article discusses PerFedPat, and application of ezDL to the important professional search area of Patent Search.

Dalianis then presents a case study in the clinical search area of Electronic Patient Records. This points out a number of practical issues in building search systems for such data, and the challenges presented by multi-linguality and automated metadata generation in this setting.

Next Fafalios and Tzitzikas look at the issue that often professional researchers need to overview the whole of a large result set. They look at metadata categorisation, clustering and named-entity extraction, in the context of two use cases: one in marine research; the other in patent search. They show their proposal can work effectively in real time, and reduce the overall time for professional search tasks. Up to this point the chapters focus on the areas of patent and clinical searching. These are of course two very important kinds of professional search, but there are many others. One such is the use of searching and mining information expressed in social media amongst marketing and other business professionals. The final chapter in this section, by Paltoglou and Giachanou, covers this important and recently emerged topic. They review recent developments in the field and the use of current techniques covered elsewhere in this volume for this new application area. In particular they review the use of named entity recognition, machine learning and lexicon-based techniques for machine learning. They conclude that genre independent opinion retrieval remains a challenging research topic.

The final section of the book covers Patent Search, which was always seen as a key case study for professional search within the MUMIA COST network which gave rise to this book. Patent Offices are legally required to classify patents according to various classification systems, most notably the International Patent Classification (IPC). Patent searchers often restrict their patent searches using this classification, effectively using the classification systems as search facets. The classification systems are very large and complex: the IPC now has over sixty thousand classes. Classification of patents and the maintenance of the patent system is a major task for the patent offices, and they have a long standing interest in effective automatic methods of classifying patents. Gomez and Moens review recent research in this area, providing an introduction to the IPC and to much recent relevant research on automatic classification. They conclude that there is an urgent need for more work on the effectiveness of modern feature selection and extraction methods for automatic patent classification.

For many professional patent searchers, improvements in the searching of the text of patents is all very well, but the time consuming and difficult work is to review image and other non-text data in the patents to determine whether a patent is relevant to their current search. Significant progress has been over the last 40 and more years with the indexing and retrieval of chemical structures [6], and some progress has been made recently with gene sequences [7], but little or no progress has been made in the commercial domain with engineering and other forms of technical drawing, flow charts, electrical circuits and a wide range of other image data which are found in patents. In the last chapter Vrochidis and colleagues review the progress which has been made in recent years towards delivering such systems commercially, and show that this is an area where technology is about to come out of the lab into the field.

There are some important issues for professional searchers which do not seem to be the focus of much research at present. Many professional searchers continue to prefer to formulate their queries as Boolean expressions, but almost all information retrieval research continues to assume that searches are formulated as so-called natural language queries (strings of ordinary human language terms or perhaps more often more or less well formed questions these days); techniques like faceting and filtering also figure in the research landscape, but these are rarely avilable in operational tools for professional searchers. Some professional searchers would also like to see better tools for visualising and manipulating the often very large result sets they have to deal with initially. Various forms of search: for example patentability search; would benefit from better estimates of recall: effectively estimates of how likely it is that further searching or results examination will yield additional relevant documents.

Because these areas are little reflected in the current research landscape, the inevitably do not appear in a volume of this sort. But I hope these remarks will stimulate researchers to build upon the work reported in this volume to undertake more work in these and the many other areas which are important for professional search.

Acknowledgements. I would like to thank Mihai Lupu and Ilkka Havukkala for assistance with tracking down some references cited in this piece.

References

1. Furnas, G.W., Landauer, T.K., Gomez, L.M., Dumais, S.T.: The vocabulary problem in human-system communication. Commun. ACM 30(11), 964–971 (1987)
2. Hunt, D., Nguyen, L., Rodgers, M.: Patent searching: Tools & techniques. Wiley (2007)
3. Trippe, A.: Revisiting an old standard 80% of technical information is found only in patents,
http://www.patinformatics.com/blog/revisiting-an-old-standard-80-of-technical-information-is-found-only-in-patents/
(accessed: June 06, 2014)

4. Lupu, M., Mayer, K., Tait, J., Trippe, A.: Preface. In: Lupu, M., Mayer, K., Tait, J., Trippe, A.J. (eds.) Current Challenges in Patent Information Retrieval. The Information Retrieval Series, vol. 29, Springer, Heidelberg (2011)
5. Gaizauskas, R., Barker, E.J.: Mice from a mountain: Reflections on current issues in evaluation of written language technology. In: Tait, J.I. (ed.) Charting a New Course: Natural Language Processing and Information Retrieval, pp. 195–238. Springer, Heidelberg (2005)
6. Holliday, J., Willett, P.: Representation and searching of chemical-structure information in patents. In: Lupu, M., Mayer, K., Tait, J., Trippe, A.J. (eds.) Current Challenges in Patent Information Retrieval. The Information Retrieval Series, vol. 29, pp. 343–355. Springer, Heidelberg (2011)
7. Li, W., Kondratowicz, B., McWilliam, H., Nauche, S., Lopez, R.: The Annotation-enriched non-redundant patent sequence databases. Database (January 2013)

A Use Case Framework
for Information Access Evaluation

Preben Hansen[1], Anni Järvelin[2], Gunnar Eriksson[1], and Jussi Karlgren[3]

[1] Department of Computer and Systems Sciences, Stockholm University
[2] School of Information Studies, University of Tampere
[3] Gavagai, Stockholm & School of Computer Science and Communication, KTH
{preben,gerik}@dsv.su.se,
anni.jarvelin@uta.fi,
jussi@gavagai.se

Abstract. Information access is no longer only a question of retrieving topical text documents in a work-task related context. Information search has become one of the most common uses of the personal computers; a daily task for millions of individual users searching for information motivated by information needs they experience for some reason, momentarily or continuously. Instead of professionally edited text documents, multilingual and multimedia content from a variety of sources of varying quality needs to be accessed. Even the scope of the research efforts in the field must therefore be broadened to better capture the mechanisms for the systems' impact, take-up and success in the marketplace. Much work has been carried out in this direction: graded relevance, and new evaluation metrics, more varied document collections used in evaluation and different search tasks evaluated. The research in the field is however fragmented. Despite that the need for a common evaluation framework is widely acknowledged, such framework is still not in place. IR system evaluation results are not regularly validated in Interactive IR or field studies; the infrastructure for generalizing Interactive IR results over tasks, users and collections is still missing. This chapter presents a use case-based framework for experimental design in the field of interactive information access. Use cases in general connect system design and evaluation to interaction and user goals, and help identifying test cases for different user groups of a system. We suggest that use cases can provide a useful link even between information access system usage and evaluation mechanisms and thus bring together research from the different related research fields. In this chapter we discuss how use cases can guide the developments of rich models of users, domains, environments, and interaction, and make explicit how the models are connected to benchmarking mechanisms. We give examples of the central features of the different models. The framework is highlighted by examples that sketch out how the framework can be productively used in experimental design and reporting with a minimal threshold for adoption.

Keywords: Evaluation, benchmarking, use cases, interaction.

G. Paltoglou et al. (Eds.): Professional Search in the Modern World, LNCS 8830, pp. 6–22, 2014.
© Springer International Publishing Switzerland 2014

1   Introduction

For decades, the Cranfield model [11, 31] has provided an effective backbone for information access research, offering a methodological vehicle for systematic and quantifiable evaluation and comparison of system components. This has contributed greatly to the success of the field, both in terms of research and in terms of practical application to task. However, the last two decades have seen a drastic broadening of information access system usage. Information access is no longer only a question of retrieving topical documents in a work-task related context. Document retrieval has become an embedded component in many systems which neither to their users nor their providers appear to be classic document retrieval systems: entertainment systems, communication platforms, time management systems, and the like.

This change in the information access landscape has rendered the classic Cranfield model insufficient as a framework for bringing together algorithm benchmarking with system and service validation: document retrieval performance is not necessarily what makes or breaks a service. Services may be popular, useful, and successful in spite of unimpressive retrieval components that are built to be satisfactory rather than optimal. Static test collections, viewed in a research context to be necessary for reproducibility of results, do not offer relevant data for testing fielded systems against a vast and vastly growing stream of human-generated data. Measurements of system quality based on classic benchmarking have thus become less reliable as a prediction mechanism for the systems' impact, user take-up, and eventual success in the marketplace. This is not news to the information retrieval field. Some of the very first discussions on the potential for interactive bibliographic retrieval pointed out the necessity of rich evaluation metrics [7, 8] and further contributions to that line of thought have continued by formulating ways to relate the usage at the interface to other human behaviour and the tasks users are concerned with to achieve a richer understanding of users, their intentions, sessions, and the evaluation thereof in formal, quantitative, or qualitative ways [5, 6, 18, 27, 34, 38] through more elaborate theoretical background models, better quantification or results, or the introduction of observational methodologies with a finer resolution better to model the task at hand [2, 15, 21, 28].

From this perspective, enriching the Cranfield-based approaches which abstract away from the user and usage situation, can be done using several contrasting approaches to evaluation. The different approaches form a continuum [14, 23]. At one end, we find laboratory based benchmarking evaluations, which seek to hold a maximal number of variables constant to be able to assess the effect of some variation as precisely as possible [31, 35, 37]. At the other end, naturalistic field studies using an ethno-methodological approach to understand the behaviour and preferences of real users with real information needs [25, 26, 33, 36]. In between a range of approaches: user studies with simulated information needs ranging from set queries to more comprehensive models of workplace tasks which users have been asked to emulate [9, 16]; and laboratory interaction simulations, which expand the user and interaction models of the traditional benchmarking evaluations [1, 3, 4, 22, 24, 32, 39].

However, performing more naturalistic user studies is not enough if they do not build up a successive body of knowledge which can be put into use for building practical systems. If we wish to see research efforts published in our field to remain relevant to commercial service providers, we must include the embedded information access components of various systems, in various contexts and domains, and cover more varied user communities, search tasks, and goals. What we still need is a framework to integrate all these components, to support richer and broader benchmarking and bring together benchmarking with system and service validation, including current research in human-computer interaction and support for industrial and commercial concerns. In this chapter, we propose such a framework based on use cases and user centered design principles.

2   Use Cases as a Model for Interaction

Use cases are a user-oriented software development methodology, first developed by Ivar Jacobson and colleagues [19, 20] for capturing interaction-based functional requirements in software development, and further developed by others, e.g. [12, 13]. Use cases are intended to capture a user's point of view; technical solutions or system implementation are not considered in a use case. The requirements are documented by describing how a user interacts with a system to carry out a task, or to reach a goal. The focus is on task modeling[1] or modeling one kind of use that a system can be put to, given a specific user role. Users may normally use a system in several ways and for different purposes. To be practical, use cases focus on a specific kind of system usage, instead of trying to cover all possible different interactions and goals. Numerous approaches to system development and software engineering, commercial and academic, consultancy-based and programmatic, take use cases as a point of departure; many leverage the information in use cases for testing protocols and quality assurance. Typically evaluation metrics in software engineering are closely tied to system effectiveness and are used as performance indicators. The aim is to verify and test functional behaviour when the system under consideration is scaled up from development operation to actual usage and to monitor system behaviour during subsequent versioning.

In the use case based framework presented in this chapter, observable patterns of human information access behavior are described through a selection of variables that can be linked to properties of the experimental design and to the system and interface features of the evaluated systems, as illustrated in Figure 1. The features of interest could be system performance variables such as those typically measured in software engineering, but in our framework, we reach further into the use case to allow for features which measure user, context, and task-related aspects of usage.

---

[1] "Task" in use cases differs from the "work tasks" often discussed in information access literature: use cases focus on users' immediate tasks when interacting with systems, the task the user expects the system to support and not the broader work tasks that the users are engaged in.

   The evaluation framework presented in this chapter integrates the features affecting information access system usage, with the constraints presented by the system and interface design on one hand and experimental design on the other. This way the framework can indicate evaluation approaches for measuring the value of an information access system to its users given some real-world constraints of the system usage, and can describe what kind of real-world information access system usages the results of a specific experiment can apply to.

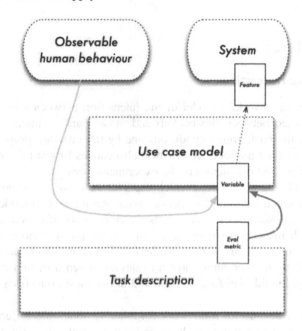

Fig. 1. Relating human behavior to system and evaluation features

The framework assists evaluation design by supporting explicit mapping between relevant features of information access system usage on the one hand, and experimental design decisions and benchmarking mechanisms on the other. This is done along a number of dimensions, held together in larger bundles of features: Interaction, Interface and System, Background, and Evaluation, cf. sections 3 and 4. The framework is called a "use case framework", as the use case, a model of system usage through the description of the user-system interaction, is at the very heart of the framework. It is in the interaction model, described in section 3.1 that the constraints and demands related to the users and usage of systems meet the evaluation mechanisms: the characteristics of the envisioned users, their tasks, contexts and environments all affect what interaction sequences are relevant to consider in evaluation. The background features, described in section 3.3, cover these aspects. In contrast with the original purpose of use cases, this is an evaluation framework and not a system design methodology. The interface and system features of the operational systems under evaluation, or of the experimental systems as defined in the experimental design, constrain the possible interaction patterns for a use case and thus limit the validity of the evaluation with respect to the users, search tasks, domains and environments covered. They are there-fore described separately in the interaction and system model (section 3.2).

For each of the three feature bundles, a corresponding checklist has been formu-lated to support thinking about, designing, and documenting a certain aspect of infor-mation access usage or evaluation, as well as noting dependencies to other aspects. In section 4, the checklists are put to use in two examples of evaluation design. In the following section, the components of the use case framework are discussed on a more general level.

3   Modelling Usage

3.1   Modeling Interaction

In the use case framework, a model of the interaction between a user and a system forms the interface between the background models and evaluation. Interaction is limited both by the background conditions and by the interface properties defined in an experiment, but the model of interaction also carries forward the requirements of the background and the interaction to the experimental design.

Correctly modeling the ways in which users interact with a system is essential for establishing the success criteria for an evaluation. An interaction model connects user goals to interaction sequences, and depicts the complexity of typical search sessions: search and result inspection strategies, result use, iterations of query reformulations, goal-orientation or randomness of the interaction. These aspects affect what results the users are likely to encounter and find relevant, given a certain time or effort of searching. They should therefore be reflected in both test collections and evaluation measures.

Use cases provide a useful framework for thinking about interaction in information access evaluation. There is no single established way of writing use cases, but use cases are typically organized around a main success scenario describing the simplest successful interaction sequence through the use case. The sequence is commonly pre-sented as ordered steps, where each step describes one interaction between the user and the system. The main success scenario is complemented by a set of extensions that describe all the other possible interaction sequences through the use case, includ-ing any alternative user actions, exceptions and failures. A typical search use case may have a simple main success scenario (1. User types a query; 2. System shows results; 3. User clicks on a result; 4. System presents result), but very many paths through the use case are possible due to the high degree of freedom of user actions. Thus iterations of the different user actions in varying order need to be modeled through extensions.

The number of interaction sequences (main success scenarios and extensions) needed for describing most information access system usages is limited however: the number of identifiable user actions is not very high, and while the number of possible paths through the use cases might be overwhelming, the types of iterations of and switches between the actions are limited and thus possible to model through a limited number of interaction sequences and extensions.

The interaction sequences are here structured following [13, 40], by dividing the scenarios into user intentions and system responsibilities that show what the user aims to do in each step of the interaction and what system responsibilities relate to each user intention. Figure 2 depicts an example of a structured main success scenario for a use case for finding an illustrative image to insert in a blog post.

insertingIllustration

USER INTENTION	SYSTEM RESPONSIBILITY
request illustration	
	show appropriate images
select image	
	show preview
confirm	
	insert image
	close

EXTENSIONS	
browsingResults	
reformulatingRequest	

Fig. 2. Example main success scenario

A goal in use cases refers to the concrete, immediate goal of a user interacting with the system, such as inserting an illustration in the above example. It defines the expected outcome of interactions and thus introduces the immediate use of information as a factor affecting evaluation criteria. Goal categories with clear impacts on interaction patterns have been recognized in previous studies, mainly based on analysis of web search logs [10, 30]. These categories offer a solid starting point for considering goals, even if new categories to cover more varied usage and more specific goals may be needed. We separately define a second aspect of user goals following Ingwersen and Järvelin [18], i.e., the type and amount of information looked for: single items or several items; ready answers, facts or notifications, or for topical content from which information can be extracted by the user.

3.2   Modeling Interface and System

Interface design is closely tied to the interaction model, as even experiments where no users or interface designs are purposely included make assumptions concerning the user interface and system functionality: depending on how the experiments are set up, the functionality may be fixed to e.g. a certain type of request formulation, or a specific type of result presentation. Such assumptions have a major effect on the applicability of the evaluation results and should be carefully modeled.

From the use case example in Figure 2, three types of user actions and thus three groups of interface and system features may be identified: request formulation, result presentation (in two levels: a set of ranked results, and image preview), and result use (inserting image). The interaction model then needs to be completed with a detailed (black-box) description of the interface features affecting the user's interaction with the system in these interaction points. The relevant aspects may include e.g.:

- Supported means for expressing requests: by querying or browsing; using different modalities; querying by examples or specifying queries by e.g. typing or humming.
- The granularity of the searchable information items: can queries target individual images, or (curated) collections or sets of images, or details in images, etc.
- Organization and presentation of the results: textual or visual results; thumbnails or full images, with context and copyright information, or without, etc.
- Result use such as manipulation, sharing, onsite consumption, exporting, ordering, etc.

3.3   Modeling Background

Individuals perceive their information needs subjectively and the way they interact with information access systems depends on their goals, personal characteristics, and attitudes. While some of the differences are genuinely individual, the users' group membership offers a strong signal of their possible needs and goals. User role models then define (abstract) user groups with respect to specific system usages. They are based on the tasks that users in specific roles are trying to accomplish while interacting with the system, but also describe the shared characteristics of those users, their interaction with the system and the information exchanged between the system and the users. The central user role model features include:

- User features, such as: user demographics (age, gender, education, social status); user knowledge and skills (with respect to the task, domain, system, language); physical characteristics ((dis)abilities); orientation and attitudes (towards the task, the system, co-searchers).
- Interaction features, related to the complexity, predictability, and frequency of the interaction; locus of control of the interaction, and information flow direction.
- Information features, related to the volume and complexity of the information exchanged between the user and the system, as well as the clarity of the users' information needs.
- Users' primary success criteria, including: efficiency and effectiveness, system reliability and comprehensibility, actionability (does results enable taking intended action?).

Information access interactions are constrained by the activities that trigger them. A domain model captures the different constraints that govern a domain of activity: how the search behavior and goals of users are constrained by the activity at large (e.g. the "work" task) and the topic of interest; by the professional, private, or social context of the activity (presence or absence of peers or collaborators while searching and sharing results with others); or by the characteristics of the data and repository accessed. A domain model may define e.g.:

- The cost of errors if search task is not duly completed (economic, social, societal, career, etc.).
- Time restrictions limiting the length of the interaction.
- Restrictions to accessing the contents of the repository (access rights, cost).
- Data and repository features such as media, genre, language quality, and dynamics of the information and repository.

Moreover, different surroundings trigger different information needs and different interactions. The physical surroundings in which a user interacts with a system affect the search goals and the preferred way of interaction. An operational environment model depicts factors related to the surroundings, mobility, and locality of the users, distractions from the search interaction, and issues related to devices and network connections. The factors include, e.g.:

- Mobility and geo-position of the users
- Device and network restrictions (small screens, limited input ergonomics, high cost, or low speed of data transfer)
- Distractions (interruptions, multiple parallel tasks, noise)

4   Evaluation

So, how do these models facilitate systematic construction of experiments based on rich models of users, domains, environments and interaction? The goal is a framework that can make explicit the functional requirements and success criteria of information access systems, and to connect them to benchmarking mechanisms, i.e., to the components of experimental settings and the criteria and metrics used for measuring system performance. Figure 3 depicts how the models are brought together.

The background models (user, domain, environment) collect the information needed for understanding the users' success criteria, and describe the preconditions of their interaction with the system: their abilities and preferences when it comes to formulating queries, inspecting results, and interpreting and processing information. This information is then used in the design of experimental settings: for defining relevant information need (e.g. topics) and query types; the test data, relevance criteria, and characteristics of the relevance assessors; interaction patterns that need to be modeled; and system interface features to cover.

The success criteria for the users under consideration together with the interaction and interface models are needed for defining reasonable evaluation criteria. Evaluation must also be based on what results are likely to be retrieved when interacting with the system: Even if high recall is a prioritized success criterion for users, there is no point to base evaluation on users ploughing through an entire result lists for one-shot queries if users typically search in sessions of several fast query reformulations and shallow result scans. The evaluation criteria as described through the interaction patterns are then operationalized in suitable metrics. Patience, time or cost parameters may be added into the standard metrics [e.g. 21, 28], but probably yet new metrics need to be developed for measuring the quality of systems, given the varied success criteria of users. The models and the process of mapping their features into experimental design can quite easily be formulated as easy-to-use checklists, similar to those used for documenting software system requirements, as implied in Figure 3.

To give an example, a classic TREC-style batch experiment starts from topics which describe well formulated, clear, topical information needs[2]. It extracts verbose keyword queries from textual topic descriptions. These are tested against static test collections with relevance assessments made by human expert assessors based on static relevance criteria. System performance is evaluated over ranked lists of document pointers returned by the system. Users' interaction with the system is modeled as sequences of one-shot queries and perusing the result list. The main success criterion used is effectiveness, as measured by MAP.

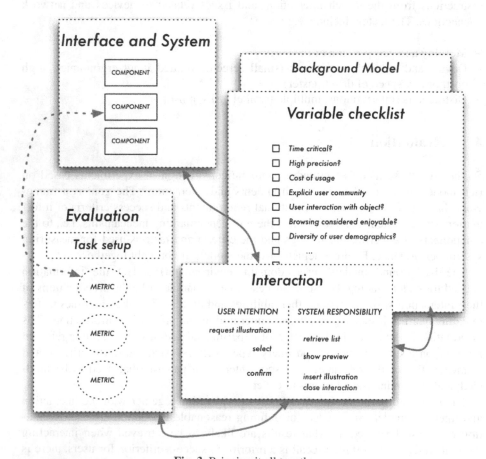

Fig. 3. Bringing it all together

---

[2] This example describes the classic experiment. Much more varied tasks, data, topics, and relevance criteria are covered in the present day evaluation campaigns in TREC, CLEF, NTCIR, and the like.

Table 1 summarizes the components of this kind of an experiment and lists some of the use case features that are (often implicitly) defined by the experimental setting. This is potentially a useful experiment for evaluation of the quality of a ranking component in a search system for a use case describing professional search tasks (e.g. on the patent domain), where the cost of missing relevant documents may be high and users are thus willing to spend considerable effort in formulating their queries and working down result lists.

Table 1. Evaluation task summary for a classic (stereotypical) TREC experiment. Depicts the components of the experimental setting and how they relate to an underlying use case.

Component	Use case features considered	Instantiation of the component
1. Test subjects	N/A	No test subjects. Minimal user model (not explicitly based on any specific users) reflected in topics, requests, relevance criteria, and metrics.
2. Topics	User role; clarity of information need; volume and complexity of information.	Topical, clear specifications of information needs and relevance criteria; created by experts.
3. Requests	User proficiency, domain know-ledge, language skills. Supported search strategies, query formulation means and modality.	Verbose, ad hoc, keyword queries.
4. Data	Repository: media, genre, language, technical quality, source dynamics. Data volume and complexity.	Static test collection of full text documents. Relatively noise-free and well-defined: clear definition of "document", few errors, standard language. Documents are independent of each other.
5. Ground truth creation	Users' domain and topic knowledge, language skills. User goals and roles.	Pooling; Manual relevance assessments using (binary liberal) relevance criteria by expert assessors.
6. Result presentation	Result presentation; user-system/ information interaction.	Ranked list of document ID's. Interaction purely based on rank.

Table 1. (*Continued*)

7. Interaction	User actions and system responses; Complexity and predictability of interaction; Users' goal-orientation and motivation, likelihood abandoning system; Restrictions.	Simple interactions of one-shot queries and deep scanning of results. Interaction is minimal and driven by the user. Patient user, no time restrictions. The encountered documents do not affect user behavior.
8. Result use	N/A	Not considered in the experiment.
9. Evaluation criteria & metrics	User goals; success/ failure criteria; motivation. Restrictions.	Ranking and recall in the absence of time or effort related restrictions; Finding as many relevant documents as possible. Operationalized as MAP.

It does not however capture the general success criteria for arbitrary other use cases. For example, a system where users access information objects for entertainment with no clear task-related information need in mind and where the browsing itself is part of the use and enjoyment of the system and where one of the central goals of interaction may be participating in a community of users, and possibly contributing to that community and to the collection needs to be evaluated using entirely different metrics [e.g., 29]. Main success criteria for such system would be e.g. high levels of user engagement manifested as users returning to the site; long sessions with protracted browsing; user adoption of site terminology and categorization schemes; and numerous user actions, such as up-votes, comments, and share actions in response to returned item lists.

To contrast with the stereotypical Cranfield experiment, Table 2 presents a (constructed) example experiment for evaluating the search component of a social video search service in the context of the typical sessions of system use. To some extent, different use case features are considered than in the Cranfield experiment presented in Table 1. The major differences are in how the components of the experiment are instantiated, when the evaluation is based on a different type of a user task or goal: The users' general task is to spend a short period of time on the service, finding something interesting to view, and interacting with their peers. Result use is an internal part of the search session, rather than something which occurs after the session. The search interaction is a success from user perspective if the user experience was pleasant and involved active participation in the social context.

The information access component is then evaluated based on (simulated) sessions [24] of information access and use with a variety of user actions included in the session model; with a test collection of linked data ranked by actionability -   the number of views, comments, votes and shares the documents have received; and measured based on a model of social interaction and gains in a time based evaluation.

The topics describe unspecific and through the search session evolving information needs - the search topic per se is not necessarily very important, but serves as an entry point to the service, where social relevance weighs heavily. Requests reflect the users' evolving understanding of the current vocabulary and conceptual model presented by the system, while the interaction patterns in general reflect the actionability of the encountered documents (social potential; peers' preferences and actions).

Table 2. Evaluation task summary for social video search: an experiment focusing on the effect of the search component on the perceived social gain and enjoyability of sessions of system use

Component	Use case features considered	Instantiation of the component
1. Test subjects	N/A	No test subjects. Users modeled through ground truth creation, interaction model and evaluation criteria.
2. Topics	User role(s), goals, clarity of information need.	Topics describe entry points to the service. They might be topically more or less specific: from known item search to very general. Each topic contains a few alternative entry points: query words, concepts or directions to search.
3. Requests	User goals. Users' service proficiency and domain knowledge. Supported search strategies, query modalities and query formulation means.	Keyword queries of varying length and quality, evolving through sessions. Reformulation guided in the interaction model as probability of query reformulation given a result, and the entry points listed in the topics.
4. Data	Repository: media, genre, language, tech. quality, source dynamics. Data volume, complexity.	Linked data with documents and related likes, comments, tags.
5. Ground truth creation	Users goals and success criteria	Extracted from test data based on user engagement: documents ranked based on the number of responses or actions they have triggered.
6. Result presentation	Result presentation; user-system and user-information interaction.	Only vaguely modelled through possible user actions in the interaction model.

Table 2. (*Continued*)

7. Interaction	Possible user actions and system responses; Complexity and predictability of interaction; Users' goal-orientation and motivation; Restrictions (time, cost, effort, social); Probability of changing role.	Modeled as probability of an encountered document triggering user actions (query formulation, browsing, perusing result, viewing video clips, commenting, up-voting, sharing).
8. Result use	Probability of user changing role. System features for enriching, use and sharing of content. User goal.	Result use is an inseparable part of the interaction. Viewing content, up-votes, comments, recommendations.
9. Evaluation criteria & metrics	User goals; success/failure criteria; motivation. Restrictions.	Actionability. Level of user engagement, time spent interacting with the results. Evaluated based on a model of costs and gains (good/bad time; social gain).

Note that not all models needed for conducting this experiment are necessary in place yet: a useful model of unpredictable interaction sequences of many possible user actions might be difficult to define. Isolating or correctly modeling the roles of the different user actions or system components for the flow or success of the interaction might be difficult based on our current knowledge. Modeling the social gain connected to different user actions, or combining the dual success criteria of social gain and having enjoyable time requires understanding of the user population and of social dynamics. These difficulties point to areas where more basic research is needed on how and why users interact with information.

If one were to evaluate the social video service search component using a standard Cranfield experiment as described in Table 1, measuring performance with respect to user goals and success criteria (social gain and having a pleasant time) would not be possible. One could evaluate how well the ranking component ranks topically relevant video clips. Changing the ground truth creation, one could evaluate how well the ranking component ranks socially relevant video clips (given that we could model social relevance satisfactorily). A different metric could be used for operationalizing the evaluation criteria for measuring e.g. the topical diversity of the top results with highest social relevance. These evaluations could be both useful and motivated in many situations, not least for the sake of their viability. They do not however evaluate the same thing as the experiment described in Table 2. Being aware of these differences is important both when designing experiments and when reporting (or reading about) them, and this is where the suggested use case framework can be useful: The goal of the use case framework is to support the analysis of the use case, to suggest possible ways of connecting use cases to experimental designs and to make explicit how the choices and simplifications made in experimental design affect the applicability and realism of the evaluation results.

5   Towards a Framework

Most experimental designs by necessity compromise between the breadth and the depth of their coverage: an experiment that aims to cover all users and all usages of a system, typically says very little concerning the systems' performance given any specific users or usages. On the other hand, the results from in-depth studies concerning the system usage patterns of specific user groups working on specific tasks are most often difficult to generalize or to transfer to other situations.

The variation in the basic interaction sequences occurring in information access systems is however limited enough to be modeled through a set of predefined interaction sequence templates. Instances of information access usage can thus be described as use cases within a use case framework and related to other instances through their shared interaction sequences. A carefully constructed model of the relationships between the interaction sequences can then notably reduce the complexity of the "evaluation landscape" by bringing together the at first glance different information access use cases that ultimately are characterized by shared interaction patterns and goals and consequently, shared evaluation criteria.

Such a framework facilitates the generalization and re-use of evaluation results of the limited in-depth evaluations in other contexts and thus provides a platform on which evaluation criteria and evaluation results can be described, debated and validated. As more use cases are described, evaluated and validated within the use case framework, the knowledge of characteristics of use cases - with respect to evaluation and success criteria - will be enriched, and the connections between distinctive use case features and patterns of interaction and success criteria become clearer.

6   Conclusions

There are many different approaches to evaluation of information access systems. Selecting the most appropriate approach must be done with attention to the use case, but also on the target (component, complete service), and the perspective of the evaluation (goals of end users, goals of customers, and goals of service providers). Essentially, all types of evaluations benefit from carefully modeling the success criteria and interaction patterns for the evaluated systems. While focusing on improving the performance of isolated system components is motivated in some phases of technology development, such evaluations should not be agnostic about the end user benefits achievable (or not) by further improvements of the components.

We do not claim that all information retrieval evaluations should add a number of variables concerning users with preferences and strategies for interacting with information retrieval systems in their experimental setting: the controlled and manageable experimental settings are one of the main strengths of the laboratory model. Instead, we claim that all information retrieval evaluations should be explicit about what they evaluate and what they believe is the applicability of the results. If the context and the purpose of the evaluation is not carefully considered, it is difficult to choose the correct evaluation measures to be used. Better description of the context of a specific evaluation also makes it easier to organize and re-use the results and thus supports the growth of knowledge and technology take-up.

Acknowledgements. This work was supported by the European Community's Seventh Framework Programme (FP7/2007-2013) under grant agreement nr 258191 (PROMISE Network of Excellence).

References

1. Ahlgren, P.: The effect of indexing strategy-query term combination on retrieval effectiveness in a Swedish full text database. Academic dissertation. Valfrid, Sweden, 166 p. (2004)
2. Azzopardi, L.: The Economics in Interactive Information Retrieval. In: Proceedings of the 34th International ACM SIGIR Conference on Research and Development in Information Retrieval, pp. 15–24. ACM (2011)
3. Baskaya, F., Keskustalo, H., Järvelin, K.: Time Drives Interaction: Simulating Sessions in Diverse Searching Environments. In: Proceedings of the 35th International ACM SIGIR Conference on Research and Development in Information Retrieval, pp. 105–114. ACM (2012)
4. Baskaya, F., Keskustalo, H., Järvelin, K.: Modeling Behavioral Factors in Interactive Information Retrieval. In: Proceedings of the 22nd ACM International Conference on Information & Knowledge Management, pp. 2297–2302. ACM (2013)
5. Bates, M.J.: Information Search Tactics. Journal of the American Society for Information Science 30(4), 205–214 (1979)
6. Bates, M.J.: The Design of Browsing and Berrypicking Techniques for the Online Search Interface. Online Review 13 (October 1989)
7. Bennett, J.L.: Interactive bibliographic search as a challenge to interface design. In: Walker, D.E. (ed.) Interactive Bibliographic Search: The User/Computer Interface, pp. 1–16 (1971)
8. Bennett, J.L.: The user interface in interactive systems. ARIST 7, 159–196 (1972)
9. Borlund, P.: The IIR evaluation model: a framework for evaluation of interactive information retrieval systems. Information Research. An International Electronic Journal 8(3) (2003)
10. Broder, A.: A taxonomy of web search. ACM SIGIR Forum 36(2) (2002)
11. Cleverdon, C.W., Keen, M.: Cranfield CERES: Aslib Cranfield research project - Factors determining the performance of indexing systems. Technical report (1966)
12. Cockburn, A.: Agile software development. Addison-Wesley (2002)
13. Constantine, L., Lockwood, L.: Software for use: A Practical guide to the models and methods of usage-centered design. Addison-Wesley (2006)
14. Fuhr, N., Belkin, N., Jose, J., van Rijsbergen, K.: Interactive Information Retrieval. Dagstuhl Seminar Proceedings: number 09101. ISSN 1862-4405. Schloss Dagstuhl -Leibniz-Zentrum fuer Informatik, Germany (2009)
15. Hansen, P., Järvelin, K.: Collaborative information retrieval in an information-intensive domain. Information Processing and Management 41(5), 1101–1119 (2005)

16. Hansen, P.: Work task-oriented studies on IS&R processes. Developing theoretical and conceptual frameworks to be applied for evaluation and design of tools and systems. In: Fisher, K., Erdelez, S., McKechnie, L. (eds.) Theories of Information Behaviour. ASIST Monograph series, pp. 392–396. ASIST, Medford (2005)
17. Hearst, M.: "Natural" Search User Interfaces. Communications of the ACM 54(11), 60–67 (2011)
18. Ingwersen, P., Järvelin, K.: The turn: Integration of Information Seeking and Retrieval in Context. Springer, Dortrecht (2005)
19. Jacobson, I.: Object-oriented development in an industrial environment. In: Procceedings of OOPSLA 1987: Sigplan Notices, 22(12) (1987)
20. Jacobson, I., Christerson, M., Jonsson, P., Overgaard, G.: Object-Oriented Software Engineering: A Use Case Driven Approach. Addison-Wesley (1992)
21. Järvelin, K., Kekäläinen, J.: Cumulated gain-based evaluation of IR techniques. ACM Transactions on Information Systems 20(4), 422–446 (2002)
22. Kanoulas, E., Carterette, B., Clough, P., Sanderson, M.: Evaluating Multi-Query Sessions. In: Proceedings of 34th International ACM SIGIR Conference on Research and Development in Information Retrieval, pp. 1053–1062 (2011)
23. Keskustalo, H.: Towards Simulating and Evaluating User Interaction in Information Retrieval using Test Collections. Ph D Dissertation. Univeristy of Tampere: Acta Universitatis Tamperensis 1563 (2010)
24. Keskustalo, H., Järvelin, K., Pirkola, A., Sharma, T., Lykke, M.: Test Collection-Based IR Evaluation Needs Extension Toward Sessions - A Case of Extremely Short Queries. In: Lee, G.G., Song, D., Lin, C.-Y., Aizawa, A., Kuriyama, K., Yoshioka, M., Sakai, T. (eds.) AIRS 2009. LNCS, vol. 5839, pp. 63–74. Springer, Heidelberg (2009)
25. Kuhlthau, C.: Inside the Search Process: Information Seeking from the User's Perspective. Journal of the American Society for Information Science 42(5), 361–371 (1991)
26. Kumpulainen, S., Järvelin, K.: Barriers to Task-Based information access in molecular medicine. Journal of the American Society for Information Science and Technology 63(1), 89–97 (2012)
27. Liu, J., Belkin, N.: Personalizing information retrieval for multi-session tasks: The roles of task stage and task type. In: Proceedings of the 33th International ACM SIGIR Conference on Research and Development in Information Retrieval, pp. 26–33. ACM (2010)
28. Moffat, A., Zobel, J.: Rank-Biased Precision for Measurement of Retrieval Effectiveness. ACM Transactions on Information Systems 27(1) (2008)
29. Murdock, V., Clarke, C., Kamps, J., Karlgren, J.: Proceedings of SEXI 2013 - Workshop on Search and Exploration of X-Rated Information at WSDM 2013 (2013)
30. Rose, D., Levinson, D.: Understanding user goals in Web search. In: Proceedings of the 13th International ACM Conference on World Wide Web, pp. 13–19. ACM (2004)
31. Sanderson, M.: Test Collection Based Evaluation of Information Retrieval Systems. Foundations and Trends in Information Retrieval 4(4), 247–375 (2010)
32. Smucker, M., Clarke, C.: Time-based Calibration of Effectiveness Measures. In: Proceedings of 35th International ACM SIGIR Conference on Research and Development in Information Retrieval, pp. 95–104. ACM
33. Spink, A., Saracevic, T.: Interaction in information retrieval: Selection and effectiveness of search terms. Journal of the American Society for Information Science 48(8), 741–761 (1997)
34. Su, L.T.: Evaluation Measures for Interactive Information Retrieval. Information Processing and Management 28(4), 503–516 (1992)

35. Tague-Sutcliffe, J.: The pragmatics of information retrieval experimentation, revisited. Information Processing and Management 28(4), 467–490 (1992)
36. Vakkari, P., Hakala, N.: Changes in Relevance Criteria and Problem Stages in Task Performance. Journal of Documentation 56(5), 540–562 (2000)
37. Voorhees, E.M.: The philosophy of information retrieval evaluation. In: Peters, C., Braschler, M., Gonzalo, J., Kluck, M. (eds.) CLEF 2001. LNCS, vol. 2406, pp. 355–370. Springer, Heidelberg (2002)
38. White, R., Dumais, S., Teevan, J.: Characterizing the influence of domain expertise on web search behavior. In: Proceedings of the Second International Conference on Web Search and Data Mining, pp. 132–141. ACM (2009)
39. White, R., Jose, J., van Rijsbergen, K., Ruthven, I.: Evaluating Implicit Feedback Models Using Searcher Simulations. ACM Transactions on Information Systems 23(3), 325–361 (2005)
40. Wirfs-Brock, R.: Designing Scenarios: Making the Case for a Use Case Framework. Smalltalk Report (November-December, 1993)

Users' Information Search Behavior in a Professional Search Environment:
A Methodological Approach

Evgenia Vassilakaki[1], Emmanouel Garoufallou[2], Frances Johnson[3],
and R.J. Hartley[3]

[1] Department of Library Science & Information Systems, Technological Educational
Institute of Athens, Egaleo, Athens, Greece
evevasilak@gmail.com
[2] Department of Library Science & Information Systems, Alexander Technological
Educational Institute of Thessaloniki, Sindos, Thessaloniki, Greece
mgarou@lib.teithe.gr
[3] Dept. Languages, Information & Communications, Manchester Metropolitan
University, Manchester, UK
{f.johnson,r.j.hartley}@mmu.ac.uk

Abstract. Searching and retrieving information, especially in the context of a professional search environment, can be an arduous task. Professional search is defined as "interactive information retrieval performed by professionals in a specific domain" [1]. These searchers have competencies and skills in searching and as such demand high quality information retrieved and are willing to spend time to find the required information. This chapter aims to analyse research into users' search behaviors in professional search enviroments. The method of systematic review was adopted and two types of studies were identified "system-centered" and "user-centered" studies. An emphasis was placed on the methods each type of study adopted to meet its purposes. It was found that system-centered studies employed mainly quantitative methods (Log analysis) to evaluate system's performance and retrieval techniques whereas user-centered studies adopted mainly qualitative methods to provide an insight into users' behaviors. In addition, system-centered studies examined users' behavior as a series of clicks, search terms employed and features used to develop systems that satisfy user's information needs. In contrast, user-centered studies explored users' behavior with the view to identify the specific search processes, thoughts and decisions made while searching as well as the factors affecting their search behaviors. This chapter contributes to providing an understanding of both the methods and approaches adopted to study users' behavior in a professional search environment.

1 Introduction

Information is considered essential for task completion and for decision making. Searching and retrieving information is performed daily to address information

G. Paltoglou et al. (Eds.): Professional Search in the Modern World, LNCS 8830, pp. 23–44, 2014.
© Springer International Publishing Switzerland 2014

needs ranging from general to specific and by searchers with diverse skills. However, searching and retrieving relevant information for a specific need can be an arduous task. Professional search is defined as "interactive information retrieval performed by professionals in a specific domain" [1]. Frequently these searchers are searching for specific information and as such are prone to spend a considerable amount of time retrieving and examining a significant number of the retrieved results [1], [2]. These searches occur across various disciplines and are more readily recognised in medicine, patent and academic document searches. In addition, they need systems that enable the creation and storage of their searches [1]. Their high demands for information derive from the understanding that failing to find the necessary information may have important consequences including huge financial losses and legal implications [2].

Professional searchers have diverse skills and competencies in searching information [3], [2]. As such, professional searching is sometimes outsourced to experts who play the role of intermediaries. In particular, professional searchers either instruct others how to develop the skills necessary to perform a professional search or perform the task of searching on their behalf [3]. This chapter focuses on the task of professional search for meeting specific information needs. In particular, this chapter reviews the literature on professional searches performed only in medicine, patent and academic document domains.

The complexity of professional searching and the diversity of searchers skills and competencies led to the realization that systems should guide the search. Developers ought to build systems which guided searchers to the right answer or to the use of the relevant information resources [2]. Therefore, significant attention has been given to developing novel systems and techniques for supporting professional search. There exists a variety of different systems designed and developed to address the needs of a professional searcher [4], [5], [6], [7], [8]. In terms of specific techniques developed to support professional search, research has focused on Boolean filters and Boolean query suggestions [9], [10], [1], clustering techniques [11], metadata exploitation [12], linked data and semantics [13], [14]. In addition, a series of specific tools have been developed [15], [16], [17], [18], models [19], [20], frameworks [21], [22] and approaches [23] to assist professional searching.

However, although these systems and techniques were developed to meet users' needs, the focus was placed more on systems' performance and features developed rather than on users' interpretation and thought processes while searching these systems. When users were considered, they were mainly employed to assess the effectiveness of retrieval techniques in these systems [24], [25], rather than inquiring into users' information needs, search behaviors and interpretations of the systems' functionality. As such this chapter sets out to analyse research that investigates users' search behavior while performing a professional search in the context of medicine, patent and academic document domains. An emphasis is given to research on the development of systems that support professional search to identify the approaches used in their evaluation. In particular, it aims to distinguish research that carries out a user evaluation of the system effectiveness from studies of the information search behavior in a professional search environment that is users reporting on their perceptions and understanding of system's functionality.

This chapter is in relation to the goal and specific objectives of the **3rd Working Group** of the MUMIA Cost Action. Specifically, it addresses the main objective of this Working Group that is to identify and review research on the user aspects of next generation search systems. It reviews literature in the medicine, patent and academic document domains to assist information exchange across disciplines. In addition, this research makes use of **information retrieval (IR)** in context and more specifically, of **interactive IR (IIR)** to provide an insight into users' thought processes and overall understanding of the search mechanism. On the whole, this research contributes to providing an insight into the methods employed to investigate users' behavior in a professional search environment in the medicine, patent and academic document domains. In addition, it helps the work of system developers by outlining both the methods and approaches adopted to examine users' behaviors and thought processes to develop efficient and effective systems and retrieval techniques. Moreover, it describes the way each method was employed to assist the work of developers and evaluators.

This chapter is structured as follows. At first, the methodological approach adopted is presented with an emphasis on the specific criteria and selection process applied; this is followed by a thorough presentation of issues regarding users' information search behavior in a professional search environment. In particular, a brief outline of the term information seeking behavior and relevant models is provided. Then, the identified studies divided in system-centered and user-centered are presented focusing on the methods adopted. Finally, issues concerning methodological approaches adopted for exploring information search behavior in a professional search environment are critically discussed.

2 Methodology

This study reviews the literature exploring users' information search behavior in a professional search environment such as the medicine, patent and academic document search domains. In this context, relevant search terms to professional search such as "professional searching", "user behavior", "information search" were performed on diverse databases (ACM Digital Library, Library, Information Science & Technology Abstracts (LISTA), Library & Information Science Abstracts (LISA), Citeseer, Google Scholar, e-prints in Library & Information Science (e-LiS), Digital Library of Information Science & Technology (DLIST), PubMed and OVID Medline). The searches were limited to 1990- 2014 and were carried out in October 2013. In total, 60 papers were retrieved and their references were also checked for any additional relevant papers. The inclusion criteria of this literature review focused on the relevance to users' seach behavior in a profeessional search environment and more specifically in medicine, patent and academic document search context. For the purposes of this chapter, studies reporting on legal and academic document search as well as library book search were excluded. By applying and refining the inclusion and exclusion criteria nineteen papers were identified focusing on users' search behavior in professional search environments such as medicine, patent and academic document search. These papers were dated from 1994 to 2012 (see Table 1).

This study has followed the rules of systematic review [26]. In this context, the full-text of the papers was read in order to identify common themes and sub-themes. The resultant categories and the assigned papers were then contrasted to resolve any discrepancies in the review process through consensus among the authors. As a result, two main themes system-centered and user-centered studies emerged. In particular, papers exploring users' judgements of a systems performance and effectiveness were defined as system-centered whereas studies focusing on users' own behaviors, perceptions and understanding of search mechanism while searching were referred to as user-centered. The relevant literature was equally assigned to the emerged themes (see Table 2). It should be noted here, that papers with more than one aim were assigned to more than one theme such as the study of Vibert [27].

This literature review reports the methods adopted in the identified research papers. As a result, the methods employed in both system-centered and user-centered studies were analysed and contrasted to report on possible emerged variations or preferences (see Table 3). In this context, the system-centered studies employed mainly quantitative methods such as Log analysis and Questionnaires whereas user-centered studies used mainly qualitative methods such as Interviews and Think aloud protocols (see Table 3). Finally, an analysis of the type of method employed each year did not reveal any significant findings (see Table 4).

A further analysis of the identified literature revealed that the nineteen papers fall into four types of publications namely journal articles, proceeding papers, reports and theses (see table 5). In an attempt to identify possible preferences for a specific source of publication, it was found that the majority of journal articles were published in *"Journal of the American Society for Information Science & Technology"* and *"Information Processing & Management"* (see Table 5). Finally, no preference to a specific type or source of publication was identified for the papers assigned to the two emerged themes of user-centered and system-centered studies (see Table 6).

3   Professional Search and Users' Behavior

For many years the development and evaluation of IR systems was the main focus of research. In this context, a variety of techniques regarding all steps of system development were adopted and tested with the view to enhancing their efficiency and effectiveness. Users assisted in the evaluation phase by judging the relevance and thus effectiveness of the data retrieved in predefined, task-based searches [28]. In most cases, users were not excluded or had minimal involvement in the development process. When they were involved, their main role concerned the improvement of system efficiency with little, if any, attention paid to users' behaviors and experiences.

For a long period, the same applied to the evaluation phase. Statistical techniques based on the use of a test collection were used to calculate the precision and recall of the retrieved results drawing on users' assessment of the relevancy of the retrieved hits. Even when users were considered, again the focus was on evaluating the system's overall performance rather than exploring users' search behaviors and system interpretation [24], [25]. Imaginary scenarios and pre-defined subject areas were given to users to search for and judge the relevance of the retrieved results. The concept of the 'simulated' user task [29] helped open up the field to allow both the evaluation of the system performance as well as the investigation of the user's behavior whilst conducting the search. However, at the same time, the distinct separation of the literature on users in retrieval system evaluation and in the study of information search behavior continued to be highlighted and questioned [30].

The complex patterns of users actions and interactions while seeking information of whatever kind and for whatever purpose is defined as Information Seeking Behavior (ISB) [31]. ISB is derived from the field of user studies and as such it can be traced back to scientific communication and information use studies. Its usage has altered over the years following developments in that field. In the beginning, the term ISB was used to refer to scientists use of formal and informal communication channels and relied in the main on quantitative methods.

ISB is a subfield of Information Science (IS) and belongs to the study of information behavior. Research in this field can be divided into three time periods: a) 1960-1985, b) 1986-1995 and c) 1996 and onwards. In the first period, four categories of study can be distinguished: user studies, use studies, information behavior studies and studies of information dissemination with a focus on information service and quality. In this context, the object of study was usually scientific behavior. Scientists seeking scholarly information tended to be the main focus of inquiry. Accordingly, the first model of information seeking regarded the user as a researcher affected by a variety of systems (see Paisley [32], Allen [33]). This model was further expanded and became more general and typically consisted of three components: the user domain, the information systems domain and the information unit domain (see Wilson [34]). This model suggested the possibility that information seeking and retrieval might be different depending on the technologies employed and on the information needs of the user. Most notably, it revealed a distinction between seeking information from human sources and retrieval behavior from information systems. Nevertheless, underpinning it was the assumption that rational information seeking behavior could be generalized to all domains. As a result, the model predicted that information retrieval would depend on information needs- and emphasized the need to investigate information needs by eliciting the reasons why users were acting in a specific way (see Taylor [35], Wilson [34]). We can characterize this research as information theoretic. That is, it is predicated on the assumption that information seeking and retrieval behavior will depend on need formation and development. Put simply, users may have specific information needs but their ability to find the information they require may be compromised in various ways. Thus and for instance, interview techniques were used in the context of information seeking (see Ingwersen [36]) in terms of an Anomalous State of Knowledge (ASK) model (see Belkin et al. [37]).

The second period was characterised by a variety of empirical studies and activity models of information seeking processes. In particular, the sense making approach to information seeking was introduced (see Dervin and Nilan [38]) encompassing the notion of knowledge gap and the information needed for bridging the gap between information situation and solution [31]. Another approach introduced in this period was the empirically based phenomenological six-phase model (see Kuhlthau [39]). This model predicts that information needs and hence information seeking behavior will depend on the work tasks associated with different domains and the problems associated with them. The six-phases consist of the following: initiation, selection, exploration, formulation, collection and presentation.

At the same time, an empirically based stage-like model was introduced encompassing eight consecutive and interacting features (see Ellis [40]). This approach also integrated work task into the model (see Jarvelin [41], Bystrom and Jarvelin [42]). Models of this kind, then, rely less on highly generic views of information seeking behavior and rely more on versions of cognitive task analysis to distinguish behaviors in different domains. They nevertheless remain committed to the general rationalistic assumption that behavior is best understood through goals-means hierarchies.

The third period of research in ISB attempts to integrate information seeking and IR research by formulating comprehensive models or frameworks and to merge already developed information seeking models. In addition, longitudinal studies of information seeking were introduced (see Wang and White [43], Vakkari [44]). In this context, a four-dimensional episode framework focusing on sixteen information seeking strategies was introduced (see Belkin et al. [45]). Work task perception, introduced in Ingwersens cognitive model connects information seeking processes in the social and organisational context to the retrieval process. Users' perception of work task is what triggers the problem situation leading to a variety of information needs (see Ingwersen [46]). As a result, the integration of work task-based information seeking and IR is done for the purposes of the design and performance of IR systems. These models typically provide the context in which studies of user information seeking take place. Therefore, relevant studies are extensive spanning key professional domains of academic documents search, library book search, patent search, medical/legal document search.

This broad characterization of research periods can be associated with the adoption of different methods. Mainly quantitative methods were employed in the first period; methods such as questionnaires and interviews, regardless of their drawbacks. During the first and second period, there was a slow progression to more qualitative methods such as observation, diaries, critical incident analysis, talking and think aloud protocols, and so on. During the 1990s, and drawing on a more explicitly sociological literature, Discourse Analysis [47] and

Grounded Theory (GT) [48] were introduced for data collection and analysis. These moves were predicated on the recognition that context informed behavior, that context in turn was defined by the meanings that people ascribed to the situations people found themselves in (an insight which derives in the main from Chigaco- school symbolic interactionist sociology [49]) and that the discovery of context meant that the generation of theory, especially of the abstract kind, was problematised.

The shift to attention to users thought processes and understanding of system's functionality occurred when there was interest in developing interactive applications, in which it was intended that user and computer collaborate and exploit the strengths of each to search more effectively [50]. Interactive information retrieval can be divided into three stages: query formulation, search and browsing [50]. In this context, two types of studies exist in the literature [51]: a) the system-centered; that is, the studies which focus on exploring systems performance by recruiting users to judge precision and relevance of the retrieved results, and b) the user-centered; that is, the studies which focus on the behavioral and cognitive aspects of users while searching and the way users interpret system's functionality. In this context, an indicative review of the papers published during 1994 to 2012 is critically presented below grouped under the headings of, system-centered and user-centered studies as defined above.

3.1   System-Centered Studies

System-centered studies employed professional users mainly during **evaluation phase**, users judged the **relevance of results** and **the effectiveness** of the systems. In particular, Spink [52] reported on a classification search term index which was developed based on users' judgements of the search terms relevance. The study employed an online interview and recorded the searches of forty professional searchers using the DIALOG database system. Analysis of log files was also conducted as a means to measure precision. It was found that search terms retrieved during term relevance feedback were more effective than those of the intermediary and database thesauri. In the same context, Spink, Goodrum & Robins [53] explored elicitations, that is verbal requests for information recorded in a triad dialogue-based model of information retrieval. Think aloud protocol was employed to explore professional searchers' actions on DIALOG. In addition, log-linear analysis was also used to observe the transitions between users' elicitations and their transactions performed. They were able to identify the different type of requests based on the elicitations of search intermediaries. In particular, these requests consisted of information on search terms, strategies, database selection, search procedures, system's output and relevance of retrieved results, users' knowledge and previous experience in searching. Based on the recorded elicitations, they could infer that systems developed to support the transactions were able to improve their perfomance.

Systems' **usefulness** and **performance** was the main focus of Tan [16]. Specifically, Tan [16] developed and tested a term relevance tool called Tag and Keyword (TKy) installed in a Web browser. It was thought to assist query reformulation and thus reduce browsing. In this context, quantitative methods were employed to identify statistical significance in query reformulation and web browsing. In addition, interviews were conducted to gain an insight into users' opinion over the specific web tool and its usefulness. Tan [16] formulated four statistical hypotheses examining whether TKy increased query formulation, decreased viewing of search result pages, web sites and web pages. The study revealed that the TKy tool shifted users' search behavior from browsing to focused searching. In addition, users reported that the tool was useful and it saved time in finding information. In the same context, Kohn et al. [5] investigated the notion of professional search and why it differed from "public search". In addition, they presented the professional search prototype YASA (Your Adaptive Search Agent) and described the initial results gained through evaluation studies. Log analysis was conducted to measure the relative use of external and in-house search engines. Kohn et al. [5] found that in-house search engines were used less than external search engines. Google was the predominant search engine mainly because of its ranking performance and access to PubMed, US patents and Wikipedia. In contrast, low usage of the Google Search Appliance that indexed an in-house file share was found mainly due to the manual log-in and unsatisfying ranking results it provided. In terms of YASA, Google remained the first search engine used but YASA surpassed all the rest. However, authors agreed that log analysis was not enough to reach safe conclusions and further evaluations by conduting user studies and surveys were needed.

In the **medical search** context, Vibert et al. [27] explored the search strategies and behavior of professional searchers on PubMed. In particular, sixteen non professional and sixteen professional searchers were asked to perform five searches for references concerning neuroscience topics. Questionnaires were employed to collect data about users' characteristics, search experience and previous knowledge of PubMed. Think aloud protocols were adopted to shed light on users' search actions and strategies. However, the focus was placed on measuring the effectiveness of the system rather than on the users' behaviors. In particular, it was found that the neuroscientists could find a sufficient number of references in the time frame provided regardless of their previous knowledge of PubMed. Life scientists with lack of knowledge in neuroscience were also able to identify a sufficient number of references. However, differences between the search behaviors of the two types of subjects were identified. Specifically, life scientists needed more time to go through the task instructions and review more abstracts before selecting the necessary references.

In terms of **audiovisual material**, Huurnink [54] examined the creation of automatic shot descriptions for audiovisual records. Log analysis was employed to analyse the purchase orders of audiovisual material, catalogue metadata and the thesaurus created for this purpose. The aim was to explore the specific terms adopted by professional searchers to retrieve audiovisual material for reuse in new productions. It was found that professionals searched for program names, person names, general subject words, locations and other names, document, identifier codes and technical metadata. Extending this research, Bron et al. [55] tested the efficiency of test tools developed for professional archivists being used by the general public online. In particular, they conducted a small-scale study with non-professional searchers performing exploratory search tasks on the Netherlands Institute for Sound and Vision (S&V), the Dutch national audiovisual broadcast archive. They argued that the search tools developed in archives were intended for professional searchers who understand the structure of the archival metadata. As such, non-professional users would find it difficult to adopt these tools and successfully retrieve the necessary information. Twenty-two first year university students carried out the searches using the advanced search mode. At first instructions on the study and a tutorial of the search interface were provided to participants. Then three specific tasks were assigned to users and a limit of fifteen minutes per task was given to complete the searches. Bron et al. [55] recorded users' search behavior and asked them to fill in a questionnaire after completion regarding their experiences with the interface.

The findings of the study were based on the results from the completed questionnaires and correct answers to the task. It was found that low precision of the retrieved results indicated that users had difficulty in finding the correct answers in the time frame given; searchers could not judge the correctness of an answer based on the metadata presented and that the amount of support offered for searching on the interface was marginal'. Users' behavior was judged based on performance. As such two groups were created based on performance, high and low performance groups. Both groups had an equal number of assigned users, eleven; either lower group did not use specific search interface components whereas the high performance group tended to go to program description pages more often but staying less time than the low performance group. Overall, it was found that there were differences in search behavior based on user's performance.

Evaluation of **clustering techniques** was another area of interest. Specifically, Jain & Mishne [11] proposed that users' professional searches would benefit from ordering word suggestions based on high-level of user intent rather than on predicting the next letters or words based on likelihood. As such they conducted a set of small-scale studies where users were employed to test and evaluate the clustering techniques. In particular, users were employed to express a preference for specific clusters and evaluate the automatic and manual clustering techniques. It was found that users' satisfaction can be substantially increased by extending the assistance layer so as to effectively group suggestions and label them. Finally, Lamm [6] focused on measuring the quality of search systems using the confirmation/disconfirmation (C/D) model that described user satisfaction. Two studies were conducted to explore the effects of users' expectations on the way systems were perceived. The users were introduced to the system and false expectations were created so as to guide users' expectations to either high or low expectations. Users were divided into four different groups which differ in expectations and system quality. Questionnaires were employed to measure users' satisfaction. Two questionnaires were distributed including statements regarding ease of use, efficiency, output display, precision, ranking of results, result quality and reuse probability. Measurements such as recall and precision were also employed to evaluate users' and system's performance. Log analysis was also employed to identify users actions and judgements of relevancy based on their retrieved results. It was found that user's expectations were both dynamic and context dependent while agreeing that further research was needed to establish reliable methods to measure user satisfaction and performance in an information retrieval environment.

3.2 User-Centered Studies

As opposed to the system-centered, user-centered studies focus on users' cognitive thoughts, perceptions and understanding of system's functionality. As such, knowledge of the user context creates potential for improving a system's overall efficiency and ultimately users' experience [56]. In terms of **evaluation**, Barry [57] performed an evaluation study in which she asked 18 students from Louisiana State University to judge the relevance of retrieved results. A set of 242 documents were provided to students who circled the portions of each document they thought relevant to pursue searching but also which they judged as irrelevant. Then interviews with the participants were undertaken inquiring about the reasons why each participant had circled a portion of the text. Barry [57] found that the main criteria of relevance were information content of documents; the user's previous experience and knowledge; the user's beliefs and preferences; other information and sources of information within the environment; sources of documents; the document as a physical entity; and the user's situation.

In the context of **interactive information retrieval**, Spink & Goodrum [58] explored the notion of encoding and external storage (EES) processes performed by professional users during mediated, interactive information retrieval. An emphasis was placed on the notes taken by professional searchers while performing a search. A micro-analysis of the notes recorded by four librarians acting as search intermediaries were analysed. They found that subjects were extensively using encoding and external storage (EES) processes whereas three types of working notes were created such as textual, numerical and graphical. Creation of working notes was identified as the fundamental element of the mediated, interactive information retrieval process. Building on this, Spink et al. [66] explored the search process of mediated information retrieval performed by professional searchers. Their goal was to record information search behavior and to identify the procedural changes and shifts in users' behavior. A mixture of methods both qualitative and quantitative was employed. In particular, three questionnaires were adopted to assist pre and post interviews, interviews were conducted both after the searches to identify specific reasons for changing search behaviors, as well as a follow up after a couple of months of the searches. The searches on the DIALOG Information service by professional searchers were audio taped and transaction logs were analysed. Spink et al. [66] were able to identify the specific users' actions while searching for information as well as the changes occurred in user's behavior over time. In particular, for each situated action, levels and regions of relevance judgements as well as other user judgements were identified.

They also found that users spent more time on performing an action, deciding and making judgements than interacting with IR or other systems.

Furthermore, Bains [59] tried to identify **an effective way of measuring the impact** of novices on interactive search retrieval systems developed for professional searchers. A variety of quantitative and qualitative methods were employed. In particular, questionnaires were used to record users' experiences and characteristics, observation to look at specific elements of users' information search, analysis of search strategies and finally interviews to inquire about users' specific reasons for employing specific search behaviors. Bains [59] discussed the advantages and disadvantages of each method in an attempt to propose a specific methodology for exploring professional searchers search behavior. Extending this research, Vibert et al. [27] explored the search strategies and behavior of professional searchers on PubMed. Specifically, they identified possible factors affecting the bibliographic search performance of life scientists. Previous experience and knowledge of the database, non domain-specific knowledge, significant difference of number of references provided, general cognitive abilities and user's age were identified as the factors significantly correlated with users' performance. It is evident, that factors apart from the system itself affected users' search behavior such as domain knowledge, cognitive abilities. These factors are directly related with the user and therefore, provide a valuable insight into users' thought processes while searching.

Building on this research, Tucker [3] investigated **the learning experiences** of information professionals and **acquisition of expertise** while searching for information. An emphasis was given to novices who aimed to acquire expertise and develop searching skills and knowledge. A mixture of both qualitative and quantitative methods was adopted to capture users' information search behavior and thought processes. In particular, think aloud protocols were employed to explain the actions and the reasons provoking specific search behaviors; interviews to further explore the reasons behind users' behaviors; and screen capture software so as to video tape the specific search behaviors of all participants. Finally, Grounded Theory was employed to identify conceptual knowledge and attributes of professional searchers. Tucker [3] identified six emerged categories describing users' search behavior such as "Broad view", "Subject domain", "Nature of Learning", "Qualities/approaches", "Tools/search knowledge", and "Work-related experiences". Threshold concept theory was employed to further justify users' search behavior. In particular, three major themes were identified such as **Concepts** adopting the attributes of threshold concepts; **Praxes** which incorporated practices, approaches and strategies; and **Traits** which referred to qualities, characteristics and attitudes.

Moreover, Iivonen & Sonnenwald [60] proposed **a model for term selection** during the information retrieval process. Thirty two professional searchers were asked to form queries based on real-life search requests. Interviews explored users' reasons for formulating the specific queries and thus search behavior. They were able to identify **six different discourses** that are users ways of talking and thinking about a certain topic. These discourses consisted of controlled vocabularies, documents and the domain, the practice of indexing, clients' search requests, databases and the users' own search experiences. Analysis of the selection process on the basis of different discourses provided another view on the way users' select of specific search terms. Building on this, Patterson et al. [61] **modelled the potential vulnerabilities** in inferential analysis under different conditions. Ten professional searchers were asked to analyse a request outside their base of expertise. The methods of think aloud protocols to capture users' search strategies and interview to identify users' characteristics and previous experience were employed. The use of software features was explored as a mean to understand the professional searchers' behaviors and reasons why they searched in specific ways. Patterson et al. [61] found that these users were prone to use narrow tactics and refine their initial results so as to reach a manageable volume of results. These results were treated as a base failing to perform additional searches or expand the results in other ways. In addition, the users articulated three different types of inaccurate statements such as assumptions that that did not apply, the incorporation of inaccurate information and reliance on outdated information. Furthermore, some of these users' adopted strategies in an attempt to reduce inaccurate statements. However, these proved to be difficult, resource-intensive and time-consuming. Finally, users presented a prematurely closed analysis process. As a result, professional searchers could degrade the quality of the final outcome, respond less effectively to the question and feel less confidence of the final outcome.

In addition, Ehrlich & Cash [62] explored **the richness** and **complexity** of professional searchers behaviors with the view to inform development of software tools. Observation of these users' search strategies as well as interviews were conducted in order to gain an insight into users' search behaviors. They found that the experience and expertise of intermediaries performing the professional searches was often invisible to the company in which they worked. Moreover, Robins [63] investigated the information problems while interacting with retrieval systems and how professional searchers change their focus during interactions. Observation was employed to record conversations between real users and professional search intermediaries while interacting with the system and performing the searches; and think aloud protocols to gain an insight into real users' and professional search intermediaries' perceptions and thought processes. Robins [63] argued that users and search intermediaries collaborate to achieve search goals in a nonlinear way. Discourse analysis showed that they changed topics on average every seven utterances. Six major focus categories of these utterances were identified such as documents, evaluation of search results, search strategies, IR system, search topic and information about the user.

Finally, Gschwandtner et al. [64] explored the information needs and search behavior of **health professionals** in the context of the KHRESMOI European Union project. The quantitative method of questionnaires was employed to explore internet access, information needs, and adoption of online resources, barriers in online searching, preferences and information search behavior. They found that physicians searched for information on drugs, treatment and medical education and empoyed mainly widely known search engines such as Google. In addition, specialists searched for information about clinical trials and expressed a preference for medical databases and professional society websites. Both physicians and specialists needed immediate and up-to-dated information. They employed search terms and were prone to go through the first three pages of the results clicking on the most relevant results. Date range and language were the main two features employed while on advanced search. Quality was judged based on source and date of last update. The ideal search engine for these users would provide access to relevant and trustworthy results.

4 Discussion

Users' information search behavior in a professional search environment is a research area of growing interest. As such, a variety of studies have been conducted exploring the characteristics of a professional search from different perspectives. The majority of studies focused on the development of systems [5], [6], [7], [8], information retrieval techniques [9], [10], [11], [1] and models [19], [20]. As such, little attention has been given to users' and their search behavior and strategies for addressing their professional information needs.

In this context, two types of studies were identified. System-centered studies employed professional users but focused on measuring systems' performance [16], [5], precision and recall [55]. As such, professional searchers were employed to judge the relevance of retrieved results and assist the work of developers and evaluators to create efficient and effective information retrieval techniques [52], [27], [6], [11], [55]. Users' behavior was documented as a sequence of searches and clicks used as a basis to extract results on systems' performance and as a way to enhance retrieval techniques [16], [52], [5]. User satisfaction was solely judged based on system's performance and amount and relevance of retrieved results [16], [55]. The same applied for all contexts of search (archival, medical) and systems [27], [54].

Log analysis was the main method employed to explore users' search actions and behaviors [52], [53], [5], [54], [6]. Analysis of the log files revealed valuable insight into users' search terms used, number of pages viewed in the search results, adoption of specific features of the system, time spent among others [6], [5]. However, there is a common belief that reliable evaluation methods are needed in system-centered studies to extract safe results on users' behavior and search strategies especially in the context of professional search environments [6], [5]. When qualitative methods were employed such as, interviews [16] and think aloud protocols [27], the focus again was on system's characteristics and performance.

In contrast, user-centered studies focused on professional users' search behavior and strategies with the view to gaining an insight into their thought processes while searching and retrieving relevant information. These studies employed mainly qualitative methods such as interviews, think aloud protocols, grounded theory, observation to explore users' search behavior [59], [61], [62],

[63], [66]. An emphasis was placed on the user, not the system, with the view to understand users' interpretation and experiences of the system and offer efficient and effective systems [57], [58], [60], [63], [66], [3].

This critical review is somewhat limited by the specific terms relating to professional search resulting in the nineteen papers found spanning two decades. Whilst this restricts the depth of the investigation, the findings discussed in this chapter serve to suggest that overall, there is still an emphasis on system development and evaluation based on measurements such as precision and recall. Users are employed to judge system's performance and effectiveness and thus mainly quantitative methods are employed. When interviews and think aloud protocols are adopted, they are used to extract quantitative data and thus are analysed as such. Professional users' search behavior in terms of their thought processes and experiences while searching is less explored. Although, when considered, the use of qualitative methods rather than quantitative is notable, placing an emphasis on understanding user search behavior through their thought processes, experiences and perceptions of the systems and of the search strategies developed to satisfy their information needs.

The methods used to study the user with respect to the 'system' performance, perhaps on the impact of a search tool or feature, thus focused on the users' activities or use of the system features in the process of finding information. In contrast, the methods used to study the user, particularly the professional searcher, focus on the cognitive aspects of the search, what the user is doing, or thinks they are doing, their resources and strategies and the impact the interaction has on them and their actions. In particular, identification of utterances [63] and discourse analysis [60], [63] provided a valuable insight into users' thinking and decision making. In addition, they highlighted the changes that occur over time in a users' behavior affecting decisions and as such search strategies. Factors affecting professional searchers behavior such as previous experience with the search interface, domain knowledge, cognitive abilities [27] were identified mainly due to the user focus in these studies and to the qualitative methods employed.

Understanding professional search is essential for the development of system and techniques designed to support this activity and, in this respect, the different approaches to the study of users are essential as well as complementary. This review, specifically distinguishes the research based on user evaluation of system effectiveness from studies of the information search behavior in a professional search environment providing a distinction into the methods employed. In addition to the potential aid in helping the work of system developers by outlining the methods adopted to examine users' behaviors in both system and user-centered studies, the review of these literatures side by side also provides essential insight into professional search behavior and the potential interrelation of system and user influences for the development of efficient and effective systems and retrieval techniques.

References

1. Kim, Y., Seo, J., Croft, W.B.: Automatic boolean query suggestion for professional search. In: Proceedings of the 34th International ACM SIGIR Conference on Research and Development in Information Retrieval. ACM (2011)
2. List, J.: The name of the game: Information seeking in a professional context. In: Lupu, M., Salampasis, M., Fuhr, N., Hanbury, A., Larsen, B., Strindberg, H. (eds.) Proceedings of the Integrating IR Technologies for Professional Search Workshop, Moscow, Russia (March 24, 2013)
3. Tucker, V.M.: Acquiring search expertise: learning experiences and threshold concepts. Queensland University of Technology (2012)
4. Koster, C.H.A., Seibert, O., Seutter, M.: The PHASAR search engine. In: Kop, C., Fliedl, G., Mayr, H.C., Métais, E. (eds.) NLDB 2006. LNCS, vol. 3999, pp. 141–152. Springer, Heidelberg (2006)
5. Kohn, A., Bry, F., Manta, A., Ifenthaler, D.: Professional search: Requirements, prototype and preliminary experience report. In: IADIS International Conference WWW/Internet, pp. 195–202 (2008), http://scholar.google.gr/scholar?start=30&q=professional+search&hl=el&as_sdt=0,5#5, (accessed January 18, 2014)
6. Lamm, K.: User experiments with search services: methodological challenges for measuring the perceived quality. In: Proceedings of the 3rd Workshop on Perceptual Quality of Systems, PQS 2010 (2010)
7. Tsai, T.H., Chang, H.T.: Surfrom: A community-oriented search engine interface. Appl. Math. 6, 389–396 (2012)
8. Salampasis, M., Giachanou, A., Paltoglou, G.: Multilayer collection selection and search of topically organized patents. Ceur-Ws.org (2013), http://ceur-ws.org/Vol-968/irps_9.pdf (accessed January 18, 2014)
9. Mitra, M., Singhal, A., Buckley, C.: Improving automatic query expansion. In: Proceedings of the 21st Annual International ACM SIGIR Conference on Research and Development in Information Retrieval. ACM (1998)
10. Kendrick, T.: The winning mindset Effective competitive intelligence research on the internet. Business Information Review 24, 228–235 (2007)
11. Jain, A., Mishne, G.: Organizing query completions for web search. In: Proceedings of the 19th ACM International Conference on Information and Knowledge Management. ACM (2010)
12. Fafalios, P., Salampasis, M., Tzitzikas, Y.: Exploratory patent search with faceted search and configurable entity mining. Ics.forth.gr (2013). http://www.ics.forth.gr/~fafalios/files/pubs/fafalios_2013_explPatSearch.pdf (accessed January 18, 2014)
13. Hollink, V., Tsikrika, T., de Vries, A.P.: Semantic search log analysis: a method and a study on professional image search. Journal of the American Society for Information Science and Technology 62, 691–713 (2011)
14. Cornacchia, R., Kamps, J.: Searching political data by strategy. In: Proceedings of the Integrating IR technologies for Professional Search Workshop (2013)
15. Cummins, R.: Choosing the right tool for the job: searchbots. The Technology Source (2001)
16. Tan, K.F.: Extending information retrieval system model to improve interactive web searching. Middlesex University (2005), http://eprints.mdx.ac.uk/8027/ (accessed January 18, 2014)

17. Chen, C., Wang, T.: Design and realization of topic search based on transfering of searching engine. Computer Engineering and Design 21, 66 (2008)
18. Baram-Tsabari, A., Segev, E.: Just Google it! exploring new web-based tools for identifying public interest in science and pseudoscience. In: Proceedings of the Chais Conference on Instructional Technologies Research (2009)
19. Spink, A., Sollenberger, M.: Elicitation purposes and tasks during mediated information search. Journal of Documentation 60, 77–91 (2004)
20. Kitsos, I., Magoutis, K., Tzitzikas, Y.: Scalable entity-based summarization of web search results using MapReduce. Distributed and Parallel Databases 1–42 (2013)
21. Petcu, P., Aps, F., Dragusin, R.: Considerations for the development of task-based search engines. Ceur-Ws.org (2013), http://ceur-ws.org/Vol-968/irps_14.pdf (accessed January 18, 2014)
22. Salampasis, M., Hanbury, A.: A generalized framework for integrated professional search systems. In: Lupu, M., Kanoulas, E., Loizides, F. (eds.) IRFC 2013. LNCS, vol. 8201, pp. 99–110. Springer, Heidelberg (2013)
23. Kohn, A.: Professional search in pharmaceutical research. Munchen, Univ., Diss., Diss. (2009)
24. Turtle, H.: Natural language vs. boolean query evaluation: A comparison of retrieval performance. In: Proceedings of the 17th Annual International ACM SIGIR Conference on Research and Development in Information Retrieval. Springer-Verlag New York, Inc. (1994)
25. Azzopardi, L., Vanderbauwhede, W., Joho, H.: Search system requirements of patent analysts. In: Proceedings of the 33rd International ACM SIGIR Conference on Research and Development in Information Retrieval. ACM (2010)
26. Hemingway, P.: What is a systematic review? Evidence-based Medicine, 1–8 (April 2009), http://www.medicine.ox.ac.uk/bandolier/painres/download/whatis/syst-review.pdf (accessed January18, 2014)
27. Vibert, N., Ros, C., Bigot, L.L.: Effects of domain knowledge on reference search with the PubMed database: An experimental study. Journal of the American Society for Information Science and Technology 60, 1423–1447 (2009)
28. Karat, J., Karat, C.: The evolution of user-centered focus in the human- computer interaction field. IBM Syst. J. 42, 532–541 (2003)
29. Borlund, P.: Experimental components for the evaluation of interactive information retrieval systems. Journal of Documentation 56, 71–90 (2000)
30. Ingwersen, P., Jrvelin, K.: The turn: Integration of information seeking and retrieval in context, vol. 18. Springer (2005)
31. Ellis, D.: Information seeking behavior. In: Feather, J., Sturges, R. (eds.) International Encyclopedia of Information and Library Science, pp. 300–301. Routledge, London (1997)
32. Paisley, W.: Information needs and uses. ARIST 3, 1–30 (1968)
33. Allen, T.J.: Information needs and uses. ARIST 4, 1–29 (1969)
34. Wilson, T.: On user studies and information needs. Journal of Documentation 37, 3–15 (1981)
35. Taylor, R.: Question negotiation and information seeking in libraries. College & Research Libraries 29, 178–194 (1968)
36. Ingwersen, P.: Search procedures in the library analysed from the cognitive point of view. Journal of Documentation 38, 165–191 (1982)
37. Belkin, N., Brooks, H., Oddy, R.: Ask for information retrieval. Journal of Documentation 38, 61–71 (1982)
38. Dervin, B., Nilan, M.: Information needs and uses. ARIST 21, 3–33 (1986)

39. Kuhlthau, G.: Inside the search process: information seeking from the users perspective. JASIST 42, 361–371 (1991)
40. Ellis, D.: A behavioral model to information retrieval system design. Journal of Information Science 15, 171–212 (1989)
41. Jarvelin, K.: On information, information technology and the development of society: An information science perspective. In: Ingwersen, P., Kajberg, L., Pejtersen, A. (eds.) Information Technology and Information Use: Towards a Unified View of Information and Information Technology, pp. 35–55. Taylor Graham, London (1986)
42. Bystrom, K., Jarvelin, K.: Task complexity affects information seeking and use. Information Processing & Management 31, 191–214 (1995)
43. Wang, P., White, M.: A cognitive model of document use during a research project: Study II Decisions at the reading and citing stages. JASIS 50, 98–114 (1999)
44. Vakkari, P.: A theory of the task-based information retrieval process: A summary and generalization of a longitudinal study. Journal of Documentation 57, 44–60 (2001)
45. Belkin, N.J., Cool, C., Stein, A., Thiel, U.: Cases, scripts, and information- seeking strategies: on the design of interactive Information Retrieval systems. Expert Systems with Applications 9, 379–395 (1995)
46. Ingwersen, P.: Cognitive perspectives of information retrieval interaction: Elements of a cognitive IR theory. Journal of Documentation 52, 3–50 (1996)
47. Brown, G., Yule, G.: Discourse analysis. Cambridge University Press, Cambridge (1983)
48. Glaser, B., Strauss, A.: The Discovery of Grounded Theory: Strategies for Qualitative Research. Aldine Transaction (1967)
49. Blumer, H.: Sociological analysis and the variable. American Sociological Review 21, 683–690 (1956)
50. Oard, D., Levow, G., Cabezas, C.: TREC-9 experiments at Maryland: Interactive CLIR. In: TREC (2000)
51. Chung, W., Zhang, Y., Huang, Z., Wang, G., Ong, T.-H., Chen, H.: Internet searching and browsing in a multilingual world: An experiment on the Chinese Business Intelligence Portal (CBizPort). Journal of the American Society for Information Science and Technology 55, 818–831 (2004)
52. Spink, A.: Term relevance feedback and mediated database searching: Implications for information retrieval practice and systems design. Information Processing & Management 31, 161–171 (1995)
53. Spink, A., Goodrum, A., Robins, D.: Elicitation behavior during mediated information retrieval. Information Processing & Management 34, 257–273 (1998)
54. Huurnink, B.: Search in audiovisual broadcast archives (2010), http://dare.uva.nl/record/358972 (accessed January 18, 2014)
55. Bron, M., Gorp, J., van, N.F., Rijke, M.: de: Exploratory search in an audio-visual archive: Evaluating a professional search tool for non-professional users, pp. 3–6 (2011)
56. Karlgren, J.: The CHORUS gap analysis on user-centered methodology for design and evaluation of multi-media information access systems. In: The Second International Workshop on Evaluating Information Access (EVIA 2008), Tokyo, Japan (December 16, 2008)
57. Barry, C.L.: User-defined relevance criteria: an exploratory study. Journal of the American Society for Information Science and Technology 45, 149–159 (1994)

58. Spink, A., Goodrum, A.: A study of search intermediary working notes: Implications for IR system design. Information Processing & Management 32, 681–695 (1996)
59. Bains, S.: End-user searching at Cranfield University. New Library World 99, 31–40 (1998)
60. Iivonen, M., Sonnenwald, D.H.: From translation to navigation of different discourses: A model of search term selection during the pre-online stage of the search process. Journal of the American Society for Information Science 49, 312–326 (1998)
61. Patterson, E.S., Woods, D.D., Tinapple, D., Roth, E.M., Finley, J.M., Kuperman, G.G.: Aiding the intelligence analyst in situations of data overload: From problem definition to design concept exploration. Institute for Ergonomics/Cognitive Systems Engineering Laboratory Report, ERGO-CSEL (2001)
62. Ehrlich, K., Cash, D.: The invisible world of intermediaries: a cautionary tale. Computer Supported Cooperative Work (CSCW) 8, 147–167 (1999)
63. Robins, D.: Shifts of focus on various aspects of user information problems during interactive information retrieval. Journal of the American Society for Information Science 51, 913–928 (2000)
64. Gschwandtner, M., Kritz, M., Boyer, C.: D8. 1.2: Requirements of the Health Professional Search. Khresmoi Project Public (2011), http://www.khresmoi.eu/assets/Deliverables/WP8/KhresmoiD812.pdf (accessed January 18, 2014)
65. Jones, R., Rey, B., Madani, O., Greiner, W.: Generating query substitutions. In: Proceedings of the 15th International Conference on World Wide Web. ACM (2006)
66. Spink, A., Wilson, T.D., Ford, N.J., Ellis, D., Foster, A.E.: Information seeking and mediated searching study. Part 3. Successive searching. Journal of the American Society for Information Science and Technology 53, 716–727 (2002)

5 Annex 1. Tables

Table 1. Year of Publication

Year	No. Paper	Papers
1994	1	Barry [57]
1995	1	Spink [52]
1996	1	Spink & Goodrum [58]
1998	3	Bains [59], Iivonen & Sonnenwald [60], Spink, Goodrum, & Robins [53]
1999	1	Ehrlich & Cash [62]
2000	1	Robins [63]
2001	1	Patterson et al. [61]
2002	1	Spink et al. [66]
2005	1	Tan [16]
2008	1	Kohn et al. [5]
2009	1	Vibert, Ros, & Bigot [27]
2010	3	Huurnink [54], Jain & Mishne [11], Lamm [6]
2011	2	Bron et al. [55], Gschwandtner, Kritz, & Boyer [64]
2012	1	Tucker [3]

In Table 1, the identified relevant literature was grouped according to year of publication. The years range from 1994 to 2012. In total nineteen papers were considered.

Table 2. Emerged Themes

A/A	Themes	No. Papers	Papers
1	System centered	9	Spink [52], Spink et al. [53], Kohn et al. [5], Vibert et al. [27], Huurnink [54], Jain & Mishne [11], Lamm [6], Bron et al. [55], Tan [16]
2	User centered	11	Barry [57], Spink & Goodrum [58], Bains [59], Iivonen & Sonnenwald [60], Ehrlich & Cash [62], Patterson et al. [61], Robins [63], Spink et al. [66], Vibert et al. [27], Gschwandtner et al. [64], Tucker [3]

In Table 2, the relevant papers were categorized in themes based on their expressed aims. As such, two themes emerged such as system-centered and user-centered studies. Both themes concentrate an almost equal number of assigned papers.

Table 3. Type of methods employed in each emerged theme

A/A	Themes	No. Papers	Papers	Methods
1	System centered	9	Spink [52], Spink et al. [53], Kohn et al. [5], Vibert et al. [27], Huurnink [54], Jain & Mishne [11], Lamm [6], Bron et al. [55], Tan [16]	Automatic multimedia content analysis, Interview, Log Analysis (2), Questionnaire (2), Role Specific ranking, Task, Think aloud protocols
2	User centered	11	Barry [57], Spink & Goodrum [58], Bains [59], Iivonen & Sonnenwald [60], Ehrlich & Cash [62], Patterson et al. [61], Robins [63], Spink et al. [66], Vibert et al. [27], Gschwandtner et al. [64], Tucker [3]	Content analysis (5) Grounded theory Interview (6) Observation (4) Questionnaire (5) Relevance Search strategy analysis Think aloud protocols (6)

In table 3., the methods employed in each emerged theme are illustrated. In terms of system- centered studies, Questionnaire and Log analysis was the most methods adopted whereas user- centered studies employed Interview, Think aloud protocols, Content analysis and Questionnaire. As such, the user- centered

studies adopted mainly qualitative methods whereas system- centered studies
mainly quantitative.

Table 4. Methods employed per year

Year	Methods
1994	Content analysis, Interview, Questionnaire, Relevance
1995	Log analysis
1996	Content analysis
1998	Content analysis, Interview, Observation, Questionnaire, Search strategy analysis, Think aloud protocols
1999	Content analysis, Interview
2000	Content analysis
2001	Observation, Think aloud protocols
2002	Interview, Questionnaire, Think aloud protocols
2005	Interview
2008	Role-specific ranking
2009	Questionnaire, Think aloud protocols,
2010	Automatic multimedia content analysis, Log analysis
2011	Interview, Questionnaire (2)
2012	Grounded Theory, Interview, Observation, Think aloud protocols

In table 4., the methods adopted each year are illustrated. A mixture of both
qualitative and quantitative methods were employed with no conclusive remarks
over a specific tendency documented over the years to a specific method.

In table 5., the identified literature was further analysed based on type of
publication. In particular, four type of papers were identified such as journal
articles, proceeding papers, reports and thesis. The majority of the relevant
papers were journal articles. In addition a tendency in terms of a specific journal
was identified since five out of the eleven articles were published in the Journal
of the American Society for Information Science & Technology and three in
Information Processing & Management.

In table 6., the identified literature was further grouped based on specific
source of publication. System-centered studies more often appeared in conference proceedings and theses, while user-centered studies more often appeared in
journal articles and reports.

Table 5. Type of publication of each paper

Kind of Papers	No. Papers	Papers	Specific source
Journal article	10	Barry [57], Spink [52], Spink & Goodrum [58], Bains [59], Iivonen & Sonnenwald [60], Spink et al. [53], Ehrlich & Cash [62], Robins [63], Spink et al. [66], Vibert et al. [27]	*Computer Supported Cooperative Work (CSCW), Information processing & management(3), Journal of the American Society for Information Science & Technology(5), New library world, Western Journal of Nursing Research*
Proceedings paper	4	Kohn et al. [5], Jain & Mishne [11], Lamm [6], Bron et al. [55]	*Proceeding CIKM 10 Proceedings of the 19th ACM international conference on Information and knowledge management, IADIS International Conference WWW/Internet PQS'10, Proceedings of the 3rd workshop on perceptual quality of systems EuroHCIR, volume 763 of CEUR Workshop Proceedings,*
Report	2	Patterson et al. [61], Gschwandtner et al. [64]	
Thesis	3	Tan [16], Huurnink [54], Tucker [3]	

Table 6. Specific source of publication for each emerged theme

A/A	Themes	No. Papers	Papers	Kind of papers	Specific source
1	System centered	9	Spink [52], Spink et al. [53], Kohn et al. [5], Vibert et al. [27], Huurnink [54], Jain & Mishne [11], Lamm [6], Bron et al. [55], Tan [16]	Journal article (3), Proceeding paper (4), Thesis (2)	EuroHCIR, volume 763 of CEUR Workshop Proceedings, IADIS International Conference WWW/Internet, Information processing & management (2), Journal of the American Society for Information Science & Technology, PQS'10, Proceedings of the 3rd workshop on perceptual quality of systems, Proceeding CIKM 10 Proceedings of the 19th ACM international conference on Information and knowledge management, Western Journal of Nursing Research
2	User centered	11	Barry [57], Spink & Goodrum [58], Bains [59], Iivonen & Sonnenwald [60], Ehrlich & Cash [62], Patterson et al. [61], Robins [63], Spink et al. [66], Vibert et al. [27], Gschwandtner et al. [64], Tucker [3]	Journal articles (7), Reports (3), Thesis	Computer Supported Cooperative Work (CSCW), Information processing & management, Journal of the American Society for Information Science & Technology (3), New library world

Information Retrieval for R&D support

Gennady Osipov, Ivan Smirnov, Ilya Tikhomirov, Ilya Sochenkov,
Artem Shelmanov, and Alexander Shvets

Institute for Systems Analysis of Russian Academy of Sciences, Moscow, Russia
{gos,ivs,tih,sochenkov,shelmanov,shvets}@isa.ru

Abstract. Research and development (R&D) involves not only researchers but also many other specialists from different areas. All of them solve a variety of tasks that require comprehensive information and analytical support. This chapter discusses the major tasks arising in R&D: study of the state of the art in a given research area, prospects assessment of research fields and forecasting their development, quality assessment of scientific publications including plagiarism detection, and automated examination of proposed R&D projects. A number of informational and analytical systems have been developed to address these tasks. The main goal of this chapter is to give a review of R&D support functions of well-known and widely-used search and analytical systems and discuss information retrieval methods behind these functions.

Keywords: Full-text search, information retrieval, R&D support, scientific publication, citation databases, scientometrics, exploratory search.

1 Introduction

Research and development (R&D) activities involve many kinds of specialists: researchers, analysts of companies interested in R&D, experts of venture capital funds, state authorities responsible for policy in science and technology. All of these specialists demand comprehensive information and analytical support to solve many different tasks arising in R&D.

One of a researcher's main needs is to study publications from reliable and authoritative sources in a given research area. This task is primarily related to specific professional information search in large-scale collections of scientific documents: papers, journals, reports, conference proceedings, patents, etc.

Venture capital funds look for the most promising innovative projects that can pay off in the near future. Analysts of these funds need to understand which research areas are developing and which are prone to stagnation. Before making decision on funding, they need to make a forecast about development of research areas, examine, and select the most promising projects.

When an R&D project is finished, the problem of evaluating its results arises. Sponsors need to assess results and make a decision about whether to fund further research. This problem is commonly related to the examination of reports and publications of the research team produced during the project.

G. Paltoglou et al. (Eds.): Professional Search in the Modern World, LNCS 8830, pp. 45–69, 2014.
© Springer International Publishing Switzerland 2014

As a result, the diversity and increasing amount of available scientific and technological (sci-tech) information as well as the specificity of the tasks of R&D induce the development of one of the contemporary branches in information retrieval – professional search and analytical processing of scientific information. Many methods and automated tools have been specially developed to process sci-tech information.

This chapter discusses the major tasks arising in R&D. It gathers and reviews information about many mature and emerging technologies, systems, resources, and approaches that are useful for solving these tasks. The chapter also suggests approaches for processing sci-tech information that can be useful for creating next generation search and analytical systems for R&D support, which is one of the main goals of the MUMIA Action.

The rest of the chapter is structured as follows. Section 2 is devoted to the problem of studying of the state of research in a given research area. Section 3 introduces systems and methods for the prospective assessment of research fields and forecasting their development. Section 4 examines techniques for the qualitative assessment of scientific publications. Section 5 discusses the problem of the expert review of proposed R&D projects. Section 6 concludes the chapter.

2   Study of a Research Area

One of the main needs of those involved in R&D is information about the state of the art in different research areas. Modern scientific and technological progress is based on the latest results achieved by researchers and scientists in different institutions all around the world. The results of R&D are published in scientific journals, conference proceedings, books, PhD theses, technical reports, patent descriptions, etc. One needs to survey and discover these sources to choose the right research goals, use modern technologies and methods, and achieve top-level results.

2.1   Tasks Behind Study of a Research Area

Every scientific project starts with the exploration of the area of research. A researcher must find the latest information about the problem and modern solutions to determine the direction of research. During research, one should familiarize oneself with the latest tendencies in the area and with the results achieved by other research groups. Continuous study of the research area helps project leaders to guide the research in the right direction. It is also helpful when evaluating the results of a project and comparing them with the state of the art in the area of research. Developers of scientific projects as well as patent attorneys, and Patent Office experts also require complete information about the latest results, inventions, and technologies in particular research areas to fulfill their professional needs. Thus, the study of a research area is an integral part of all R&D activities.

Study a research area comprises the following tasks.

The first task is *information search*. A user needs to find answers to questions, particular facts, or documents, which they know are characterized by keywords, key phrases, and some metadata.

The second task is *exploratory search* [1]. It assumes that a user needs information about a topic or a particular problem in a research area, but they are unfamiliar with the domain of their goals (i.e. the user needs to learn about the topic in order to understand how to achieve their goal) or unsure about ways to achieve their goals [2].

The third task is *fast familiarization* with the topic and the content of a particular document in the focus of a user's attention. This can be achieved by presenting keywords and abstracts of documents, which are provided by authors as metadata or built automatically using methods for keyword extraction and text summarization.

2.2   Scientific Analytical Systems to Support Study of a Research Area

In the modern world, the full and comprehensive study of a research area cannot be performed without search and analytical systems. The common way to find required information is to use a global web search engine like Google, Bing, Yahoo, or Yandex. Although these systems provide advanced capabilities for information search on the Web, they cannot satisfy information needs arising from R&D activities and cannot solve the tasks mentioned above. The reasons for this are the following:

- Functionalities of the global search engines are *limited to the keyword search*;
- The global search engines focus on requests that are *limited to a short phrase*;
- The global search engines suffer from *low precision* due to large numbers of irrelevant documents among search results, such as advertisements, paper descriptions, and announcements, which clog up information returned to users;
- The global search engines have a *low recall* due to an incomplete coverage of specific information sources such as scientific journals, patent databases, etc.

To solve the tasks of the study of a research area, the following scientific analytical systems were developed: digital scientific libraries, patent databases and search engines, academic search engines, and scientific citation indexing services and databases. They provide a varied set of scientific search and analytical functions. Table 1 gives succinct overview of these systems.

Digital scientific libraries specialize in particular scientific fields and provide extended search functionality including paper metadata indexing, predefined taxonomies for document topic identification, thesauri for query expansion, and specific user interfaces for complex query construction.

Patent databases are mostly similar to digital scientific libraries but have extended metadata sets and cover all scientific and technical fields. Therefore, patent databases use complex hierarchical taxonomies, such as the International Patent

Table 1. Scientific analytical systems

Category	System	Comment
Digital scientific libraries	ArXiv[1]	Contains e-prints in physics, mathematics, computer science
	PubMed[2]	Contains papers on life sciences and biomedical topics
	IEEE Xplore[3]	Contains scientific and technical content published by the IEEE
	NGC[4]	Contains evidence-based clinical practice guidelines in medicine
Patent databases	European Patent Organisation (EPO)[5], The United States Patent and Trademark Office (USPTO)[6], Federal Institute of Industrial Property (FIPS)[7]	Contain patents and patent application topically classified by experts
Patent search engines	Google Patents[8], FPO[9]	Aggregate data from different patent databases
Academic search engines	Scirus[10], CiteSeer^X [11], Google Scholar[12] [3], Microsoft Academic Search[13], Exactus Expert[14] [4]	Aggregate scientific semi-structured data from the Web
Scientific citation indexing services and databases	Elsevier Scopus[15], Thomson Reuters Web of Science (WoS)[16], eLIBRARY.RU[17]	Import structured bibliographic data from publisher databases and scientific journals

[1] http://arxiv.org/
[2] https://www.ncbi.nlm.nih.gov/pubmed/
[3] http://ieeexplore.ieee.org/
[4] http://www.guideline.gov/
[5] http://www.epo.org/
[6] http://www.uspto.gov/
[7] http://www1.fips.ru/wps/wcm/connect/content_en/en/main/
[8] https://www.google.com/?tbm=pts
[9] http://www.freepatentsonline.com/
[10] http://www.scirus.com/
[11] http://citeseerx.ist.psu.edu
[12] http://scholar.google.com
[13] http://academic.research.microsoft.com/
[14] http://expert.exactus.ru/
[15] http://www.scopus.com/
[16] http://thomsonreuters.com/web-of-science-core-collection/
[17] http://elibrary.ru

Classification (IPC)[18] or the Cooperative Patent Classification (CPC)[19] to specify the category of an invention presented in a patent. There are patent search engines that automatically aggregate data from different patent databases.

Academic search engines aggregate scientific information from different sources including web sites of scientific journals, publisher databases, and digital libraries. The *scientific citation indexing services and databases* also focus on scientific information and provide advanced metadata analysis features (e.g., bibliographic reference analysis).

CiteSeer^X, Google Scholar, and Exactus Expert focus on indexing scientific information that is freely published on the Web. The considered academic search engines extract descriptive metadata of scientific documents (e.g., titles, authors, affiliations, etc.) directly from their entire texts. For example, Google Scholar uses information extraction algorithms, which take into account information about fonts and layout of a text[20]. Descriptive metadata extracted from documents without markup (PDF, PS, etc.) often contains some errors. Therefore, some systems (e.g., Google Scholar and Exactus Expert) extract descriptive metadata not only from the texts of target documents, but also from web pages containing paper descriptions or tables of contents. The extracted metadata is linked with the corresponding full-text documents.

Automated web-crawling, indexing, and metadata extraction often produce inconsistent data due to different citation formats, different spellings of authors' surnames, misspellings, full-text duplicates, and other difficulties. Thus, the tasks of author disambiguation [5,6], bibliographic reference identification [7,8,9], and duplicate documents filtering arise.

Digital scientific libraries and patent databases use quite a different approach to update their databases. The editors and administrators of these systems store the full texts of scientific documents to repositories with descriptive and bibliographic metadata along with structured bibliographic references manually. Most of digital scientific libraries export structured bibliographic metadata and bibliographic references to citation indexing services and databases. Thus, data inconsistency rarely arises with such an approach, and the main challenges lie in complexity of manual updates and full-text indexing.

2.3   Information Search in Scientific Analytical Systems

Although all of the aforementioned systems support search through metadata as the main entry point to system databases, not all of them provide full-text search.

---

[18] International Patent Classification. Available at:
   `http://www.wipo.int/classifications/ipc/en/`, last accessed July 5, 2014.
[19] Cooperative Patent Classification. Available at:
   `http://www.cooperativepatentclassification.org/index.html;`
   `jsessionid=1ujqr7669rr4i`, last accessed July 5, 2014.
[20] Inclusion Guidelines for Webmasters. Available at:
   `http://scholar.google.com/intl/en/scholar/inclusion.html`, last accessed July 5, 2014.

Web of Science and Scopus do not work with semi-structured full-text data at all, but focus on processing of bibliographical data aggregated from scientific journals and publisher databases. Microsoft Academic Search and eLIBRARY.RU support limited text search through abstracts and descriptions of scientific documents.

Patent databases, digital scientific libraries, and the mentioned academic search engines provide *full-text search* along with advanced search capabilities. In general, these systems support the *Boolean query language*, implement different methods for ranking search results by relevance, and provide the ability to precisely specify search areas (e.g., by bibliographic metadata constraints).

Digital scientific libraries and academic search engines work with search queries in natural language. The information search functions of these systems use inverted indices [10] and provide complex relevance ranking of search results along with the extended Boolean model [11]. Google Scholar considers citation counts and words included in the title of a document[21] [12]. Exactus Expert uses the complex text comparison algorithm [13], which combines statistical features of words (like TF-IDF or BM ranking [14,15] used in most of search engines) with linguistic features of a query and indexed texts [16].

CiteSeer^X [17] and Exactus Expert process full texts of scientific papers to extract bibliographic references and provide the ability to search through citations.

2.4 Exploratory Search in Scientific Analytical Systems

Search and analytical systems can help to solve this task in several ways. The first one is to use the *topic identification* methods to assign documents to categories and restrict search to particular categories. The second way is to use *thesauri for query expansion* [18] with conventional domain-specific lexis, which helps to find documents that belong to the user's area of interest. The third way is to *recommend search requests* similar to the original one [19]. The fourth way is to implement the search for *documents that are thematically similar* to the set of documents specified by a user.

Aforementioned scientific analytical systems usually do not utilize automatic methods for topic identification. It is mostly performed by editors and administrators or by the authors of papers using a predefined *taxonomy*. Documents corresponding to each topic can be accessed by navigating through the taxonomy, which is another access point to the search and analytical database [20].

Digital libraries containing materials on a particular research area offer the taxonomy related to that area. For example, ArXiv has a one-level hierarchy structure for each research area, which is convenient to explore. Users can select the particular category and get a list of recent documents to discover the latest published results. Users can also perform keyword search inside the chosen category.

Patent databases offer Boolean search as the main information search tool. Search results are sorted by date or patent / application number. Using this

---

[21] How does Google Scholar work? Available at:
https://www.lib.umn.edu/faq/5342, last accessed July 5, 2014.

approach, selection of relevant patents from the desired research area is a complicated task because of a huge number of search results. One should specify all keywords that characterize the desired domain along with the particular IPC categories. If a user wants to find all patents / applications thematically similar to the particular one, they must make an assumption about the keywords and construct an appropriate search query [21].

Some practical problems arise in the case of *global taxonomies* presenting a structure of all research areas. Because of the large multi-level hierarchy of such taxonomies, it is impossible to keep in mind all categories. Therefore, WIPO[22] provides a complex search and browsing tool to navigate across IPC[23]. However, this tool is integrated neither with patent databases nor with any patent search engines mentioned above.

The Universal Decimal Classification[24] is another global taxonomy for bibliographic and library classification. However, it is not widely used in academic search engines and digital libraries due to its complexity and size. eLIBRARY.RU uses the National Classification for Scientific and Technical Information (NCSTI)[25,26], as an alternative version of the UDC created by VINITI [22]. Most Russian scientific journals have predefined sets of NCSTI categories according to the topic of published papers. Therefore, papers published in interdisciplinary scientific journals automatically belong to all NCSTI categories associated with the respective journal. Such an approach lowers precision of classification.

To summarize, the global taxonomies for topic identification and exploratory search have the following main problems:

- Large multi-level hierarchies are complex and intransparent to users;
- Global taxonomies are volatile, since they are often reviewed and restructured (e.g., IPC);
- Scientific search and analytical services use incompatible taxonomies with different structure and no mappings between them are available;
- Manual assignment of topics is ambiguous in most cases. Moreover, there is a lot of information, which is potentially cannot be classified into predefined taxonomy [23].

[22] World Intellectual Property Indicators. Available at: http://www.wipo.int/portal/en/, last accessed July 5, 2014.

[23] IPC publication – WIPO. Available at: http://web2.wipo.int/ipcpub/#refresh=page, last accessed July 5, 2014.

[24] UDC Consortium. Available at: http://www.udcc.org/, last accessed July 5, 2014.

[25] State Classificator of Scientific and Technical Information. Available at: http://www2.viniti.ru/index.php?option=content&task=view&id=57, last accessed July 5, 2014.

[26] State Classificator of Scientific and Technical Information of Russia. Available at: http://scs.viniti.ru/rubtree/main.aspx?tree=RGNTI, last accessed July 5, 2014.

Some *scientific analytical services and databases* (e.g., Scirus, Microsoft Academic Search, and Exactus Expert) offer their *own flat classification systems* to overcome these problems. In practice, these classifications contain about 20-30 categories. Generally, documents are assigned to categories with the help of mappings from taxonomies used by scientific journals. These flat classifications are useful only for the constriction of search areas and they are not suitable for exploratory search.

Scientific citation indexing services and databases Scopus and Web of Science also have their own classification systems that are created from taxonomies used by journals, which export their data to these systems.

The PubMed system offers a different approach to exploratory search. It uses the MeSH *thesaurus*[27] as a controlled vocabulary and an interactive user interface tool for *query construction*. Because of its size, the thesaurus cannot be browsed easily. Therefore, indexed papers are available through the search, which takes into account MeSH descriptors as keywords or tags and other metadata constraints. An interactive form for query construction analyses user's input and shows matching descriptors from MeSH. In PubMed, users can sort search results by dates to browse the latest papers in the area of interest.

A more comprehensive tool for exploratory search is searching for *documents that are thematically similar* to a particular document or a set of documents. This function is called "similar" (IEEE Xplore, Scirus, and Exactus Expert) or "related" (PubMed, Google Patents, and Google Scholar) document search as well as "co-citations" and "clustered documents" (CiteSeer^X). Different approaches are used to implement these features in the aforementioned systems.

Analysis of bibliographic references and *comparison of papers by citations* is the most common approach. IEEE Xplore, Scirus, CiteSeer^X, PubMed, and Google Scholar consider papers similar if the first one cites the second one and they both have joint references. Although this approach has a simple implementation over the structured citation database and provides a good quality of exploratory search, it has some disadvantages. Citation distribution highly depends on a research area [24,25], language of scientific papers, affiliations of authors, their self-citations, and collaborations [26]. Thus, there is no guarantee that found information is representative and covers the research area entirely rather than just small part of it. However, Google Scholar uses this approach to characterize users' areas of interest and provide recommendations of recently published and indexed papers, in which they may be interested [27].

A lot of documents (e.g., patents) do no have references at all [28]. Therefore calculating similarity between these documents using citation analysis is not possible. An alternative approach is to use *keywords and phrases* as subject descriptors for the similar document search. In contrast to the first approach, which assumes that scientific documents in a particular research area share the same citations, the keyword-based approach relies on the hypothesis that papers in a particular research area contain the same lexis. This approach is implemented in Exactus

---

[27] Medical Subject Headings. Available at: http://www.nlm.nih.gov/mesh/, last accessed July 5, 2014.

Expert and Google Patents. The latter extracts key phrases from document text and provides full-text search for patent documents relevant to different combinations of these phrases. No more than 10-15 key phrases are usually offered to users. Exactus Expert extracts single and compound lexemes from texts with the help of a syntactic parser, puts them into inverted indexes, and provides the ability to search for similar documents on that basis. About 50-200 of the most significant words are used to characterize each document. Search results can be sorted by measure of similarity or by date.

2.5 Fast Familiarization with Documents in Scientific Analytical Systems

Both in information and exploratory search users have to deal with many found documents. Sci-tech documents are long and complex. Reading all of them is a very arduous and time-intensive task [29]. Therefore users need some tools to determine quickly the topic and content of found documents and separate the relevant results from the irrelevant ones.

The systems that provide the full-text search commonly offer a user the brief description of found documents through *snippets*. Snippets are usually short extracts of text containing terms of a user's query.

To help users to perform the exploratory search most of the aforementioned systems characterize documents with *keywords and abstracts* provided by authors. This function is very useful, but sometimes these lists of keywords and abstracts are incomplete and do not present enough information about documents.

There is an alternative approach to introducing to users the topics and content of documents based on *text summarization* methods. Scientific analytical systems (Microsoft Academic Search, Google Patents, and Exactus Expert) provide keywords and key phrases automatically extracted from abstracts and full texts. Exactus Expert implements the text summarization algorithm, which builds a document summary on a user's demand. A summary consists of the most important sentences containing the most significant keywords of a document. There is also an ability to build the summary of a paper that contains sentences with definitions introduced by the authors and sentences that characterize the results of the paper.

2.6 Summary

Study of a research area is a complex task demanded by different categories of specialists involved in R&D. The considered search and analytical systems provide a large set of services that help users to study the most recent state of research in different domains. With the assistance of modern analytical systems, users are able to search for required information, understand the structure of the research area of their interest, and make themselves familiar with the topic and content of sci-tech documents. Table 2 summarizes features of the discussed analytical systems.

Table 2. Scientific analytical systems

System	Database update	Metadata search	Full-text search	Classification system	Similar / related document search	Summarization
ArXiv	manual	✓	✓	✓own one-level	–	✓**
PubMed	manual	✓	✓	✓MeSH	✓(citation based)	✓**
IEEE Xplore	manual	✓	✓	✓own one-level	✓(citation based)	✓**
NGC	manual	✓	✓	✓MeSH	–	✓**
EPO	manual	✓	✓	✓IPC	–	✓*
USPTO	manual	✓	✓	✓IPC	–	✓*
FIPS	manual	✓	✓	✓IPC	–	✓*
Google Patents	automated	✓	✓	✓IPC	✓(keyword-based)	✓*
FPO	automated	✓	✓	✓IPC	–	✓*
Scirus	automated	✓	✓	✓own one-level	✓(citation-based)	–
CiteSeer^X	automated	✓	✓	✓own one-level	✓(citation-based)	✓**
Google Scholar	automated	✓	✓	–	✓(citation-based)	✓*
Microsoft Academic Search	automated	✓	✓(abstracts and descriptions only)	✓own one-level	✓(citation based)	✓**
Exactus Expert	automated	✓	✓	✓own one-level	✓(keyword-based)	✓***
Scopus	manual	✓	–	✓own one-level	–	✓**
WoS	manual	✓	–	✓own one-level	–	✓**
eLIBRARY .RU	manual	✓	✓(abstracts and descriptions only)	✓NCSTI	–	✓**

* – abstracts provided by authors
** – abstracts and keywords, provided by authors
*** – automatically full-text extracted keywords and automatically generated summaries

There are still many unresolved tasks in the area of scientific semi-structured information processing. The information retrieval methods for solving these tasks are in focus of the modern research. There are conferences, which purpose is to compare new information search and retrieval methods, and speed up the technology transfer from research labs to industrial analytical systems, e.g., TREC[28], NTCIR[29], CLEF[30], SemEval[31], and ROMIP[32]. Despite growing quality of experimental methods, in practice, the widely used industrial analytical systems rarely use advanced information retrieval methods due to their computational complexity and prefer simple solutions for the real-world problems. Bringing new advanced methods to the widely used scientific analytical systems is a challenge.

3   Prospects Assessment of Research Fields and Forecast of Their Development

Another problem that arises in R&D activities is search for promising research fields and research groups. This problem involves the prospects assessment of research fields and forecasting their development.

3.1   Users and Their Goals

There are several categories of users whose needs and goals are related to the prospects assessment of research fields and forecast of their development.

Public state funds and venture companies look for the most promising innovative projects that can pay off in the near future to bring funding to them. Firstly, analysts of these funds should understand which research fields are developing and which have a tendency to stagnate. They need to evaluate a performance of the known research fields and *discover unseen or multi-disciplinary research fields* and directions that may be emerging. Secondly, analysts should find the most productive research groups that can advance in a given field and successfully accomplish a sci-tech project. Therefore, they need a way to *discover research groups*, determine in which scientific directions they work, and evaluate them.

Research institutions and managers should plan their research activity and guide their projects in the most perspective directions. They also search for promising researchers and experts qualified in certain areas to involve them in sci-tech projects.

---

[28] Text REtrieval Conference (TREC). Available at: `http://trec.nist.gov/`, last accessed June 17, 2014.

[29] NTCIR. Available at: `http://research.nii.ac.jp/ntcir/index-en.html`, last accessed June 17, 2014.

[30] The CLEF Initiative (Conference and Labs of the Evaluation Forum). Available at: `http://www.clef-initiative.eu/`, last accessed June 17, 2014.

[31] SemEval-2014 : Semantic Evaluation Exercises. Available at: `http://alt.qcri.org/semeval2014/index.php?id=tasks`, last accessed June 17, 2014.

[32] ROMIP: Russian Information Retrieval Evaluation Seminar.   Available at: `http://romip.ru/en/`, last accessed June 17, 2014.

Research groups and researchers themselves should assess the prospects of research topics, productivity, and their place in the global scientific context. They need to discover related research groups and fields to be aware of the state of the art. In addition, the subject of the study of researchers related to scientometrics lies in progress of research groups and their impact, relationships between the scientific communities, and their influence on each other.

3.2   Approaches and Tools

The tasks related to the prospects assessment of research fields and forecast of their development can be solved by experts. However, this can be ineffective due to the subjectivity of experts and the complexity of the tasks. Traditionally scientometric problems were automatically solved using *bibliometric analysis* [30] and most of the aforementioned tasks are solved with the help of citation indexing services and databases.

The arsenal of bibliometric analysis tasks and approaches includes:

– *Calculating indices* or indicators that reflect the performance, impact or influence of a publication, researcher, institution, state, etc. This task is solved by methods for citation network analysis, which involve counting the number of citations, clustering, and co-citation analysis [31].
– *Analyzing research trends* for understanding the evolution, progress or regress of research processes. This task is solved by building trends for publication activity and other indicators of researchers, organizations, states, etc.
– *Structuring research fields*, which is also called mapping, assumes retrieving unseen research fields and sub-fields. For this task, methods for clustering of publications are usually applied. Similarity is calculated between bags of terms that are extracted from the metafields of publications such as titles, abstracts, and keywords.

There are several tools [32] and datasets [33,34] for analysis of citation networks. Scientometric problems are widely considered in the journal Scientometrics[33].

State-of-the-art scientific analytical systems – SciVal[34], Illumin8[35] and Web of Knowledge[36] – partially solve the tasks of searching for promising fields of research and research groups.

SciVal is the set of products and services based on Elsevier's bibliographic database Scopus that supports decision making in research. The most signifi-cant functions of SciVal are the following: *building tailored reports* to analyze

---

[33] Scientometrics. Available at: `http://link.springer.com/journal/11192`, last accessed July 6, 2014.
[34] Products & Services — SciVal. Available at: `http://www.elsevier.com/online-tools/research-intelligence/products-and-services/scival`, last accessed July 6, 2014.
[35] illumin8 Elsevier. Available at: `http://www.elsevier.com/online-tools/illumin8`, last accessed July 6, 2014.
[36] Web of Knowledge. Available at: `http://thomsonreuters.com/content/science/pdf/Web_of_Knowledge_factsheet.pdf`, last accessed July 6, 2014.

the achievements of researchers, teams, departments or custom-defined groups; *searching for experts or partners* by terms or free text identifying the topic of research; searching for comprehensive, accurate and current *funding opportunity* content; searching for unique *research strengths* of institutions to identify competitive advantages, threats, and opportunities; *identifying multidisciplinary strengths* to determine areas for further investment; *measuring the institution performance* against others through an easy comparison of research strengths; *understanding research trends* in the institution, country, and region to establish research strategy; *identifying the specific areas of research* excellence and the emerging strengths of an institution; *finding rapidly emerging research areas* and potential areas for further investment; *evaluating the productivity* of researchers and teams and their impact on other researchers and consumers of scientific information.

Many of these functions are implemented using *bibliometric analysis*. However, more advanced technologies are also used. One of the core components of SciVal is Elsevier Fingerprint Engine[37]. Using a variety of Natural Language Processing (NLP) techniques and thesauri, it extracts and indexes weighted terms from the texts of scientific documents – publication abstracts, funding announcements, awards, project summaries, patents, proposals / applications, and other sources. The extracted *weighted terms* are called *"Fingerprint"* because they succinctly define scientific texts. Matching "Fingerprints" helps to find reviewers, funding opportunities, and suitable journals for publishing papers.

Illumin8 is another tool from Elsevier for exploring new processes and technologies, locating promising partners, monitoring competitors, and learning about the possible risks and benefits of trying novel approaches or getting into unfamiliar markets. Illumin8 indexes *full-text articles* from ScienceDirect[38] and *abstracts* from Scopus.

Web of Knowledge offers a variety of solutions for evaluating R&D performance[39]. They mainly use the Web of Science citation base and support most of the functions implemented in SciVal. Essential Science Indicators[SM] is a single environment for research and bibliometric assessment and evaluation[40] with the following abilities: analyzing the *research performance* of companies, institutions, and journals; identifying *significant trends* in the sciences; *ranking* top countries, journals, scientists, papers, and institutions by the fields of research areas; determining the *level of research results* and *impact* in specific fields of research.

---

[37] Elsevier Fingerprint Engine — SciVal. Available at: `http://info.scival.com/fingerprint`, last accessed July 6, 2014.

[38] ScienceDirect. Available at: `http://www.sciencedirect.com`, last accessed July 7, 2014.

[39] Research Analytics – Research Analytics – Thomson Reuters. Available at: `http://researchanalytics.thomsonreuters.com/`, last accessed July 6, 2014.

[40] Essential Science Indicators – IP & Science – Thomson Reuters. Available at: `http://wokinfo.com/products_tools/analytical/essentialscienceindicators/`, last accessed July 6, 2014.

Although the SciVal and Web of Knowledge provide some services that can partially solve the tasks of the prospects assessment of research fields and forecast of their development, in some cases such analysis could be unreliable due to incompleteness of their databases. Publications that are written in regional non-English languages are covered poorly in Scopus and Web of Science. The state-of-the-art scientific analytical systems analyze textual meta-information from names, titles, keywords, and abstracts, however full texts are hardly processed. Keywords and abstracts given by the author of a paper may present its content incorrectly, but the full text contains more useful information for processing than metafields.

Many scientific publications with full texts in different languages are freely accessible in the Web. These full-text publications can be a source for deep scientometric analysis, which can overcome aforementioned problems. In the recent years, the role of textual components has been growing and the combination of citation analysis and text-mining techniques has been used more often [35,36]. For example, Exactus Expert[14] integrates both the generally accepted principles of bibliometric indicator assessment and methods for semantic analysis of textual information. The main idea of Exactus Expert is to use deep linguistic processing of full texts for retrieving useful information from unstructured scientific papers that helps solving many tasks more efficiently [13].

4   Quality Assessment of Scientific Publications

This section is devoted to the techniques of quality assessment of scientific publications. Such techniques could be useful for researchers who describe the results of their studies (especially for students), for peer reviewers, the editors of scientific journals, and experts who would like to evaluate the quality of a publication before reading it. The following approaches based on the automatic analysis of texts could be applied to the assessment of the quality of scientific publications:

- Plagiarism and improper citation detection;
- Verification of compliance with the standard rules for writing primary scientific texts.

These approaches are considered in detail below.

4.1   Plagiarism Detection

Improper citations and plagiarism often occur in research papers written by students and inexperienced researchers. Since the number of publications and citations measure a scientist's success, there is a temptation to usurp the scientific results published by other authors. Self-plagiarism as duplication of earlier

---

[14] Exactus Expert. Available at: http://expert.exactus.ru/, last accessed July 5, 2014.

research papers is also used to improve scientific indicators. Plagiarism is a serious problem in education too. It constitutes a serious misconduct, which can damage the integrity and prestige of the scientific community [37]. Therefore, improper citations detection is an important task that arises in R&D. The peer reviewers and editors of scientific journals should detect plagiarism in all its forms and prevent substandard papers from being published.

Thus, plagiarism and improper citations detection is the highly demanded feature of modern scientific analytical systems. There are numerous *computer-assisted plagiarism detection* (CaPD) systems (commercial or free services on the Web) that implement different approaches to this task: The Plagiarism Checker[41], PlagScan[42], Grammarly[43], Chimpsky[44], Copyscape[45], PlagTracker[46], Plagiarisma.ru[47], Antiplagiat.ru[48]. The Plagiarism Checker, PlagTracker, and Antiplagiat.ru are designed specifically to detect potential plagiarism in sci-tech content.

Most of the systems do not have their own databases and textual indexes for text matching. Usually they use the *API of web search engines* to perform search over the most valuable fragments of a given text (e.g., Chimpsky[49], Copyscape[50], PlagScan[51], Plagiarisma.ru[52]). The difference between these systems lies in search engines that are used to find similar textual fragments, ranking schemas, and reports presentation. They use various modifications of the Zipf's law [38,39] and *TF-IDF weighting schemas* [40] to determine the most valuable fragments of a given text.

---

[41] The Plagiarism Checker. Available at: http://www.dustball.com/cs/plagiarism.checker/, last accessed July 6, 2014.

[42] PlagScan – Plagiarism checker. Available at: http://www.plagscan.com, last accessed July 6, 2014.

[43] Grammarly — Instant Grammar Check. Available at: http://www.grammarly.com, last accessed July 6, 2014.

[44] Chimpsky – Index – University of Waterloo. Available at: http://chimpsky.uwaterloo.ca, last accessed July 6, 2014.

[45] Copyscape Plagiarism Checker. Available at: http://www.copyscape.com/, last accessed July 6, 2014.

[46] PlagTracker. Available at: http://www.plagtracker.com/, last accessed July 6, 2014.

[47] Plagiarisma.ru. Available at: http://plagiarisma.ru/, last accessed July 6, 2014.

[48] Antiplagiat.ru. Available at: http://www.antiplagiat.ru, last accessed July 6, 2014.

[49] Overview - Help on chimpsky. Available at: http://chimpsky.uwaterloo.ca/help, last accessed July 6, 2014.

[50] About Copyscape. Available at: http://www.copyscape.com/about.php, last accessed July 6, 2014.

[51] PlagScan – Our Technology. Available at: http://www.plagscan.com/technology, last accessed July 6, 2014.

[52] FAQ Plagiarisma. Available at: http://plagiarisma.ru/faq.php, last accessed July 6, 2014.

Antiplagiat.ru has its own database, which it uses to find matching text fragments. The database contains scientific papers, students' essays, reports, theses from web sites along with Wikipedia and documents uploaded by users. It seems that the algorithm of Antiplagiat.ru is based on the modified fingerprint comparison described in [41,42].

The quality of improper citation detection strongly depends on how the database of a system covers potential plagiarism sources. Therefore, to provide the better recall of detection, PlagTracker combines both the considered approaches: it has its own database containing texts from academic sources and utilizes web search engines.

It is important to measure quality of systems for plagiarism and improper citations detection and compare them to each other. A good survey over the plagiarism detection software is presented in [43]. There is a special track on plagiarism detection at CLEF[53]. The mentioned solutions are good enough to find simple "copy-and-paste" plagiarism, but they do not find paraphrased sentences, in which some words and phrases are replaced with synonyms and other wordings, since the bag-of-words and fingerprint analysis cannot deal with such cases. Moreover, none of the aforementioned CaPD systems provides the deep analysis of texts to distinguish improper and proper citations, whereas in the latter case references to sources are presented in a text.

4.2 Verification of Compliance to Standard Rules for Writing Primary Scientific Texts

Many publications describe rules and standards, which should be complied by scientific paper [44,45], or rules to assess the quality of scientific research manually [46,47], but only few studies are devoted to automatic text quality assessment and a couple of them consider scientific publications.

According to standard requirements, a primary scientific text:

- Should have a *specific structure* that meets the paper design requirements of experiment- and theory-oriented literature;
- Should have a *specific scientific vocabulary* and contain phrases expressing the implementation of certain intellectual operations;
- Should contain *references* to other scientific publications;
- Should *not* be written in an *unscientific offensive language* or contain a *pseudo-scientific lexis*.

There is the general standard of scientific publication structure. The majority of scientific journal articles are written in the *IMRAD format*. That means that a text is typically divided into the following sections: "Introduction", "Methods (Materials and Methods)", "Results", and "Discussion". If an article is devoted to theoretical research, the "Methods" section is replaced by the "Theoretical Basis" [48]. In the English biological and medical periodicals, the share of articles

---

[53] PAN 2014. Available at: http://pan.webis.de/, last accessed June 17, 2014.

structured in the IMRAD format was 80% by 1970, and since 1980 texts written in a different style are not accepted for publication [49]. Now this format has become the universal standard accepted by the majority of scientific journals.

A few researches investigate the problem of *structural components detection in a scientific publication*. This problem is often considered as the classification task. For instance, in [50] support vector machines (SVM) are used for the automatic classification of sentences in full-text biomedical articles into the IMRAD categories. Explored features included words, n-grams, the presence of a citation, verb tenses, and the positions of sentences in a text. This classifier achieved 81.3% accuracy, which is significantly higher than results of predecessors presented in [50].

Liakata et al. [51] proposed a method for the automatic recognition of conceptualization zones in scientific articles. There are 11 categories at the sentence level: "Hypothesis", "Motivation", "Goal", "Object", "Background", "Method", "Experiment", "Model", "Observation", "Result", and "Conclusion". They trained machine-learning classifiers (support vector machines and conditional random fields) on a corpus of 265 full-text articles in biochemistry and chemistry. Acceptable results were obtained, some paper sections were recognized with a high accuracy and recall (for categories "Experiment", "Background", and "Model", F-measure was 76%, 62%, and 53%, respectively). However, the method can currently be applied to only two scientific fields.

Another approach provides the ability to check the structure of publications from different scientific fields [52]. To determine the presence or absence of the structural components of an article, special markers were chosen. The markers are semantic constructs that describe the typical and unique designs (of the author) of the structural components of a primary scientific text. For identification of markers, morphological, grammatical, syntactic, and semantic analysis of the verbal material, which is located within each structural component, was carried out. Lists of semantic and syntactic constructs that most likely belong to the one of the structural components of a publication were automatically obtained. It was shown that the automatic detection of such markers could be applied for the determination of paper sections independently from the topic of a paper.

Identifying section with results also gives an opportunity to understand the coherence of results obtained by authors with results published earlier. If the same results has been already described, the new paper is not worth publishing separately. To distinguish authors' results in an article, the method described in [53] could be used. It is proposed to detect a particular piece of knowledge that may represent the author's current work, or work reported elsewhere by using machine learning.

The *lexicon of scientific writing* consists of three main layers: *common words*, *general scientific words*, and *scientific terms*. In any scientific text, the common lexicon is a basis. General scientific words are used to describe phenomena in the different areas of science and technology. Term saturation is the characteristic feature of the style of scientific papers. Several approaches could be used for the estimation of scientific language level in an article.

Nenkova [54] proposed a method for *predicting general and specific sentences* and automatic assessment of sentence fluency in machine translation and summary coherence in text summarization. The author claims that a well-written text contains the balanced mix of general overview statements and specific detailed sentences. If a text contains too many general sentences it will be perceived as insufficiently informative, and too much specificity can be confusing for a reader. A logistic regression classifier trained on around the 2,800 examples of general and specific sentences from news articles marked by human annotators distinguished such sentences rather well. For sentences, in which all five annotators agreed about the class, the classifier could predict the correct class with 95% accuracy; for sentences, in which only four out of five annotators agreed, the accuracy was 85%. For sentences, which annotators found hard to classify in terms of general and specific, the accuracy of prediction was 75%. This method could be applied to scientific papers, which in terms of readability are distinguished from news articles by the higher percentage of specific detailed sentences.

Some studies are devoted to the *creation of a scientific lexicon*. The various corpora of scientific and unscientific material are processed and automatic analysis is applied for highlighting various phrases and utterances that are inherent to a general scientific writing. These items make up the vocabulary, which could be used to determine the level of the general scientific expressions in an article.

The presence of the *bibliography section* is an indispensable condition for an article to be published. However, there are articles (most often conference proceedings), in which the bibliography is absent or formatted so badly that it is hard to recover accurately what sources the author refers to. ParsCit [55] is the state-of-the-art reference extraction system that uses heuristics to detect and segment references within a scientific article. Roman Kern et al. [56] proposed the extraction of references using layout and formatting information from scientific articles that increases in some cases F-measure by 3% comparing to ParsCit on the same dataset. Both systems are based on finding reference headers, which could be one of "References", "Bibliography", "References and Notes", "Literature cited". However, when an article does not contain such a header, the accuracy of the system decreases. Therefore, these methods still should be improved. ParsCit also can detect citations within a text. This useful function helps to find the lack of citations that might indicate the that the quality of a publication is low: if authors do not cite previous studies, it is the sign of their incompetence in a research subject.

Another important rule for a primary research paper is the *absence of unscientific and quasi-scientific lexis*. It is necessary to avoid the ambiguities and polysemy of various scientific concepts. Authors should not introduce new terms and definitions needlessly. Methods for the identification of texts written in unnatural language, which were automatically generated by computer programs, are being investigated. For example, methods designed for spam detection based on machine learning techniques could also be used for the detection of unusual unscientific lexicon. It could help to identify generated articles as well as quasi-scientific articles with questionable studies.

Distinguishing *speculative statements* from factual ones could be useful for the identification of texts that consist only of phrases, which convey uncertainty about the inferred conclusions. An approach, which is based on solving two sub-problems to identify speculative sentence fragments, is introduced in [57]. The first sub-problem is identifying the speculation keywords in the sentences and the second one is resolving their linguistic scopes. The first sub-problem is formulated as a supervised classification task, where potential keywords are classified as real speculation keywords or not by using the diverse set of linguistic features that represent the contexts of the keywords. After detecting the actual speculation keywords, the syntactic structures of sentences are used to determine their scopes. Linear SVM models are built for classification in this case as in many other systems described above. Good results were obtained (F-measure is 82% for full-text articles and 91% for abstracts), which is signicantly better than the baseline methods considered in [57].

Thus, to establish whether an article is a complete primary scientific publication it is possible to perform the following types of analysis: determination of the *structural components* of the publication, checking presence of *references*, determining the level of the *general scientific lexicon*, *detection of unscientific and quasi-scientific lexis*.

5   Expert Reviews of Proposed R&D Projects

One of the main tasks of R&D support is providing the expert review of proposed projects. When governments or private companies are looking for R&D projects, they are interested in modern technologies, original ideas, novel research, and, of course, the feasibility of a project. Though these factors seem simple at the first sight, they are much more complex in practice, and the question of how to rank R&D projects is not an easy one.

The expert reviews of R&D projects are mostly done by human experts. This difficult task requires great responsibility. The entire process is divided into three main steps:

- Finding and assigning experts to projects.
- Examination of the projects by the experts.
- Ranking the projects.

The first step is to find experts for projects. There are several requirements for an expert: an expert has to be a person with good scientific papers and results; their research area has to be similar to the goals of a project, an expert cannot have any affiliations with a proposed project that can cause conflicts of interest. This task can be solved using the registry of experts[54] or a scientific database[15]. An expert's area of interest can be determined by examining their

---

[54] Corpus expertov. Available at: http://www.expertcorps.ru/, last accessed July 6, 2014.

[15] Scopus. Available at: http://www.scopus.com/, last accessed July 5, 2014.

publications and keywords in their expert profile[15]. However, it is not always possible to reveal a conflict of interest with a proposed project. To solve this task it is necessary to have brief overview of an expert's affiliation (a project group and an expert should not be co-workers). It is also a good idea to check an expert's papers for joint publications with researchers involved in a project.

The second step is the examination of the proposed projects. There are many criteria to examine projects: novelty, originality of ideas, area of application, competence of a project team, resource availability, etc. Most of these criteria can be checked by experts using a certain system. For example, it is possible to assess the quality of scientific texts, as described in section 4 of this chapter. The better the quality of the text is, the greater the chance is that the project will be accepted. The originality of ideas can be determined using the similar documents search. For example, some of the aforementioned analytical systems can find thematically similar papers.

The important part of R&D projects is a patent search. With the help of patent databases, it is possible to find documents in the same area of research. However, the quality of current patent database search engines is still not perfect. It can take a long time to find patents that are sufficiently similar to the project goals.

Another important factor is the qualifications of the project team. In general, the leader of a project has to be a well-respected person with good scientific results in the area of a project. A project team has to be balanced and include scientists, engineers, PhD students, post doctoral, secondary staff, etc. For the evaluation of project teams, it is possible to apply methods of scientometrics (citations, indices, impact factors) [58] to profiles from scientific databases[15,16,12]. The better the team is, the greater the chances of success of the project are.

The third step is ranking of the projects. Usually, the criteria are divided into several groups: the scientific level of projects and its prospects, the leader of a project and a project team, and resource provision of the project. Groups and criteria depend on the rules of a funding organization. Each group and criteria has a weighting coefficient and the final place on the list of a project is calculated as a weighted total. Of course, special expert opinions can be taken into consideration. It is common for experts' opinions to be very different and achieving agreement among experts can be a problem. The questions of decision making support are difficult, well-discussed elsewhere, and beyond the scope of this chapter. However, it is always possible to use certain instruments to check why experts have differing opinions. For example, if an expert gives a high rating to a weak research team, it may be the sign of a bias caused by conflict of interest. In this case, an additional examination and possibly the change of the expert are required. An expert's review tends to be more responsible, when the expert is aware of the possibility that their review will be verified.

[16] Web of Science. Available at:
http://thomsonreuters.com/web-of-science-core-collection/, last accessed July 5, 2014.

[12] Google Scholar. Available at: http://scholar.google.ru/, last accessed July 5, 2014.

6   Conclusion

The task of supporting scientific and technical activities is far from being solved. Rapid scientific development and the overgrowth of research areas, which are becoming immense, make the activities of R&D more and more complicated. To overcome obstacles arising around R&D it is important to develop and upgrade scientific search and analytical systems that could take on some of the common tasks. We believe that state-of-the-art systems fall seriously behind the today's needs of people involved in R&D. We are looking forward to the following two major problems being solved in the near future.

Many activities on the different stages of R&D lack automated information and analytical support. Scientometrics in addition to citation analysis will benefit from advanced IR techniques like deep full-text search, exploratory search, and metadata extraction from full texts. The study of research areas will be assisted by methods for thematic clustering analysis and automatic summarization. Automatic tools that help experts to check the quality of scientific publications and detect plagiarism will become widespread.

The problem of isolation and incompleteness of scientific information sources should also be a focus. To alleviate this problem, public scientific databases will continue to develop and gain significant influence compared to the commercial databases. Integrating the research published in regional languages with global science is also needed.

Acknowledgements. The chapter is supported by the Russian Academy of Sciences; project ONIT 2.9 "Development of methods and technologies Exactus Expert for semantic search and analysis of scientific publications".

References

1. Marchionini, G.: Exploratory search: From finding to understanding. Communications of the ACM 49(4), 41–46 (2006)
2. White, R.W., Roth, R.A.: Exploratory search: Beyond the query-response paradigm. Synthesis Lectures on Information Concepts, Retrieval, and Services 1(1), 1–98 (2009)
3. Connor, J.: Google Scholar Blog, http://googlescholar.blogspot.ru/2013/11/google-scholar-library.html (last accessed July 6, 2014)
4. Osipov, G., Smirnov, I., Tikhomirov, I.: Relational-situational method for text search and analysis and its applications. Scientific and Technical Information Processing 37(6), 432–437 (2010)
5. Ferreira, A.A., Gonçalves, M.A., Laender, A.H.: A brief survey of automatic methods for author name disambiguation. SIGMOD Rec. 41(2), 15–26 (2012)
6. Huang, J., Ertekin, S., Giles, C.L.: Fast author name disambiguation in CiteSeer. ISI Technical Report (2006)

7. Connan, J., Omlin, C.W.: Bibliography extraction with hidden markov models. Technical report, Department of Computer Science, University of Stel-lenbosch (February 2000)
8. Hetzner, E.: A simple method for citation metadata extraction using hidden markov models. In: Proceedings of the 8th ACM/IEEE-CS Joint Conference on Digital libraries, pp. 280–284. ACM (2008)
9. Gupta, D., Morris, B., Catapano, T., Sautter, G.: A new approach towards bibliographic reference identification, parsing and inline citation matching. In: Ranka, S., Aluru, S., Buyya, R., Chung, Y.-C., Dua, S., Grama, A., Gupta, S.K.S., Kumar, R., Phoha, V.V. (eds.) IC3 2009. CCIS, vol. 40, pp. 93–102. Springer, Heidelberg (2009)
10. Frakes, W.B., Baeza-Yates, R. (eds.): Information Retrieval: Data Structures and Algorithms. Prentice-Hall, Inc., Upper Saddle River (1992)
11. Salton, G., Fox, E.A., Wu, H.: Extended Boolean information retrieval. Communications of the ACM 26(11), 1022–1036 (1983)
12. Beel, J., Gipp, B.: Google Scholar's ranking algorithm: An introductory overview. In: Proceedings of the 12th International Conference on Scientometrics and Informetrics (ISSI 2009), vol. 1, pp. 230–241 (2009)
13. Osipov, G., Smirnov, I., Tikhomirov, I., Vybornova, O.: Technologies for semantic analysis of scientific publications. In: 2012 6th IEEE International Conference on Intelligent Systems (IS), pp. 58–62. IEEE (2012)
14. Maron, M.E., Kuhns, J.L.: On relevance, probabilistic indexing and information retrieval. Journal of the ACM (JACM) 7(3), 216–244 (1960)
15. Robertson, S.E., van Rijsbergen, C.J., Porter, M.F.: Probabilistic models of indexing and searching. In: Proceedings of the 3rd Annual ACM Conference on Research and Development in Information Retrieval, pp. 35–56. Butterworth & Co. (1980)
16. Osipov, G., Smirnov, I., Tikhomirov, I., Zavjalova, O.: Application of linguistic knowledge to search precision improvement. In: Proceedings of 4th International IEEE Conference on Intelligent Systems, vol. 2, pp. 17–12 (2008)
17. Giles, C.L., Bollacker, K.D., Lawrence, S.: Citeseer: An automatic citation indexing system. In: Proceedings of the Third ACM Conference on Digital Libraries, pp. 89–98. ACM (1998)
18. Qiu, Y., Frei, H.P.: Concept based query expansion. In: Proceedings of the 16th Annual International ACM SIGIR Conference on Research and Development in Information Retrieval, pp. 160–169. ACM (1993)
19. Huang, C.K., Chien, L.F., Oyang, Y.J.: Relevant term suggestion in interactive web search based on contextual information in query session logs. Journal of the American Society for Information Science and Technology 54(7), 638–649 (2003)
20. Wilson, M.L., Kules, B., Shneiderman, B., et al.: From keyword search to exploration: Designing future search interfaces for the web. Foundations and Trends in Web Science 2(1), 1–97 (2010)
21. Fafalios, P., Salampasis, M., Tzitzikas, Y.: Exploratory patent search with faceted search and configurable entity mining. In: Proceedings of the Workshop on Integrating IR technologies for Professional Search, in Conjunction with the 35th European Conference on Information Retrieval (ECIR 2013), vol. 968. CEUR Workshop Proceedings, Moscow (2013)
22. Markusova, V.: All Russian institute for scientific and technical information (VINITI) of the Russian academy of sciences. Acta Informatica Medica 20(2), 113–117 (2012)

23. Hanbury, A., Lupu, M.: Toward a model of domain-specific search. In: Proceedings of the 10th Conference on Open Research Areas in Information Retrieval, Lisbon, Portugal, pp. 33–36 (2013)
24. Vieira, E.S., Gomes, J.A.: Citations to scientific articles: Its distribution and dependence on the article features. Journal of Informetrics 4(1), 1–13 (2010)
25. Adler, R., Ewing, J., Taylor, P.: Citation statistics: A report from the international mathematical union (IMU) in cooperation with the international council of industrial and applied mathematics (ICIAM) and the Institute of Mathematical Statistics (IMS). Statistical Science, 1–14 (2009)
26. Figg, W.D., Dunn, L., Liewehr, D.J., Steinberg, S.M., Thurman, P.W., Barrett, J.C., Birkinshaw, J.: Scientific collaboration results in higher citation rates of published articles. Pharmacotherapy: The Journal of Human Pharmacology and Drug Therapy 26(6), 759–767 (2006)
27. Connor, J.: Google Scholar Blog, http://googlescholar.blogspot.ru/2012/08/scholar-updates-making-new-connections.html (last accessed July 6, 2014)
28. Hall, B.H., Jaffe, A., Trajtenberg, M.: Market value and patent citations. RAND Journal of Economics, 16–38 (2005)
29. Lupu, M., Hanbury, A.: Patent retrieval. Foundations and Trends in Information Retrieval 7, 1–97 (2013)
30. De Bellis, N.: Bibliometrics and citation analysis: From the science citation index to cybermetrics. Scarecrow Press (2009)
31. Ding, Y.: Scientific collaboration and endorsement: Network analysis of coauthorship and citation networks. Journal of Informetrics 5(1), 187–203 (2011)
32. Cobo, M.J., López-Herrera, A.G., Herrera-Viedma, E., Herrera, F.: Science mapping software tools: Review, analysis, and cooperative study among tools. Journal of the American Society for Information Science and Technology 62(7), 1382–1402 (2011)
33. Tang, J., Zhang, J., Yao, L., Li, J., Zhang, L., Su, Z.: Arnetminer: Extraction and mining of academic social networks. In: Proceedings of the 14th ACM SIGKDD International Conference on Knowledge Discovery and Data Mining, pp. 990–998. ACM (2008)
34. Radev, D.R., Muthukrishnan, P., Qazvinian, V.: The ACL anthology network corpus. In: Proceedings of the 2009 Workshop on Text and Citation Analysis for Scholarly Digital Libraries, pp. 54–61. Association for Computational Linguistics (2009)
35. Glänzel, W.: Bibliometric methods for detecting and analysing emerging research topics. El profesional de la Información 21(2), 194–201 (2012)
36. Liu, X., Zhang, J., Guo, C.: Full-text citation analysis: A new method to enhance scholarly networks. Journal of the American Society for Information Science and Technology 64(9), 1852–1863 (2013)
37. Horrom, T.A.: The perils of copy and paste: Plagiarism in scientific publishing. Journal of Rehabilitation Research and Development 49(8), 7–12 (2012), http://www.rehab.research.va.gov/jour/2012/498/horrom498.html
38. Eissen, S.M.z., Stein, B.: Intrinsic plagiarism detection. In: Lalmas, M., MacFarlane, A., Rüger, S.M., Tombros, A., Tsikrika, T., Yavlinsky, A. (eds.) ECIR 2006. LNCS, vol. 3936, pp. 565–569. Springer, Heidelberg (2006)

39. Bravo-Marquez, F., L'Huillier, G., Ríos, S.A., Velásquez, J.D.: Hypergeometric language model and Zipf-like scoring function for web document similarity retrieval. In: Chavez, E., Lonardi, S. (eds.) SPIRE 2010. LNCS, vol. 6393, pp. 303–308. Springer, Heidelberg (2010)
40. Potthast, M., Gollub, T., Hagen, M., Kiesel, J., Michel, M., Oberländer, A., Tippmann, M., Barrón-Cedeño, A., Gupta, P., Rosso, P., et al.: Overview of the 4th international competition on plagiarism detection. In: CLEF (Online Working Notes/Labs/Workshop) (2012)
41. Brin, S., Davis, J., Garcia-Molina, H.: Copy detection mechanisms for digital documents. In: ACM SIGMOD Record, vol. 24, pp. 398–409. ACM (1995)
42. Stein, B.: Fuzzy-fingerprints for text-based information retrieval. In: Proceedings of the 5th International Conference on Knowledge Management (I-KNOW 2005), pp. 572–579. Journal of Universal Computer Science, Graz (2005)
43. Weber-Wulff1, D., Mller1, C., Touras2, J., Zincke, E.: Plagiarism detection software test (2013), http://plagiat.htw-berlin.de/wp-content/uploads/Testbericht-2013-color.pdf (last accessed June 17, 2014)
44. Steingraber, S., Jolls, C., Goldberg, D.: Guidelines for Writing Scientific Papers. Technical report (1985)
45. Szklo, M.: Quality of scientific articles. Revista de Saúde Pública 40(SPE), 30–35 (2006)
46. Gray, C.: Quality assurance and assessment of scholarly research. Research Information Network 23 (2010)
47. Kmet, L.M., Lee, R.C., Cook, L.S.: Standard quality assessment criteria for evaluating primary research papers from a variety of fields, vol. 13. Alberta Heritage Foundation for Medical Research (2004)
48. Day, R.A.: The origins of the scientific paper: the IMRAD format. Journal of the American Medical Writers Association 4(2), 16–18 (1989)
49. Sollaci, L.B., Pereira, M.G.: The introduction, methods, results, and discussion (IMRAD) structure: A fifty-year survey. Journal of the Medical Library Association 92(3), 364 (2004)
50. Agarwal, S., Yu, H.: Automatically classifying sentences in full-text biomedical articles into introduction, methods, results and discussion. Bioinformatics 25(23), 3174–3180 (2009)
51. Liakata, M., Saha, S., Dobnik, S., Batchelor, C., Rebholz-Schuhmann, D.: Automatic recognition of conceptualization zones in scientific articles and two life science applications. Bioinformatics 28(7), 991–1000 (2012)
52. Kuznetsova, J., Osipov, G., Chudova, N., Nad Shvets, A.: Automatic assessment of article conformity to the standards for scientific publications. Proceedings of ISA RAS 62(3), 132–138 (2012) (in Russian)
53. Waard, A.D., Thompson, P., Liakata, M., Nawaz, R., Anani-adou, S.: Comparing scientific discourse annotation schemes for enhanced knowledge extraction. In: Proceedings of Workshop Beyond the PDF (2011)
54. Nenkova, A.: Automatic text understanding of content and text quality. In: Frontiers of Engineering 2011: Reports on Leading-Edge Engineering from the 2011 Symposium, pp. 49–54 (2012)
55. Councill, I.G., Giles, C.L., Kan, M.Y.: Parscit: An open-source CRF reference string parsing package. In: Proceedings of LREC, vol. 28, pp. 661–667 (2008)

56. Kern, R., Kampfl, S.: Extraction of references using layout and formatting information from scientific articles. D-Lib Magazine 19(9), 2 (2013)
57. Özgür, A., Radev, D.R.: Detecting speculations and their scopes in scientific text. In: Proceedings of the 2009 Conference on Empirical Methods in Natural Language Processing, vol. 3, pp. 1398–1407. Association for Computational Linguistics (2009)
58. Hirsch, J.E.: An index to quantify an individual's scientific research output. Proceedings of the National academy of Sciences of the United States of America 102(46), 16569–16572 (2005)

21st Century Search and Recommendation: Exploiting Personalisation and Social Media

Morgan Harvey and Fabio Crestani

Faculty of Informatics, University of Lugano, Switzerland
{morgan.harvey,fabio.crestani}@usi.ch

Abstract. Using the Internet to find information and interesting content is now one of the most common tasks performed on a computer. Up until recently, search algorithms returned only one-size-fits-all rankings, resulting in very poor performance for ambiguous search queries. Recent work has demonstrated that contextual information - such as the interests of the searcher - can be utilised to provide more accurate results which have been "personalised" and adapted to the user's current information need and situation. Likewise, information about the user can be brought to bear to mitigate the problem of information overload and filter content so that users are only shown items they are likely to be interested in.

In this book chapter we explore new methods for assisting users to find the information they want by reducing the complexity of the search task through *personalisation*. We explore this problem from the perspective of web search and then by considering a very common form of new socially-generated data - microblogs. We first tackle the problem of search result personalisation in the face of extremely sparse and noisy data from a query log. We describe a novel approach which uses query logs to build personalised ranking models in which user profiles are constructed based on the representation of clicked documents over a topic space. Our experiments show that this model can provide personalised ranked lists of documents which improve significantly over a non-personalised baseline. Further examination shows that the performance of the personalised system is particularly good in cases where prior knowledge of the search query is limited.

We then turn our attention to the related problem of recommendation (where the user profile is itself the query) and, more specifically, discuss the possibility of learning user interests from social media data (specifically micro blog posts). We present a short introduction to early work focussing on the difficult task of making use of this vast array of ever-changing data. We demonstrate via experiment that our methods are able to predict, with a high level of precision, which posts will be of interest to users and comment on possibilities for future work.

1   Personalised Search and the Vocabulary Problem

As discussed in the MUMIA memorandum of understanding, the sheer volume of data which has become available in the last decade as a result of web becoming

G. Paltoglou et al. (Eds.): Professional Search in the Modern World, LNCS 8830, pp. 70–95, 2014.
© Springer International Publishing Switzerland 2014

more social (the so called *web 2.0*) will require a new generation of search systems to be developed. This huge new resource will only be useful if the raw data can be transformed into high value information which users can easily manage, understand and exploit. One of the ways to help in making sense of all this data is to use context to intelligently narrow down the amount which is presented to individual users, especially when searching.

Search, particularly on the web, is undeniably an important topic in computer science with several very large companies such as Google, Microsoft and Yahoo dedicating large sums of money to research and development in this field. Using a search engine to find information is often listed as one of the most common tasks performed on the Internet [41]. Up until recently, focus was placed primarily on matching short textual queries with documents, resulting in generally excellent performance for a large proportion of search tasks. Modern search systems consider a large number of features when attempting to determine relevant documents and then to optimally rank these documents in a list. Notable breakthroughs have been made by considering features other than simply the content of the documents, such as the Google PageRank algorithm [7] which also considers the hyperlinks between web pages.

Search engines provide us with the means to rapidly access information and to narrow down the overwhelming number of web pages and resources available on the web in order to find a small number of relevant items. This is usually achieved via the submission of a - typically very short - textual query which the search engine must interpret in order to retrieve the most appropriate pages to present to the user [33]. However, understanding a user's information needs given such a small amount of information is far from a trivial task, especially in cases where the user himself only has a very vague idea of what he is looking for. The traditional approach in Information Retrieval (IR) is to simply return the documents which are in some sense most similar to the query terms, with this often being determined by either proximity in a vector space or via probability theory [16].

As search engines have developed, the scope for dramatically improving result quality has narrowed, making it necessary that researchers focus on more niche problems or leverage new sources of data. A large percentage of searches can now be handled optimally by modern search systems, in the sense that the result the user was looking for is returned at the top rank position, by applying standard IR technology. However, for a smaller number of more "difficult" search queries the opportunity still exists to make significant improvements. These queries are often difficult because they are ambiguous and could potentially be referring to more than one concept or information need (related to the "vocabulary problem", where people use the same terms to describe different needs [23]). In this case the query terms are not sufficient to return useful results and it is not possible to create a ranked list which is optimal for all users. This is where more contextual information, particularly about the user's interests, can be utilised to augment the scanty information provided by the query.

Other basic forms of context can be put to use, such as time and location [35], however a developing source of additional information for search is the plethora of modern social media sites. These sites do not present simply static content, but rather allow users to interact with each other to share information and thoughts and to connect with each other, forming complex social networks [25]. The sheer volume of information submitted to these services gives a far greater insight into human language and behaviour than has previously been possible.

This new data represents an additional source of information about users, their interests, their thoughts and feelings. Users often post web sites they have found and want to share with others, information which could be used to learn what is popular on the web right now and which could be fed into search engines and recommendation algorithms to augment their existing data streams. The responses to questions posted to social networks could even be mined to provide intelligent yet instantaneous answers to similar questions posed by search engine users.

Difficult queries (i.e. those which would benefit most from additional context) can often be detected by measures such as *click entropy* - which is simply the entropy of the distribution of prior clicks on different URLs, given the query of interest - or by looking at the length of the query [48]. Consider an unambiguous query such as "facebook" where almost all users will want to click on the same URL. In cases such as this, a sensible option is to simply rank the documents in descending order of prior click frequency [19]. Conversely, queries with high click entropy are more complicated to deal with and thus the ideal ranking will likely depend on the person who submitted the query and so a ranking personalised to the interest profile of the user is likely to yield better results.

Such profiles are often built by considering searches made by the user prior to the current one and, for each of these, the query terms used and the documents clicked. Alternative sources of profile data, such as a user's social media history, are often easier to gain access to and may be more abundant, potentially leading to a more granular understanding of the user's interests. There is however at present little work where this new source of data is exploited, however work has shown that the terms used on Twitter to describe a given URL are useful as descriptions of that web page [28]. In early approaches user profiles were constructed using the raw terms of prior queries or the content of the clicked documents, usually in the form of language models, however this often proves to be ineffective, perhaps because such a representation of interests is too fine-grained given the limited amount of data available. An approach for dealing with this sparsity is to instead base the profile on the main topics discussed in each document.

In this work we use query logs to build personalised ranking models in which user profiles are constructed based on the representation of clicked documents over a topic space. However, instead of employing a human-generated ontology, we use latent topic models to determine these topics. This means that the topic space is extracted directly from the query log itself and there is no need for human intervention to define the topics. Our experiments show that by subtly introducing user profiles as part of the ranking algorithm, rather than by re-ranking an existing list, we can provide personalised ranked lists of documents which improve significantly over a non-personalised baseline. Further examination shows that the performance of the personalised system is particularly good in cases where prior knowledge of the search query is limited. This is especially useful as these are the cases where we are unable to rely on prior clicks to determine a good ranked list and must instead rely on the ranking model.

2 Related Work

An idealised IR system should, given all the information available, rank documents in descending order of their expected relevance to an information need, usually expressed as a short keyword-based query [44]. Most early retrieval systems considered the query in isolation and while this is obviously an extremely strong indicator of what information or resources the searcher is looking for, there are other - perhaps less obvious - clues which can be used, particularly in cases where the query itself is ambiguous. In this section we outline work already conducted in the areas of contextual search and user profiles, personalised search and, lastly, topic modelling.

2.1 Context and User Profiles

There are many different sources of context that can potentially be exploited when attempting to improve search engine rankings, often by subtly altering an existing ranked list [39]. This extra contextual information should allow the system a better understanding of the current search "situation," beyond the often meagre but essential information given by the query. For example, the user's location can be used to select which language(s) should be considered and to focus search results so that they are geographically close to the user [2]. Results can be tailored towards the age and/or linguistic ability of the user by considering factors such as reading level [15] (i.e. how complex the use of language within the document is). A perhaps more obvious source of contextual data is the interests and preferences of the searcher which must be expressed in such a way that the system can make use of them to improve search effectiveness. These representations of preference are often referred to as *user profiles* and can be defined by the users themselves [36,14] or, instead, automatically by learning from the user's prior interactions with the system.

The idea of using previous interactions of a user with a search system to construct a user profile has been around since the mid-1990s [43], and there is significant variation in the ways that the problem has been tackled [1]. The approaches differ based on what length of profile data is used, which data is used and how the data chosen is then turned into a suitable user profile. In some cases researchers have considered only the information from the current search session in order to build short-term profiles [17,50], whereas other work has attempted to identify longer-term user interests [37,42]. Recent work by Bennett et al. [3] has even shown how these short and long-term profiles can be effectively combined. In general, short-term data is often too sparse to allow for robust personalisation performance and only delivers solid improvements late in long search sessions, which are relatively rare. In this work we focus on long-term click data to build user profiles as it provides a richer source of information about the user's true interests and preferences.

Once prior interaction data has been chosen, it must then be converted into a user profile which should form a representation of the user's interests. These profiles can be generated in a number of different ways. Some approaches use vectors of the original terms [17,37] from the queries or the URLs clicked, often weighted in some fashion. Others attempt to map the user's interests onto a set of topics extracted from large online ontologies of web sites, such as the Open Directory Project (ODP) [14,45,24]. Some methods do not make use of any terms, but rather rely solely on which URLs were clicked, given different queries. For example Cao et al. [9] modelled the sequence of queries and clicks on URLs in order to create sequential estimates of most probable future clicks. In this work we use topic modelling techniques to map the original query terms onto a lower-dimensional space which itself is derived from the original data.

2.2 Personalising Search

Dou et al. [19] investigated a number of methods for creating user profiles and generating personalised rankings using query logs. Their approach was to use a set of pre-defined interest categories and a K-nearest neighbour approach for clustering similar users. In this chapter we take a similar view that by reducing the dimensionality of the data we can get better results, however we use more principled techniques that do not rely on predefined categories but derive these from the data as part of the estimation process. Dou et al. found that personalisation is not appropriate for all users and/or queries and may even harm performance. For example, in the case of highly unambiguous queries (e.g. navigational queries such as "google"), where the unpersonalised ranking is close to optimal for all users. In fact, for queries which are both unambiguous and common, optimal results can be obtained by simply ranking documents in order of their prior probability of being clicked for that query. However, this approach is clearly not feasible for the large number of queries where either scant or no prior click data is available.

Teevan et al. [48] confirmed these results and investigated for what kinds of queries personalisation techniques most improved ranking performance. They found that the level of ambiguity of the query provides a good indication of how much benefit will be gained from personalisation. For queries of low ambiguity (where all users tend to find the same results relevant) the personalisation can have a negative impact on performance. This work indicates that we must be careful when designing such systems to ensure that too much weight is not given to prior user preferences in deference to the unpersonalised document score. Building on this earlier work, Teevan et al. [47] later demonstrated that the potential that each user/query pair holds for effective personalisation can in some cases be predicted a-priori, allowing the system to select between personalised and unpersonalised rankings.

Matthijs et al. [37] constructed user profiles using different textual summaries from each previously-clicked URL including summaries derived from a page's title, content and metadata as well as set of "important keywords" as determined by a Term Extraction algorithm. Term candidates form a summarisation of the full text and were found using a number of linguistic patterns and are assigned a weight based on the frequency of the term and its sub-terms. These profiles were then used to subtlety rerank the top 50 results returned by Google. Their method was tested via a user study in which users were asked to download and use a browser plugin, some participants being then shown the reranked results when performing a Google search, the others receiving the unaltered ranked list. This method was reported to deliver good results, however unfortunately the authors did not attempt to apply it to any large-scale data sets such as a query log.

Rather than re-ranking search results by using profiles based on raw terms, many approaches instead attempt to map user interests and documents onto a set of categories or topics. Doing so can potentially alleviate many of the issues resulting from discordant term use since exact matches between terms in the query and in documents are no longer necessary. Most personalised search models which employ topics use sets of pre-defined, human-curated categories, such as those provided by the Open Directory Project (ODP) [14,45,24]. While this is a straightforward approach to acquiring sets of topics, it suffers from the fact that the topics are not derived from the data being categorised and therefore may not be an especially good match, necessitating that some documents are "pigeon-holed" into topics to which they do not clearly belong. Furthermore this method either requires humans to manually label each document - an extremely expensive and time-consuming task - or some method of automatically assigning documents to topics must be devised, often replying on similar approaches to classical IR document matching with all of the inherent vocabulary issues. Instead, it is possible to automatically derive sets of topics from the document collection itself, an idea which has been investigated in recent years [27,11].

2.3 Topic Models

The idea of automatically modelling the topical content of documents has been present in the IR field for some time and developed from early work - termed Latent Semantic Indexing or LSI - which used a Singular Value Decomposition of document-term matrices to represent the documents in a lower-dimensional space [18]. This idea was reformulated as a probabilistic generative model by Hofmann [30] and then further improved upon by Blei and Jordan [4], who developed the Latent Dirichlet Allocation (LDA) model. Both probabilistic models attempt to uncover the underlying semantic structure of a collection of documents based on analysis of their vocabulary. This latent topical structure is modelled over an often pre-defined number of topics, which are assumed to be present in the collection.

LDA has served as the basic building block for a large number of more complex models, dealing with problems such as image categorisation [22], movie recommendation [29] and even to determine the ancestry of people based on their genes [21]. While early methods of inferring topics from documents [4] were somewhat cumbersome and complex, making it quite a difficult task to extend upon them, more recent approaches are more straightforward and easier to develop and build upon [26]. Wei et al. [49] showed that it was possible to use topic models to improve the performance of search systems by matching queries to documents at a semantic level.

Topic models have been considered as a solution to personalisation. Harvey et al. [27] and Carman et al. [11] introduced new models based on LDA for the problem of personalised search which both include a user-topic distribution directly in the model, thereby considering the user as part of the generative process. When evaluating these models using query log data it was found that they had an overall negative effect on the ranked lists produced and were therefore unable to improve upon the unpersonalised LDA baseline. Both authors note that this is perhaps due to the user becoming too influential in the model and overpowering the perhaps generally more useful information from the documents themselves.

We now present an approach to query log-based search personalisation using sets of latent topics derived directly from the log data itself where the user is not specifically included as part of the generative process but rather is subtly introduced as part of the ranking formula. By means of a large-scale experiment we are able to demonstrate performance improvements over an unpersonalised baseline and show that this new model is particularly effective in cases of sparse prior data where click frequencies cannot be utilised to generate good ranked lists.

3   A Topic Model for Personalised Search

As already stated, a basic tenet of personalisation is the idea that information regarding a user's interests and preferences can be garnered from their previous interactions with a search system. More concretely, the idea is to use the terms from the query the user submitted and the specific document(s) (or, in the case of web search, URLs) that they clicked on in the results list, to build a topic level description of the user. The clicked documents should then represent solutions to the actual information need that the user expressed via the query. For example, given a potentially ambiguous query such as "java", a user interested in computer science is likely to click very different documents from a user who is interested in coffee.

For a document (URL) d, we consider all of the query terms in the log which resulted in the user clicking on d, conflating these terms over all users and queries. This follows the theory that queries should be random draws from the Language Models of the documents for which they are relevant and it has been shown that queries and URL content are strongly correlated [10]. Therefore, provided we

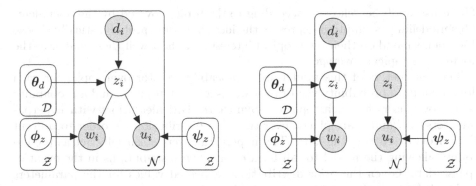

Fig. 1. Simple topic model for personalised retrieval (used for ranking)

Fig. 2. Actual model used for parameter estimation

ensure enough queries exist to represent each URL, they should describe them well. Once we have these document-specific language models we must determine how best to represent them.

Due to the relatively sparse nature of these language models and the success of using such methods on short documents [27,49], we investigate the use of topic models to represent the documents over a reduced-dimensionality latent topic space. In doing so we take a similar approach to many existing personalisation models [14,45,24], namely that lower-dimensional categories are a better representation of a document's topical coverage than its raw terms. However, instead of obtaining topic allocations from an online ontology, which may have poor coverage, low levels of granularity and a lack of novel vocabulary, we attempt to derive topics from the data itself.

Ideally this approach should allow us to: (1) generalise vocabulary terms to deal with synonymy and polysemy and (2) generalise the resource representations based on the similarity to other resources in the data set. These models operate using Bayesian inference which is useful when reasoning from noisy data; this is particularly appealing in this context as we expect the distributions of query terms over URLs to be both sparse and noisy.

Figure 1 shows a graphical model diagram for a personalisation topic model. The model involves an observed document d, a latent topic variable z, an observed word w and an observed user u. This structure is repeated for all words in a user's query[1], all queries by the user and all users in the log. Here we make the modelling assumption that the user, as well as the word, is dependant on the topic. That is, given the topic distribution of the document, there will be a number of words chosen at random from those topics to describe that document and there will be a number of users who chose to click on that document.

---

[1] We also experimented with a model in which a single topic variable was associated with each query as opposed to each keyword within the query (effectively holding the topic constant over the terms in the query) but observed poorer performance with respect to the model presented.

These users will be "chosen" according to the topics covered by the document. This modelling assumption expresses the idea that users probabilistically choose documents based on their own topical interests and how well these match to the document's topical coverage.

The parameters of this model are a probability vector over topics for each document θ_d, a probability vector over words for each topic ϕ_z and a probability vector over users for each topic ψ_z. Symmetric Dirichlet priors with hyperparameters α, β and γ are placed over the three distributions in order to prevent them from overfitting the data. The hyperparameters essentially act as pseudo counts allowing the model to fall back on uniform distributions in the event of sparse data. Given the prior distributions, expected values for the parameters under their respective posterior distributions are simply:

$$\hat{\phi}_{w|z} = \frac{N_{w,z} + \beta \frac{1}{W}}{N_z + \beta} \tag{1}$$

$$\hat{\theta}_{z|d} = \frac{N_{z,d} + \alpha \frac{1}{Z}}{N_d + \alpha} \tag{2}$$

$$\hat{\psi}_{u|z} = \frac{N_{u,z} + \gamma \frac{1}{U}}{N_z + \gamma} \tag{3}$$

Here $N_{w,z}$, $N_{z,d}$ and $N_{u,z}$ are counts denoting the number of times the topic z appears together with the word w, document d and user u respectively. N_z and N_d are the number of times topic z and the document d occur in total. W is the vocabulary size, Z is the number of topics and U is the number of users.

Exact inference for topic models is intractable, however a number of methods of approximating the posterior distribution have been proposed including mean field variational inference [4] and Gibbs sampling [26]. Gibbs sampling is a Markov chain Monte Carlo method where a Markov chain is constructed that slowly converges to the target distribution of interest over a number of iterations. In our case, each state of the Markov chain is a complete assignment of topics to words in the queries. In Gibbs sampling the next state in the chain is reached by resampling all variables from their distribution when conditioned on the current values of all the other variables. After sufficient iterations of the sampler, the Markov chain converges and the parameters of the model can then be estimated. We assume that the chain has converged when we observe minimal change in the model likelihood over successive samples. For increased accuracy, we average parameter estimates over consecutive samples from the Markov chain.

Using the distributions obtained from this model we should be able to construct a ranking formula which, given a query, will consider the probability of each document given both the words in the query and the interests of the user who submitted it. However, as outlined earlier in the paper, in order for personalisation to work it must be applied very subtly. By directly including the user in the topic model we are saying that his/her topical interests are equally important when describing a document he/she has clicked as the words assigned to that document to describe it. The work of Carman et al. [11] demonstrated that this assumption is clearly far too strong as they were unable to obtain successful results from similar models. Instead we consider a different model which does not explicitly include the user in the Markov chain topic sampling but instead calculates an interest distribution for each user after the sampler has converged.

This alternative approach is depicted in Figure 2 where we see that the user does not play a part in the sampling. After the Markov chain has converged, samples from the chain are used (as per normal) to calculate the 3 posterior means (using Equations 1-3 above). The estimates for each user's interests over the topic space (or more precisely the distribution over users for each topic ψ_z) are still obtained. However, the sampler does not use these estimates to calculate the conditional distribution over topics when sampling the topic to assign to each word position.

The intuition behind this model (i.e. calculating the probability of a user given a topic and not vice-versa) is that we wish to capture the idea that a user clicks on a document given a specific query due, in part, to his/her interests which are expressed over the topic space. We know from our estimates for θ_d which topics are covered by a document and therefore by multiplying this with $P(u|z)$ we can express (a quantity proportional to) the probability that the user u would have clicked on this document, given the user's interests. This means that if the model is confronted with a new query in which none of the constituent terms have been used by the user previously, it should still be able to map the query onto the user's topic-based profile. This would clearly not be the case if we were to instead use the raw (unigram) terms to build the user profiles.

Now, given a query, we wish to construct ranking formulae to order the documents in the collection based on the distributions obtained from the latent topic models. In the case of the personalised model, the ranking should in some sense "perturb" the non-personalised ranking to give higher weight to documents which more closely correspond to the user profile.

4   Ranking Documents

We now describe formulas for ranking resources using the parameters that were estimated based on the topic models described above. Given a query q we wish to return to the user a ranked set of documents ($d \in \mathcal{D}$) according to their likelihood given the query under the model, which in the case of an unpersonalised (LDA) model can be estimated as follows:

$$P(d|q) \propto P(d)P(q|d) = P(d) \prod_{w \in q} P(w|d)$$

$$= P(d) \prod_{w \in q} \sum_{z} P(w|z)\, P(z|d)$$

Notice that the ranking formula consists of the product of 2 distinct parts; a prior on the probability of the document $P(d)$, and the probability of the query given the document $P(q|d)$, with the latter being estimated using parameters from the topic model. In our experiments we use the available click information to set the document prior $P(d)$ to be a Dirichlet smoothed estimate based on the relative frequency of clicks on that particular url in the query log:

$$\hat{\pi}_d = \frac{\#click(d) + \delta\frac{1}{|\mathcal{D}|}}{\sum_d \#click(d) + \delta}$$

So in terms of the parameters from the topic model we can write the ranking formula as:

$$score(d, q) = \hat{\pi}_d \prod_{w \in q} \sum_z \hat{\phi}_{w|z}\,\hat{\theta}_{z|d}$$

For the personalised ranking model, we also know which user issued the query and can therefore include that user's preferences into the ranking formula. We do that by simply ranking documents according to their likelihood given both the query *and the user* as follows:

$$P(d|q, u) \propto P(d) \prod_{w \in q} P(w, u|d)$$

$$P(d) \prod_{w \in q} \sum_z P(w|z)\,P(u|z)\,P(z|d)$$

Now the estimate of the probability of a document includes the probability of the user clicking it, given its similarity to the user's interests over the topic space.

We extend this basic personalisation model by introducing an additional parameter λ in the range zero to one, which we use to weight the probability of a user given a particular topic $P(u|z)$ as follows:

$$\tilde{P}(d|q, u) \propto P(d) \prod_{w \in q} \sum_z P(w|z)\,P(u|z)^\lambda\,P(z|d)$$

Thus we now rank documents according to:

$$score(d, q, u) = \hat{\pi}_d \prod_{w \in q} \sum_z \hat{\phi}_{w|z}\,\hat{\psi}_{u|z}^\lambda\,\hat{\theta}_{z|d}$$

This new parameter is of critical importance since it allows us to control, in a coherent and discriminative fashion, the amount of influence that the user's topical interests have on the overall ranking. The intuition behind the introduction of this parameter is that documents likely tell us more about their own topic distribution than the users who click on them do.

Note that the estimates of relevance to the query as computed here could be combined linearly with standard IR features such as term frequency, as demonstrated by Wei [49]. However, since we are interested in understanding the effect of personalisation on rankings, and not absolute retrieval performance, in this work we experiment purely with the topic model-based ranking algorithms.

Table 1. Counts and statistics for the AOL dataset used for experimentation

Dataset	Data set
users	6,581
URLs	15,996
vocabulary size	53,132
queries	2,236,156
word occurrences	6,289,262
average queries/user	340
average queries/url	140
average words/query	2.9
queries/vocab word	56.3

5   How Effective Is Personalisation?

To evaluate our models on real-world data where each query was made in context we used the AOL Query Log dataset. The log contains the queries of 657,426 anonymous users over a 3 month period from March to May, 2006. It is, as far as we know, the only publicly available dataset of sufficient size to perform our analysis. Users' personalised details were protected by analysing results only over aggregate data. We separated the dataset into training and testing subsets by retaining the *last 5%* of query log entries for each user for testing, rather than a random split. In doing so we ensure that the test data is distributed over users in the same way as the training data. This also ensures the data are in the correct chronological order. We use each query in the test set as the input query and since we know for each query which document (URL) was clicked, we can classify a ranked resource as being relevant if it is the same URL the user actually clicked. Therefore our relevance assessments for each query are obtained directly from the log and are determined by the author of each query.

In order to clean the data, we first selected those queries which resulted in a click on a URL. Secondly, we selected only those URLs for which more than 100 users had clicked on at least once. Finally, we selected only those users with more than 100 remaining queries. This ensures that all users in the dataset have a reasonably large number of queries from which to build the personalisation models and that the documents constructed for each URL from the queries are of a reasonable size. In order to parse the queries we first separated the words according to whitespace. All punctuation was removed and Porter's algorithm was used for stemming. We did not remove any stopwords but did remove any singleton terms as it is not possible that such a term would exist in both training and testing sets and therefore they would be useless for ranking. The resulting reduced data set is described in more detail in Table 1.

We report two standard Information Retrieval evaluation metrics - Success at rank k (S@k) and Mean Reciprocal Rank (MRR). $S@k$ is the proportion of instances where the relevant document is ranked at position k or higher. For example S@1 indicates the proportion of queries for which the ranking algorithm is able to return the relevant document at the top rank. MRR is the inverse of the rank of the relevant document averaged over all queries. In addition to these metrics we also report Personalisation Gain (P-gain), which simply compares the number of times the personalisation algorithm improves the ranking with the number of times it worsens it. Using this metric a value of 0 indicates no overall change in the rankings due to personalisation, a positive value indicates an improvement in performance and a negative value indicates a degradation in performance. We compare the new personalised model against a competitive topic-based, but unpersonalised, baseline (Latent Dirichlet Allocation - LDA). Note that we experimented with a variety of different settings for Z (the number of latent topics) and found that for both models the performance peaked at somewhere between 125 and 150 topics. The following analysis is conducted on models with 150 latent topics.

5.1   Results

Table 2. Ranking performance on the test data set

	S@1	S@10	MRR@10	P-gain
LDA	0.2341	0.4766	0.1403	–
PTM	0.2646*	0.4991*	0.1599*	0.1962*
% improv.	11.5%	4.5%	12.3%	–

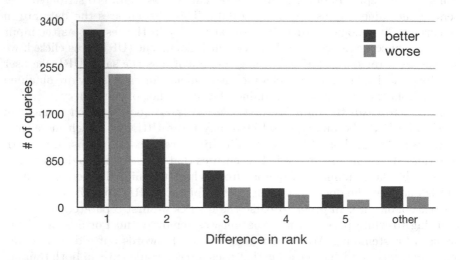

Fig. 3. Difference in rank position between the 2 models

Table 2 shows the results for the two models. We can see that the personalised model is able to deliver much better results in comparison to the non-personalised baseline, registering an improvement in rank in 19.62% of cases. In fact the difference in performance over all metrics is significant[2] (p-value $\ll 0.01$).

---

[2] As determined by 2 sample proportion z-test.

The improvements are particularly noticeable in the lower ranks, resulting in a considerable increase in S@1 and MRR.

The difference in ranking performance between the two models can be better understood by considering the difference in the ranks of the relevant document. Figure 3 shows the distribution of the difference in the ranking of the relevant document for each query between the two models. The darker bars show the number of queries where the ranking was improved, the lighter bars show where the ranking deteriorated, "other" refers to all rank changes greater than 5. The distribution shows, importantly, that the ratio between improved and deteriorated queries increases with the change in rank position. At a rank change of 1 the ratio is only 1.33:1, however it becomes as high as 1.91:1 when we look at queries where the change in rank was greater than 5. This indicates that for a number of queries the personalisation is able to move the relevant document much higher in the rankings, however the opposite case occurs very infrequently.

5.2   Impact of Query Difficulty

Table 3. Performance as query "difficulty" changes

Query length	1	2	3	4	> 4
# better	615	1,893	1,685	1,242	1,449
# worse	203	1,082	1,145	953	1,243
P-gain	0.504	0.273	0.191	0.132	0.077
Entropy	0 0.2	0.2-0.4	0.4-0.6	0.6-0.8	0.8-1.0
# better	398	429	669	605	630
# worse	236	262	319	343	267
P-gain	0.256	0.242	0.354	0.276	0.405

As mentioned earlier, we would expect a personalised model to be most beneficial in the case of short and ambiguous queries and perhaps less so for longer queries where the information need has been more thoroughly described. Queries can be described in terms of their "difficulty", with short ambiguous queries being more "difficult" than longer less ambiguous ones. There are a number of measures of query difficulty [12,48], however 2 common approaches are to look at the length of the query and (when click data is available) the click entropy for that query.

Table 3:top details how the performance of our model changes as the length of the queries change. The performance gain of the personalised model is clearly much better for shorter queries, particularly for queries of length 1 or 2, however as the query length increases, the performance of the personalised model - relative to the unpersonalised one - decreases. Regardless of query length, the personalised model is still able to outperform the LDA baseline, however the number of queries for which it is able to produce a better ranking decrease as query length increases. This ties in nicely with the idea that personalisation is much more effective for ambiguous queries where there is likely to be much more variation between different users. In the case of longer queries, the extra information included in the query reduces the uncertainty and renders the user profile information much less useful. As one would expect the general performance of both models decreases as the query length increases (i.e. as the queries become increasingly less ambiguous). For example, by focusing purely on queries of length 3 or less, we can achieve an overall p-gain of 0.265. This is an important observation since queries tend to be short and therefore the better performance is obtained for the most common query lengths. In our testing data set queries of length 3 or less account for 70.69% of all queries (72666/102790).

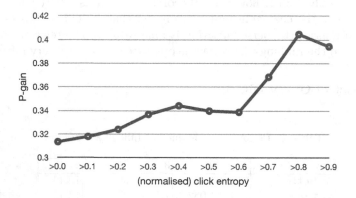

Fig. 4. Personalisation performance depends on query ambiguity as this plot demonstrates: For high values of normalised click-entropy the personalisation performance is much higher

For the more common queries we can measure the query difficulty (ambiguity) more directly in terms of the click-entropy. When initially looking at the click entropy, we did not observe the same relationship. For this metric we actually observed the opposite relationship, although it is not very clear: in general, as the click entropy of the query increases, the relative performance of the personalised model appears to decrease. However, upon further investigation it became clear that quite a large proportion of these entropies were being calculated based on very small numbers of data points, in fact in over 10% of cases the entropy was calculated based on fewer than 5 data points. Clearly when the entropy calculation is based on such a small sample it is highly unlikely to approximate the "true" value over the greater user population. To account for this we considered only the queries for which 20 or more data points were present in the training data set. Table 3:bottom shows how the performance of the models changed as the (normalised) click entropy of the queries increased. By restricting our analysis to only queries that were well represented in the training set we of course reduce the number of data points quite significantly, however the numbers are still large enough to identify general trends. Although the trend is not nearly as clear as it was for the query lengths, we can see that as the click entropy of the

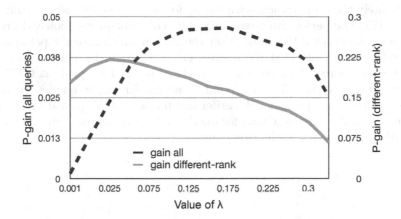

Fig. 5. The effect of varying the λ parameter in the personalised ranking algorithm

query increases, so too does the relative performance of the personalised model (correlation = 0.71). This relationship is more obvious as depicted in figure 4 which shows in finer granularity how performance changes as the click-entropy of the queries increase.

5.3   The Effect of λ

We introduced a parameter λ into the ranking formula for the personalised model to allow control over the amount of influence the user profile has on the document scores. We tested the effect of this parameter within the range of 0...0.5, where the extreme setting $\lambda = 0$ should collapse the model back to the same estimates as LDA. The effect on performance, in terms of P-gain, over all queries (dashed line) and over just the different-rank queries (solid line) is shown in figure 5. Looking at the different-rank queries we can see that as the parameter value is decreased, the performance seems to increase. However as λ decreases the total number of different-rank queries also decreases, since the differences between the two models are becoming increasingly smaller. That being the case, we do not necessarily want to optimise this parameter based purely on performance over this set of queries as we also want to ensure that the positive impact of the personalisation is affecting as many queries as possible. For example in setting λ to 0.025, which appears to yield the best performance, the number of different-rank queries is reduced to just 5,331 (5.2% of the total). If λ is instead optimised for performance over all queries ($\lambda = 0.175$) then the improvement over the subset of different-rank queries is still very high, however the size of this set is increased to 14,656 (14.25%). Note that we have not included points in the plot for $\lambda = 0$ because in this case the algorithm simply collapses back the unpersonalised model and all p-gains are 0.

Figures 6 and 7 further illustrate the effect of varying λ and its relationship with the length of the queries. When comparing these plots to figure 5 we observe approximately the same trends, with the performance over all queries peaking at around 0.175. The performance over only different-rank queries slowly decreases as λ increases, except if the value is set too low, in which case the performance is generally poor. Note that for queries of length one, the performance over different-rank queries does not appear to have reached its peak at 0.175 and continues to slowly rise after this point. However for longer queries we notice that the performance peaks much earlier and has already degraded by the time λ has reached 0.3, so much so that for queries of length greater than 4 the p-gain is actually slightly negative by this point.

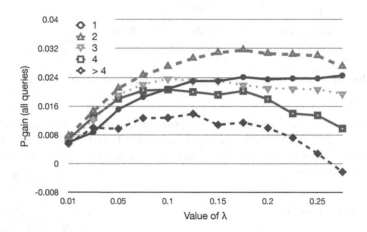

Fig. 6. Performance effects of different values of λ for queries of different lengths, showing all queries (not just different-rank queries). Note that short and likely more ambiguous queries of length 1 have a much larger optimal value for λ (greater than 0.25) as compared to queries of length 3 or more, indicating that the importance of the user profile is higher for the shorter queries.

5.4   Model Performance Summary

The results of our analysis indicate that it is possible to improve performance through personalisation by making use of topic-model based user profiles. While in theory, personalisation can offer a path to achieving substantial gains in retrieval performance, in practice performance improvements over all queries will be quite small with respect to the performance of the un-personalised retrieval system. Thus personalisation needs to be introduced with great care in order to obtain gains without adversely affecting average performance. We have shown that the performance gains for our model are significant for a smaller subset of queries, which can be identified by using query difficulty metrics such as click entropy and query length. Query length was shown to be an excellent indicator of performance and it was shown that there is some correlation between click entropy and performance, although this was not perhaps quite as clear as we might have expected.

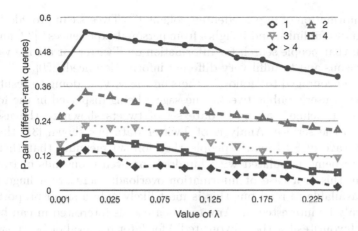

Fig. 7. Performance effects of different values of λ for queries of different lengths, showing only different-rank queries

6 Recommending Tweets

It can be argued that personalisation and recommendation are in fact two sides of the same coin as they both use knowledge about the user - usually some kind of profile - to filter down a large list of possible items to present to the user. The key difference being that in the case of personalised search the system is given an input query, whereas in the case of recommendation there is no query, rather the user's interests (as well as other contextual data) alone must be used to narrow the candidate items [1,40]. Therefore, having shown how personalisation can be used to improve the ranking performance of a search engine, we now turn briefly to the related problem of recommendation and present the preliminary stages of research into personalised suggestion of interesting Tweets.

Search on the web evolves constantly, with social media having an ever-increasing impact and even being included in mainstream search engine results. In the 1990s the main concerns for a search engine were ensuring a good match between query terms and documents returned and to keep spam at bay. However as the web has matured, issues such as freshness, trustworthiness and serendipity have slowly become more important [8]. The rapid growth of social media in in the last decade has provided an unprecedented volume and breadth of data, yet the sheer scale of this new data source can be overwhelming for users [5,46]. Perhaps the most well-known and popular example of social media is the short messaging service Twitter.

Twitter is a socially-focussed short messaging ("micro-blogging") service that allows users to post and read short messages - known as "tweets" - of up to 140 characters in length. In these tweets users post about what they are currently reading, thinking and doing and often post URLs to web sites of interest to them [34,38]. In addition to being a platform for socially sharing thoughts and opinions, work has shown that Twitter also represents a valuable, user-driven source of information of unprecedented volume [5]. Tweets can provide "specific information, useful links, and insights from personal experiences" [32] and it has been shown that people search for information on Twitter for a wide variety of different reasons and to fulfil very different information needs [20].

Users are encouraged to "follow" others on the service, doing so results in all of the followed user's public tweets (messages) being displayed in the following user's "home timeline;" an up-to-date set of tweets shown to the user after logging in to the service. Analysis of Twitter data has shown [31] that users have an average of 80 friends (people they follow) meaning that their home timelines are being populated with hundreds or even thousands of tweets per day. Clearly this is a case of information overload: there are a huge number of Tweets available to read but this is most likely only a small proportion the user will truly be interested in. Any tweets a user is interested in can be either added to a favourites list (be "favourited") for later retrieval or be "retweeted," meaning that the original Tweet is shared with followers of the retweeting user.

A system able to identify which tweets from a user's home timeline are likely to be favourited or retweeted by that user would therefore be useful in coping with this information overload and would allow Twitter users to narrow down the huge number of posts and focus on the most interesting for them. We can define this as a classification problem by considering the list of tweets appearing on a user's home timeline and considering all those which are favourited or retweeted as belonging to the positive class with all others being negative. Of course in order to make accurate classifications we need to develop a number of features of the tweets which will allow us to distinguish between those which are interesting and those which aren't. A further consideration is that the features which best describe favourited tweets may not be the same as those which best describe retweets, perhaps necessitating that separate models be developed.

6.1   Understanding What Makes a Tweet Interesting

In order to build prediction models we need to have some data on which to train and data which can be used to test the performance of the suggestions made. To do so we collected data from the Twitter API for a sample of 27 users over a period of 2 months. These users were recruited via a combination of direct mails and tweets advertising the study and asking users to take part. Users were simply directed to a page where the Twitter API asked them to confirm that they were willing to allow us access to their data. During this time we polled the API [3] once per hour and collected information about all tweets which appeared on each user's home timeline and in particularly whether the user subsequently favourited or retweeted each one, yielding tweets from around 7 thousand different authors. We also queried the API for information about each of these authors. Having access to each user's full Twitter data made it possible to ensure that the home timelines we were downloading were exactly the same as those really seen by each user.

---

[3] Twitter REST API version 1.1: https://dev.twitter.com/docs/api/1.1

Table 4. Useful features for predicting retweets and favourites on Twitter

Feature	Description	RT	Fav
RTSim	Similarity between post content and user's retweet profile	×	
FavSim	Similarity between post content and user's favourites profile		×
RTCount	Total number of times post has been retweeted by other users	×	−
MentionCount	Number of users mentioned in post (@username)	×	×
URLCount	Number of URLs included in the post		−
FavCount	Total number of times post has been favourited by other users	×	×
Mention	Whether of not the target user is mentioned in the post	×	×
FollowerCount	The follower count of the author	−	−

To learn more about the users' interests, so that personal profiles could be constructed, we queried the API for all retweets and favourites made by each user. This data was then used to construct a pair of profiles based on the terms appearing in all of the user's favourited and retweeted posts. Profiles were constructed by considering all of the terms derived from the posts after they had been lower-cased and a list of Twitter-specific stop words had been removed. In addition, terms only appearing once in any given profile were removed and two bag-of-words models were created from the resulting profiles to represent each user.

With the collected data we computed a large number of different features (n−24) which could potentially hint at how interesting or useful a tweet might be. These included features describing the post itself such as the bag-of-words of terms in the post, the number of photographs, user mentions or URLs embedded in the tweet and the number of times it had been retweeted or favourited by other users. To determine if the content of the tweet might be interesting to the user we calculated the Cosine similarity between the user's profiles and the bag-of-words representation of the tweet. As is standard in Information Retrieval, TD-IDF weighting was applied to the term weights. Features were also constructed describing the post's author including how many followers the author had and how many times they had tweeted since joining the service.

Using a simple logistic regression model we are able to identify which features contribute significantly to the prediction task. A description of the most statistically powerful features is given in Table 4 as well as which of the two models (retweets and favourites) the features pertain to. × indicates that the feature correlated positively with the target class, − indicates a negative correlation. Note that different combinations of features are useful for the two different classification model, hinting that while the problem may be similar, the features which encourage a retweet are somewhat different to those encouraging the user to favourite.

We trained our models on a sample of the data collection comprising a total of 20,454 tweets, only 133 of which were favourited and 356 retweeted. These numbers highlight one of the key difficulties with this task: the sheer imbalance of the classes. If we consider favourites prediction then the class imbalance is 153:1! Although the regression models mentioned earlier were able to identify useful features and could return fairly accurate class predictions, we do not use them as our final classifier due to their inability to cope well in the case of imbalanced data. Instead, to train the final classifier, we used random forests [6], a modern and highly competitive [13] tree-based classification algorithm. In this ensemble learning method a large number of decision trees are computed based on different random samples (subsets) of the training data. When classifying a new data point, all of the decision trees calculated during training vote on the correct output class and a final classification is made based on the mode of the classes output by the individual trees. Given a new tweet (represented by its set of features), this method returns the probability that it belongs to the positive class.

Since the classifier is optimised based on classification accuracy, we cannot simply assign tweets to the positive class if the predicted probability is greater than 0.5, as would normally be the case. To understand why, consider that it is possibly to design a trivial classifier for this task by simply returning the negative class regardless of the input. Such as classifier would achieve an "accuracy" of 99.3% when predicting favourites however it would be of little use as it would never return a single "interesting" tweet. To deal with this issue we also train a threshold value on the outputted probabilities, above which the tweet will be classified as positive. We selected this threshold by choosing the value which returned the best F1 score on the training data, which is an appropriate metric as it is the harmonic mean of precision and recall. This means that a high F1 score indicates that the classifier is able to return a good proportion of the positively-classed tweets (the true positives) whilst making few mistakes (i.e. returning false positives). For both prediction tasks the threshold was optimised to 0.15.

Despite the complexity of the classification problem at hand, our favourites prediction model is able to achieve an F1 score of 0.491 (precision: 0.455, recall: 0.534) and an accuracy of 0.993%, the retweet model achieves 0.394 (precision: 0.354, recall: 0.444) and 0.976%. Both models are able to simultaneously achieve very good F1 scores and overall prediction accuracy. In both cases the recall scores are better than the precision scores indicating that the models are retrieving a larger percentage of the positively-classed tweets at the cost of introducing more false positives.

It appears that the similarity between a post's content and user's profile is a good indicator of interestingness and it also seems that there is a difference between the terms of tweets users retweet and those they favourite (removing the user profile similarity from the favourites model reduces the F1 score significantly to 0.3). Interestingly, the number of times the post has been retweeted by other users is a positive feature for detecting retweets but negative when detecting favourites. Perhaps people feel encouraged to retweet a post which they have observed has been already retweeted by some of the people they follow. For both models the number of users mentioned in the post is a positive feature as is the number of times the post has been favourited. When the target user is mentioned in the post, the probability of it being retweeted or favourited increases dramatically, particularly for some users. This hints that ego plays some part in choosing tweets or that users want to ensure easy refinding of tweets which were specifically directed at them. The number of URLs in the post and the follower count of the author are both negative features, perhaps because posts with large numbers of URLs are often SPAM, advertisements or automatic posts from news sources.

7 Conclusions and Future Work

With the explosive growth of new data available on the web everyday from both traditional static web pages and newer social-generated sources, it is becoming increasingly difficult to filter out what is important and interesting, often leading to "information overload". In this book chapter we have considered two instances where users could be assisted in finding resources of interest to them from the vast array of potential candidate items available. In the first case we illustrated how a web search can be improved by means of personalising the results and in the second case we showed how items can be recommended to the user. We argue that these two scenarios are in fact two sides of the the same coin, the difference being that in the first case the user provides a query as input whereas in the second instance the user profile itself is the query.

We built models to learn about a person's interests and use of terminology based purely on their previous search queries which were then used to develop personalised search algorithms and were tested on real search log data. The re sults of our analysis indicate that it is possible to improve performance through personalisation by making use of topic model based user profiles. While, in the ory, personalisation can offer a path to achieving substantial gains in retrieval performance, in practice performance improvements over all queries will be quite small with respect to the performance of the un-personalised retrieval system. Thus personalisation needs to be introduced with great care in order to obtain gains without adversely affecting average performance.

We have shown that the performance gains for our model are significant for a smaller subset of queries, which can be identified by using query difficulty metrics such as click entropy and query length. Query length was shown to be an excellent indicator of performance and it was shown that there is some correlation between click entropy and performance, although this was not perhaps quite as clear as we might have expected. A better quantity for predicting personalisation performance may take both the click entropy and the query length into account and perhaps even the interaction between these metrics. For example it may be possible to normalise the click entropy by the expected entropy at that query length or it may be useful to consider some linear combination of the metrics to identify when to personalise and when not to.

We believe that there are further gains to be achieved by taking into account to what extent the user profile differs from that of the "average user", whereby the more particular the interests of the user, the more likely personalisation is to have a positive effect. More generally, we would like to estimate the extent to which the user profile reduces the ambiguity of the query and use that to decide for which query-user pairs to personalise the results. If we can determine that the profile is useful for disambiguating the query, then it makes sense to personalise, otherwise it doesn't. Such a metric would give a sense of how "contrary" a given user is. For example, if (for most queries) the user regularly clicks on the same URL as the majority of other users then we can say that they are not contrary and should reduce the influence of the user profile accordingly (via λ). If, on the other hand, the user very often chooses URLs contrary to other users then it is likely that an increase in the value of λ will yield better results.

To recommend social media posts to users we collected a large sample of data from Twitter and attempted to predict which posts a user would retweet or favourite (both indicators of interest in the post). By defining a number of features describing the post itself, its similarity to the user's interests (as determined by previous posts they showed interest in) and the author we were able to build classification models with high levels of both precision and recall. In future work we could consider more complex features, for example features based on the Twitter social network (i.e. the network of links between users defined by friendships and follower relationships). With this information we could use graph theory techniques to gain a better understanding of how the social links contribute to interestingness. We also acknowledge that our method of constructing user profiles is somewhat rudimentary and could certainly be improved by either implementing some intelligent term selection routines or even using topic models.

In summary we have shown that there is much to be gained from considering contextual information about the user, whether from web logs or social media, when personalising search results and recommending items of interest. However, we have also demonstrated that this information must be incorporated in a subtle manner if it is to be of benefit. The directions indicated for future work have the potential to further increase the existing performance gains and lower further the information load imposed upon users.

References

1. Adomavicius, G., Tuzhilin, A.: Toward the Next Generation of Recommender Systems: A Survey of the State-of-the-Art and Possible Extensions. IEEE Transactions on Knowledge and Data Engineering 17(6), 734–749 (2005)
2. Bennett, P.N., Radlinski, F., White, R.W., Yilmaz, E.: Inferring and using location metadata to personalize web search. In: 34th ACM Conference on Research and Development in Information Retrieval, SIGIR 2011, pp. 135–144. ACM (2011)
3. Bennett, P.N., White, R.W., Chu, W., Dumais, S.T., Bailey, P., Borisyuk, F., Cui, X.: Modeling the impact of short- and long-term behavior on search personalization. In: 35th ACM Conference on Research and Development in Information Retrieval, SIGIR 2012, pp. 185–194. ACM (2012)
4. Blei, D., Ng, A., Jordan, M.: Latent dirichlet allocation. Journal of Machine Learning Research 3, 993–1022 (2003)
5. Boyd, D., Golder, S., Lotan, G.: Tweet, tweet, retweet: Conversational aspects of retweeting on twitter. In: 43rd Hawaii Conference on System Sciences, HICSS 2010, pp. 1–10. IEEE Computer Society (2010)

6. Breiman, L.: Random forests. Machine Learning 45(1), 5–32 (2001)
7. Brin, S., Page The, L.: The anatomy of a large-scale hypertextual Web search engine. Computer Networks and ISDN Systems 30, 107–117 (1998)
8. Cambazoglu, B., Junqueira, F., Plachouras, V., Banachowski, S., Cui, B., Lim, S., Bridge, B.: A Refreshing Perspective of Search Engine Caching. In: 19th International Conference on World Wide Web, WWW 2010, pp. 181–190. ACM (2010)
9. Cao, H., Hu, D.H., Shen, D., Jiang, D., Sun, J.-T., Chen, E., Yang, Q.: Context-aware query classification. In: 32nd ACM Conference on Research and Development in Information Retrieval, pp. 3–10. ACM (2009)
10. Carman, M.J., Baillie, M., Gwadera, R., Crestani, F.: A statistical comparison of tag and query logs. In: 32nd ACM Conference on Research and development in Information Retrieval, SIGIR 2009, pp. 123–130. ACM (2009)
11. Carman, M.J., Crestani, F., Harvey, M., Baillie, M.: Towards query log based personalization using topic models. In: 19th ACM Conference on Information and Knowledge Management, CIKM 2010, pp. 1849–1852. ACM (2010)
12. Carmel, D., Yom-Tov, E., Darlow, A., Pelleg, D.: What makes a query difficult? In: 29th ACM Conference on Research and Development in Information Retrieval, SIGIR 2006, pp. 390–397. ACM (2006)
13. Caruana, R., Niculescu-Mizil, A.: An Empirical Comparison of Supervised Learning Algorithms. In: 23rd International Conference on Machine Learning, ICML 2006, pp. 161–168. ACM (2006)
14. Chirita, P.A., Nejdl, W., Paiu, R., Kohlschütter, C.: Using odp metadata to personalize search. In: 28th ACM Conference on Research and development in Information Retrieval, SIGIR 2005, pp. 178–185. ACM (2005)
15. Collins-Thompson, K., Bennett, P.N., White, R.W., de la Chica, S., Sontag, D.: Personalizing web search results by reading level. In: 20th ACM Conference on Information and Knowledge Management, CIKM 2011, pp. 403–412. ACM (2011)
16. Croft, B., Metzler, D., Strohman, T.: Search Engines: Information Retrieval in Practice. Addison-Wesley Publishing Company, USA (2009)
17. Daoud, M., Tamine-Lechani, L., Boughanem, M., Chebaro, B.: A session based personalized search using an ontological user profile. In: 2009 ACM symposium on Applied Computing, SAC 2009, pp. 1732–1736. ACM (2009)
18. Deerwester, S., Dumais, S.T., Furnas, G.W., Landauer, T.K., Harshman, R.: Indexing by latent semantic analysis. Journal of the American Society for Information Science 41, 391–407 (1990)
19. Dou, Z., Song, R., Wen, J.-R.: A large-scale evaluation and analysis of personalized search strategies. In: 16th Conference on World Wide Web, WWW 2007, pp. 581–590. ACM (2007)
20. Elsweiler, D., Harvey, M.: Engaging and maintaing a sense of being informed: Understanding the tasks motivating twitter search. Journal of the American Society for Information Science and Technology, JASIST (2014)
21. Falush, D., Stephens, M., Pritchard, J.K.: Inference of population structure using multilocus genotype data: linked loci and correlated allele frequencies. Genetics 164(4), 1567–1587 (2003)
22. Fei-Fei, L., Perona, P.: A bayesian hierarchical model for learning natural scene categories. In: IEEE Computer Society Conference on Computer Vision and Pattern Recognition, CVPR 2005, vol. 2, pp. 524–531. IEEE (2005)
23. Furnas, G., Landauer, T., Gomez, L., Dumais, S.: The Vocabulary Problem in Human-System Communicatio. Communications of the ACM 30(11), 964–971 (1987)

24. Gauch, S., Chaffee, J., Pretschner, A.: Ontology-based user profiles for search and browsing. Web Intelligence and Agent Systems 1(3-4), 219–234 (2003)
25. Golder, S., Huberman, B.: The structure of collaborative tagging systems. Journal of Information Science 32(2), 198–208 (2005)
26. Griffiths, T., Steyvers, M.: Finding scientific topics. National Academy of Science 101, 5228–5235 (2004)
27. Harvey, M., Carman, M., Ruthven, I.: Improving social bookmark search using personalised latent variable language models. In: 4th ACM Conference on Web Search and Data Mining, WSDM 2011, pp. 485–494. ACM (2011)
28. Harvey, M., Carman, M., Elsweiler, D.: Comparing tweets and tags for urls. In: Baeza-Yates, R., de Vries, A.P., Zaragoza, H., Cambazoglu, B.B., Murdock, V., Lempel, R., Silvestri, F. (eds.) ECIR 2012. LNCS, vol. 7224, pp. 73–84. Springer, Heidelberg (2012)
29. Harvey, M., Ruthven, I., Crestani, F., Carman, M.: Bayesian latent variable models for collaborative item rating prediction. In: 20th ACM Conference on Information and Knowledge Management, CIKM 2011, pp. 699–708. ACM (2011)
30. Hofmann, T.: Probabilistic latent semantic indexing. In: 22nd ACM Conference on Research and Development in Information Retrieval, SIGIR 1999, pp. 50–57. ACM (1999)
31. Huberman, B.A., Romero, D.M., Wu, F.: Social networks that matter: Twitter under the microscope. First Monday 14(1) (2009)
32. Hurlock, J., Wilson, M.L.: Searching twitter: Separating the tweet from the chaff. In: 5th AAAI Conference on Weblogs and Social Media, ICWSM 2011. AAAI (2011)
33. Jansen, B.J., Spink, A.: How are we searching the World Wide Web? A comparison of nine search engine transaction logs. Information Processing and Management (IPM) 42, 248–263 (2006)
34. Java, A., Song, X., Finin, T., Tseng, B.: Why we twitter: understanding microblogging usage and communities. In: 9th WebKDD and 1st SNA-KDD 2007 Workshop on Web mining and Social Network Analysis, pp. 56–65 (2007)
35. Lawrence, S.: Context in Web Search. IEEE Data Engineering Bulletin 23, 25–32 (2000)
36. Ma, Z., Pant, G., Sheng, O.R.L.: Interest-based personalized search. ACM Transactions on Information Systems 25(1) (February 2007)
37. Matthijs, N., Radlinski, F.: Personalizing web search using long term browsing history. In: 4th ACM Conference on Web Search and Data Mining, WSDM 2011, pp. 25–34. ACM (2011)
38. McFedries, P.: Technically speaking: All a-twitter. IEEE Spectrum 44(10), 84–84 (2007)
39. Melucci, M.: A basis for information retrieval in context. ACM Transactions of Information Systems 26(3), 14:1–14:41 (2008)
40. Nakamura, S., Konishi, S., Jatowt, A., Ohshima, H., Kondo, H., Tezuka, T., Oyama, S., Tanaka, K.: Trustworthiness analysis of web search results. In: Kovács, L., Fuhr, N., Meghini, C. (eds.) ECDL 2007. LNCS, vol. 4675, pp. 38–49. Springer, Heidelberg (2007)
41. Purcell, K.: Search and email still top the list of most popular online activities. Pew Internet Center (August 2011)
42. Qiu, F., Cho, J.: Automatic identification of user interest for personalized search. In: 15th Conference on World Wide Web, WWW 2006, pp. 727–736. ACM (2006)

43. Resnick, P., Iacovou, N., Suchak, M., Bergstrom, P., Riedl, J.: GroupLens: An open architecture for collaborative filtering of netnews. In: Proceedings of the 1994 ACM Conference on Computer Supported Cooperative Work (CSCW), pp. 175–186 (1994)
44. Robertson, S.E.: The Probability Ranking Principle in IR. In: Readings in Information Retrieval, pp. 281–286. Morgan Kaufmann Publishers Inc. (1997)
45. Sieg, A., Mobasher, B., Burke, R.: Web search personalization with ontological user profiles. In: 16th ACM Conference on Conference on Information and Knowledge Management, CIKM 2007, pp. 525–534. ACM (2007)
46. Soboroff, I., McCullough, D., Macdonald, C., Ounis, I., McCreadie, R.: Evaluating real-time search over tweets. In: 6th AAAI Conference on Weblogs and Social Media, ICWSM 2012. AAAI (2012)
47. Teevan, J., Dumais, S.T., Horvitz, E.: Potential for personalization. ACM Transactions on Computer-Human Interaction 17(1), 4:1–4:31 (2010)
48. Teevan, J., Dumais, S.T., Liebling, D.J.: To personalize or not to personalize: Modeling queries with variation in user intent. In: 31st ACM Conference on Research and Development in Information Retrieval, SIGIR 2008, pp. 163–170. ACM (2008)
49. Wei, X., Croft, W.: Lda-based document models for ad-hoc retrieval. In: 29th ACM Conference on Research and Development in Information Retrieval, SIGIR 2006, pp. 178–185. ACM (2006)
50. White, R.W., Bailey, P., Chen, L.: Predicting user interests from contextual information. In: 32nd ACM Conference on Research and Development in Information Retrieval, SIGIR 2009, pp. 363–370. ACM (2009)

Domain Specific Search

Mihai Lupu, Michail Salampasis, and Allan Hanbury

Institute for Software Technology and Interactive Systems
Vienna University of Technology
{lastname}@ifs.tuwien.ac.at

Abstract. This chapter takes a look at the existing search landscape to observe that there are a myriad of search systems, covering all possible domains, which share a handful of theoretical retrieval models and are separated by a series of pre- and post-processing steps as well as a finite set of parameters. We also observe that given the infinite variety of real-world search tasks and domains, it is unlikely that any one combination of these steps and parameters would yield a renaissance-engine — a search engine that can answer any questions about art, sciences, law or entertainment. We therefore set forth to analyze the different components of a search system and propose a model for domain specific search, including a definition thereof, as well as a technical framework to build a domain specific search system.

1 Introduction

The need for information is primarily answered today by some form of search technology. The ubiquity of casual web search in daily life may, on superficial observation, lead one to believe that there is one type of information need and that therefore one type of search system is needed. The success of web search engines has produced a generation of digital natives that have grown up with instant access to information and for whom the first ten hits in Google are the truth [26]. We know very well that this is not the case — information seeking tasks have been studied extensively in the literature [24,19]. For instance, when search technologies are used for professional search (i.e. search for a professional reason or aim) there are a number of characteristics which differentiate them from web search: lengthy search sessions which may be suspended and resumed, different notions of relevance, different sources searched separately, and the use of specific domain knowledge.

It has already been shown that the same retrieval engine shows significant performance differences across test collections [38]. It seems somewhat intuitive that if we are to handle a specific type of information request optimally, the search engine needs to be fine-tuned. This may imply many changes, ranging from changing the search space to the designing of an appropriate interface.

We refer to this fine-tuning process as *Domain-Specific Search*. The phrase has been used before in the information retrieval literature [32,40] but focusing on the data aspects of the problem. In fact, domain-specificity goes beyond the

G. Paltoglou et al. (Eds.): Professional Search in the Modern World, LNCS 8830, pp. 96–117, 2014.
© Springer International Publishing Switzerland 2014

data itself. Even on the same data, different information needs may need to be answered differently, as evidenced by the research on information seeking tasks mentioned above. Recently, we have proposed a definition for Domain Specific Search [4], and we shall expand on it in this chapter.

1.1 Motivation

Even though many domains have similar characteristics and challenges, there is currently no general framework for developing domain-specific search solutions, and no way of characterising a domain to allow the best approach or tools to be chosen. The general approach is to take a domain and develop search solutions for challenges in that domain. This silo-based development of domain-specific IR solutions is inefficient, as many solutions are developed for a specific domain, and then not applied to, or possibly even redeveloped for another domain. For example, research has been done on estimating the level of specificity of medical documents by using medical vocabularies [44], but this also has potential in the Intellectual Property search area. This has been identified as a major problem in the field of information retrieval [15] and our objective is to align the different areas of IR into a framework that would allow us to identify similarities and dissimilarities between systems, as well as to think about and plan future systems.

Therefore, another objective of this chapter is to present a general framework for designing domain-specific search systems. Based on the definition we propose, we introduce a model to assist the search solution designer in thinking about the components that will go into an integrated search system. The methodology stops short of providing a formal model, in the mathematical sense, but rather focuses on the components that a domain-specific IR system would need to consider.

1.2 Related Work

So far, the different aspects of domain-specific IR have been considered separately, and in a largely ad-hoc manner. For instance, we have seen over the past 20 years a significant number of evaluation campaigns targeting different domains and languages. They have demonstrated the utility of customizing tools for the task at hand, provided a set of lessons for each domain and made an impact on industry [33]. However even with these results, when working toward a search solution for a specific domain, the approaches are generally ad-hoc and combined arbitrarily depending on the perceived requirements of the domain.

The lack of a unified approach to domain-specific IR is illustrated by a few specific examples. We begin with global approaches to designing and creating domain-specific search engines. In 2002, Chao et al. [10] looked at a search engine for nanotechnology documents. Their approach was symptomatic of early domain-specific IR: restriction of the documents indexed and application of general purpose IR tools. Later, Luo and Tang [27] showed the other extreme of domain-specificity: a full adaption to the existing manual practices of the medical search domain. In this case, the adaptation is not only with respect to the data used, but to the search process itself. Given these two quite different approaches to creating a domain-specific search engine, it is not clear what one can learn from these experiences that is generalizable to further domains.

The majority of the work on domain-specific search, in particular in the evaluation campaigns, has been at a higher granularity, focussing on adapting various components of search engines to domains. For example, Fautsch and Savoy looked into tweaking *tf-idf* for domain-specific search [14], after having also looked at the relative performance of automatic or morphology-based stemmers [13]. Even these two papers are difficult to reconcile, as some of their results are conflicting. In general the results at this granularity are difficult to generalise beyond the specific tasks modelled in the evaluation campaigns, due to poor characterisation of all aspects of the domain around the tasks.

Finally, we should note that there are a series of systems which allow different components to be plugged in and therefore to be adapted to one domain or another. Most open source search engines have this capacity (Lucene, Terrier, Indri/Galago), and some take it a step further and allow the specification of search strategies [12]. This work complements these efforts with a framework to consider the different aspects to be taken into account when designing a new search tool or studying a search strategy.

2   A Conceptual Description

The search engine is now part of the life of many people. A large amount of research effort is justifiably dedicated to improving the search experience of the majority of the users. This is generally referred to as Web Search. It is however a very broad term, potentially encompassing many different tasks. People can use the Web to perform a wide range of search tasks, privately or professionally. They may use the Web to access a specific search engine which indexes only some documents available online, or documents not present anywhere else online. Often this is what is understood by Domain Specific Search: a system that *"limits its index to pages corresponding to a particular subject area, publisher or purpose"* [40]. In a previous article [4], we have proposed a new definition for Domain Specific Search, one that takes into account all the variable components in a search system. We will repeat it here for completeness.

A **Domain-specific search [engine | process]** *is a search [engine | process] that specifies one or more of the following five dimensions:*

1. **subject areas** *e.g. chemical, biomedical, healthcare*
2. **modality** *e.g. text, images, videos, sounds*
3. **users** *e.g. a patent examiner, a professor of medicine, a project manager*
4. **tasks** *e.g. prior art patent search, technology survey, literature search, diagnosis search*
5. **tools, techniques and algorithms required** *to complete the tasks, e.g. query completion limited to specific vocabularies, cross-lingual search, possibility to store search results*

The five aspects of this definition can be arguably grouped in only three: information sources (*subject areas* and *modality*), user aspects (*users* and *tasks*), and technical aspects. However, it is clear that although the five dimensions are not orthogonal (e.g. some users have only some tasks and apply only some tools on a specific modality in a specific subject area), they are distinguishable, and we argue that this distinction is important for defining the domain specific search system.

We can think of a search system as a shape in the 5D space defined by the definition's components. Figure 1 shows how this might look on a radar plot. Such a plot allows us to visualize where two existing systems (or an existing system and a set of requirements) meet and diverge.

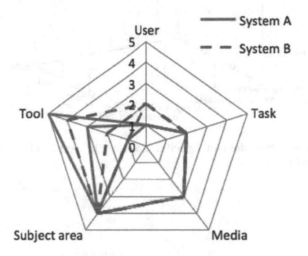

Fig. 1. Comparing two domain specific systems in terms of users, tasks, media, domains, and tools

Projections of this space in 3D may be more useful to visualize the idea. Pairs of axes can be merged in a standard, multiplicative way. For instance, we can combine users and tasks. We may have two users: a patient and a physician, and two tasks: known item search or explorative search, generating a new axis with a four point domain. Similarly, domains and modalities may be viewed together. The 3D space thus created can be used to compare domain specific systems, by comparing the vectors defined by the points at the intersections of users/tasks, domains/modalities, and tools. Figure 2 shows such a possible comparison. We would observe from it that Systems A and B are comparable in many aspects (blue thick lines), but address different users in their deployment of, for instance, *tool2* on *media1/subject area1*. We might then chose to evaluate this particular difference, instead of focusing on all the other common aspects.

Alternatively, we can orthogonally project the 5 dimensional space into one of its 3 dimensional subspaces. The result is a space where each point contains pairs of the additional two dimensions. For instance, Figure 3 shows such a projection on the <users, tasks, subject area> space, where the points tell us which tools have to be used to process each media in each case. Compared with the previous type of projection, the orthogonal one is more suited to the analysis of one system in order to identify specific components, rather than the comparison of two or more systems.

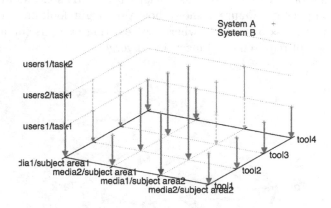

Fig. 2. Comparing two domain specific systems in terms of users/tasks, media/domains, and tools

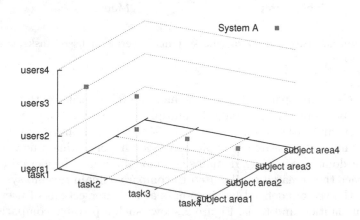

Fig. 3. Orthogonal projection in 3D subspace

To validate our definition, the following two sections show two use-cases, from the intellectual property and healthcare domains.

2.1   Intellectual Property Domain

This section presents an instantiation of the proposed model based on the results of a study on intellectual property specific search, more precisely on patent search systems. The information was collected in user studies performed in the *anonymized* [1] and *anonymized* [2] projects [2].

Gathering Information: In order to populate the model, a series of surveys has been performed over the past two years. Unlike the medical domain, which covers a very large set of users, the patent domain is generally limited to a set of professionals. Arguably, any citizen can freely look into any patent collection because these are public data and the patent system is designed around the idea of exchanging the disclosure of new methods and devices for a guaranteed monopoly. In practice however, the users who actually consider these documents are limited to information professionals, lawyers and inventors. The surveys were therefore targeted to these categories of users and focused on a qualitative approach rather than a quantitative one. This meant also discussions and interviews with respondents.

Preparatory Survey: Approaching professional users is best done after a thorough examination of the literature describing their work. The complex nature and high economic value of the patent domain has generated series of books and articles describing the tasks, processes, data sources, and objectives of patent search. A starting point was Adams's book on information sources for the patent domain [1]. Another reference book in the area is by Hunt, Nguyen and Rogers [23]. If Adams's book is more about where to get patent data and general search practices, the book of Hunt et al. focuses on how precisely to do patent search. While the technology has changed substantially in the past five years, it is still considered a reference book in the field. The results of the studies were verified through user surveys. We synthesized one of the tasks into a written, bullet-pointed scenario, and asked users to tell us how correct and complete the scenario was. This was done via a survey and interview at the Greek Patent Office, as well as through online surveys. A previous survey [6] had identified a set of general search requirements in the patent domain. This was followed up by a survey focused on image retrieval tools, done among the patent professionals participating in the 2nd Information Retrieval Facility Conference. In both, questions were grouped into what is being done now, and what is still missing. Based on the results and analysis of the surveys and interviews, we can now populate the five axes defined above for the specific case of the patent domain.

Users: The following people search for information in the intellectual property domain: **Inventor/Researcher** – a technically skilled person, without any or

---

[1] anonymized
[2] anonymized

with very limited knowledge of the patent legal system; **Librarian/Information specialist** – is skilled in the science of information organization. Generally also technically skilled, and with limited to moderate knowledge of the patent system; **Patent Lawyer** – has deep knowledge of the patent legal system, generally only superficially technically skilled; **Patent Office Examiner** – a technically skilled person, particularly familiar with the granting and examination procedures of a specific patent office.

Tasks: A relatively well defined set of tasks are performed in the patent domain [28]. They include: *State of the art search*, *Patentability* or *Validity* search. The different tasks focus on precision and recall at different degrees [41]. For instance, Validity focuses more on precision in the sense that the relevant documents must match very closely the information request. Alternatively. State of the Art search is a much more recall oriented search in the sense that the task is to collect many potentially relevant documents.

As observed in Section 2, the axes in this model are not quite orthogonal. From the list above we can observe that if the user is the *Patent Office Examiner*, than the only search task possible is *Patentability*. However, this task can be also performed by other users. Equally, an *Inventor* is very unlikely to ever perform a *Patent Portfolio Search*.

Subject Areas: The patent domain focuses on industry-applicable inventions, and is therefore technical in nature. If we were to use the Dewey Decimal Classification (DDC) commonly used in Libraries, the entire domain would be restricted to the Technology division (DDC number 600), potentially also including the computer science, information and general works division (DDC number 000) and the Science division (DDC number 500).

In the patent system there exist also a set of different subject area classifications. The only one used globally is the International Patent Classification (IPC), managed by the World Intellectual Property Organisation (WIPO). In the case of the Intellectual Property search, the subject areas do not provide a separation between this and other domains, as all subject areas are covered by Intellectual Property.

Media: The media that users consult for this domain is in practice limited to text and images. DNA sequences, chemical formulae and names are also represented in textual format, but clearly should not be subjected to a default indexing procedure that may include stemmers. Patent images can be grouped in different categories, each of which should be treated with a different tool [18].

Tools: The toolbox used in patent search contains the full set of components of a general purpose search engine, to which a set of specific ones are added, to appropriately handle meta-data, named entities and images. It is fairly clear that this dimension is not orthogonal to the previous ones, particularly the *Subject* *areas* and *Media.* For instance, given the *Chemistry* subject area and *Image* media, it is very likely that we will need a chemical structure recognizer, to transform the bitmap representation into a semantic one. However, other tools may be needed, such as flowchart or table recognizers. Overall, this dimension is potentially the most difficult to fill, because it is bounded only by the imagination of tool designers and perhaps computational resources.

2.2 Medical Domain

This section discusses the instantiation of the model for search in the medical domain by members of the general public and physicians. The case of search within medical literature is covered (knowledge-based information), not search within patient-specific information such as Health Records.

Gathering Information: In order to build the model, extensive consultation with the end users was carried out. This was done in the following steps: performing an online survey, categorization of user profiles, identification of user scenarios, and the verification of this identification. The steps carried out are summarised below. More detail on the latter three steps is available in *a document withheld due to anonymisation.*

Online Survey: Two online surveys on current practices in medical search and perceived requirements were conducted, one of members of the general public (385 responses) and one of physicians (500 responses). Detailed analysis of the results of the surveys are reported in *two documents withheld due to anonymisation.* To obtain additional, quantitative insight, additional studies were conducted: query log analysis and interviews. The results obtained through these additional studies helped test the use cases in real-life circumstances.

Identification: The second step involved implementation of user requirements within the context of real-life search scenarios for each of the proposed groups. The structure of the scenarios was inspired by [11]. Each scenario included information about the scenario itself, user specific characteristics (pre-condition, log-in status, willingness to pay, context, time available, and language skills), goal/intention of the search, ideal search process (link description, automatic categorization, manual categorization, tools, and suggested websites), successful search scenario and alternative scenarios (unsuccessful scenario and suggested settings for a log-in scenario). In addition, further information on examples of useful data resources for each use case scenario was provided.

Verification: After this, the user scenarios were verified and validated using semi-structured interviews with physicians and the general public. Interviews helped to gain some qualitative insight on the topic whilst ensuring that the proposed scenarios had validity in real life. Preliminary results of query log analysis done on search logs available from the Health on the Net search engine[3] and PubMed [21] have also been taken into account.

Users: The analysis of a survey for physicians [25] demonstrated that search behaviour and information needs were primarily determined by the level of specialisation, status of employment, and level of qualification. As a result, five distinct user groups were identified: self-employed general practitioners, self-employed specialists, hospital clinicians, physicians in training, and research physicians. These user groups were found to differ in the level of search, expected resources, location of search, role of multilinguality, level of access (mobile device vs. fixed device), priority of output ranking (last update, simplicity, quality rating), and digital social support.

Analysis of the results of a survey among the general public [31] led to the identification of user profiles with unique patterns of search behaviour and information needs, reflecting the user's level of health literacy:

- generally healthy, browsing for self-education.
- just diagnosed with an acute condition, searching for information about an acute condition.
- just diagnosed with a chronic condition, searching for a wide variety of information about a chronic condition from a definition of disease and treatment to a social worker assistance.
- a chronic patient for a certain period of time, an "expert patient".

However, based on the survey results, it would also make sense to group the users based on age and gender.

Tasks: We have identified six types of searches: two performed by the general public and four by physicians [9]:

Basic: characterized by definition and easily accessible health content search (as in symptoms of a disease, drug description etc.) by members of the general public.

Advanced: characterized by more profound, detailed search by members of general public, typically by "expert patients".

Wide: performed when a physician (typically a general practitioner or physician in training) seeks out definitional, general or descriptive information from secondary resources.

Narrow: performed when a physician (typically a self-employed specialist or hospital clinician) seeks information in his/her field of specialisation, usually from specialised resources, to answer a usually concrete, complex question.

Research: performed when a physician (typically a research physician or hospital clinician) seeks information, usually from primary resources, describing the newest findings or "state of the art" on a topic.

---

[3] http://www.healthonnet.org

Continuing Medical Education (CME): performed when a physician seeks local, online CME content to pursue required levels of medical updating.

The connection between the search tasks defined above and the users is shown in Table 1. In terms of the model, this table represents the sub-space spanning the *users* and *tasks* axes.

Table 1. The search types (columns) typically carried out by each user category (rows) are shown by the shaded cells

Users \ Search Tasks	General Public Tasks		Physician Tasks			
	Basic Search	Advanced Srch	Wide Search	Narrow Search	Research Srch	CME Search
Public — Generally Healthy Person	■					
Just Diagnosed Acute	■					
Just Diagnosed Chronic	■					
Chronic for longer period		■				
Physicians — Self-Employed GP			■			■
Self-Employed Specialist				■		■
Physician in Training			■			■
Research Physician			■		■	
Hospital Clinician			■	■	■	

Subject Areas: Table 2 shows the type of resources expected to be covered by each type of search, corresponding to the *subject areas* and *tasks* axes (and through Table 1 to the *users* axis) of the model. The distinction between *primary* and *secondary* resources is important in the medical domain. Primary information (primary literature) consists of original research in journals, conferences, reports, etc. Secondary resources review, condense and synthesize the primary literature [20]. In general, physicians working in a clinical environment find secondary literature of more use, while physicians working in research are most interested in primary literature, as also visible from the table. A detailed list of specific resources falling into the categories required by medical practitioners is given in [36].

Media: Text is the main source of information for this domain. However, medical images (potentially volume images) also play an important role.

Tools: In the surveys of the physicians and general public, participants were asked to rate the importance of various aspects of a search engine in the context of medical search, and also given the possibility to suggest tools or features important to them. From the responses, it was possible to identify various search tools that would be useful for these groups. These include various types of ranking and query completion. An unexpected request from survey participants was the ability to rank result documents based on social ratings, where social ratings

Table 2. The types of resources (rows) typically needed to be searched for each search type (columns)

Resources	General Public Tasks		Physician Tasks			
	Basic Search	Advanced Srch	Wide Search	Narrow Search	Research Srch	CME Search
Primary resources		▨		▨	■	
Secondary resources		■			▨	
Guidelines			■	■	■	
Certified Web Pages	■		■	■	■	
Specialised Web Pages (Medical societies, hospitals)	■		■			
Drug information	■		■	■	■	
Further product information beyond drugs (glucometers, syringes, lenses)	■			■		
News	■		■	■		
Forums	■					
CME courses	■					■
Wikipedia	■					
Local career websites						
Physician Directory	■		■			
Local healthcare information (patients/physician associations, health insurance, social security)	■		■			
Events (conferences)						■

of physicians should be treated differently from social ratings of the general public, as shown in Table 4. For query completion, the integration of patient data in a process of formulating a query is specific to medical professionals. The general public require assistance with medical terminology in specifying the query, or assistance in specifying the type of search results that they expect, such as diagnosis, treatment, symptoms, etc. All survey analysis results are available in [3]. Some of the results obtained are shown in Tables 3 to 5 (all results are available in *a document hidden due to anonymisation*). These tables correspond to the *tools, techniques and algorithms required* and *tasks* axes of the model. Table 3 shows various types of result ranking requested.

Finally, Table 5 shows the types of query completion or support typically requested for each search type. While some are common, the integration of patient data in a process of formulating a query is specific to medical professionals. The final three rows are specific to the general public, who require assistance with medical terminology in specifying the query, or assistance in specifying the type of search results that they expect, such as diagnosis, treatment, symptoms, etc.

3   The Electra Framework

In the use-cases described in the previous section we have seen that the combination of different tools and components that can be used to instantiate a domain specific search system may become quite complex. In fact, any specific domain and any specific task will very likely require a specific combination of a set of pre-existing tools or new tools, potentially accompanied by custom-designed components.

Table 3. The types of ranking typically required (rows) for each search type (columns)

	General Public Tasks		Physician Tasks			
	Basic Search	Advanced Srch	Wide Search	Narrow Search	Research Srch	CME Search
Ranking by						
Relevance						
Language	Mother tongue	Mother tongue	Mother tongue	Mother tongue	English	Mother tongue
Location (independent of language)	Local	Local	Local	Local	International	Local
Physician Social Ratings						
General Public Social Ratings						
Level of accessibility (open, firewall, ...)						
Date of publication						

Table 4. The types of collaborative tools requested (rows) for each search type (columns)

	General Public Tasks		Physician Tasks			
	Basic Search	Advanced Srch	Wide Search	Narrow Search	Research Srch	CME Search
Collaborative/Social Aspects						
Physician quality rating	Sees	Sees	Mostly uses	Uses and rates	Uses and rates	Uses and rates
General public quality rating	Uses and rates	Uses and rates	Sees			

Table 5. The types of query completion or support typically requested (rows) for each search type (columns)

	General Public Tasks		Physician Tasks			
	Basic Search	Advanced Srch	Wide Search	Narrow Search	Research Srch	CME Search
Query Completion/Support						
Suggested query completion/expansion						
Integration of patient data						
Search history						
Spelling correction						
Suggestion of Scientific/Medical Synonym						
Term definition shown below search bar						
Query categorisation (content type)						

While the five dimension model provides a contextual description to identify and analyse the needs and requirements of a domain specific search system, the design of such domain specific search systems remains to a large extent an open issue. For this task of designing domain specific search systems we propose a general framework, namely Electra, for *Integrated Domain Specific Search systems* [5]. In that perspective the five dimension model and the Electra framework are complementary as conceptual tools to analyse and design domain specific search systems respectively. The main utilities of the Electra framework during the design process are: a) provide an analytic method to study and understand the design space of domain specific search systems, b) classify different IR and Natural Language Processing (NLP) technologies according to the functionality and services they provide to different modules, c) describe and compare domain specific search systems in a more systematic and independent way and, d) provide an architecture for developing interoperable search systems based on a set of cooperating IR/NLP tools.

The proposed framework makes explicit four functional models in domain specific search systems: a) information and information sources, b) metadata and semantics, c) session and d) information views and user interaction. It provides an underlying architecture based on which different IR and NLP technologies can coexist and tools interoperate to provide a set of search services in an integrated and uniform manner. The four functional modules of the framework are shown in Figure 4. The bordered areas around the functional modules depict the communication or other protocols which may be used between tools residing in different modules.

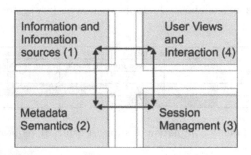

Fig. 4. Electra: a framework for Domain Specific Search Systems

Functional module 1 (Information and Information Sources) is where all primitive information in different modalities (text, image, audio etc.) is stored. Information can be organized in a single collection (logically or physically) as in most search systems, or it can be found in many different collections which are physically distributed in different servers. For example, an instantiation of the framework for a federated search system approach would show that multiple information sources exist, sources queried by the searcher through automated source selection and results merging services.

The framework captures the traditional IR model as this model is already encapsulated in the functional modules 1 (Information Sources) and 4 (View-Interact). However the framework additionally offers a much wider range of design space capable of capturing more comprehensively the extensive range of research and development activities of modern IR and NLP tools and systems.

For example, functional module 2 (Metadata-Semantics) explicitly captures and incorporates into the design space of domain specific search systems the importance of the so-called Knowledge Extraction and Organization, e.g. classification schemes, taxonomies, ontologies. These are important prerequisites and resources for developing intelligent search tools and search systems that no longer just do what the searcher says but also what he/she means [43]. This explicit distinction between raw information and metadata/semantics emphasizes the importance of IR and NLP technologies such as entity mining and extraction, faceted and semantic search and generally methods seeking to improve search accuracy by understanding the contextual meaning of terms to generate more relevant results.

The right section of the framework, i.e. functional modules 3 and 4 are concerned with the runtime and user aspects of the information seeking process. It is important to observe in the framework that having functional module 3 (Session), which is fully separated from the more static left part of the framework (information and metadata), has the important implication that instantiations of information and metadata during a session can be treated and managed separately from their original sources, and therefore can be stored as first-class objects. This means that the session data produced during a search process can become information itself and therefore stored, searched, processed and analyzed. An important implication for search systems developing this module of the framework is that they can manage and store session data as first-class objects and therefore increase the reproducibility of a search process and preserve complete sessions that can be stored and managed at a later stage. This is a very important requirement for many domain specific search systems.

The last functional module of the Electra framework is View/Interact. The main innovative feature the framework suggests is the potentially parallel coordinated use of multiple views produced from various search services accessing the data source(s) under examination. These views can be a "simple" ranked list of documents produced out of a retrieval algorithm aiming to deliver the "best" ten results, but other views may be produced as a result of combining or filtering information (using Linked Open Data for example) or using metadata (e.g. using faceted search based on already produced or dynamically extracted entities).

The framework can be used in different levels of abstraction in order to study and classify a domain specific search system, or compare a number of different search systems. However, there is a need to define a clear communication and coordination architecture before the framework can be useful as a complete architecture and a starting point for the development of an integrated domain specific search system. The framework addresses this opportunity for becoming an underlying platform for designing and developing domain specific search systems by explicitly stating the existence of protocols between the four functional modules. These protocols can take various forms based on the work that has been produced in the past or relatively recently in various fields of computing such as workflow management [42], multi-agent systems [35], agent-based software engineering [39], service oriented computing[29], and web services [22].

3.1   The Framework as a Tool for Designing Search Systems

We follow up the two instantiations of the conceptual model, regarding patent search (Section 2.1) and medical search (Section 2.2) with the case study of two systems addressing these two topics. We look at them from the perspective of the Electra framework in the following two sections.

3.2   Intellectual Property Search System

The PerFedPat[4] system is a federated patent search system based on ezDL [7], a system for developing interactive search applications. PerFedPat provides core services and operations to search, using a federated method, multiple online patent resources (currently Esp@cenet, Google patents, Patentscope and the CLEF-IP collection), thus providing access to multiple patent sources while hiding complexity from the end user who uses a common query tool for querying all patent datasets at the same time. Wrappers are used which convert PerFed-Pat's internal query model into the queries that each remote service can accept. "Translated" queries are routed to remote search systems and their returned results are internally re-ranked and merged as a single list presented to the patent searcher. In addition to patent resources, there are resources already supported by ezDL, most of them offering access to online bibliographic search services. Based on this architecture, PerFedPat aims to become a pluggable system that puts together the following components: retrieval, selection, integration, presentation and adaptation.

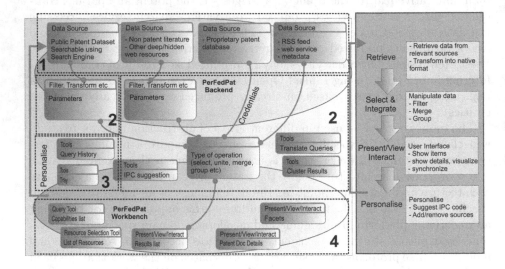

Fig. 5. PerFedPat architecture and component overview

Figure 5 depicts the relationships between the Electra framework and the PerFedPat search system. At the top of the diagram there are the information sources (marked area 1), which are available in PerFedPat and which are accessed using appropriate PerFedPat wrappers to federated remote resources. The marked area 2 shows the tools using semantic information and metadata (e.g. IPC). They provide elaborated knowledge management services and tools to the searcher. Note that tools and services in these two areas (1 & 2) are mostly

---
[4] http://www.perfedpat.eu

implemented as software running at the PerFedPat backend (server). Marked areas 3 and 4 illustrate the tools that the user interacts with and are -respectively- about providing session management and information views. Information views are provided at different levels and complexities, ranging from a simple ranked list of documents, filtered views, clusters of documents, to faceted navigation.

One innovative feature of PerFedPat is that it enables the use of multiple search tools which are integrated in PerFedPat. The tools that a designer will decide to integrate into a patent search system do not only have to do with existing IR technologies, but probably more with the context in which a patent search is conducted and the searcher's attitude. Furthermore, it is also very important to understand a search process and how a specific tool can attain a specific objective of this process and therefore increase its efficiency.

Currently the search tools which are integrated are a) an International Patent Classification (IPC) selection tool, b) a tool for faceted search producing different facets of the results retrieved based on existing metadata in patents, c) a tool producing clustered views of patent search results, and d) a Machine Translation (MT) tool for translating queries. The first tool aims to support a specific objective during prior art search, i.e. to narrow the search by identifying relevant IPC codes and the effectiveness of the IPC selection tool method has been evaluated [34]. Here we focus on the approach that has been used to integrate this and the other tools into PerFedPat.

From the perspective of the Electra framework it is also important to note that the integration of the IPC suggestion tool was implemented sending HTTP requests to an external server providing the IPC selection services. The server hosting the IPC selection tool receives the requests and sends a response back about the IPC codes suggested. It is important also to mention that for the IPC tool to operate there is a need to access certain metadata that are produced using Distributed IR core services (resource representation) and are managed locally by the IPC selection server. This data could also exist in the original PerFedPat server and could be sent on request to different tools which need to access such data. It is therefore important to mention that interoperability at the process level is achieved, however this process level interoperability is not based on full exchange of metadata but some form of regular updates may be necessary.

In PerFedPat there are more search tools integrated in similar way (tools for faceted search, clustered views of results). From an information seeking process perspective, the integration of different search tools in addition to the basic ranked list of patent documents returned from the Distributed IR retrieval engine allows different views of patent information to coexist.

This process-oriented integration provides some useful services to the PerFedPat patent search system but synchronization between the tools is required so that one event or action in one tool can update the views produced from the other tools. For example selecting an IPC code may affect the results presented in the faceted search tool.

3.3   Medical Search System

The Khresmoi project[5] has built an integrated search system for multilingual, multimodal health and medical information. Like PerFedPat, the Khresmoi search system is based on a Service-Oriented Architecture (SOA), using a Service Component Architecture (SCA) model. The Khresmoi system provides the ability to search both text and images, but only the text components will be considered here. The text search components for Khresmoi Professional, the search engine instantiation aimed at medical professionals, are shown in Figure 6.

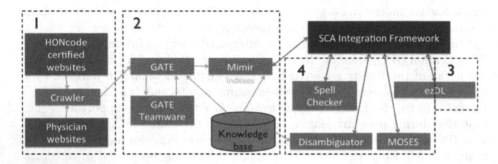

Fig. 6. Khresmoi text search Service-Oriented Architecture. The dotted lines and numbers represent the functional modules of the Electra framework.

As in the case of PerFedPat, ezDL is used as the search interface for Khresmoi Professional. Khresmoi is based to a large extent on open source software, including GATE, the General Architecture for Text Engineering, and Mimir, a search engine that makes use of GATE text annotations [17]. Furthermore, it makes use of the MOSES machine translation software trained on medical documents to translate both queries and document sections [30]. Further components such as a spell checker and disambiguator for queries are called. A knowledge base supports the annotation and disambiguation components [16].

We now briefly analyze Khresmoi in terms of the Electra framework. For this specialized health and medical search engine, attention needs to be paid to the resources indexed (functional module 1), to ensure that they are of sufficient quality. The project indexes websites certified by the Health on the Net foundation [8], as well as web-sites manually selected as being important to physicians [37]. For the metadata (functional module 2), there exist many medical ontologies and vocabularies. For this reason Khresmoi settled on the Linked Life Data, which fuses and cross-links over 30 biomedical knowledge resources. The GATE and Mimir tools make use of the metadata by annotating the texts, and searching based partly on the annotations. Through the use of the ezDL framework [7], session management (functional module 3) is included in the system, which stores a detailed query log and allows users to place documents in their personal

---

[5] http://www.khresmoi.eu

library, tag them and share them with other users. Finally, the user can interact with the information (functional module 4) by machine translating it through transparent calls to the MOSES service, or using tools provided by ezDL such as filtering results through the use of facets or search within the results, or generating summaries in the form of word clouds. As for PerFedPat, it is important to note that the integration was done by making all components available through web service interfaces and defining data exchange protocols between the web services.

3.4   Discussion

Based on the previous case-studies, we are now perhaps in a better position to consider the links between the domain-specific search engine definition of Section 2 and the Electra framework of Section 3. It is clear that there is no one-to-one mapping between the five dimensions of domain-specific search and the four components of the framework. Instead, the question to ask is what components of the Electra framework are affected by a change in one of the five dimensions of the definition, if the remaining four remain fixed. For the *subject areas*, *tasks* and *tools, techniques and algorithms required* dimensions, their broad nature implies possible changes in all of the four Electra components. The *modality* dimension implies changes in the Information and Information Sources and User Views and Interaction components, since new data is to be processed and displayed to the user. Finally, changes in the *users* dimension imply changes in the User views and Interaction and Session Management components.

This mapping is seen in Figure 7 and can be used for the design of future domain-specific systems by identifying the components that need to be changed when one of the five dimensions of the definition needs to cover a new element. In three of the five cases we will have to look at all of them, but at least we have

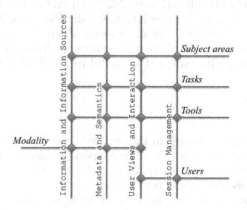

Fig. 7. Interactions between Electra components and Domain-specific search process definition

something similar to a check-list we can go through in order to design the new system.

Such a mapping allows us to think about the relative benefits of two similar, potentially competing systems. For instance, in the case of patent search, we might look at two publicly available systems such as Google Patents[6] and Espacenet[7] and observe that they are similar in the set of modalities and subject areas they handle, but their tools, users and tasks are slightly different. While Google Patents seems to focus more on general users searching for content, Espacenet focuses apparently more on users already familiar with the patent domain and does not provide full text search.

4   Conclusions

There is a perceived limitation in how we are dealing today with domain specific information retrieval. Different methods are applied to different domains, performance improvements are demonstrated over systems, but it is difficult to communicate the nature of the differences in the domains. This, in turn, makes it difficult to reason about which components need to be changed in a system to handle a new domain. We have therefore proposed here both a definition of domain specific IR, for which we have identified five dimensions, as well as a framework to design and conceptualise a search system. Looking at two domains, Patent IR and Medical Search, we have observed that the model and the framework can be used to describe the two, leading us to be optimistic about their validity and utility for other domains as well.

Acknowledgements. The research leading to the results presented in this chapter was partially funded by the European Union Seventh Framework Programme (FP7/2007-2013) under grant agreement no. 257528 (KHRESMOI), under grant agreement no. 275522 (PerFedPat), and the Austrian Science Fund (FWF) under projects MUCKE (I 1094-N23) and ADmIRE (P25905-N23). The authors thank Célia Boyer, Marlene Kritz, Natalia Pletneva, Matthias Samwald and Veronika Stefanov for the useful discussions about the results in the medical domain. Also we would to thank patent examiners from the Greek Industrial Property Organization who provided us useful feedback about PerFedPat.

References

1. Adams, S.: Information Sources in Patents, 3rd edn. G. Saur (2011)
2. Authors, A.: Anonymized Title. Technical report, Anonymized Venue (2011)
3. Authors, A.: Anonymized Title. Anonymized Venue (2012)
4. Authors, A.: Anonymized Title. In: Booktitle (2013)
5. Authors, A.: Anonymized Title. In: Proc. of Anonym (2013)

---

[6] http://patents.google.com
[7] http://worldwide.espacenet.com/

6. Azzopardi, L., Vanderbauwhede, W., Joho, H.: Search system requirements of patent analysts. In: Proceeding of the 33rd International ACM SIGIR Conference on Research and Development in Information Retrieval, SIGIR 2010, pp. 775–776. ACM, New York (2010)

7. Beckers, T., Dungs, S., Fuhr, N., Jordan, M., Kriewel, S.: ezDL: An interactive search and evaluation system. In: Proceedings of the SIGIR 2012 Workshop on Open Source Information Retrieval (2012)

8. Boyer, C., Baujard, V., Geissbuhler, A.: Evolution of health web certification through the honcode experience. Stud. Health Technol. Inform. 169, 53–57 (2011)

9. Boyer, C., Gschwandtner, M., Hanbury, A., Kritz, M., Pletneva, N., Samwald, M., Vargas, A.: Use case definition including concrete data requirements. Khresmoi Public Deliverable D8.2 (February 2012)

10. Chau, M., Chen, H., Qin, J., Zhou, Y., Qin, Y., Sung, W.-K., Mcdonald, D.: Comparison of two approaches to building a vertical search tool: A case study in the nanotechnology domain. In: Proceedings of the Second ACM/IEEE-CS Joint Conference on Digital Libraries (JCDL 2002), pp. 135–144. ACM Press (2002)

11. Cockburn, A.: Writing Effective Use Cases. Addison-Wesley Professional (2000)

12. Cornacchia, R., de Vries, A.P.: A parameterised search system. In: Amati, G., Carpineto, C., Romano, G. (eds.) ECiR 2007. LNCS, vol. 4425, pp. 4–15. Springer, Heidelberg (2007)

13. Fautsch, C., Savoy, J.: Algorithmic Stemmers of Morphological Analysis? An Evaluation. Journal of the American Society for Information Science and Technology (2009)

14. Fautsch, C., Savoy, J.: Adapting the tf idf vector-space model to domain specific information retrieval. In: Proc. of SAC (2010)

15. Fuhr, N.: Salton award lecture information retrieval as engineering science. SIGIR Forum 46(2), 19–28 (2012)

16. Georgiev, G., Pentchev, K., Avramov, A., Primov, T., Momtchev, V.: Scalable interlinking of bio-medical entities and scientific literature in linked life data. In: Proc. CALBC Workshop (March 2011)

17. Greenwood, M.A., Tablan, V., Maynard, D.: GATE Mimir: Answering questions google can't. In: Proceedings of the 10th International Semantic Web Conference, ISWC (2011)

18. Hanbury, A., Bhatti, N., Lupu, M., Mörzinger, R.: Patent image retrieval: A survey. In: Proc. of PaIR (2011)

19. Hansen, P.: Task-Based Information Seeking and Retrieval in the Patent Domain. Processes and Relationships. PhD thesis, University of Tampere (2011)

20. Hersh, W.: Information Retrieval: A Health and Biomedical Perspective, 3rd edn. Springer (2009)

21. Herskovic, J.R., Tanaka, L.Y., Hersh, W., Bernstam, E.V.: A day in the life of PubMed: Analysis of a typical day's query log. Journal of the American Medical Informatics Association 14(2), 212–220 (2007)

22. Huhns, M.N.: Agents as web services. IEEE Internet Computing 6(4), 93–95 (2002)

23. Hunt, D., Nguyen, L., Rodgers, M.: Patent Searching. Wiley, Hoboken (2007)

24. Ingwersen, P., Järvelin, K.: The Turn: Integration of Information Seeking and Retrieval in Context. Springer (2005)

25. Kritz, M., Gschwandtner, M., Stefanov, V., Hanbury, A., Samwald, M.: Utilisation and perceived problems of online medical resources and search tools among different groups of European physicians. Journal of Medical Internet Research (2013)

26. Lagemaat, W.G.: The future of information tools and technology - our joint effort. World Patent Information 35(2), 93–94 (2013)
27. Luo, G., Tang, C.: On iterative intelligent medical search. In: Proc. of SIGIR (2008)
28. Lupu, M., Hanbury, A.: Patent Retrieval. Foundations and Trends in Information Retrieval 7(1) (2013)
29. Papazoglou, M.P., Georgakopoulos, D.: Introduction: Service-oriented computing. Commun. ACM 46(10), 24–28 (2003)
30. Pecina, P., Dušek, O., Goeuriot, L., Hajič, J., Hlaváčová, J., Jones, G.J., Kelly, L., Leveling, J., Mareček, D., Novák, M., Popel, M., Rosa, R., Tamchyna, A., Urešová, Z.: Adaptation of machine translation for multilingual information retrieval in the medical domain. In: Artificial Intelligence in Medicine (2014)
31. Pletneva, N., Vargas, A., Boyer, C.: Requirements for the general public health search. Khresmoi Public Deliverable D8.1.1 (May 2011)
32. Qin, J., Zhou, Y., Chau, M.: Building domain-specific web collections for scientific digital libraries: A meta-search enhanced focused crawling method. In: Proceedings of the 4th ACM/IEEE-CS Joint Conference on Digital Libraries, JCDL 2004, pp. 135–141. ACM, New York (2004)
33. Rowe, B., Wood, D., Link, A., Simoni, D.: Economic Impact Assessment of NIST's Text REtrieval Conference (TREC) Program. Technical report, National Institute of Standards and Technology (2010)
34. Salampasis, M., Paltoglou, G., Giahanou, A.: Report on the clef-ip 2012 experiments: Search of topically organized patents. In: CLEF (Online Working Notes/Labs/Workshop) (2012)
35. Salampasis, M., Tait, J., Hardy, C.: An agent-based hypermedia framework for designing and developing digital libraries. In: Proceedings of the 3rd International Forum on Research and Technology Advances in Digital Libraries, ADL 1996. IEEE Computer Society, Washington, DC (1996)
36. Samwald, M., Kritz, M., Gschwandtner, M., Hanbury, A.: A curated index of high-quality web resources for medical practitioners. In: Proc. Medical Informatics Europe, MIE (2012)
37. Samwald, M., Kritz, M., Gschwandtner, M., Hanbury, A.: A curated index of high-quality web resources for medical practitioners. In: Proceedings of Medical Informatics Europe, MIE (2012)
38. Sanderson, M., Turpin, A., Zhang, Y., Scholer, F.: Differences in Effectiveness Across Sub-collections. In: Proc. of CIKM (2012)
39. Sharma, D., Ma, W., Tran, D., Anderson, M.: A novel approach to programming: Agent based software engineering. In: Gabrys, B., Howlett, R.J., Jain, L.C. (eds.) KES 2006. Part III. LNCS (LNAI), vol. 4253, pp. 1184–1191. Springer, Heidelberg (2006)
40. Tang, T., Craswell, N., Hawking, D., Griffiths, K., Christensen, H.: Quality and relevance of domain-specific search: A case study in mental health. Information Retrieval 9, 207–225 (2006)
41. Trippe, A., Ruthven, I.: Current Challenges in Patent Information Retrieval. Evaluating Real Patent Retrieval Effectiveness, ch. 6. Springer (2011)
42. Wolstencroft, K., Haines, R., Fellows, D., Williams, A., Withers, D., Owen, S., Soiland-Reyes, S., Dunlop, I., Nenadic, A., Fisher, P., Bhagat, J., Belhajjame, K., Bacall, F., Hardisty, A., Nieva de la Hidalga, A., Balcazar Vargas, M.P., Sufi, S., Goble, C.: The taverna workflow suite: Designing and executing workflows of web services on the desktop, web or in the cloud. Nucleic. Acids. Res. 41(web server issue), W557–W561 (2013)

43. Wolter, B.: It takes all kinds to make a world – some thoughts on the use of classification in patent searching. World Patent Information 34(1) (2012)
44. Yan, X., Lau, R.Y., Song, D., Li, X., Ma, J.: Toward a semantic granularity model for domain-specific information retrieval. ACM Trans. Inf. Syst. 15, 1–15 (2011)

ezDL: An Interactive IR Framework, Search Tool, and Evaluation System

Thomas Beckers[1], Sebastian Dungs[1], Norbert Fuhr[1], Matthias Jordan[1],
Georgios Kontokotsios[2], Sascha Kriewel[1], Yiannis Paraskeuopoulos[2],
and Michail Salampasis[2]

[1] Information Engineering, University of Duisburg-Essen, Duisburg, Germany
`firstname.lastname@uni-due.de`
[2] Information and Software Engineering, Vienna University of Technology, Austria
`firstname.lastname@tuwien.ac.at`

Abstract. *ezDL* is an open-source IR frontend system supporting proactivity, higher level search activities, the digital library life cycle, and collaboration of searchers. The *ezDL* framework is based on an extensible, service-oriented architecture, with user clients running on the desktop, in a browser or as a smartphone app. For performing user-centered evaluations, *ezDL* has a builtin evaluation mode that addresses many of the major challenges inherent in setting up evaluation tasks and tracking user activity during the experiments.

Currently, *ezDL* is employed in three major application areas. For searching computer science literature, it connects to several different digital libraries. In the medical domain *ezDL* provides literature search for general practitioners, as well as allowing for retrieval of medical images, including 3D data. PerFedPat is an application of *ezDL* in the patent retrieval domain comprising tools for supporting the International Patent Classification, faceted navigation of results, clustered views of patent search results and cross lingual retrieval.

Keywords: interactive search system, framework, user studies.

1   Introduction

In this chapter we present *ezDL*, an open-source[1] software for building highly interactive search user interfaces which are based on cognitive models of seeking and searching as well as state of the art user interface design principles.

Beginning with the popular SMART system [40], research in the area of information retrieval (IR) has produced a number of open source search engines over the last three decades. However, this work has focused on the backend side of retrieval, while little attention has been paid to the user interface side —

---

[1] *ezDL* is licensed under GPL v3. Other licenses can be used on request. The main web site for developers and further information can be found here: `http://www.ezdl.de/guide/`

G. Paltoglou et al. (Eds.): Professional Search in the Modern World, LNCS 8830, pp. 118–146, 2014.
© Springer International Publishing Switzerland 2014

some systems were designed solely for system-oriented experiments, or they provide only a basic interface (e.g. Indri [2] or Terrier [35]) that falls short of the interfaces that users are accustomed to nowadays.

ezDL is a successor of the Daffodil (Distributed Agents For user-Friendly access Of Digital Libraries) project, which started in 1998 [24]. The original idea was to develop a new type of federated search engine: First, the system should not only combine digital libraries, but also other kinds of Web services ("agents") that provide useful functions like e.g. proposing related terms or translating the query to other languages. Second, for enhanced user-friendliness, the system aimed to implement support for cognitive models of seeking and searching, proactivity and collaboration (see Section 3) [18,29,25].

Based on the experiences with Daffodil, we started the development of the successor *ezDL* in 2009, using more modern software technologies and interface design methods (see also [9]). Most important, we formulated three clear goals for the new system:

1. *ezDL* is a powerful frontend tool that can be easily configured for searching a heterogeneous collection of digital libraries.
2. *ezDL* is a flexible and extensible software platform providing a solid base for writing customized applications, both at the functional and the presentation level.
3. *ezDL* is also an evaluation framework providing a rich functionality for performing a broad variety of user evaluations.

ezDL is highly correlated to the goals of the MUMIA network since it represents a powerful search tool and implements coordinated federated search, as stated in MUMIA's memorandum of understanding. *ezDL* contributes especially to the WG3 (user-centered aspects: exploratory search, interactive IR) by providing an advanced user-friendly retrieval interface and to WG5 (distributed and social search) due to its features for federated search and collaboration.

The remainder of this chapter is structured as follows: After a survey over related work (Section 2), we first introduce the basic concepts underlying *ezDL*. Section 4 describes the extensible architecture of the system, while Section 5 highlights the evaluation tool aspect of *ezDL*. Three major use cases are discussed in some detail in Section 6, before the final section concludes the paper.

2   Related Work

Today many systems covering one or more aspects of *ezDL* exist but to the best of our knowledge the concept of unifying them into one single framework is unique. In the following paragraphs similar systems related to the different aspects of *ezDL* are presented.

Interactive Search Tools. Querium [19] is an interactive search system featuring a concept that focuses on complex recall oriented searches. It aims at preserving the context of searches and allows relevance feedback to generate alternative result sets. At the moment, the system is limited to only one Lucene-based index.

Numerous tools exist that focus on storing and managing a personal library or citations. A popular example is Mendeley[2] which also offers different front ends and collaborative features. Other citation tools include CiteULike[3] and Connotea[4]

CoSearch [3] is a collaborative web search tool. It offers a user interface that can simultaneously take input from different users sharing a single machine. Mobile devices can be used to contribute to a collaborative search session. Data is acquired by using a popular web search engine.

Development Platforms for Search Systems. SpidersRUs Digital Library Toolkit [15] is a search engine development tool. The developers strove for a balance between easiness of use and customizability. The toolkit also features a GUI for the process of search engine creation. Results presentation follows common standards of popular web search engines. Support for complex search sessions, e.g. a tray or citation management tool are not included.

Evaluation Systems. The Lemur project [2] includes a query log tool bar that can be used to capture usage data. It can collect queries as well as user interaction such as mouse activity and is available as open source.

Bierig et al. [13] presented an evaluation and logging framework for user-centered and task-based experiments in interactive information retrieval that focuses on "multidimensional logging to obtain rich behavioural data" of searchers.

Hall et al. [20] describe a pluggable workbench for creating interactive IR interfaces to make evaluations more comparable and reproducable. Based on a simple configuration a corresponding user interface can be created and used for evaluation purposes.

Conclusion. The software systems presented here focus on one or very few applications. *ezDL* integrates support for more complex exploratory searches with easy extensibility in terms of features and data sources and functions that make building evaluation systems easier. The next sections introduce the concepts in *ezDL* and show how *ezDL* can be used in daily searches, system building and interactive IR evaluations.

3   Concepts

As a re-implementation and revision of the Daffodil project [18], *ezDL* builds on many of the same concepts and principles as Daffodil. Like Daffodil it is a

---

[2] http://www.mendeley.com/
[3] http://www.citeulike.org/
[4] http://www.connotea.org/

"search system for digital libraries aiming at strategic support during the information search process" [29]. Its primary target group is not that of casual users using a search system for short ad-hoc queries. Instead the software aims to support searchers during complex information tasks by addressing all the steps in the *Digital Library Life Cycle*, as well as integrating search models originally proposed by Marcia Bates [6,7,8].

The Digital Library Lifecycle. The *Digital Library Life Cycle* divides the information workflow into five phases [36], beginning with the *discovery* of information resources, which in *ezDL* is supported through the Library Choice view. This is followed by the *retrieval* phase of information search, the *collating* of found information using the personal library and tagging, *interpreting* the information, and finally the *re-presenting* phase where new information is generated. In all phases, different so-called tactics or stratagems can be employed by searchers or information workers, which we try to support through *ezDL*.

Higher-Level Search Activities. The notion of tactics and stratagems as higher-level search activities was introduced by Bates [6,7,8]. Based on search tactics used by librarians and expert searchers, Bates describes basic *moves*, as well as higher-level *tactics*, *stratagems*, and finally *strategies* that build on lower-level activities.

ezDL already offers direct support for some of those higher-level activities through term suggestions of synonyms or spelling variants, extraction of common results terms, or through icons in the result items that allow easy monitoring of performed activities.

Tran [46] implemented a prototype tool to support the pearl growing stratagem. Pearl growing or citation pearl growing [22] is an interactive process that starts with an initial, relevant document and uses the references contained within that document as well as citation relationships to find more documents. The pearl growing tool visualizes citation relationships between documents in a graph and allows the user to follow these relationships and keep track of the search progress using document annotations. Figure 1 shows a screenshot of a pearl growing session with some documents marked as relevant. It is planned to include this tool in *ezDL* in the near future.

Proactivity. During query formulation, *ezDL* provides term suggestions to the user (e.g. synonyms and related terms). These are an example for the concept of proactive system support. Bates describes "five levels of system involvement (SI) in searching" [8]. The proactive support of *ezDL* belongs to the third level, where a search system (through monitoring of user activities) can react to the search situation without prompting by the user. Users are informed of improvement options for their current move. Jansen and Pooch [23] demonstrated that proactive software agents assisting users during their search can result in improved performance of users. The effectiveness of such suggestions has also been shown for the Daffodil system [41].

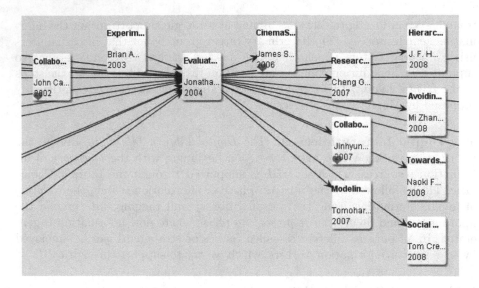

Fig. 1. A close-up of the pearl growing tool

Proactive support of higher-level activities, such as suggestion of tactics and stratagems for improvable search situations [27,28] or suggestion of search strategies with scaffolding support has been integrated as part of the Khresmoi project (cf. Section 6.1). A suggestion framework analyzes the user's current situation using parameters like the number of results, used query fields, search operators or query terms, the most common terms from the search results, and other aspects of the most recent search. Using this parametrised situation, case–based reasoning is employed to fetch the most similar previous situations of other users from a case base and suggest the adapted tactics and stratagems which where successful in those situations to the users [44,43] (see Figure 2). This can be combined with a guided search that helps inexperienced searchers to specify their information need and decompose the search task into sub tasks. Users can use a classification view that allows browsing and selecting from a hierarchy of topics and common, domain specific information tasks.

Collaboration. *ezDL* supports collaboration between users by allowing sharing of documents in the personal library. Documents can be shared with a set of users but also with a set of user groups. The user can accept or decline incoming sharing requests.

Furthermore, the user can annotate shared or unshared documents. An annotation is a short text created by the user that is attached to a document. There are different privacy levels: Private annotations are only visible for the user that has created the annotation. Public annotations are visible for all users. This annotation facility allows discussions about documents.

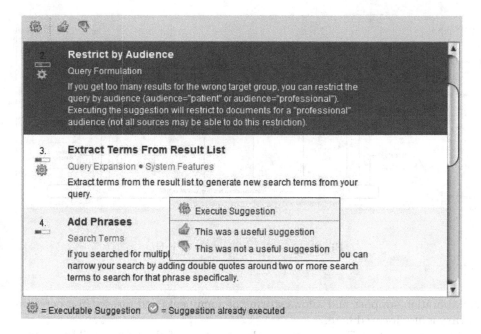

Fig. 2. Tactical search suggestions

In the Daffodil system there was a chat tool that allowed the users to communicate with each other or e.g. to consult a search expert. It is planned to extend *ezDL* with chat functionality.

4   Architecture

ezDL's overall architecture has inherited many features from Daffodil. Figure 3 provides a high-level overview of the system.

The system architecture makes extensive use of separation of concerns to keep interdependencies to a minimum and make the system more stable. This is true on the system level where a clear separation exists between clients and backend, but also within the backend itself, where individual "agent" processes handle specific parts of the functionality, and even within these agents. The desktop client, too, is separated into multiple independent components called "tools". *ezDL* is completely written in Java using common frameworks and libraries.

4.1   The Backend

The backend provides a large part of the core functionality of *ezDL*: the meta-search facility, user authorization, a knowledge base about collected documents, as well as wrappers and services that connect to external services. Functionality that provides

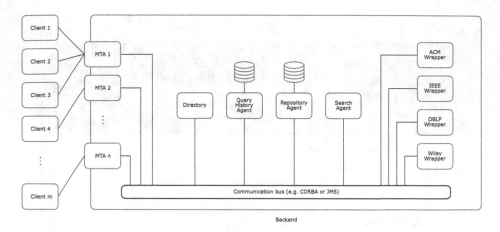

Fig. 3. Overall architecture of *ezDL*

collaboration support and allows storing of documents and queries in a personal library is also located here.

The right part of Figure 3 shows the structure of the backend. The components of the backend are agents: independent processes that provide a specific functionality to the system. Agents use a common communication bus for transferring messages between each other.

The Service-Based Agent Infrastructure. Agents are subdivided into the main agent behaviour (registering with the Directory, sending and receiving messages, managing resources) and components that deal with specific requests. These components—the request handlers—are independent and process requests concurrently.

Starting from the left, an MTA (Message Transfer Agent) is an agent that provides clients with a connection point to the backend. MTAs are responsible for authenticating users and translating requests from clients into messages to certain agents. E.g., if a client requests a search for a given query, the query from the client is translated into a message to the Search Agent. This mechanism creates a clear separation between the client view of the system and the internal workings: the client doesn't have to know how many agents are serving search queries and new search agents could be instantiated as the system load demands. Currently there is only one MTA implementation, which uses a binary protocol over a TCP connection, but it is possible to provide other protocols—e.g. SOAP—by using separate MTA implementations.

The Directory is a special agent that keeps a list of agents and the services they provide. Upon start, each agent registers with the Directory and announces the services it provides.

Since every kind of functionality is taken care of by different agents, the crash of one agent generally only disrupts this particular functionality. For example, if the search agent crashes, detail requests and the personal library are still working. Also, this compartmentalization can be used as the basis for future extensions like running multiple agents of each kind for load balancing and as a fail-safe mechanism.

The connection to remote (or local) search services (e.g., digital libraries or information retrieval systems) is managed by wrapper agents—in Figure 3 the four agents on the right hand side. They translate the internal query representation of *ezDL* into one that the remote service can parse and translates the response of the remote service into an appropriate document representations to be handled by *ezDL*. Such wrappers are already available for Apache Lucene or Solr[5].

To illustrate the interplay between the different agents, let us look at the example of running search queries. When a client requests a search, it sends a request to the MTA with a query in *ezDL* syntax and a list of remote services that the query should be run on. The request is handled by the MTA which forwards it to the Search agent. The Search agent asks the Directory for the name of agents that provide a connection to the remote services requested by the client. After receiving that list, the Search agent forwards the query to each of these agents. The agents then translate the query into something that the remote service understands and sends the answer of the remote service back to the Search agent. The Search agent collects all answers from all the remote services, merges duplicates and reranks them. By default the reranking is done by using the reciprocal original ranks from the original results [34]. The answer set is then sent back to the MTA that requested the search. The MTA relays the answer to the client. The search agent also forwards the collected documents to the repository agent which is responsible for serving requests for details on documents (e.g., if the user wants to see the full text).

4.2   The Desktop Frontend

ezDL comes with multiple frontends, of which the most mature ones are the basic desktop client and a mobile client. Specialized frontends exist for various applications (see use cases in Section 6). This subsection details the architecture of the desktop client, since this is the main client of *ezDL*.

Tools and Perspectives. A *tool* comprises a set of logically connected functionalities. Each tool has one or more *tool views*, interactive display components that can be placed somewhere on the desktop. A configuration of available tools and the specific layout of their tool views on the desktop is called a *perspective*. Figure 4 shows the perspective for searching, while Figure 5 shows the perspective for organizing documents and sharing documents with other users. Users can modify existing predefined perspectives as well as create custom perspectives. The desktop client already has many built-in tools and functionalities and can be easily extended (see Figures 4 and 5):

---

[5] http://lucene.apache.org/solr/

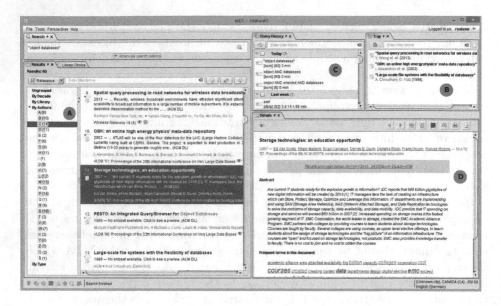

Fig. 4. The search perspective of the desktop client

- The Search Tool (A) offers a variety of query forms for different purposes and views to present the results in list or grid form, as well as a Library Choice view for selecting information sources. Results can be sorted or grouped by different criteria, filtered, and exported. An extraction function can be used to extract frequent terms, authors, or other features from the result and visualize them in form of a list, a bar chart or a term cloud. Grouping criteria, extraction strategies or renderers for result surrogates are handled by internal registry classes and a developer can easily add new ones for different result types or use cases.
- A Tray (B) can be used to temporarily collect relevant documents within a search session.
- The Search History (C) lists past queries for re-use and allows grouping by date and filtering.
- The Detail View (D) shows additional details on individual documents, such as thumbnails or short summaries where available, or additional metadata not included in the surrogate that is shown in the result list. A detail link can be provided to retrieve the fulltext.
- The Personal Library (E) allows to store documents or queries persistently for authenticated users. Within their personal collection, users can filter, group and sort (e.g. by date of addition), organize the documents with personal tags, and share them with other users or groups. Additional documents can be imported into the personal library as long as their metadata is available in BibTeX format.

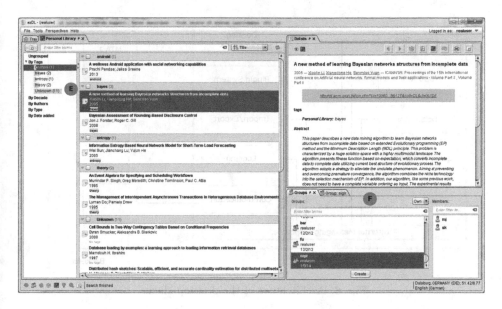

Fig. 5. The organisation and sharing perspective of the desktop client

- The Group Management Tool (F) lists all user groups in the system. The user can join existing groups or he can create his own groups that can be visible to the public or private for a predefined set of users. These groups can be used in the Personal Library tool to share documents with other users or groups. User groups are also be utilized for annotations by users on documents.

Communication with the Backend. Like the backend, the desktop client uses a messaging infrastructure for communication between otherwise independent components. In Figure 6 a diagram of the components is shown. On the left, four of the available tools can be seen with their connection to the internal communication infrastructure (search, personal library, details, and query history). On the right hand side, a few subsystems are presented, one of which is the external communication facility that connects the client to the backend.

As an example, if the user enters a query in the search tool and presses the "search" button, an internal message is sent to the communication facility, which transmits the query to the backend. When the answer is received, the communication facility routes the message back to the search tool.

Since from the client's point of view the backend is hidden behind the MTA, further details are omitted in the backend part of Figure 6.

Query Processing and Proactive Support. Documents in *ezDL* are field-oriented and so are queries. Many fields are pre-defined, such as "Author", "Title",

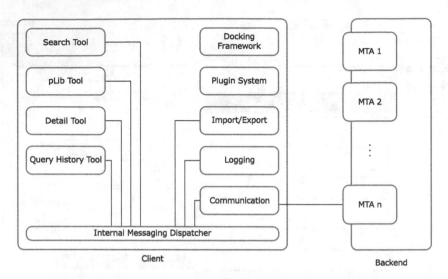

Fig. 6. Architecture of the desktop client

"DOI", but developers can add own field definitions. In a query, searching for a keyword "foo" in document titles is represented by an explicit comparison between the field "Title" and the keyword "foo".

There is a special field called "Text". What exactly that "Text" field refers to is subject to the implementation of each data source and the implementation of the wrapper that connects the data source to *ezDL*. A general convention in *ezDL* is that the "Text" field denotes a (conceptual) concatenation of all text-based fields that a data source provides, but this set of text-based fields differs from data source to data source. Also, individual data sources might have text-based fields that are not suitable for including in a search—e.g. internal comments. So, from the user's point of view, the field "Text" is only vaguely defined.

Users can specify queries by entering text in a text input box, called "query text field"[6]. The query text field is used to build several query forms. One form uses only one query text field for saving screen estate on small screen devices. Another uses four query text fields, each of which deals with one of four frequently used document fields, such as title and author.

The queries that users enter are expressed in a grammar specific to *ezDL* that is quite flexible and allows simple queries like `term1 term2 term3` as well as more complicated ones like `Title=term1 AND (term2 NEAR/2 term3)`. Internally, the query is represented as a tree structure that can also keep images as comparison values so *ezDL* can be used to specify image search queries.[7]

---

[6] The confusion between those fields that make a document and those that the user enters queries in stems from similar terminology used for different things in information retrieval and Java, respectively.

[7] This mechanism is used in the Khresmoi project (see Subsections 6.1 and 6.2) to allow general physicians and radiologists to search by using medical example images.

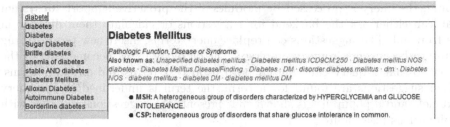

Fig. 7. Suggestion popup with explanations on mouse-over

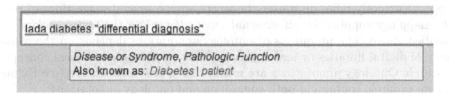

Fig. 8. Annotated query tokens with mouse-over explanations

But users generally don't want to enter too much text into a query text field. So query text fields have a default field and keywords that are not marked with a field identifier are considered to refer to the default field. E.g. the simplest query text field has the default field "Text". So a query "foo" would imply to search for "foo" in the "Text" field, while a query "foo AND Author=bar" would search for "foo" in "Text" and for "bar" in "Author".

Internally, the query text field uses a software object called the "query factory", which is concerned with translating back and forth between the user input and an internal representation. The query factory is the only object that knows about the query syntax that users deal with. Since the query text field relies entirely on the query factory for information about the query syntax, and since there can be multiple different query factory objects, the syntax can, in principle, vary between *ezDL* versions or even between different query text fields in a single *ezDL* client: there could be one query interface that accepts the standard *ezDL* query syntax and another that accepts a legacy syntax to help users move over from a different system.

Another feature of the query text field is that each token of the query (as defined by the query factory) can be annotated. Annotations can take many forms. Currently, the following annotations are supported: Errors, ontology terms, and proactive suggestions.

Terms marked with an error annotation are underlined with a curly red line. Proactive suggestions contain advice the user might try to improve the query and are underlined in blue. The desktop client offers proactive support during query formulation on a term-by-term basis. During query formulation, the user's interaction is observed by the system. If the system notices a break in the user's typing, the query is processed by modules of the proactive support subsystem that can either ask the backend for suggestions or calculate them directly in the frontend. The suggestions can replace query terms, insert new terms, or tag terms with concepts from an ontology. The ontology items become part of the query so that a query can contain both plain text terms and ontology terms. When suggestions are found for a term, the term is underlined in the query text field and a popup list is shown that presents the suggestions together with explanations (see Figure 7).

If a query term has been marked with an ontology term, this represents a mapping to a specific concept in an ontology for easier disambiguation. The mapping currently relies on a user choosing between several suggestions of *possible* mappings supplied by an external service (based on the textual token) as described above. The usefulness of ontology annotations depends on the availability of digital libraries or search services that uses those ontological concepts for search. Ontology annotations are marked by yellow highlighting (see Figure 8 for an example containing both suggestion and ontology annotations).

Examples for these suggestions are spelling corrections, related terms, synonyms, translations to foreign languages and terms from a medical ontology. All of these examples are implemented in some versions of *ezDL*.

4.3   The Frontend for Mobile Devices

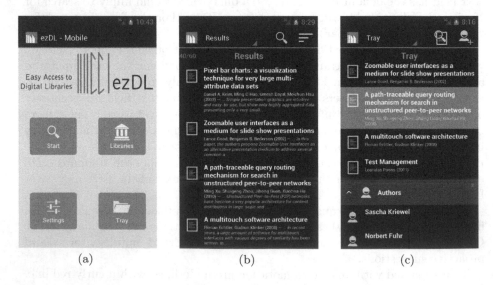

       (a)   (b)   (c)

Fig. 9. The start screen (a), the result list (b) and the tray tool (c)

Fig. 10. The action bar

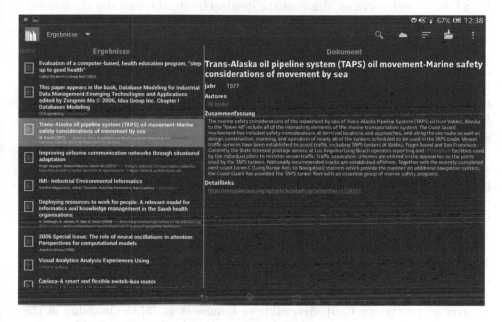

Fig. 11. The result list and details on a tablet

The mobile frontend of *ezDL* is implemented as an Android[8] app [32]. The app is available from the Google Play Store[9]. Mobile devices differ from desktop-based applications in several important aspects: The available screen space is much smaller and a mouse or keyboard is usually not present. Instead, a touch-based user interface is common. Thus, the app for mobile devices cannot be a one-to-one implementation of the desktop client. The *ezDL* app is based on Android 4+ to support not only smartphones but also tablets and other devices with bigger screen size. The main user interface component is the so-called *action bar* (see Figure 10). The action bar is placed at the top of the screen. From there the user can easily switch to the different tools. Figure 9 (a) shows the start screen that comprises links to the most important functionalities. After submitting a query in the query view the result list is displayed (Figure 9 (b)). The user can request details for a document from the result list, start a new search or storing documents in the tray tool (Figure 9 (c)). The tray can also

---

[8] http://www.android.com/

[9] https://play.google.com/store/apps/details?id=de.unidue.inf.is.ezdl.androidfrontend

store terms or author names for later usage. The tray is persistent when closing and restarting the app. Objects in the tray can be exported as BibTeX or simple text to other apps using the default sharing intent[10]. Figure 11 shows the result list and the details of a document on a 10 inch tablet.

The communication between the app and the *ezDL* backend is realized by REST-based web services. Whereas the desktop frontend uses a stateful connection to the backend this mechanism is not suitable for an Android-based mobile application. The connection to the backend is usually much more instable on mobile devices than on desktop computers. Additionally, there are incompatibilities between the Java and Android platforms. Thus, the messages send between frontend and backend cannot be just serialized plain Java objects. To overcome these issues we implemented a *proxy* that translates REST requests in JSON format from the app via HTTP to the backend. The responses from the backend are transformed into JSON objects which are then send back to the app.

Since most usability problems can be found with only four or five users [50] the usability of the app has been evaluated in a small user study [32,31]. Eight participants (average age: 28) were asked to solve several common information seeking tasks with the app, e.g. such as storing documents in the tray or finding a document with a specific title. Most (seven of eight) participants had experiences using smartphones or other mobile devices. For measuring the usability the SUS questionnaire [14] was used. The analysis of the questionnaire shows a SUS score 72.5 of 100 points. Four of the eight participants had previous experiences with the desktop frontend of *ezDL*. The SUS score for these advanced users is 83 on average (std. dev: 9) while the SUS score for the unexperienced users is only 62 on average (std. dev.: 12.5). According to Bangor et al. [5] the usability of the app can be considered as *good* (on the following scale: worst imaginable > poor > ok > good > excellent > best imaginable) for the advanced users and *ok* for all users.

4.4 Extending and Customizing ezDL

As mentioned already in the introduction, one of the goals in the development of *ezDL* is to provide an extensible framework that allows for easy modification and extension of both its functional and the presentation level components. Below, we describe the various possibilities provided for modifying the system.

Plugins. Each agent and the desktop client are extensible using a plugin system. Plugins are registered at a central component that can later be asked to return plugin objects of a specific type. There are two different ways to announce plugins: the first possibility is by loading them as an OSGi[11] bundle when the affected subsystem starts (e.g. an agent or a client). The other way is by announcing them in statically linked code. Using the OSGi way makes it easier for

---

[10] http://developer.android.com/training/sharing/send.html
[11] A module system for the Java platform, managed by the OSGi Alliance (http://www.osgi.org)

end-users to extend their personal clients while using the latter way makes it easier to maintain and deploy centrally developed extensions.

As an example, it is possible to add a new proactive suggestion module to the system that implements a new way of retrieving suggestions. The popup list that shows the suggestions can likewise be replaced by an alternative. Further uses of the plugin system are export and import modules and modules that extract information from the result list. Even entirely new tools can be added by the end-user; an option that makes it easier to maintain different versions of the client for use in an experiment.

Services (Agents). Adding a new service is usually done by implementing a new agent. There is an abstract class that takes care of most issues but the actual functionality. This is usually implemented using specialized classes (request handlers) for which there are abstract implementations, too. Thus, developers can concentrate on the business logic. It is also possible to extend existing agents by new request handlers. An interesting special case is the user agent, which offers services to deal with users (authenticating them, getting profile information) and also offers a wrapper (see below) so users can search the users of the system the same way they search remote digital libraries.

Connecting More Collections and Services. Connecting to a new collection for searching (a digital library, a local IR system, a BibTeX file, etc.) is accomplished by implementing a wrapper agent. These are agents specialized in translating between *ezDL* and a remote system. Remote systems can be those that provide a stable API like SOAP or SQL but also those that only have a web site and a search form. *ezDL* has built-in support for most common fields (e.g. title, author, publication year, abstract) and data types (e.g. text, numbers, images). There are abstract wrappers available to quickly connect to Solr servers. There is also a library of code for translating the *ezDL* query representation into other languages, e.g. Lucene and Solr ones. If required, web pages can be scraped using an elaborate tool kit that is configured by an XML file. This file contains information on how to issue a query to a remote collection, how to process the resulting document (e.g. web page) and how to interpret the result in terms of document information. Using this toolkit, even digital libraries without a proper API can be connected.

Agents—and, thus, wrapper agents—announce themselves to the Directory agent when started. The client can ask the backend for a list of known wrapper agents, so there is no need to change any code or configuration outside of the agent. This also enables developers to store the code and put it under version control independent from the main *ezDL* code.

5   Evaluating Search Systems

To support user-centred evaluations, *ezDL* has a builtin evaluation mode that addresses many of the major challenges inherent in setting up evaluation tasks and tracking user activity during the experiments. The following is a brief overview of those functionalities within *ezDL* directly designed to support evaluations.

Logging User Actions. For evaluations with actual users all user actions performed with the system should be logged for later inspection and analysis. *ezDL* has a built-in logging facility that stores all the interaction data of the user in a relational database (currently *MySQL* is used). A *log session* comprises all *log events* that a user or the system has triggered. A log event has *i*) a unique name identifying this type of event, *ii*) timestamps from the frontend and the backend, *iii*) a sequence number to ensure the correct order, and *iv*) parameters as multiple key/value pairs. For example, when a user performs a search for `information retrieval` in the DBLP and ACM digital library the corresponding log event may look like this:

```
event:
  name: "search"
  clientTimestamp: 1/4/2012 15:26:32,1234
  timestamp: 1/4/2012 15:26:32,3456
  sequenceNumber: 10
  parameters:
      query: "information retrieval"
      sources: dblp, acm
```

The logging facility takes care of allocating activities to sessions and users. If it is required to log some previously unlogged action (e.g. because a new tool has been integrated), this can easily be integrated by sending a corresponding logging message to the backend.

Dynamic AOIs. Gaze tracking is a method for user-centred evaluation that has recently gained popularity within the IR field [10,13]. For analyzing fixation data of users, the standard eye tracking software allows for the definition of so-called *Areas of Interest* (AOIs), which are rectangular areas on the screen, e.g. for collecting data about the duration of fixations of an AOI, as well as the transitions between different AOIs. Usually, AOIs are defined for a static screen image, where each AOI corresponds to a certain object displayed in that area. However, for a highly interactive systems with the possibility of resizing frames, scrolling and pop-up windows, there is a need for keeping track of the objects displayed at any given time. For this purpose, we have developed the *AOILog* framework [12,48,47] and integrated it into *ezDL*. This way, it is e.g. possible to keep track of the result items looked at, while the user scrolls through this list.

Fixed Layout on Screen. The layout of the desktop can be locked to keep UI-related variance low. With a fixed layout it is no longer possible for a test subject to open additional tool views or change the layout of the desktop.

Loading Predefined Perspectives. Predefined perspectives can be loaded immediately after the system has been started. This allows the evaluator to create custom perspectives that can be used for an evaluation without selecting them manually.

Splash Screen for Choosing Evaluation Settings. A splash screen can be enabled that is shown before starting the system. It can be used to choose and set settings for the evaluation session, e.g. a search task description or the system variant when doing a comparison of different UIs or system features.

Web Application for Controlling Experiments. A specific experimentation web-based application controls experimental sessions by scheduling user tasks and questionnaires. This application was used for the INEX Interactive Track [37].

Several user studies have been performed and experimental systems have been implemented using *ezDL* as a base system. The next section presents some of them in more detail.

6   Use Cases

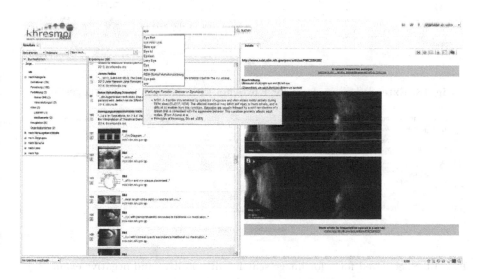

Fig. 12. The web client used in the Khresmoi project

ezDL is currently running as a live system, and is being used and extended in a number of projects of various sizes.

The live system[12] features all core functionalities which are also available in the more specific projects. These include a simple and an advanced search function, various result manipulation options, a temporary document store, and exporting of meta information. Registered users can also use a personal library to store, annotate and share found or imported documents. Currently, nine different digital libraries are connected to the system. The selection of libraries focuses on computer science libraries but includes others like Pubmed and the Amazon catalogue. The system is publicly available, still under constant development and updated regularly.

6.1   Medical Search: Khresmoi Professional

Khresmoi is an EU funded research project with the goal to provide consumers as well as medical professionals with a multi–lingual and multi–modal search engine for trustworthy, health-related information and documents [4,21]. Specialized search interfaces are being developed for the different user groups and supported tasks. These targeted user interfaces are meant to support and improve access to medical information.

Fig. 13. Extended query form for Khresmoi with disambiguation suggestions

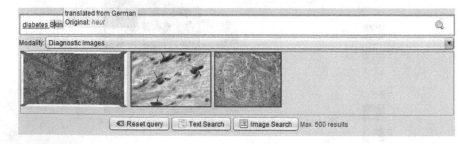

Fig. 14. Specialized form for image search (with positive and negative examples)

Using the *ezDL* reference implementation three clients for health professionals have been developed under the name of Khresmoi Professional: a simple web

---

[12] http://www.ezdl.de/

client implemented using Google Web Toolkit (see Figure 12)[13], a desktop client based on the standard *ezDL* client and a mobile client for Android 4.0.2+[14]. These clients support users in coping with some of the difficulties that they might encounter while searching for medical information online. They provide new query forms that expand on the standard search fields, or allow image search using example images and relevance feedback (see Figures 13 and 14).

From a functional point of view, new data sources have been made available for the Khresmoi version of *ezDL* including new searchable data types to cover the specific demands of the medical domain. For search support the Khresmoi client offers query completion, tactical search suggestions and automatic translation. A guided search for health–related information needs has been evaluated [44,43].

Social and collaborative functionalities are being integrated that will allow health professionals to work and search together on cases and also to indirectly profit from other users' interaction with the system. Search results can be shared with other users and annotated, automatic translations of the systems can be corrected and will improve translations for other users. A system for user rating of resources and search results is planned, and users already can leave comments on other users' profile pages.

6.2   Medical Search: Khresmoi Radiology

Another variant of the stand–alone desktop client is specifically targeted at radiologists and other medical practitioners who are mainly searching for medical images, including 3D data (see Figure 15). The radiologist can select an existing case from a hospital case base and mark interesting regions in the image data. 3D images, so called *volumes*, are separated into slices. Each slice represents a cut through the volume along a given orientation. Using the marked regions in the example slices, similar images from previous cases are fetched along with their diagnoses, as well as additional images from the literature and text documents based on the most common diagnosis present in the case reports of the results [30].

Figure 15 shows the interface after a set of results has been received. On the left the query volume is shown as a reference. A marked region of interest is also indicated by a red box. Search results are displayed on the right hand side. Between these two areas details of result items are shown. In this case the user selected a full 3D volume. The diagnosis corresponding to the case is visible below the image data. Several mouse gestures are implemented that allow quick interaction with the volume. Commonly radiologists tend to scroll a lot between the different slices. They can do so slice-based by using the mouse wheel or very rapidly by holding a mouse button and moving the mouse. Users also need to change the brightness and contrast settings, which is possible via a mouse gesture as well. All changes made to the query volume's settings are automatically applied to the result items as well to keep them comparable. Furthermore, slices

---

[13]   available at http://professional.khresmoi.eu
[14]   available at the Google Play Store

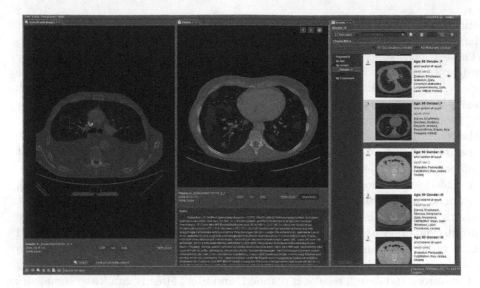

Fig. 15. Khresmoi client for radiologists

can be zoomed and moved. Additional types of results, like text documents, can be accessed by using the tabs visible above the result list.

6.3   Patent Search: PerFedPat

PerFedPat is an interactive patent search system based on the federated search approach and the *ezDL* framework. Federated Search [42] represents a Distributed Information Retrieval (DIR) scenario and allows the simultaneous search of multiple searchable, remote and physically distributed resources [33]. PerFedPat provides core services and operations for being able to search, using a federated method, multiple online patent resources (currently Espacenet[15], Google patents[16], Patentscope[17] and the MAREC[18] collection), thus providing unified single-point access to multiple patent sources while hiding complexity from the end user who uses a common query tool for querying all patent datasets at the same time. Wrappers are used which convert the PerFedPat internal query model into the queries that each remote system can process. Queries are routed to remote search systems and their returned results are internally re-ranked and merged as a single list presented to the patent searcher. PerFedPat is developed

---

[15] http://worldwide.espacenet.com/

[16] http://www.google.com/patents

[17] http://patentscope.wipo.int/

[18] MAREC is a static collection of over 19 million patent applications and granted patents in a unified file format normalized from EP, WO, US, and JP sources, spanning a range from 1976 to June 2008.
http://www.ifs.tuwien.ac.at/imp/marec.shtml

upon *ezDL* therefore, in addition to the patent resources which are provided in PerFedPat, there are other resources already provided by *ezDL*, most of them offering access to online bibliographic search services (e.g. ACM DL, DBLP, Springer, PubMed) for non-patent literature.

The second idea that is explored in PerFedPat is the utilization of *ezDL*'s open framework for patent search using a variety of patent search tools and User Interfaces. To achieve this goal PerFedPat uses *ezDL*'s pluggable and extensible architecture, thereby providing multiple patent search tools and UIs. Consequently in PerFedPat federated search is used beyond the way that it is used in traditional Distributed IR, i.e. to provide a single merged list of multiple ranked results. Hence, the second innovative feature of PerFedPat is that it enables the use of multiple search tools which are integrated in PerFedPat. Currently the search tools which are integrated are a) an International Patent Classification (IPC) selection tool, b) a tool for faceted navigation of the results retrieved based on existing metadata in patents, c) a tool producing clustered views of patent search results d) a Machine Translation (MT) tool for translating queries for cross lingual information retrieval.

The two basic principles explained above define PerFedPat as an Integrated Professional Federated Search System. Although it is relatively easy to differentiate professional search from 'public search' with a number of characteristics (e.g. classification schemes are extensively used, lengthy search sessions, high recall is usually important, focus is on specific domain knowledge, reason about how the results have been produced, ability to reproduce accurately a search session), the concept of an integrated search system is not clear. Most definitions found in the Information Retrieval literature converge to use the term "integrated" to define search systems that simultaneously access a number of different data sources providing a single point of search. This view is much more compatible with the Federated Search view that allows the simultaneous search of multiple resources. In PerFedPat we expand the meaning of the term integrated to define search system designs where multiple search tools can be used (in parallel or in a pipeline) by the professional searcher. As a result our definition of integrated professional search systems primarily describes a rich information seeking environment for different types of searches, utilizing multiple search tools and exploiting a diverse set of integrated IR and Natural Language Processing (NLP) technologies.

Based on this integrated architecture PerFedPat is a pluggable system which puts together the following components: retrieval, selection, integration, presentation and adaptation (Figure 16).

The screenshot (Figure 17) shows some of the core *ezDL* tools as they are adapted or configured for the PerFedPat application. It shows the Query Tool (A) as it has been adapted to address the needs of multiple fields in patent search, the Library Choice Tool (B) with the four patent datasets which are currently supported and the Results (C) and the Details tools (D). The Cluster Explorer and the Entities Explorer Tools (E) which are specifically developed for patent search in PerFedPat are also shown.

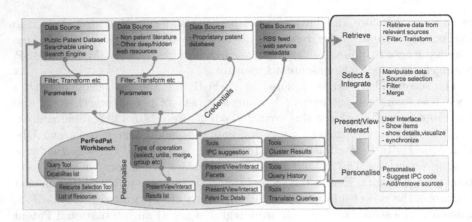

Fig. 16. PerFedPat architecture and component overview

In the remainder of this section we discuss the tools that have been integrated into PerFedPat to experiment and to set the ground for improving patent search in PerFedPat.

The IPC Suggestion Tool. The IPC suggestion tool aims, given a query, to select a number of IPC codes, at different levels of the classification hierarchy if requested, which include patents related to this query. The algorithm and the method which we used to implement this tool is based on DIR techniques for collection selection which we extended for patent search and they are already reported in the literature [39,38]. We cannot discuss the algorithm in more detail here, but the essence of the method is that it identifies relevant IPC codes not by searching the textual description of IPC classes, groups, subgroups etc., but by using an indirect method. First it retrieves patents which are already allocated to IPC codes, and then indirectly builds a probability estimation of the relevance of the allocated IPC codes to the query.

The functionality that the IPC suggestion tool provides relates to the very fundamental step in professional patent search which is "defining a text query, potentially by Boolean operators and specific field filters". In prior art search probably the most important filter is based on the IPC (CPC now) classification [49,1]. Selecting the most promising/relevant IPC codes depends of course on the prior knowledge of a patent professional in the technical area under examination, but sometimes the area of a patent application may not be easily distinguishable or usually a patent uses various technical concepts represented by multiple IPC codes. To identify all these relevant IPC codes could be a difficult, error prone and time-consuming task, especially for a not very knowledgeable patent professional in some technical area.

The IPC suggestion tool supports this step automatically; this is, given a query, it selects the most appropriate IPC codes, passes these IPC codes to the

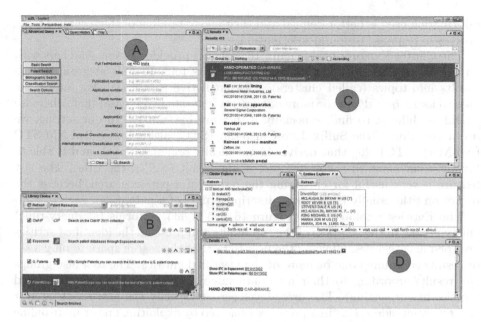

Fig. 17. Screenshot of the PerFedPat system

Query tool. The query tool then initiates a filtered search based on the automatically selected IPC codes. This process naturally resembles the way patent professionals conduct various types of patent search. Also, the patent searcher may use the tool not only to produce IPC-based filters automatically to narrow his/her search, but also as a classification search which will be used as a starting point to identify and closer examine technical concepts as these are expressed in IPC codes and to which a patent could be related and should be examined more vigorously. This ground understanding step helps soon after in formulating better queries with higher precision which will usually include expansion with noun-phrases from the IPC codes which deemed relevant. Of course the patent searcher has the flexibility to add the IPC codes that he assumes relevant in addition to the ones suggested by the IPC suggestion tool.

The Cluster Explorer and the Entities Explorer Tools. The Faceted Search tool supports an exploratory strategy for patent search that exploits the metadata already available in patents in addition to the results of clustering and entity mining that can be performed at query time. The results (metadata, clusters and entities grouped in categories) can complement the ranked lists of patents produced from the core patent search engine with information useful for the user (e.g. providing a concise overview of the search results) which are further exploited in a faceted and session-based interaction scheme that allows the users to focus their searches gradually and to change between search methods as their information need is better defined and their understanding of the technical topic evolves in response to found information.

The Cluster Explorer tool (Figure 16, (E) left) provides patent searchers with an overview of the results shown in the Results tool. It aims at grouping the results into topics (called clusters), with predictive names (labels), aiding the user to locate quickly one or more documents (patents in our case) that otherwise would be difficult to find, especially if they are low ranked. In our setting, we use a variation of the Suffix Tree Clustering (STC) algorithm, called NM-STC (No-Merge STC) [26], that derives hierarchically organized labels and is able to favour occurrences in a specific part of the result (e.g. in the title). The last feature is very useful for clustering the results of a patent search, because the invention title usually is the most descriptive part of a patent.

The Entities Explorer tool (Figure 16, (E) right) performs (at query-time) entity mining in the snippets of the top results and presents the identified entities grouped in categories, allowing the user to restrict the search space to only a set of results containing one or more of the identified entities. The tool also groups the results according to their metadata values (which can also be considered entities in our setting). The user/developer can specify the entities of interest (currently outside *ezDL*) in a preprocessing step by exploiting one or more online Semantic Knowledge Bases (Linked Data). Thereby, the entity mining process can be configured for different contexts and domains. The Knowledge Bases are also exploited at real-time for retrieving more (semantic) information about an identified entity allowing the user to explore its properties and other related entities.

The algorithms and the methods of these two PerFedPat tools are reported in detail in [17,16]. Currently the two tools work with the MAREC patent resource only, but it is straightforward to support any patent resource in PerFedPat federation as both tools attain their functionality fully at query time only (i.e. no preprocessing or indexing is necessary). In the current version, the Entities Explorer tool has been configured to group the results according to the following metadata categories: Publication Country, Application Country, IPC, Inventor, Applicant, Application Year, Publication Number, Publication Year and ECLA. Also, entity mining has been configured for the biomedical domain and can identify the following types of entities: Diseases, Drugs and Proteins.

The Machine Translation Tool. The Machine Translation tool uses third party MT services (e.g. Microsoft's Bing) in order to translate queries into different languages so that Cross-Language Information Retrieval (CLIR) can be conducted to retrieve patents in more languages. To initiate a CLIR process the user needs to press translate and query. If this happens the query tool sends a message to the machine translation tool which in its turns sends the appropriate requests to one or more MT services. The translation is sent back to the query tool and the translated query is subsequently sent to the selected patent resources (which in their turn build the appropriate request to retrieve results from them).

7   Conclusion and Outlook

We presented *ezDL*, which is a flexible, extensible framework system for interactive retrieval and its evaluation. Building upon state-of-the art interface technology and usability concepts, *ezDL* can provide an advanced user interface for many IR applications. The system can also be easily extended, at the functionality level as well as at the presentation level; thus, new concepts for the design of IR user interfaces can be integrated into *ezDL* with little effort. Furthermore, the system provides extensive support for performing user-oriented evaluations. In the same way as there are various experimental IR backend systems, there is now an IR frontend system that allows for easy experimentation and application of interactive retrieval.

Future work on the *ezDL* system will focus on a more flexible interface and enhanced proactive behavior. For the former, we follow the select-organise-project model described in [11]: a retrieval system should provide a number of specialized retrieval methods (like e.g. Web search engines do after classifying th submitted query first), offer further variants of result organisation (besides the grouping and sorting functions already available), and implement a variety of projections, i.e. structure and content of the surrogates in the result list. On the proactive side, we want to improve user guidance by applying quantitative modeling methods and proposing a list of promising next steps at each stage of the search process [45]. The combination of these two approaches will lead to a both more flexible and more effective search tool.

Acknowledgments. The research leading to these results has received funding from the European Union Seventh Framework Programme (FP7/2007-2013) under grant agreement №257528 (KHRESMOI), and by the German Science Foundation (DFG) under grant FU 205/24-1 (HIIR). The research leading to the results referring to PerFedPat has received funding from the European Union Seventh Framework Programme (FP7/2007-2013) under grant agreement №275522 (PerFedPat).

References

1. Adams, S.: Using the international patent classification in an online environment. World Patent Information 22(4), 291–300 (2000)
2. Allan, J., Callan, J., Collins-Thompson, K., Croft, B., Feng, F., Fisher, D., Lafferty, J., Larkey, L., Truong, T.N., Ogilvie, P., et al.: The Lemur toolkit for language modeling and information retrieval (2003)
3. Amershi, S., Morris, M.R.: Cosearch: A system for co-located collaborative web search. In: Proceedings of the Twenty-sixth Annual SIGCHI Conference on Human Factors in Computing Systems, CHI 2008, pp. 1647–1656. ACM, New York (2008)

4. Aswani, N., Beckers, T., Birngruber, E., Boyer, C., Burner, A., Bystron, J., Choukri, K., Cruchet, S., Cunningham, H., Dedek, J., Dolamic, L., Donner, R., Dungs, S., Eggel, I., Foncubierta, A., Fuhr, N., Funk, A., Garcia, A., de Herrera, S., Gaudinat, A., Georgiev, G., Gobeill, J., Goeuriot, L., Gomez, P., Greenwood, M., Gschwandtner, M., Hanbury, A., Hajic, J., Hlavácová, J., Holzer, M., Jones, G., Jordan, B., Jordan, M., Kaderk, K., Kainberger, F., Kelly, L., Kriewel, S., Kritz, M., Langs, G., Lawson, N., Markonis, D., Martinez, I., Momtchev, V., Masselot, A., Mazo, H., Müller, H., Pecina, P., Pentchev, K., Peychev, D., Pletneva, N., Pottecher, D., Roberts, A., Ruch, P., Samwald, M., Schneller, P., Stefanov, V., Tinte, M.A., Uresová, Z., Vargas, A., Vishnyakova, D.: Khresmoi professional: Multilingual semantic search for medical professionals. In: ACM SIGIR Workshop on Health Search and Discovery: Helping Users and Advancing Medicine (2013)
5. Bangor, A., Kortum, P., Miller, J.: Determining what individual sus scores mean: Adding an adjective rating scale. Journal of Usability Studies 4(3), 114–123 (2009)
6. Bates, M.J.: Idea tactics. Journal of the American Society for Information Science 30(5), 280–289 (1979)
7. Bates, M.J.: Information search tactics. Journal of the American Society for Information Science 30(4), 205–214 (1979)
8. Bates, M.J.: Where should the person stop and the search interface start? Information Processing and Management 26(5), 575–591 (1990)
9. Beckers, T., Dungs, S., Fuhr, N., Jordan, M., Kriewel, S.: ezDL: An interactive search and evaluation system. In: SIGIR 2012 Workshop on Open Source Information Retrieval (OSIR 2012) (August 2012)
10. Beckers, T., Fuhr, N.: User-oriented and eye-tracking-based evaluation of an interactive search system. In: 4th Workshop on Human-Computer Interaction and Information Retrieval (HCIR 2010) @ IIiX 2010 (2010)
11. Beckers, T., Fuhr, N.: Search system functions for supporting search modes. In: 2nd European Workshop on Human-Computer Interaction and Information Retrieval (EuroHCIR) @ IIiX 2012 (August 2012)
12. Beckers, T., Korbar, D.: Using eye-tracking for the evaluation of interactive information retrieval. In: Geva, S., Kamps, J., Schenkel, R., Trotman, A. (eds.) INEX 2010. LNCS, vol. 6932, pp. 236–240. Springer, Heidelberg (2011)
13. Bierig, R., Gwizdka, J., Cole, M.: A user-centered experiment and logging framework for interactive information retrieval. In: Understanding the user - Workshop in Conjuction with SIGIR (2009)
14. Brooke, J.: SUS: A quick and dirty usability scale. In: Usability Evaluation in Industry, pp. 189–194 (1996)
15. Chau, M., Wong, C.H.: Designing the user interface and functions of a search engine development tool. Decision Support Systems 48(2), 369–382 (2010)
16. Fafalios, P., Kitsos, I., Marketakis, Y., Baldassarre, C., Salampasis, M., Tzitzikas, Y.: Web Searching with Entity Mining at Query Time. In: Salampasis, M., Larsen, B. (eds.) IRFC 2012. LNCS, vol. 7356, pp. 73–88. Springer, Heidelberg (2012)
17. Fafalios, P., Salampasis, M., Tzitzikas, Y.: Exploratory patent search with faceted search and (configurable) entity mining. In: Proceedings of the Integrating IR Technologies for Professional Search (in conjuction with ECIR 2013) (2013)
18. Fuhr, N., Klas, C.-P., Schaefer, A., Mutschke, P.: Daffodil: An integrated desktop for supporting high-level search activities in federated digital libraries. In: Agosti, M., Thanos, C. (eds.) ECDL 2002. LNCS, vol. 2458, pp. 597–612. Springer, Heidelberg (2002)

19. Golovchinsky, G., Diriye, A., Dunnigan, T.: The future is in the past: Designing for exploratory search. In: Proceedings of the 4th Information Interaction in Context Symposium, IIIX 2012, pp. 52–61. ACM, New York (2012)
20. Hall, M.M., Katsaris, S., Toms, E.: A pluggable work-bench for creating interactive ir interfaces. In: Proceeding of the the 3rd European Workshop on Human-Computer Interaction and Information Retrieval, EuroHCIR 2013 (2013)
21. Hanbury, A., Belle, W., Lawson, N., Dolamic, L., Pletneva, N., Samwald, M., Boyer, C.: Prototype of a first search system for intensive tests. Deliverable D8.2, Khresmoi (2012)
22. Harter, S.P.: Online information retrieval: concepts, principles, and techniques. Academic Press Professional, Inc., San Diego (1986)
23. Jansen, B.J., Pooch, U.: Assisting the searcher: utilizing software agents for web search systems. Internet Research: Electronic Networking Applications and Policy 14(1), 19–33 (2004)
24. Klas, C.-P., Gövert, N., Fuhr, N.: Distributed agents for user-friendly access of digital libraries. In: Searching for Information: Artificial Intelligence and Information Retrieval Approaches, Savoy Place, London WC2R 0BL, UK, vol. 17, pp. 1–3. IEE Informatics (1999) ISSN 0963-3308
25. Klas, C.-P., Kriewel, S., Schaefer, A.: Daffodil - Nutzerorientiertes Zugangssystem für heterogene digitale Bibliotheken. dvs Band (2004)
26. Kopidaki, S., Papadakos, P., Tzitzikas, Y.: STC+ and NM-STC: Two Novel Online Results Clustering Methods for Web Searching. In: Vossen, G., Long, D.D.E., Yu, J.X. (eds.) WISE 2009. LNCS, vol. 5802, pp. 523–537. Springer, Heidelberg (2009)
27. Kriewel, S.: Unterstützung beim Finden und Durchführen von Suchstrategien in Digitalen Bibliotheken. PhD thesis, University of Duisburg-Essen (2010)
28. Kriewel, S., Fuhr, N.: Evaluation of an adaptive search suggestion system. In: Gurrin, C., He, Y., Kazai, G., Kruschwitz, U., Little, S., Roelleke, T., Rüger, S., van Rijsbergen, K. (eds.) ECIR 2010. LNCS, vol. 5993, pp. 544–555. Springer, Heidelberg (2010)
29. Kriewel, S., Klas, C.-P., Schaefer, A., Fuhr, N.: Daffodil - strategic support for user-oriented access to heterogeneous digital libraries. D-Lib Magazine 10(6) (June 2004), http://www.dlib.org/dlib/june04/kriewel/06kriewel.html
30. Markonis, D., Donner, R., Holzer, M., Schlegl, T., Dungs, S., Kriewel, S., Langs, G., Müller, H.: A visual information retrieval system for radiology reports and the medical literature. In: Gurrin, C., Hopfgartner, F., Hurst, W., Johansen, H., Lee, H., O'Connor, N. (eds.) MMM 2014, Part II. LNCS, vol. 8326, pp. 390–393. Springer, Heidelberg (2014)
31. Muno, S.: Entwicklung eines Android-Frontends fü ezDL. Diplomarbeit. Universität Duisburg-Essen (2013)
32. Muno, S., Beckers, T., Kriewel, S.: Konzeption und Implementierung einer Android-App für das ezDL-System. In: Proceedings of the IR Workshop at Lernen, Wissen, Adaption (LWA 2013) (October 2013)
33. Nottelmann, H., Fuhr, N.: Evaluating different methods of estimating retrieval quality for resource selection. In: Proceedings of the 26th Annual International ACM SIGIR Conference on Research and Development in Informaion Retrieval, SIGIR 2003, pp. 290–297. ACM, New York (2003)
34. Nuray, R., Can, F.: Automatic ranking of information retrieval systems using data fusion. Information Processing & Management 42(3), 595–614 (2006)
35. Ounis, I., Amati, G., Plachouras, V., He, B., Macdonald, C., Johnson, D.: Terrier information retrieval platform. In: Losada, D.E., Fernández-Luna, J.M. (eds.) ECIR 2005. LNCS, vol. 3408, pp. 517–519. Springer, Heidelberg (2005)

36. Paepcke, A.: Digital libraries: Searching is not enough–what we learned on-site. D-Lib Magazine 2(5) (1996), http://www.dlib.org/dlib/may96/stanford/05paepcke.html
37. Pharo, N., Beckers, T., Nordlie, R., Fuhr, N.: Overview of the inex 2010 interactive track. In: Geva, S., Kamps, J., Schenkel, R., Trotman, A. (eds.) INEX 2010. LNCS, vol. 6932, pp. 227–235. Springer, Heidelberg (2011)
38. Salampasis, M., Giachanou, A.: Multilayer collection selection and search of topically organized patents. In: Proceedings of the Integrating IR Technologies for Professional Search (in conjuction with ECIR 2013), pp. 48–56 (2013)
39. Salampasis, M., Paltoglou, G., Giahanou, A.: Report on the clef-ip 2012 experiments: Search of topically organized patents. In: Forner, P., Karlgren, J. (eds.) CLEF (Online Working Notes/Labs/Workshop) (2012)
40. Salton, G., Buckley, C.: Term-weighting approaches in automatic text retrieval. Information Processing & Management 24(5), 513–523 (1988)
41. Schaefer, A., Jordan, M., Klas, C.-P., Fuhr, N.: Active support for query formulation in virtual digital libraries: A case study with DAFFODIL. In: Rauber, A., Christodoulakis, S., Tjoa, A.M. (eds.) ECDL 2005. LNCS, vol. 3652, pp. 414–425. Springer, Heidelberg (2005)
42. Shokouhi, M., Si, L.: Federated search. Found. Trends Inf. Retr. 5(1), 1–102 (2011)
43. Tacke, A., Kriewel, S.: Strategische Suchunterstützung auf Makro- und Mikroebene. In: Proc. IR Workshop at Lernen, Wissen, Adaption (LWA 2013) (Oktober 2013)
44. Tacke, A., Kriewel, S.: Strategic search support on macro and micro level. In: Datenbank-Spektrum (2014)
45. Tran, V.T., Fuhr, N.: Markov modeling for user interaction in retrieval. In: SIGIR 2013 Workshop on Modeling User Behavior for Information Retrieval Evaluation (MUBE 2013) (August 2013)
46. Tran, V.T.: Entwicklung einer Unterstützung für Pearl Growing. Masters thesis, University of Duisburg-Essen (2011)
47. Tran, T.V., Fuhr, N.: Quantitative analysis of search sessions enhanced by gaze tracking with dynamic areas of interest. In: Zaphiris, P., Buchanan, G., Rasmussen, E., Loizides, F. (eds.) TPDL 2012. LNCS, vol. 7489, pp. 468–473. Springer, Heidelberg (2012)
48. Tran, V.T., Fuhr, N.: Using eye-tracking with dynamic areas of interest for analyzing interactive information retrieval. In: Proceedings of the 35th International ACM SIGIR Conference on Research and Development in Information Retrieval. ACM (August 2012)
49. Vijvers, W.G.: The international patent classification as a search tool. World Patent Information 12(1), 26–30 (1990)
50. Virzi, R.A.: Refining the test phase of usability evaluation: How many subjects is enough? Hum. Factors 34(4), 457–468 (1992)

Clinical Text Retrieval - An Overview of Basic Building Blocks and Applications

Hercules Dalianis

Department of Computer and Systems Sciences
Stockholm University
P.O. Box 7003, 164 07 Kista
Sweden
hercules@dsv.su.se

Abstract. This article describes information retrieval, natural language processing and text mining of electronic patient record text, also called clinical text. Clinical text is written by physicians and nurses to document the health care process of the patient. First we describe some characteristics of clinical text, followed by the automatic preprocessing of the text that is necessary for making it usable for some applications. We also describe some applications for clinicians including spelling and grammar checking, ICD-10 diagnosis code assignment, as well as other applications for hospital management such as ICD-10 diagnosis code validation and detection of adverse events such as hospital acquired infections. Part of the preprocessing makes the clinical text useful for faceted search, although clinical text already has some keys for performing faceted search such as gender, age, ICD-10 diagnosis codes, ATC drug codes, etc. Preprocessing makes use of ICD-10 codes and the SNOMED-CT textual descriptions. ICD-10 codes and SNOMED-CT are available in several languages and can be considered the modern Greek or Latin of medical language. The basic research presented here has its roots in the challenges described by the health care sector. These challenges have been partially solved in academia, and we believe the solutions will be adapted to the health care sector in real world applications.

Keywords: Information retrieval, electronic patient records, clinical text, spell checking, ICD-10, SNOMED-CT, Swedish.

1 Introduction

In this article we aim to describe the problems that may be encountered when processing and retrieving clinical text written in Swedish. We also describe how to solve some of these problems. We specifically address one key objective of the EU Cost Action Multilingual and Multifaceted Interactive Information Access (MUMIA)[1] namely: *Integrating and Managing Language Resources* as well as one general objective *Bridging the gap between Science and Industry.*

---

[1] http://www.mumia-network.eu

G. Paltoglou et al. (Eds.): Professional Search in the Modern World, LNCS 8830, pp. 147–165, 2014.
© Springer International Publishing Switzerland 2014

For the objective Integrating and Managing Language Resources we focus on the use of the ICD-10 diagnosis codes and SNOMED-CT terminologies within one language, with the aim of showing how these methods can be used to cross domains within the health care sector as well as to transfer them across languages. In the general objective Bridging the Gap between Science and Industry, we focus on the use of clinical information retrieval in industry, which in our context means health care.

There are a multitude of important problems the health care sector would like to solve, but health care personnel are busy treating patients and have no spare time to reflect over their work and how to improve it by using state of the art techniques. By learning how health care processes are carried out, we as researchers can propose solutions from academia that few health care personnel have heard about. One example is how to use and reuse unstructured patient record repositories. We believe that some of the problems can be solved using faceted search. In our context, faceted search tries to hook up to important parts of the text and then use the hooks to explore the unstructured text in a faceted way.

A patient record is written by physicians and nurses to document the health care process of a patient. The reasons for this are twofold. One is to write notes concerning how the health care process is proceeding in order to transfer the care of the patient to other physicians and nurses, but the documentation is also a memory note written by the author of the record. The other reason, at least in Sweden, is a legal reason; a clinician is obliged to document the health care process.

The Electronic Patient Records (EPRs) for primary care and hospital care have been developed during the past 30 years. In the early days of the EPRs they only contained free text and some structured information about the patient. Electronic Patient Record Systems (EPRs) were only used at some large clinics or hospitals, but today, at least in Sweden, the computerized systems predominate, and almost no paper based records are used. Nilsson [30], carried out an extensive and historical overview of the patient record. Nowadays, structured information about patient care from various systems in the hospital, such as laboratory and blood values, is automatically inserted into the EPR of the patient, and the EPRs have become very information rich, with information on millions of patients treated for long periods of time. Usually each patient record, and specifically the discharge letter, contains a diagnosis code called the ICD-10 code [53]. This code is mainly used for economic and administrative purposes.

During the past five years EPRs have also become available in large repositories, which can be defined as data warehouses. Because of the vast size of these databases, the healthcare and research community is considering whether these large repositories can be used as more than just a storage place, such as for performing text and data mining to find adverse events, to discover adverse drug events or to find new methods for curing patients.

There is, however, a drawback, since the EPRs contain sensitive information. Physicians make notes in the EPR on the medical status and treatment of the patient, as well as concerning sensitive or personal information including the patient's name and address. This combination of information makes these documents unreachable or very difficult for researchers and developers to access in order to develop tools for information retrieval or to perform natural language processing. At the same time, users of EPRs in hospitals have started to require various support tools when entering text, such as spelling and grammar checking, as well as different dictionaries for terminology and ICD-10 diagnosis code assignment.

2 Background

Information retrieval in a clinical context is an unexplored area because of the lack of patient record text that can be used as test data for developed tools. Patient records are protected by a number of laws for safeguarding the privacy of the patient. To get access to these records, ethical permission is required and even then it is difficult to get access to clinical text.

It is very difficult to get access to such records. First, approval from the regional ethics review board is required, and then approval must be obtained from the hospital manager or clinic manager. It is then necessary to get an appointment with the database manager at the hospital, communicate with the database manager concerning what parts of the records you would like to obtain, manage to get the data out of the electronic patient records system in the right format, and then transfer the data in the right format to your research database or system. Thereafter you must determine that you have not missed getting some of the information from the source. Only then can you start to carry out experiments on the clinical text. It is also necessary to have access to infrastructure with encrypted safe servers to which no non-authorized person has access.

However, there are some early articles that have elaborated on future systems. For example, Gardner 1997, [15] described one such scenario for extracting essential information about the patient record, including symptom lists, problem descriptions, previous appointments, ICD-10 diagnosis codes and laboratory values, and structuring it in a simple menu for the physician to select from together with the physician's own keywords. These keywords would then be used for the information retrieval system to search part of or the entire Internet to answer the question as to what disease the patient has. This simple menu could also be used by the patient before and after the visit. A later article by Meystre et al. 2009, [29], elaborates on various applications and constitutes a good review of the area.

2.1 Clinical Corpora

There are some larger clinical databases or corpora available for research including the i2b2[2] clinical corpus consisting of approximately 1,000 notes in English, the CMC[3] corpus containing 2,216 patient records in English [34], the

---

[2] http://www.i2b2.org
[3] http://computationalmedicine.org/catalog

MIMIC[4] (De-id) corpus consisting of 1,934 discharge summaries and 412,509 nursing notes written in English [38], a Finnish clinical corpus[5] containing 2,800 sentences from nursing notes and finally the THIN[6] database, containing 11 million English patient records from general practices [27]. Another corpora, the Stockholm EPR Corpus is described in Dalianis et al. [9,10]. The Stockholm EPR Corpus contains over one million patients from over 500 clinical units at Karolinska University Hospital. The records encompass the period 2006-2013. The corpus is de-identified with regard to patient personal names and personal identity numbers. The personal identity number is replaced by a serial number so that the patient can be followed through the care process.

The Stockholm EPR Corpus contains both unstructured clinical text in Swedish and structured information. The unstructured text contains both physicians' notes and nurses' narratives as well as other notes about the patient from other professionals in the care process. The structured information includes gender and age of the patient, admission and discharge date and time, ICD-10 diagnosis codes, drugs, both the name and the ATC-code, blood values, laboratory values, etc.

2.2   Characteristics of Clinical Text

Research has been carried out on the Stockholm EPR Corpora for almost seven years. The first study was an overview of what type of data it contained and the characteristics of this data, and this information can be studied in more detail in Dalianis et al. [10], and in Allvin et al. [1]. The authors investigated and found that the clinical text contained a lot of spelling errors, non standard abbreviations but also incomplete sentences with missing subject, mainly the patient subject was not mentioned, see Figure 2.2 for an example in Swedish. The language was very telegraphic and sometimes very economical and implicit. As an example of the economy or aggregation of the text, see Figure 2.2. Dalianis [7], described these types of aggregation rules.

Medical terms have many different spelling variations; either the spelling is transcribed directly from Greek/Latin to Swedish or transcribed from English, German or French spelling of Greek/Latin words into Swedish. Usually Greek terms are used for diseases and symptoms while Latin terms are used for anatomical parts.

Swedish as well as German create compounds in a very productive manner that we can also see in clinical Swedish; one example from [10] is:

strålbehandlingsplaneringsdatortomografi
(radiation-treatment-planning-computer-tomography)

or

leverkirurgkonferens (conference for liver surgeons)

---

[4] http://www.physionet.org/physiotools/deid
[5] http://bionlp.utu.fi/clinicalcorpus.html
[6] http://www.ucl.ac.uk/pcph/research-groups-themes/thin-pub/database

Septisk pat, oklart fokus, rundodlas före Zinacef. (in Eng. Septic pat,
unclear origin, roundcultured before Zinacef)

which means:

Patienten har sepsis med oklart ursprung, bakterieodling tas från
samtliga möjliga infektionsfokus, inklusive blododling, innan behan-
dling med Zinacef inleds. (in Eng. The patient has sepsis of unclear
origin, bacterial culture samples taken from all possible foci for infec-
tion, including blood culture samples, before commencing treatment
with Zinacef.

Fig. 1. An example of aggregated clinical text. It has been rephrased so as not to contain any redundant information, and it presumes background knowledge of the reader. *The text example is courtesy of Dr. Maria Kvist.*

Beklagar nissförstånd rek ayt provar mindre smaker som innehåller
mindre Kolhydrater 8vilket pat benämner som smaken sött som di-
asip, komplett näring naturell samt provide x-tra tomat. Ut tar upp
dessa till avd för utprovning . Vi ska se vad vi kna göra med de
näringsdrycker som finns i hemmet då pat är åter hemma... (in Eng;
Sorry for the nisunderstanding rec tto try less flavours that contain
less Carbohydrates 8which pat name as taste sweet like diasip, com-
plete nutrition natural as well as provide x-tra tomato. Ut takes these
to clin for try out . Let's see what we cna do with the nutrition drinks
in the house when pat is back home...).

Fig. 2. Example of clinical text from [10]

The Stockholm EPR Corpus has been studied regarding the amount of abbreviations and it was found that around 10 percent of the clinical text contained abbreviations [23]. Patrick & Nguyen [33], found 1 percent abbreviations in English clinical text, and 3.2 percent acronyms.

Regarding misspellings, it was found that French clinical text contained around 10 percent misspelled words, see Ruch et al. [37], and in the Stockholm EPR Corpus there were 7.6 percent misspellings [31], while Patrick & Nguyen [33] found that English clinical text contained only 2 percent misspellings. According to Pakhomov et al. [32], there are 30 percent non-word tokens, abbreviations, acronyms, misspellings, wrongly used grammar, etc., in clinical text. This large difference can be due to the types of clinical text used for assessment, but it can also be due to the classification of spelling errors, abbreviations and acronyms.

Ehrentraut et al. [12], compared the amount of spelling errors in clinical text with that in standard text, and it was found that the 10 percent misspellings in clinical text is as high as in SMS messages. The normal spelling error rate is below 0.8 percent.

2.3 Reasoning in Clinical Text

When physicians reason about what diagnosis a patient has, they try to exclude what symptoms the patient does not have. Groopman [18], has explained these reasoning processes used by physicians. These processes are also found in the English BioScope clinical corpus, [50], where 13.6 percent of the clinical texts contain negations and 14.0 percent contain speculative keywords. In the Swedish Stockholm EPR Corpus, the area of assessment in various clinical units was studied and it was found that negated sentences or expressions comprised 13.5 percent of the texts [11].

In a study by Chapman et al. [3], more than half of the expressions in American radiology reports were found to contain negations. However, we believe that radiology reports contain more negations than ordinary patient records with both physician notes and nursing narratives. This is because physicians use more negations than nurses while reasoning about symptoms and diagnoses, while nurses write more about the daily status of the patient.

Diagnosing expressions used by physicians are very vague and are difficult for both a layman and a computer to understand. With that dilemma in mind, Velupillai [49], studied Swedish clinical text. She built a model with two polarities and three gradations: *Positive* and *Negative* along with the gradations *Certain, Probable* and *Possible* i.e. *Certainly Positive, Probably Positive, Possibly Positive, Possibly Negative, Probably Probable* and finally *Certainly Negative,* Velupillai assessed the model using annotation experiments and also carried out machine learning experiments to evaluate her results.

Considered together, misspelling, non standard abbreviations, incomplete sentences and speculative and negated sentences make the clinical text noisy and difficult to process. Therefore, we believe that to obtain good results in natural language processing or text mining of clinic text we need to normalize the text.

3   Normalization before Retrieval

In Figures 2.2 and 2.2 in the previous chapter we saw examples of the noisiness and the telegraphic style of the clinical texts. We believe it is necessary to normalize the text, i.e. to preprocess it by performing lemmatization and compound splitting of the words in the text, as well as to expand the abbreviations in the text. Together, these measures will make the text easier to process, both for parsing and tagging purposes but also for pure information retrieval leading to increased precision and recall.

According to Patrick & Nguyen [33], on the other hand, the normalization process means changing the text in a way so that a human finds it normal, while standardization means changing the text in a way that has been defined as standard by an expert community. Unfortunately, it is not that easy. Physicians find a clinical text normal if it contains familiar expressions, such as different types of jargon. Below we will define normalization as various ways to make the text better from the viewpoint of information retrieval.

3.1 ICD-10 Diagnosis Codes and SNOMED-CT Medical Terminology

In medicine there are two standard terminology systems: ICD-10 diagnosis codes and SNOMED-CT, which are available in several languages.

ICD-10 is the 10th revision of the International Statistical Classification of Diseases, and is available in the six official languages of the WHO (Arabic, Chinese, English, French, Russian and Spanish) as well as in 36 other languages, including Swedish. It contains 32 000 different diagnosis codes divided into 22 chapters or groups [53].

SNOMED-CT stands for Systematized Nomenclature of Medicine-Clinical Terms and is available in US English, UK English, Argentine Spanish, Danish and Swedish. Translations into French, Lithuanian, and several other languages underway, [22]. SNOMED-CT is a clinical hierarchical health care terminology containing medical terms and their relations as well as synonyms including over 320,000 terms. SNOMED-CT contains clinical findings (symptoms), disorders (diagnoses), procedures, body structures, organisms etc.

We can consider these terminologies as the new Greek and Latin of medicine, since when an ICD-10 diagnosis code is mentioned, for example *J12* everyone, regardless of their mother tongue, knows that *J12*, means the disease *pneumonia* even if we call it *lunginflammation* in Sweden. Likewise, if we look at SNOMED-CT we can identify disorder number *disorder number 53084003*, as the disease *pneumonia* expressed in English. However it is worth to mention that physicians still might interpret the ICD-10 codes different both intra-language wise and inter-language wise.

Both of these terminologies are used and can be used for cross language information retrieval but also as plain terminologies for various preprocessing steps. In the next sub-chapters we will show where these common terminologies has been used.

3.2 Stemming and Lemmatization

We can return to our definition of normalization and our proposed methods, stemming and lemmatization, for performing normalization.

Stemming is a technique that conflates a word to its stem. A stem does not to be the lemma or base form of the word; two different but very closely related words can be stemmed to one stem. For example, *hospital* and *hospitalisation* might be stemmed to the same stem, namely *hospital.*

Lemmatization is a technique that makes a complete morphological analysis of a word and also produces the base form of the word. It is considerably more expensive, in terms of time and effort, to develop a well performing lemmatizer than to develop a well performing stemmer. It is also more expensive, in terms of computational power and run time, to use a lemmatizer than to use a stemmer. The reason for this is that the stemmer can use ad-hoc suffix and prefix stripping rules and exception lists while the lemmatizer must do a complete morphological analysis.

Another important point is that a stemmer can deliberately "bring together" semantically related words belonging to different word classes to the same stem, which a lemmatizer cannot do.

One standard method for information retrieval is stemming or lemmatization of the words in the document collection before being indexed, but also of the queries being matched to the index. However, this standard method does not work for carrying out a phrase search, since then the phrase will not match the stemmed word in the index. One way of solving this problem is also to store the fullform word in case a phrase search is going to be used.

For highly inflective (non-English) languages such as Swedish, German, Polish, etc., better precision and recall can be obtained when retrieving documents if the documents and the search queries have been stemmed beforehand [2,24]. Several other studies also show this.

3.3   Compound Splitting

Swedish, German, Dutch and Finnish creates compounds in a creative way. We also know that compound splitting in these languages improves precision and recall in an information retrieval setting. For example, Tomlinson [48], showed that a compound splitter/decompounder gave good results in increasing precision and recall for Finnish and German but gave decreased precision and recall for other languages, Spanish, Dutch, French, Italian, Swedish and English. However, stemming and compound splitting were used in an other experiment where the authors obtained 14 percent higher precision for Dutch, 37 percent higher precision for German and 30 percent higher precision for Swedish and Finnish respectively [5].

We also know that compounds are an obstacle for Swedes, who tend to search Swedish in an English non compounding manner, writing search terms in de-compounded form.

An example on the Swedish public medical website Vårdguiden, is when some-one is searching for *diabetespatient* and obtains no hits. The system then tries to split the compound word into *diabetes patient* and the resulting hit becomes *patienter med diabetes* (patients with diabetes). Notice that the stemmer will make it possible to automatically find the word patienter (plural form of pa-tients). The other situation is when the user uses two search words *streptokock infektion* and does not obtain any hit then the system can propose the compound *streptokockinfektioner* (plural form) that gives several relevant hits. Therefore it is necessary to carry out word splitting before indexing the document, or some-times to perform word compounding of the search term [8].

Clinical text uses a many words of Greek and Latin origin. Compounds will therefore use morphology and stems based on Greek and Latin origin. Conse-quently standard compound splitters will therefore be delimited for clinical text. In an experiment using a state of the art compound splitter for Swedish applied to 200 highly frequent compounds from a Swedish clinical text the authors ob-tained up to 80 percent accuracy, precision and recall. Most of the errors were due to the medical terminology [13].

To construct compound splitters they need to be adapted for clinical text. One way to do this would be to follow the study by Schulz and Hahn [39] on the different variants of German compounds and adapt it for Swedish clinical text and then implement it.

3.4 Spell Checking

Regarding spell checking during information retrieval it is well known that search queries are misspelled. Dalianis [6], reported 10 percent spelling errors in a public search engine at the Swedish tax authorities. Wang et al. [52], reported more than 26 percent spelling errors in an academic search engine. Dalianis also shows that 90 percent of the misspelled search queries can be corrected before matching the index for retrieval.

According to Kukich [25], the four edit error types (also called Damerau–Levenshtein distance); insertion, deletion, substitution and transposition, that encompass 80 percent of all spelling errors; therefore, connecting a spell checker with a search engine will assist the searcher a great deal. Normally, spell checkers use string matching techniques to a specific dictionary. In a search engine the spell checker uses the index as a lexicon. Otherwise it might propose words that are not in the index, and therefore not searchable, and of course not useful in a search situation. Edit-distance is the number of insertions, deletions, substitutions and transpositions needed to make a new spelling suggestion. A good spelling suggestion is one that needs a short edit-distance, and it is also one that proposes a word that is frequent on the web site.

Patrick & Nguyen [33], used SNOMED-CT for English as the dictionary for performing proof reading of clinical text. The coded content increased by 15 percent after the automatic correction process and the number of unique codes increased by 4.7 percent However, they do not report the number of spelling errors in the text.

In a rule based approach to match Swedish SNOMED-CT terms to a Swedish clinical text it was found that spelling correction using Levenshtein distance improved the recall slightly [41]. In a machine learning experiment using CRF++ in retrieving symptoms, diagnosis, body parts and drugs in Swedish clinical text Skeppstedt [42], observed that compound splitting had a large effect on retrieving symptoms and increasing recall without diminishing precision. The compound splitter that was used utilized textual descriptions from both the Swedish ICD-10 diagnosis code and from the Swedish SNOMED-CT terminology as well as from the Swedish MESH (Medical Subject Headings) and Swedish FASS (list of all drugs in Swedish) and the Parole Dictionary of General Swedish [42].

When comparing rule based and machine learning-based retrieval of clinical entities the best results were obtained using the machine learning based system with an over 80 percent F-score in finding the above entities. Wong & Glance [54], described a very effective normalization process where the system corrects spelling, and expands abbreviations and acronyms. When evaluated the system obtained an accuracy of 88.73 percent.

3.5   Negation

In the previous sub-chapter 2.3, we have described the uncertain and speculative text physicians produce while reasoning about the disorder of a patient has before deciding which disorder it is.

When retrieving symptoms and diagnoses and not wanting to obtain hits on negated symptoms and diagnoses as for example *no cough* or *no fever*, NegEx can be used, [4]; it can distinguish between affirmed and non-affirmed symptoms and diagnoses expressed in English.

NegEx uses a trigger list containing three different types of negations, post-negations, pre-negations and pseudo-negations. NegEx also uses a list of findings and disorders that it matches in the text and calculates the distance to the negation in the sentence. Skeppstedt [40], has adapted the rule based NegEx to Swedish and has obtained slightly poorer results than for the English version. The English version obtained a precision of 84.5 percent and a recall of 82.4 percent when applied to English discharge summaries, while the Swedish adaption of NegEx obtained a precision of 75.2 per cent and a recall of 81.9 percent.

4   Some Applications

There is a spectrum of applications within clinical text mining, from spelling and grammar correction, to named entity recognition, such as de-identification, clinical entity recognition, and classification of patient records, to information retrieval of individual patient records.

First of all a spelling and grammar checking system or proof reading system would be very valuable. In sub chapter 2.2 we reported the large amount of spelling errors contained in clinical text.

Until now, little has been done in the area of clinical proof reading. This is probably because of the difficulty in getting hold of textual data in order to develop such tools due to the sensitivity of patient records. It can also be due to the low demand on the part of users for development of such tools.

4.1   Information Retrieval from Electronic Patient Records

There have been a number of shared tasks within clinical text mining, for example the TREC 2013 Medical Record Track and then the ShARe/CLEF eHealth Evaluation Lab 2014. Basically all shared tasks using electronic patients records need de-identified records and special care when sharing the texts among the teams that are going to compete, due to sensitivity of the records.

In TREC 2013 the task was to retrieve a specific topic from 50 possible topics. The 50 topics contained in total 17,264 patient records each corresponding to a patient visit. All participants had to perform some sort of normalization of the clinical text to make the noisy clinical text less noisy. The participants also used the ICD-9[7], to retrieve the topics. Problems with negated findings and disorders were also reported [51],

---

[7] ICD-9 diagnosis code is used in the U.S., and is an earlier revision of ICD-10.

ShARe/CLEF eHealth Evaluation encompassed three tasks, all regarding clinical text in English. The first task was the identification and normalization of disorders by mapping them to SNOMED-CT, the second task was to expand abbreviation and acronyms and the third task was more of a traditional Q&A task for patients, but for clinical reports [47].

4.2 Patient-Adapted Text Simplification of Patient Records

The Swedish Government has prioritized the patient's right to have access to his/her patient records. In some county councils in Sweden today, individual patient records are therefore available for the patient to read on the Internet. Kvist & Velupillai [26], described their initial analysis of Swedish radiology reports, where a few categories such as body parts, findings, procedures, and administrative information can be translated to layman vocabulary. Other approaches to letting patients read their records have been carried out in the U.S.

Polepalli et al [35], described an experiment where the patient record was enhanced with popup information explaining difficult concepts, and it was found that the NoteAid system improved comprehension of patient records for lay people by 23 to 40 percent.

A qualified guess is that the clinicians, physicians and nurses will demand spelling and grammar tools since they know that the patient records they are authoring will be spread to a wider audience, but also that patients will require different support tools to understand the patient record.

4.3 De-Identification of Patient Records

Since the clinical texts are sensitive and contain information that can reveal a patient's identity, there has been a great demand to anonymize patient records. An important research area is therefore the de-identification of patient records. First, identification of sensitive information about the patient must take place. After the information is identified, it is either removed, *de-identified*, or the sensitive information is replaced with fake or surrogate information, *pseudonymized*, so that the patient records can be used for research purposes.

The HIPAA (Health Insurance Portability and Accountability Act) is a framework defined by the U.S. Department of Health and Human Services stipulating which sets of classes need to be de-identified in patient records to make them safe or non sensitive for use by researchers. The HIPAA classes are used in different variants by different researchers. Examples on the classes are *personal names, addresses, phone numbers, hospital names*, etc. All together there are 18 different classes [20].

There are both rule-based (hand-crafted) and machine learning-based de-identifications systems, and the best de-identification systems obtain a precision, recall and F-score of at least of 96 percent. Nevertheless, it is still necessary to read the patient record manually to ensure that no sensitive information remains.

Meystre et al. [28] have published a good overview of different de-identification systems. However, there has been some debate concerning the value of using pseudonymized records for developing natural language processing tools, since the text and semantics have been distorted. The HIPAA has become a de facto standard, and is used by many different research groups outside the U.S. in an adapted form based on specific needs.

4.4   ICD-10 Diagnosis Code Assignment and Validation

The ICD-10 is a diagnostic coding system that is used to classify diseases. There are around 35,000 ICD-10 codes distributed in 22 different chapters. The ICD-10 codes have been translated and used in several languages throughout the world, [53]. In an investigation carried out by the National Board of Health and Welfare (Socialstyrelsen) in Sweden, 4,200 patient records and their ICD-10 coding were reviewed, and the Board found that the percentage of errors in the main diagnoses was 20 percent [44]. In another investigation the National Board of Health and Welfare found that 1.2 percent of main diagnoses were missing in 1.5 million patient records [45].

Several systems have been developed that automatically assign ICD-10 codes to diagnosis text, see Stanfill et al. [46], for a good overview. The best performing systems obtain F-scores of around 90 percent.

For an interesting approach using a variant of latent semantic indexing called random indexing to retrieve ICD-10 diagnosis codes, see [19], where an approximate 82 percent match is reported within the rheumatology domain.

Care episode: discharge – admission > 48 hours

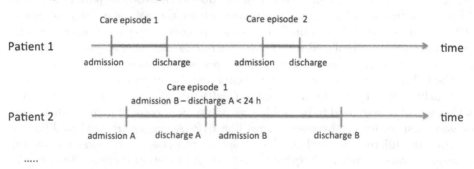

Fig. 3. If a patient (Patient 2) is discharged from one clinical unit and admitted to another within 24 hours and the whole period is more than 48 hours then that patient considered to be admitted for whole care episode and can therefore be analyzed for HAI. The figure is a courtesy of Mr. Hideyuki Tanushi.

4.5   Detection of Hospital Acquired or Nosocomical Infections

An important area is detection, measurement and prediction (early warnings) of hospital acquired infections (HAI), or nosocomial infections, sometimes also called healthcare-associated infections. These infections can include pneumonia, urinary tract infection, sepsis and various wound infections. Around 10 percent of all patients who are admitted and treated as inpatients at hospitals may acquire an infection due to the treatment [21]. Included in the definition of an HAI is that the patient must have been admitted to the hospital for more than 48 hours before an infection can be defined as an HAI. The patient can be admitted and discharged and re-admitted within 24 hours to another ward as long as the patient has a more than 48-hour care episode at the hospital. See also Figure 3.

When a hospital acquired infection occurs, by law it must be reported. However, HAIs are greatly underreported. To solve this problem the National Board of Health and Welfare in Sweden requires that all caregivers report how many inpatients in each clinic have HAIs during one particular day. These measurements are carried out twice a year and are called Point Prevalence Measurements, PPM. In this way the authorities can at least get a clue regarding the level of HAIs. Since PPM is only performed twice a year and unfortunately does not give the whole picture, hospital management would like to have continuous measurements. For example, documentation of how many patients get HAIs each moment 24 hours per day on each ward, clinic and hospital. If specific measures or routines are carried out to avoid HAIs, then it would be of value to have feedback on their effect on HAIs.

Generally speaking, the HAI detection systems investigate the clinical text for *infection specific terms* that may indicate an HAI, for use of specific antibiotics for treating HAI infections, for microbiological results containing typical HAI bacteria, and for elevated body temperatures. Risk-prone patients are also patients with catheters and patients who have been newly operated on, and patients with open wounds.

There have been a number of approaches for detecting HAIs, both rule-based (hand-crafted) and machine learning-based, using both microbiological results and the clinical text. The best systems have reached up to 97 percent precision and recall. Freeman et al. [14], have done an extensive overview of the different systems.

Proux et al, [36], describe a French rule based detection system, while Ehrentraut et al. [12], describe a Swedish machine learning system Detect-HAI. See Figure 4.5 for input to the Detect-HAI system.

4.6   GTT, the Global Trigger Tool

The Global Trigger Tool is a manual method for reviewing patient records to find adverse events. The reviewer is only allowed to use 20 minutes per patient record. Usually the initial reviewers are clinicians such as physicians and nurses who perform a first scan of the patient records to find patients with risks for adverse events. Thereafter a second review is carried out by a physician who assesses whether that particular patient record describes a patient with an HAI [17].

```
123 H - IVA 322916614D 2007-08-21 9:12 1944 Woman
Anamnesis
Got a urine catheter two days ago. Done a lab test
on the urine and gave antibiotics.
<ICD-10 code>
I110 Pneumonia.
I509 Heart failure, unspecified.

<Current medication>
Penomax

<Body temperature>
38
38
38.5

123 H - IVA 322916614D 2007-08-22 16:12 1944 Woman
<Body temperature>
37
36.8
36.9

<Blood culture>
pseudomonas
```

Fig. 4. An example of an electronic patient record text translated to English. The text is in a format prepared for processing by a computer program for detecting HAIs. The important features are extracted from the patient record and the program can check the status of the patient day by day. This particular patient got an HAI.

The method has been developed in Sweden and is today called *markörbaserad journalgranskning*, (in English: marker-based patient record review). The instructions contain seven groups of markers of adverse events with over 44 different markers (previously called triggers) [43]. The method has been further developed and is now semi-automatic. The first step, finding patients with risks for HAI, is carried out by a module that has been trained using previous manual extracts.

The semi-automatic method has been implemented both in Sweden and Denmark by the SAS Institute. In the Danish approach, 500 manually reviewed patient records were used as input to an SAS NLP preprocessing and Text Mining system and they obtained a precision of 56 percent and a recall of 70 percent in correctly identifying risks for pressure ulcers (all grades). These percentages were calculated, based on the data in [16], by the authors of this article. After the first step, the clinicians have to decide which records contain patients who have acquired HAIs.

5   Conclusion and Future Research

Our conclusions are that clinical text is noisy and difficult to process and that standard information retrieval technology cannot be used to retrieve information from clinical text. Clinical text needs to be preprocessed using the above-described preprocessing tools, spelling checking, abbreviation expansions, lemmatizers, compound splitters, negation detection, and diagnosis assertion classification, to make the clinical text more information retrieval friendly, or in other words to normalize it.

Many of these tools can make use of ICD-10 diagnosis codes and SNOMED-CT terminologies. These terminologies can be used both in the cross-language and the cross health care domains. Use in the cross-language domain means using the terminologies as a resource for employing technology developed for one language in the other language. Use in the cross health care domain means that we can apply the terminologies as a support when moving between domains in the clinical setting. For example, when moving from an intensive care unit to a heart clinic or rheumatology clinic using a unified terminology. Matching by using terminologies and other natural language processing and text mining tools makes it possible to perform high quality clinical entity recognition that, together with the structured fields of the patient records, make it possible to make faceted searches.

We anticipate that in the future, electronic patient record systems will contain spelling and possibly also grammar checking, but also automatic proposals of ICD-10 diagnosis codes for the discharge letter module. We also believe that each electronic patient record system will contain an information retrieval engine that can extract the most important symptoms and diagnoses from the record, but also the drugs used and the microbiological tests performed, and present them for the physician so he or she can get an overview of each individual patient. In addition, we can also foresee translation tools that describe the patient record in a way patient laymen will understand.

Acknowledgments. I would like to thank the members from the Clinical Text Mining group at the Department of Computer and Systems Sciences, Stockholm University: Martin Duneld, Claudia Ehrentraut, Aron Henriksson, Maria Kvist, Gunnar Nilsson, Maria Skeppstedt, Hideyuki Tanushi, Sumithra Velupillai for inspiring ideas, discussions and fantastic joint research work.

I would also like to thank the Karolinska University Hospital and specifically Ann-Britt Bolin Wiechel, Elda Sparrelid and Bo Wikström for giving us access to the Stockholm Electronic Patient Record (EPR) Corpus that has been crucial for our research. I would also like to thank Gunnar Ekeving at Karolinska University Hospital for invaluable data extraction assistance.

For funding I would like to thank VINNOVA (Swedish Governmental Agency for Innovation Systems), Nordforsk (part of Nordic Council of Ministers) and SSF (Swedish Foundation for Strategic Research).

References

1. Allvin, H., Carlsson, E., Dalianis, H., Danielsson-Ojala, R., Daudaravicius, V., Hassel, M., Kokkinakis, D., Lundgrén-Laine, H., Nilsson, G.H., Nytrø, Ø., Sanna, S., Hanna, S., Sumithra, V.: Characteristics of Finnish and Swedish intensive care nursing narratives: A comparative analysis to support the development of clinical language technologies. Journal of Biomedical Semantics 2(suppl. 3), 1–11 (2011)
2. Carlberger, J., Dalianis, H., Hassel, M., Knutsson, O.: Improving precision in information retrieval for Swedish using stemming. In: Proceedings of NODALIDA 2001 - 13th Nordic Conference on Computational Linguistics (2001)
3. Chapman, W.W., Bridewell, W., Hanbury, P., Cooper, G.F., Buchanan, B.G.: Evaluation of negation phrases in narrative clinical reports. In: Proceedings of the AMIA Symposium, p. 105. American Medical Informatics Association (2001)
4. Chapman, W.W., Bridewell, W., Hanbury, P., Cooper, G.F., Buchanan, B.G.: A simple algorithm for identifying negated findings and diseases in discharge summaries. Journal of Biomedical Informatics 34(5), 301–310 (2001)
5. Chen, A., Gey, F.C.: Combining query translation and document translation in cross-language retrieval. In: Peters, C., Gonzalo, J., Braschler, M., Kluck, M. (eds.) CLEF 2003. LNCS, vol. 3237, pp. 108–121. Springer, Heidelberg (2004)
6. Dalianis, H.: Evaluating a spelling support in a search engine. In: Andersson, B., Bergholtz, M., Johannesson, P. (eds.) NLDB 2002. LNCS, vol. 2253, pp. 183–190. Springer, Heidelberg (2002)
7. Dalianis, H.: Aggregation in natural language generation. Computational Intelligence 15(4), 384–414 (1999)
8. Dalianis, H.: Improving search engine retrieval using a compound splitter for Swedish. In: Proceedings of the 15th Nordic Conference of Computational Linguistics, Joensuu, Finland, University of Joensuu, pp. 38–42. Citeseer (2005)
9. Dalianis, H., Hassel, M., Henriksson, A., Skeppstedt, M.: Stockholm EPR Corpus: A clinical database used to improve health care. In: Swedish Language Technology Conference, pp. 17–18 (2012)
10. Dalianis, H., Hassel, M., Velupillai, S.: The Stockholm EPR Corpus-Characteristics and Some Initial Findings. In: Proceedings of ISHIMR 2009, Evaluation and Implementation of e-Health and Health Information Initiatives: International Perspectives, 14th International Symposium for Health Information Management Research, pp. 243–249 (2009)
11. Dalianis, H., Skeppstedt, M.: Creating and evaluating a consensus for negated and speculative words in a Swedish clinical corpus. In: Proceedings of the Workshop on Negation and Speculation in Natural Language Processing, pp. 5–13. Association for Computational Linguistics (2010)
12. Ehrentraut, C., Tanushi, H., Tiedemann, J., Dalianis, H.: Detection of hospital acquired infections in sparse and noisy Swedish patient records. In: Proceedings of the Sixth Workshop on Analytics for Noisy Unstructured Text Data (AND 2012) held in conjunction with Coling 2012, Bombay (2012)
13. Falck, L., Samadi, O.: Compound splitting of Swedish medical words - An evaluation of the Compound Splitter software. Scientific course report, Stockholm University (2012), http://dsv.su.se/health/Falck_Samadi_Compound_splitting.pdf
14. Freeman, R., Moore, L.S.P., Álvarez, L.G., Charlett, A., Holmes, A.: Advances in electronic surveillance for healthcare-associated infections in the 21st century: A systematic review. Journal of Hospital Infection (2013)

15. Gardner, M.: Information retrieval for patient care. BMJ 314(7085), 950 (1997)
16. Gerdes, L.U., Hardahl, C.: Text mining electronic health records to identify hospital adverse events. Studies in Health Technology and Informatics 192, 1145–1145 (2012)
17. Griffin, F.A., Resar, R.K.: IHI global trigger tool for measuring adverse events. IHI Innovation Series White Paper (2009)
18. Groopman, J.E.: How doctors think. Houghton Mifflin Company, New York (2007)
19. Henriksson, A., Hassel, M.: Optimizing the dimensionality of clinical term spaces for improved diagnosis coding support. In: Proceedings of Louhi 2013 4th International Workshop on Health Document Text Mining and Information Analysis (2013)
20. HIPAA Health Insurance Portability and Accountability (HIPAA): U.S. Department of Health and Human Services (2003), http://www.cdc.gov/mmwr/preview/mmwrhtml/m2e411a1.htm
21. Humphreys, H., Smyth, E.T.: Prevalence surveys of healthcare-associated infections: what do they tell us, if anything? Clinical Microbiology and Infection 12(1), 2–4 (2006)
22. IHTSDO: SNOMED-CT, Systematized Nomenclature of Medicine-Clinical Terms, http://www.ihtsdo.org/snomed-ct/ (accessed April 09, 2014)
23. Isenius, N., Velupillai, S., Kvist, M.: Initial results in the development of SCAN. a Swedish clinical abbreviation normalizer. In: CLEFeHealth 2012 Workshop on Cross-Language Evaluation of Methods, Applications, and Resources for eHealth Document Analysis, Rome (2012)
24. Jongejan, B., Dalianis, H.: Automatic training of lemmatization rules that handle morphological changes in pre-, in- and suffixes alike. In: Proceedings of the 47th Annual Meeting of the ACL and the 4th IJCNLP of the AFNLP, pp. 145–153 (2009)
25. Kukich, K.: Techniques for automatically correcting words in text. ACM Computing Surveys (CSUR) 24(4), 377–439 (1992)
26. Kvist, M., Velupillai, S.: Professional language in swedish radiology reports–characterization for patient-adapted text simplification. In: Scandinavian Conference on Health Informatics 2013. Linköping University Electronic Press (2013)
27. Lewis, J.D., Schinnar, R., Bilker, W.B., Wang, X., Strom, B.L.: Validation studies of the health improvement network (thin) database for pharmacoepidemiology research. Pharmacoepidemiology and Drug Safety 16(4), 393–401 (2007)
28. Meystre, S., Friedlin, F., South, B., Shen, S., Samore, M.: Automatic de-identification of textual documents in the electronic health record: A review of recent research. BMC Medical Research Methodology 10(1), 70 (2010)
29. Meystre, S.M., Savova, G.K., Kipper-Schuler, K.C., Hurdle, J.F.: Extracting information from textual documents in the electronic health record: A review of recent research. Yearb Med. Inform. 35, 128–144 (2008)
30. Nilsson, I.: Medicinsk dokumentation genom tiderna: En studie av den svenska patientjournalens utveckling under 1700-talet, 1800-talet och 1900-talet. Enheten för medicinens historia, Medicinska fakulteten, Lunds universitet (2007) (in Swedish)
31. Nizamuddin, N., Dalianis, H.: Detection of spelling errors in Swedish clinical text (submitted, 2014)
32. Pakhomov, S., Pedersen, T., Chute, C.G.: Abbreviation and acronym disambiguation in clinical discourse. In: AMIA Annual Symposium Proceedings, vol. 2005, p. 589. American Medical Informatics Association (2005)

33. Patrick, J., Nguyen, D.: Automated proof reading of clinical notes. In: PACLIC, 25th Pacific Asia Conference on Language, Information and Computation, pp. 303–312 (2011)
34. Pestian, J.P., Brew, C., Matykiewicz, P., Hovermale, D., Johnson, N., Cohen, K.B., Duch, W.: A shared task involving multi-label classification of clinical free text. In: Proceedings of the Workshop on BioNLP 2007: Biological, Translational, and Clinical Language Processing, pp. 97–104. Association for Computational Linguistics (2007)
35. Polepalli, R.B., Houston, T., Brandt, C., Fang, H., Yu, H.: Improving patients' electronic health record comprehension with noteaid. Studies in Health Technology and Informatics 192, 714–718 (2012)
36. Proux, D., Hagège, C., et al.: Architecture and systems for monitoring hospital acquired infections inside a hospital information workflow. In: Proceedings of the Workshop on Biomedical Natural Language Processing, pp. 43–48 (2011)
37. Ruch, P., Baud, R., Geissbühler, A.: Using lexical disambiguation and named-entity recognition to improve spelling correction in the electronic patient record. Artificial Intelligence in Medicine 29(1), 169–184 (2003)
38. Saeed, M., Villarroel, M., Reisner, A.T., Clifford, G., Lehman, L.W., Moody, G., Heldt, T., Kyaw, T.H., Moody, B., Mark, R.G.: Multiparameter intelligent monitoring in intensive care ii (mimic-ii): A public-access intensive care unit database. Critical Care Medicine 39(5), 952 (2011)
39. Schulz, S., Hahn, U.: Morpheme-based, cross-lingual indexing for medical document retrieval. International Journal of Medical Informatics 58, 87–99 (2000)
40. Skeppstedt, M.: Negation detection in Swedish clinical text: An adaption of NegEx to Swedish. Journal of Biomedical Semantics 2(suppl. 3), S3 (2011)
41. Skeppstedt, M., Kvist, M., Dalianis, H.: Rule-based entity recognition and coverage of SNOMED CT in Swedish clinical text. In: Proceedings of the Eighth International Conference on Language Resources and Evaluation, LREC 2012, pp. 1250–1257 (2012)
42. Skeppstedt, M., Kvist, M., Nilsson, G., Dalianis, H.: Automatic recognition of disorders, findings, pharmaceuticals and body structures from clinical text: An annotation and machine learning study. Journal of Biomedical Informatics 49, 148–158 (2014)
43. SKL: Sveriges Kommuner och Landsting, Swedish Association of Local Authorities and Regions (SALAR), Markörbaserad journalgranskning för att identifiera och mäta skador i vården (2012), http://webbutik.skl.se/bilder/artiklar/pdf/7164-847-1.pdf (in Swedish)
44. Socialstyrelsen: The National Board of Health and Welfare, Diagnosgranskningar utförda i Sverige 1997-2005 samt råd inför granskning (2006), http://www.socialstyrelsen.se/Lists/Artikelkatalog/Attachments/9740/2006-131-30_200613131.pdf (in Swedish)
45. Socialstyrelsen: The National Board of Health and Welfare, Kodningskvalitet i patientregistret, Slutenvård 2008 (2010), http://www.socialstyrelsen.se/Lists/Artikelkatalog/Attachments/18082/2010-6-27.pdf (in Swedish)
46. Stanfill, M.H., Williams, M., Fenton, S.H., Jenders, R.A., Hersh, W.R.: A systematic literature review of automated clinical coding and classification systems. J. Am. Med. Inform. Assoc. 17, 646–651 (2010)
47. Suominen, H., et al.: Overview of the ShARe/CLEF eHealth Evaluation Lab 2013. In: Forner, P., Müller, H., Paredes, R., Rosso, P., Stein, B. (eds.) CLEF 2013. LNCS, vol. 8138, pp. 212–231. Springer, Heidelberg (2013)

48. Tomlinson, S.: Experiments in 8 European languages with Hummingbird Search-serverTM at CLEF 2002. In: Advances in Cross-Language Information Retrieval, pp. 242–256. Springer (2003)

49. Velupillai, S.: Shades of Certainty: Annotation and Classification of Swedish Medical Records. Ph.D. thesis, Stockholm University (2012)

50. Vincze, V., Szarvas, G., Farkas, R., Móra, G., Csirik, J.: The BioScope Corpus: Biomedical texts annotated for uncertainty, negation and their scopes. BMC Bioinformatics 9(suppl. 11), S9 (2008)

51. Voorhees, E., Tong, R.: Overview of the TREC 2011 medical records track. In: Proc. of TREC (2011)

52. Wang, P., Berry, M.W., Yang, Y.: Mining longitudinal web queries: Trends and patterns. Journal of the American Society for Information Science and Technology 54(8), 743–758 (2003)

53. WHO: International Classification of Diseases (ICD), http://www.who.int/classifications/icd/en/ (accessed April 09, 2014)

54. Wong, W., Glance, D.: Statistical semantic and clinician confidence analysis for real-time clinical progress note cleaning. Artificial Intelligence in Medicine 53, 171–180 (2011)

Exploratory Professional Search through Semantic Post-Analysis of Search Results

Pavlos Fafalios and Yannis Tzitzikas

Institute of Computer Science, FORTH-ICS,
and Computer Science Department, University of Crete, Greece
{fafalios,tzitzik}@ics.forth.gr

Abstract. Professional Search is usually a recall-oriented problem. For
helping the user to get efficiently a concise overview, to quickly restrict
the search space and to make sense of the results, in this article we present
an exploratory strategy for professional search that is based on semantic
post-analysis of the classical search results (of keyword based queries).
The described strategy can exploit the metadata that are already available, as well as the results of textual clustering and entity mining that
can be performed at query time. The outcome of this process (i.e. metadata, clusters and entities grouped in categories) complement the ranked
list of results produced from the core search engine with useful information for the user. This extra information is useful not only for providing
a concise overview of the search results, but also for supporting a faceted
and session-based interaction scheme that allows the users to restrict
their focus gradually and to explore other related information. To tackle
the corresponding configuration requirements of this process, we show
how one can exploit the (constantly evolving) Linked Data for specifying
the entities of interest and for providing further information about the
identified entities. In this article, apart from detailing the steps of this
process, we present applications of this approach in the *marine* domain
and in the domain of *patent* search.

Keywords: exploratory search, professional search, entity mining and
exploration, linked data, faceted search.

1 Introduction

In professional search (e.g. medical search, patent search, bibliography search),
it is often unacceptable to miss relevant documents, therefore the retrieval (and
inspection) of nearly all relevant documents is sometimes necessary. In that context, the grouping of the numerous search results through *facets* that correspond
to various kinds of *metadata* or *extracted entities* can help the user to get efficiently a concise overview, to quickly restrict the search space, and to make
better sense of the results. Moreover, the integration of unstructured documents
that usually appear in the search results, with the emerging Web of Data can
bring significant benefits and is nowadays a challenging vision.

In this chapter, we describe a search process for recall-oriented information
needs (i.e. focusing on retrieving as much as possible relevant documents) that

G. Paltoglou et al. (Eds.): Professional Search in the Modern World, LNCS 8830, pp. 166–192, 2014.
© Springer International Publishing Switzerland 2014

is based on post-processing of the search results. It can also be considered as an integration approach that takes place during *searching* and aims at enriching the responses of non-semantic professional search systems with semantic information. Specifically, we analyze an exploratory search process which combines the following methods:

- Exploitation of the static metadata of the (top) search results
- Textual Clustering of the (top) search results
- Named Entity Extraction in the (top) search results
- Semantic enrichment and exploration of the identified entities using external (online) Knowledge Bases (KB), i.e. Linked Data.
- Session-based interactive exploration of the above information

The results of this process (metadata, clusters and entities grouped in categories) complement the query answers with useful information for the user which is further exploited in a faceted and long session interaction scheme that allows users to restrict their focus gradually as their information need is better defined[1]. This is important because a high percentage of search tasks are *exploratory* and focalized search very commonly leads to inadequate interactions and poor results [58,42]. This interaction scheme can also save a lot of time in professional searches as it allows locating very quickly hits which are low ranked.

We could say that the issue of *integrated professional search systems* is addressed from two perspectives. From an *information integration* perspective, we can say that entity names are used as the "glue" for automatically connecting documents with data (and knowledge). This approach does not require designing or deciding on an integrated schema/view (e.g. [55]), nor mappings between concepts as in KBs (e.g. [54,33]), or mappings in the form of queries as in the case of databases (e.g. [32]). Entities can be identified in documents, data, database cells, metadata attributes and KBs.

From an *information seeking* process perspective we present the tight integration of different search tools for a) faceted search using existing metadata, b) entity extraction and c) textual clustering, with the main retrieval engine which produces ranked lists of documents in response to a query. This integration allows different search interfaces to coexist in an information seeker's search system.

Correlation to the MUMIA Cost Action. Part of the work in this chapter has been done in the context of MUMIA Cost Action[2]. Specifically, the Working Group 4 *(Semantic Search, Faceted Search and Visualization)* has the objective to identify and critically review the aspects of next generation search related to Semantic and Faceted search, as well as to study visualization techniques that can be applied as multiplying "gain" factor to both types of search. In

---

[1] Faceted search is a technique for accessing information organized according to an analytic-synthetic classification scheme, allowing users to explore a collection of information by applying multiple filters [49].

[2] http://www.mumia-network.eu/

this chapter, we present an approach for *semantic search* which is based on the post-analysis (by performing entity mining at query-time) of the results of a professional search system. In addition, we show how the result of the above process, as well as the result of textual clustering and of metadata-based grouping, can be integrated and exploited in a *faceted interaction scheme*. In a nutshell, and in correspondence to the objective of this Working Group, this chapter proposes a generic model of how Semantic and Faceted Search can be applied in next generation professional search.

The rest of this chapter is organized as follows: Section 2 describes in detail the post-analysis process. Section 3 analyzes the interaction model that can support this functionality. Section 4 reports experimental results regarding effectiveness and efficiency, ways of improving the efficiency of the proposed approaches and limitations that arise when exploiting online KBs. Section 5 presents two application examples that demonstrate how this process can be applied in the *marine* domain as well as in the domain of *patent* search. Finally, Section 6 concludes and identifies directions for future research.

2   Post-Analysis of Search Results

This section first presents the motivation, the context, some related works, and the steps of the overall process. Then, it describes the main post-analysis functions (metadata-based grouping, textual clustering, entity mining) and discusses issues of ranking and connectivity that arise in such context.

2.1   Motivation

The *analysis of search results* is a useful feature as it has been shown by several user studies. For instance, the results in [36] show that categorizing the search results improves the search speed and increases the accuracy of the selected results. A user study [35] shows that categories are successfully used as part of users' search habits. Specifically, users are able to access results that are located far in the rank order list and formulate simpler queries in order to find the needed results. In addition, the categories are beneficial when more than one result is needed like in an *exploratory* or *undirected search* task. According to [40] and [59], recall-oriented information can play an important role not only in understanding an information space, but also in helping users select promising sub-topics for further exploration.

Recognizing entities and grouping hits with respect to entities is not only useful to public web search, but is also particularly useful in *professional search* that is, search in the workplace, e.g. in industrial research and development [38]. A user study [47] indicated that categorizing dynamically the results of a search process in a *medical* search system provides an organization of the results that is clearer, easier to use, more precise, and in general more helpful than simple relevance ranking. As another example, in professional *patent search*, in many cases one has to look beyond keywords to find and analyse patents based on a more sophisticated understanding of the patent's content and meaning [34]. We should also stress that professional search sometimes requires a long time. For instance, in the domain of patent search, the persons working in patent offices spend days for a particular patent search request. The same happens in bibliographic and medical search.

Technologies such as entity identification and analysis could become a significant aid to such searches and can be seen, together with other text analysis technologies, as becoming the cutting edge of information retrieval science [15]. Analogous results have been reported for search over collections of *structured* artifacts, e.g. ontologies. For instance, [8] showed that making explicit the relationships between ontologies and using them to structure (or categorize) the results of a Semantic Web Search Engine led to a more efficient ontology search process.

Finally, the usefulness of the various analysis services (over search results) is subject of current research, e.g. [19] comparatively evaluates *clustering* versus *diversification* services.

2.2   Context and Related Works

The idea of enriching the classical *query-and-response* process of current Web search engines, with *static* and *dynamic* metadata for supporting *exploratory search* was proposed in [45] and it is described in more detail (enriched with the results of a user-based evaluation) in [44]. In that work the notion of *dynamic metadata* refers to the outcome of *results clustering* algorithms which take as input the *snippets* of hits, where snippets are *query word dependent* (and thus they cannot be extracted, stored and indexed a-priori). Note that the result of entity mining if applied over the textual snippets also falls into the case of *dynamic metadata*.

There is also a plethora of works and systems that offer a kind of entity search. EntityCube[3] generates *summaries of entities* from Web pages and allows the exploration of their relationships. However it supports only three categories of entities (people, locations and organizations) and for complex or long queries that do not contain the entity of interest the results are poor. In [21], the authors propose a framework with two indexing and partition schemes for efficient entity search in which users formulate queries that directly describe what types of entities they are looking for (using the prefix #, e.g. #phone). [11] presents ESTER, a modular search system that combines full-text and ontology search. ESTER supports entity recognition by assigning words or phrases in the corpus to the entities from the ontology they refer to. It is domain-specific and elaborates well on a small set of predefined categories of entities (ontology classes). Finally, [57] discovers (offline) *entity structures* in Web pages regarding the computer science domain, and constructs a heterogeneous network of bibliographic information (which is then analyzed) for offering keyword-based entity search.

---

[3] http://entitycube.research.microsoft.com/

In contrast to the works listed in the previous paragraph (which focus on entity search and retrieval), the approach that we describe in this article does not change the (user-friendly) way users search for information, but acts as a mediator between any search system and semantic information; users still get documents as search results, but also get and interact with semantic information that helps them locate and explore fast possible useful results.

2.3   The Steps of the Post-Analysis Process

Hereafter we consider the following, quite general, process for post-analysis of search results (also depicted in Figure 1):

1) The user submits a keyword query to the professional search system.
2) The search system retrieves the top-K results that correspond to the submitted query together with the static metadata of each result.
3) The search system uses a component, we call it PProc from "Post-Processor", which derives (ideally at real-time) the *cluster labels* and the *entities* that correspond to the top-K results (Sections 2.5 and 2.6 detail this step).
4) PProc *groups* the metadata values according to their category and the entities according to their class.
5) PProc *ranks* the metadata values of each category, the clusters and the entities of each class (cf. Section 2.7).
6) The results (i.e. groups of ranked metadata values, clusters and entities) are visualized and exploited in a faceted and session-based interaction scheme [49] that allows the user to restrict his/her focus or information need *gradually*, and exploits the results of the previous steps (cf. Section 3). Apart from gradual exploration, the user can also retrieve more information about an identified entity by exploiting the Linked Open Data (LOD) [14].

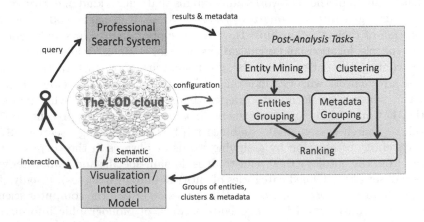

Fig. 1. Semantic post-analysis of search results

Fig. 2. A prototype offering real-time exploratory patent search

To grasp the idea and what the outcome of this process can be, Figure 2 depicts an indicative screen dump of a prototype patent-search system that offers the aforementioned functionality. Note that the user has many options for restricting the search space by selecting one or more metadata values of the category International Patent Classification (A), one or more entities of type Drug (B), or one or more cluster labels (C). For instance, in the current example the user has focused on the Drug ibuprofen, the International Patent Classification A61531/185, and the Cluster behandlung, restricting the search space to only 2 results which correspond to the selected facets (D). Furthermore, the user is able to retrieve (at real-time) more information about an entity (E) by exploiting online semantic KBs (e.g. DBpedia [10]).

2.4 Metadata-Based Grouping

For grouping the results according to their static metadata values, one has to decide which metadata elements are important in a professional search process, i.e. which of them are the more useful and likely to be used in a faceted search-like process for narrowing the search space. For example, in the context of patent searching, a patent document has numerous metadata elements. Indicatively, a patent document of the *Matrixware Research Collection* (**MAREC**) data corpus[4] may contain more than 20 metadata elements including *document identification fields, concerned parties, filing and priority information, national and international classification codes, titles, abstracts and descriptions (in many languages), citations, related applications, claims,* etc.

For selecting the fields which are most useful and likely to be used in a faceted search-like interface, one approach is to gather opinions from profes-

---

[4] http://www.ir-facility.org/prototypes/marec

sionals in the corresponding domain. For example, [27] gathered opinions during interviews with patent examiners from the *Industrial Property Organization of Greece*[5], in a visit aiming to observe patent examiners searching in their working environment. They also did an one-on-one interview with a very experienced patent examiner specifically to learn about their attitudes and beliefs accompanying the usefulness of different types of metadata in patent search. The expert mentioned the following nine metadata fields as being important in a faceted patent search: *International Patent Classification (IPC), European Classification (ECLA), Applicant, Inventor, publication number, publication country, publication year, application country, application year*. Thus, they decided to offer the above metadata fields for faceted exploration in their patent search system.

2.5 Textual Clustering

Results clustering aims at grouping the search results into topics (called clusters), with predictive names (labels), aiding the user to locate quickly one or more documents that otherwise it would be laborious to find, especially if they are low ranked. Results clustering is very useful in cases where there are no metadata elements (e.g. in cases where only textual snippets of the hits are available), or in cases of metadata elements that contain long textual descriptions.

There are many algorithms for results clustering. In our applications we adopt the clustering method described in [39] which is actually a variation of the Suffix Tree Clustering (STC) algorithm [60], called NM-STC (No-Merge STC), that derives hierarchically organized labels and is able to favor occurrences in a specific part of the result (e.g. in the title). Figure 3 depicts the result of the NM-STC algorithm applied in the top-200 snippets returned by Bing Search Engine for the query **tuna species**. By clicking for example the cluster label "seafood (7)", the user can inspect the seven results that contain information about tuna species and seafood.

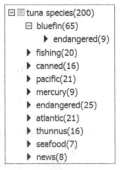

Fig. 3. Top-10 cluster labels for the query **tuna species**

The main advantage of the STC-based algorithms is that they do not rely on external resources or training data, and thus they have broad applicability

---
[5] http://www.obi.gr/

(e.g. for different natural languages). For supporting a different language, the user/administrator must only provide a list with the *stop words* of this language. This feature is particularly useful in patent search where the patent descriptions may be in different languages. In addition, the *invention title* is usually the most important and descriptive part of a patent, therefore NM-STC can favor occurrences of labels (topics) in the title.

2.6 Discovering Entities

Named Entity Extraction (NEE), also referred as *semantic annotation*, is the process of identifying entities in texts and linking them to relevant semantic resources. NEE often consists of two main sub-processes: *named entity recognition* (or *entity mining*) which is the task of identifying entities belonging to a set of class labels (such as Person, Location, Organization, etc.), and *entity linking* which tries to link a named entity with a resource in a KB.

There are several tools that support NEE and that could be exploited by a professional search system. Below we briefly describe some of them.

DBpedia Spotlight: DBpedia Spotlight [43] is a tool for annotating mentions of DBpedia resources in text, providing a solution for linking unstructured information sources to the LOD. It performs NEE, including entity resolution. It finds and returns entities that exist in a text, ranks them depending on how relevant they are with the text content, and links them with URIs from DBpedia.

AlchemyAPI: AlchemyAPI [1] is a Natural Language Processing (NLP) service which provides cloud-based and on-premise text analysis infrastructure. AlchemyAPI eliminates the expense and difficulty of integrating NLP systems into an application, service or data processing pipeline. It provides a platform for analyzing Web pages, documents and tweets along with APIs for integration. In addition, the named entity extractor is able to disambiguate the detected entities, link them to various datasets on the LOD and resolve co-references.

OpenCalais: Calais [3] is a toolkit of capabilities that allows incorporating semantic functionality within a blog, content management system, Web site or application. The OpenCalais Web Service automatically creates semantic metadata for the submitted content. Using NLP, Machine Learning (ML) and other methods, Calais analyzes a document, finds the entities within it and gives them a score based on their text relevance. It also supports automatic connection to the LOD.

Wikimeta: Wikimeta [7] is a NLP semantic tagging and annotation system that allows incorporating semantic knowledge within a document, Web site or content management system. It tries to link each detected named entity to some entity in DBpedia based on a disambiguation process that is described in [20]. The dataset used to train the NLP tools of Wikimeta, are derived from Wikipedia and are also available to download to build customized applications, gazetteers (i.e. dictionaries) or training corpora.

Lupedia: Lupedia [2] uses a gazetteer which is a list of surface forms that are associated to a subset of entities in DBpedia and LinkedMDB (a dataset that contains movies descriptions). The default configuration takes the longest sequence of consecutive words that corresponds to some entry in the gazetteer and annotates it with the corresponding entity in the KB.

Gate ANNIE: Gate ANNIE [22,16] is a ready-made information extraction system which contains several components (e.g. Tokeniser, Gazetteer, Sentence Splitter, etc.) and supports both gazetteers and NLP functions.

We should note that we are interesting only in the result of the NEE process. Thus, the approach that we propose can use any NEE system, independently of the underlying NLP algorithm. This also means that the support of several capabilities involved in the entity mining process (e.g. support of multiple languages, stemming, lemmatization, etc.) are in the responsibility of the NEE system.

Configuring the Entities of Interest

The useful entities are not the same in every domain. To tackle the corresponding configuration requirements of the considered process, here we show how one can exploit the (constantly evolving) LOD for specifying and updating the entities of interest, and for providing further information about the identified entities.

In case a NEE system supports *gazetteers* for named entity recognition (apart from NLP and ML techniques), like `Gate ANNIE`, we can exploit the LOD for creating new (supported) categories of entities. Specifically, we can query a semantic KB (that is accessible through a SPARQL [6] endpoint) for retrieving a list of names that belong to a particular *resource class*[6] or which are described by a *SPARQL query*.

For example, Figure 4 shows an example of a SPARQL query that returns a list of Fish names (using DBpedia's SPARQL endpoint as the underlying KB). The URI "`http://dbpedia.org/ontology/Fish`" is the resource class of the category Fish. Likewise, we can create a complex SPARQL query that describes a set of entities with some specific characteristics, or we can use *federated SPARQL queries* [5] and gather information from multiple KBs. Thereby, we can also support the identification of entities in any language, e.g. we can run a query that returns a list of entity names in a specific language by exploiting the `FILTER` operator of SPARQL 1.1. In addition, by exploiting the LOD, and since the LOD constantly changes and increases, we can keep "fresh" the entities of the supported categories or update (at any time) a category with names of entities coming from a new KB.

```
SELECT DISTINCT str(?label) WHERE {
  ?uri rdf:type <http://dbpedia.org/ontology/Fish> .
  ?uri rdfs:label ?label }
```

Fig. 4. Example of a SPARQL query for retrieving a list of Fish names from DBpedia

---

[6] A resource class actually represents a category of entities.

Note that there are many tools that can facilitate the construction of the SPARQL queries, without requiring any advanced knowledge in SPARQL (like [9] and [48]). Furthermore, there are natural language approaches that guide users in formulating queries in a language seemingly akin to English and translate them to SPARQL [24].

Figure 5 depicts the result of entity mining applied in the top-200 snippets returned by Bing Search Engine for the query **tuna species**. In this example, the NEE system has been configured to identify fish species, countries and water areas. By clicking for example the entity "yellowfin tuna (9)" from the category Species, the user can inspect the nine results that contain information about the species "yellowfin tuna".

Fig. 5. The result of entity mining (configured to identify fish species, countries and water areas) for the query **tuna species**

2.7   Ranking

The identified entities, the clusters and the metadata values may be numerous. Thereby, we need an effective method for ranking them and promoting the most important. [25] and [27] proposed a ranking scheme for entity mining that promotes the entities that have been identified in the top positions of the ranked list of results. We can adapt this formula for ranking also the clusters and the metadata values. However, most clustering algorithms rank the derived clusters, thus in this case we can avoid ranking them. Specifically, consider that the user submits a keyword query q, and let R be the set of the top-K results (e.g. $K = 200$) returned by the underlying search system. For a $r \in R$, let $rank(r)$ be its position in the answer (the first result has rank equal to 1, the second 2, and so on). We apply entity mining and clustering in R, and get a set of entities E and a set of cluster labels C. We also have a set of metadata values M. Now, we can rank each element e in $E \cup C \cup M$ according to the formula:

$$Score(e) = \frac{\sum_{r \in hits(e)} ((|R| + 1) - rank(r))}{\frac{|R|(|R|+1)}{2}} \tag{1}$$

where $hits(e)$ denotes the results (i.e. the elements of R) in which an entity e has been identified. We can see that the elements (i.e. metadata values, entities and cluster labels) occurring in the top results are promoted. The rational behind this ranking formula is that the top hits in the ranked list probably contain more useful elements that the last hits since they are considered "better" results. On this account (and considering that we analyze only the top-K results), the ranking algorithm of the underlying search system is very important.

[25] comparatively evaluated with users three formulas for entity ranking in the context of Web searching. The first ranking formula is the one described above (Formula 1). The second formula takes into account the words of the entity names and of the query, and promotes the entities that exist in the query string. The third formula considers both perspectives, i.e. it promotes both the entities identified in the top search results and the entities that exist in the query string. The results showed that the string similarity between the query and the entity names did not improve entity ranking.

An issue is how to also rank the categories of entities (or the metadata categories) if they are numerous. In this case, the system must decide which categories to promote (e.g. in order for the user to see them without needing to scroll). Various methods can be applied, however this is an issue that is worth further research.

2.8 Inspecting the Connectivity of the Identified Entities

So far, the user can only inspect a *list* of entities identified in the search results. The structured knowledge that may be available as LOD for the identified entities is not exploited. For instance and regarding the marine domain, an identified fish species (e.g. the *yellowfin tuna*) may have many properties (e.g. *family, genus, kingdom*, etc.) and related entities (e.g. *predators, binomial authority*, etc.), and can belong to multiple categories (e.g. *Fish, Eukaryote, Fish of Hawaii*, etc.). Moreover, some species may share one or more common properties or related entities (e.g. two species belong to the same *genus* or *family*). All this information should be exploitable as it can provide useful information about the *context* of these entities. In addition, it allows the user to instantly inspect information that may lie in different places and that may be laborious and time consuming to locate, e.g. how the detected species *papuan seerfish* and *kanadi kingfish* are related, why the species *pacific bonito* was detected in the search results for the query *tuna*, etc. Furthermore, all this information can be integrated in the search process helping the user (apart from restricting the search space) to get a more sophisticated overview and to make better sense of the results.

However, the amount of structured information that is available for these entities can be very high (i.e. their associations and properties). Therefore, there is a need for methods for ranking all this semantic information in order to promote and present to the end-users the most important associations and properties.

To tackle the above challenges, [29] proposes a method founded on Link Analysis. Specifically, this work introduces an appropriately biased PageRank-like algorithm for ranking entities and properties, which is also exploited for producing (and showing to the user) *top-K semantic graphs*. A top-K semantic graph can complement the query answer with useful information regarding the *connectivity* of the identified entities. The keypoint is that this approach can exploit associations and it is quite general and configurable. Moreover, it promotes the entities identified in the top ranked results, as well as the semantic information that is linked with many important (i.e. highly ranked) entities.

For example and regarding the marine domain, by analyzing the snippets of the top-100 results that Bing returns for the query *yellowfin tuna* (with *fish species* as the entities of interest), and exploiting DBpedia at real-time for retrieving the properties of the identified entities, in the top semantic graphs the user gets information about the taxonomy of the *yellowfin tuna* (family, order, etc.), other tuna species that belong to the same family or the same conservation status system (e.g. the *bigeye tuna*), how all these entities are connected, etc. The user gets all this information in only 3 seconds without performing any additional query. Figure 6 depicts an example of a top-5 semantic graph.

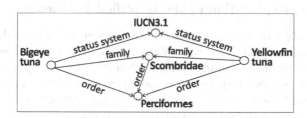

Fig. 6. A top-5 semantic graph

3   Interaction Model

This section focuses on how the user can interact with the result of the post-analysis process.

3.1   Faceted Search-Like Exploration of the Results

The results of entity mining, clustering and metadata-based grouping can be visualized and exploited according to the *faceted exploration* interaction paradigm [49]; when the user clicks on an entity, cluster or metadata value, the hits are restricted to those that contain that entity, cluster or metadata value. The user is able to gradually select elements from one or more categories and refine the answer set accordingly (the mechanism is session-based). Figure 7 depicts an indicative example regarding the marine domain in which the user has selected to inspect the results containing information for three species.

There are several approaches for supporting this functionality. For instance, if such selections belong to the same category, they can have disjunctive (OR) semantics and if they belong to separate categories they can have conjunctive (AND) semantics [27]. In addition, in order to avoid overloading the interface, we can display only the top-L (e.g. L=5) values of each category, and by clicking a hyperlink (e.g. a "show all" button), the user will be able to inspect all of them.

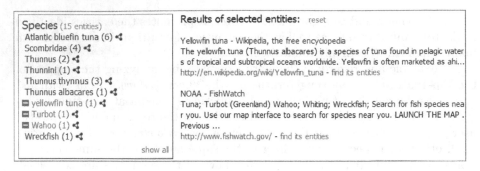

Fig. 7. Example of faceted exploration of the results

3.2 Semantic Exploration of the Identified Entities

There are already vast amounts of structured information published according to the principles of LOD. The availability of such datasets enables not only to configure easily the entity names that are interesting for the application at hand (as described in Section 2.6), but also the enrichment of the entities with more information about them. In this way, users not only can get *useful information* about one entity without having to submit a new query, but they can also start *browsing* the entities that are linked to that entity. Note that many of the *static metadata* can also be considered entities (e.g. the Author of a document).

Another important point is that exploiting LOD is more dynamic, affordable and feasible, than an approach that requires each search system to keep stored and maintain its own KB of entities and facts. Returning to our setting, a question is which LOD dataset(s) to use. An approach is to identify and specify one or more appropriate dataset(s) for each category of entities. For example, GeoNames[7] can be exploited for *geographic data*, DrugBank[8] for *drugs*, DBpedia, YAGO [52] and FactForge [13] contain data related to many domains, etc.

Running one (SPARQL) query for each entity would be a very expensive task, especially if the system has discovered a lot of entities. For this reason, one can offer this service *on demand*. Specifically when the user requests to inspect more information about an entity, e.g. by clicking a button, the system *at that time* can collect semantic resources that "match" the name of the selected entity by querying one or more SPARQL endpoints.

For example, Figure 8 shows an example of a SPARQL *template* query which tries to find a resource of type (`rdf:type`) Fish whose label (`rdfs:label`) contains the name of the selected entity (ignoring case). Note that the SPARQL template query contains the character sequence [ENTITY]. At request time, the system reads the endpoint and the corresponding template query of the category in which the identified entity belongs, replaces each occurrence of [ENTITY] in the template query with the entity's name, and finally runs the query.

---

[7] http://www.geonames.org/

[8] http://www.drugbank.ca/

For instance, for the entity name "salmon" (of type Fish) and having defined DB-pedia as the underlying KB, the matching resources are 16. Some of them follow:

- http://dbpedia.org/resource/Chum_salmon
- http://dbpedia.org/resource/Coho_salmon
- http://dbpedia.org/resource/Giant_salmon_carp
- http://dbpedia.org/resource/Salmon_shark
- http://dbpedia.org/resource/Chinook_salmon

```
SELECT DISTINCT ?uri WHERE {
  ?uri rdf:type <http://dbpedia.org/ontology/Fish> .
  ?uri rdfs:label ?label
    FILTER(regex(str(?label), '[ENTITY]', 'i')) }
```

Fig. 8. Example of a SPARQL *template* query for matching an identified Fish name with resources in DBpedia

The derived semantic information can be visualized in a popup window as shown in Figure 2 (E). Then, the user is able to continue browsing by further exploring the properties of the related resources. For example, Figure 9 shows an example of a SPARQL template query for retrieving all the outgoing properties of a resource. The SPARQL template query contains the character sequence [URI] (including the [and]) which at request time is replaced by the resource's URI. Alternatively, someone could provide a query that retrieves only a subset of the properties, literals in a specific language, images, etc. Figure 10 depicts an example of a pop-up window showing some of the properties (from DBpedia) of the entity "Chum salmon" (resource class: http://dbpedia.org/resource/Chum_salmon).

```
SELECT DISTINCT ?propertyName ?propertyValue WHERE {
  <[URI]> ?propertyName ?propertyValue }
```

Fig. 9. Example of a SPARQL *template* query for retrieving the outgoing properties of resource

4   Experimental Results

Several works have pointed out the value (for the end users) of categorizing the search results in both Web and Professional search. We should note that the post-analysis approaches that we have described in this chapter also fall into this case, i.e. they are ways of categorizing search results.

In this section, we first review the results of several experimental evaluations that demonstrate the *effectiveness* and the *usefulness* of such approaches (Section 4.1). In the sequel, we report experimental results regarding the *efficiency* of the post-analysis processes and we also discuss ways for improving it

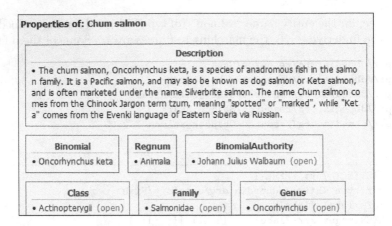

Fig. 10. Pop-up window showing some of the properties of the fish "Chum salmon"

(Section 4.2). Finally, we present experimental results regarding the efficiency of the semantic exploration of the identified entities, we discuss limitations that arise when exploiting online KBs at query time, and also we show ways to improve the reliability of this process (Section 4.3).

4.1   Effectiveness and Usefulness

In [36], an experiment with 20 participants was conducted to compare an interface that categorizes the search results to the de facto standard solution (ranked list, 10 results per page interface). This interface provides an overview of the results by presenting a list of the most frequent words and phrases as categories next to the actual results. The results showed that the users were 25% faster and 21% more accurate with a system that categorizes the search results. In more details, the results showed that it is possible to browse through more results because the searching speed is higher. This is important, since many times the search results are unreliable and it is thus desirable to be able to access alternative results quickly. In addition, categorizing the search results not only gives the users more options but gives them more relevant options. The results showed that the increase in the number of results was due to the increase in the number of relevant results, while the speed of finding relevant results was about 40% higher. Furthermore, the users found the first relevant result earlier (with fewer selections).

In another experimental evaluation [35], the same interface was provided to 16 users for a two-month period. The interactions with the system were logged and the users' opinions were elicited with two questionnaires. The results showed that categories are successfully used as part of users' search habits. Specifically, categories are helpful when the result ranking of the search engine fails. In this case, the users are able to access results that locate far in the rank order list. Moreover, by exploiting the categories, there were fewer cases where user did not find any results. This means that when the query formulation fails, the user may still be able to find results using the categories. Finally, the results showed that the categories are beneficial when more than one result is needed like in an *exploratory* search task.

The user study in [40] examined how searchers interacted with a web-based, faceted library catalog when conducting exploratory searches. It applied eye tracking, stimulated recall interviews and direct observation to investigate important aspects of gaze behavior in a faceted search interface. Three facets (i.e. categories of results) were used in the evaluation: *Subject, Region* and *Time Period*. The results showed that facets played a major role in the exploratory search process, accounting for about one-half the amount of time spent looking at actual results.

[59] presented the results of a four-week longitudinal study investigating the use of both exploratory and keyword forms of search within an online video archive, where both forms of search were available concurrently in a single user interface. The results showed that there was a balance of exploratory and keyword searches and that they were often used together. Specifically, the facets were used as often as keyword searches, and also they were used both passively to understand the structure of the collection and actively to produce more expressive queries.

Finally, [47] conducted a task-based user study of a *medical* search system for evaluating a dynamic categorization technique. The goal was to determine whether this technique for organizing search results is more useful than two existing techniques: relevance ranking (i.e. ordered list of search results) and SONIA document-clustering [50]. Fifteen users completed query-related tasks using all three tools. The authors measured the time it took the subjects to accomplish their tasks, the number of answers to the query that the subjects found in four minutes, and the number of new answers that they could recall at the end of the study. Subjects also completed a user-satisfaction questionnaire. The results showed that users could find significantly more answers in a fixed amount of time and were significantly more satisfied with their search experience when they used the dynamic categorization tool. In addition, the users indicated that this categorization provided an organization of search results that was more clear, easy to use, accurate, precise, and helpful.

4.2   Efficiency of Real-Time Post-Analysis

[27] measured the average time required for a) grouping the top-K results according the their metadata values (each result is actually a patent document), b) applying clustering (at real-time) on the title and abstract of the top-K results (using NM-STC), c) applying entity mining (at real-time) on the title and abstract of the top-K results (using Gate ANNIE), for several values of K. The results showed that the metadata-based grouping requires about 0.8 ms per result, the clustering about 3 ms per result, while entity mining is the most time consuming task requiring about 10 ms per result. The total time for analyzing the top-200 results is about 3 seconds. However, the three tasks can be performed in parallel, i.e. the results of a task are not required for running another task.

Note also that the time depends not on the size of the underlying data sources but on the number of the top results that we want to analyze; the more results we analyze, the more time is required for grouping, clustering and mining them.

In addition, [25] showed that performing real-time entity mining (using Gate ANNIE) in the *full contents* of the top-50 results returned by a Web search system (Google) costs about one minute (including the time for downloading the content of each result). Nevertheless, in that case one can adopt a distributed approach. A scalable method for entity-based summarization of Web search results at query time using the MapReduce programming framework [23] is described in [37]. That work shows how to decompose a sequential entity mining algorithm into an equivalent distributed MapReduce algorithm (the logical decomposition is sketched in Figure 11) and deploy it on the cloud for speedup the process.

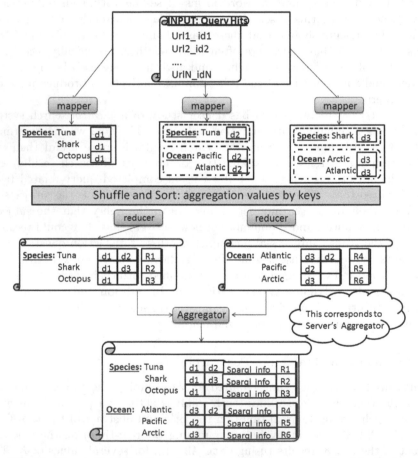

Fig. 11. Example of distributed entity mining processing using MapReduce

Alternatively, instead of offering *real-time* entity mining of the snippets or the full contents of the top hits of the answer, one could analyze the entire corpus *offline* (assuming that the corpus is available), and build an appropriate index (or database) for using it at run time. Then, for each incoming query, the entities of the top-K (e.g. $K = 1,000$) hits of the answer are fetched from the index, and are given to the user. An important observation is that the size of the entity index in the worst case could be in the scale of the corpus. Also note that this approach cannot be applied at meta (uncooperative) search level.

Another approach is to process the top hits of the answer of only the *frequent queries*. In that case, for each frequent query of the log file (e.g. for those which are used for query suggestions), we compute its answer, fetch the top-K hits, apply textual clustering and entity mining and finally save its results as they should be shown using the approach and indexes described at [28,26]. The benefit of this approach (apart from the *instant response*) is that here we do not have to process the entire collection but only the top hits (e.g. top-200) of the most frequent queries. This significantly reduces the required computational effort and storage space. The downside of this approach is that if a user submits a query which does not belong to the frequent queries, and thus it has not been processed, then the system cannot offer results. In that case the system could offer to the user the "real-time" approach as it was described earlier. Finally, we should note that this approach is applicable also at a meta search level, but periodically the index has to be refreshed, mainly incrementally.

4.3 Efficiency of Semantic Exploration

According to [27], the time for matching an entity with semantic resources (by querying the LOD) highly depends on the SPARQL endpoint (i.e. the underlying KB) and the SPARQL template query. The authors noticed that the more data (i.e. labels of entities) a category of entities contains in the underlying KB, the more time is required for matching an entity that belongs to this category.

Indicatively (and for the time being), DBpedia's endpoint contains about 1 million labels of type Geographical Area. For retrieving information about a geographical area, about 5 seconds are required (including network delay time). However, for retrieving information about a Physical Entity (DBpedia contains about 6 millions labels of this type), the time required is about 20 seconds. On the contrary, the time for retrieving the properties of a semantic resource is very low because we already know its URI (no string comparisons are required like in the case of entity matching).

Limitations. The existing publicly available online KBs (like DBpedia) are not reliable since they mainly serve demonstration purposes. The fact that everyone can query them affects their efficiency and availability. They also do not serve multiple concurrent requests in order to avoid overloading their systems.

In addition, if an entity belongs to a category with millions of entities then the time for retrieving related resources (i.e. URIs) can be high. The same is true in case the underlying application requires to retrieve semantic information for numerous entities at once, i.e. when this functionality is not offered on-demand. In such cases, adopting a *caching mechanism* or *indexing* a part of the underlying

KB (with the cost of loosing the freshness of the results) will highly improve the response times and the throughput that can be served.

Of course, in a real application the underlying KBs may not be publicly available, or a *dedicated Warehouse* can be constructed that will only serve a particular application (like the *MarineTLO-based warehouse* described in [53]). The KBs (or the Warehouse) could also be *distributed* in many servers, so the system can apply a load balancing technique [18] for serving the requests. Furthermore, as it is proposed in [56], one could keep a local copy of data that hardly changes and offer a hybrid query execution approach for improving the response time and reducing the load on the endpoints, while keeping the results fresh. All the above can highly improve the performance and the scalability of the underlying professional search system.

Finally, we should stress that even if the post-analysis services require some time to complete, and therefore are not "real-time", in various kinds of professional search, this time is really low. For instance, in the domain of patent search, the persons working in patent offices spend days for a particular patent search request. In bibliographic search, a few minutes is a rather short period considering the time that could be saved if a useful hit corresponding to a low ranked document gets retrieved because a mined entity allowed the user to locate it.

5   Application Examples

This section presents two applications of the described approach. Specifically, Section 5.1 describes an application for the marine domain, while Section 5.2 describes an application for patent search.

5.1   X-Search: Exploring Marine Resources

X-Search is a meta-search engine that reads the description of an underlying search source (OpenSearch [4] compliant), queries that source, analyzes the returned results in various ways and also exploits the availability of semantic repositories. It also has a gCube version in which the underlying search system is gCube Search. gCube [17] is a service-oriented application framework that supports the on-demand sharing of resources for computation, content and application services. gCube enables the realization of e-infrastructures that support the notion of Virtual Research Environments (VREs), i.e. collaborative digital environments through which scientists, addressing common research challenges, exchange information and produce new knowledge.

X-Search has been developed in the context of the iMarine project[9]. iMarine exploits gCube and offers an operational distributed infrastructure that serves hundreds of scientists from the marine domain. The key features of X-Search are the following:

---

[9] http:/www.i-marine.eu/

– *Provision of textual clustering of the results* (supporting the following algorithms: STC, STC+, NM-STC, STC++ and NM-STC+ [39]). Clustering is performed on the textual snippets of the returned results, but clustering of the entire contents is also supported.
– *Provision of entity mining of the results.* Entity mining can be performed either over the textual snippets or over the entire contents. It also supports ranking of the identified entities [25].
– *Faceted search-like exploration of the results.* The results of clustering and entity mining are visualized and exploited according to the faceted exploration interaction paradigm: when the user clicks on a cluster or entity, the results are restricted to those that contain that cluster or entity.
– *On-click semantic exploration of a KB.* X-Search provides the necessary linkage between the mined entities and semantic information. In particular, by exploiting the *MarineTLO-based Warehouse* [53], the user can retrieve more information about an entity by querying and browsing over this KB. The *MarineTLO-based Warehouse* integrates information coming from Fish-Base [31], WoRMS[10], ECOSCOPE[11], FLOD[12] and DBpedia, and currently contains information (more than 4M triples) about marine species (40,000), ecosystems, water areas, vessels, etc.
– *Entity discovery and exploration during plain Web browsing.* X-Search also offers entity discovery and exploration while user is browsing on the Web. Specifically, the user is able to inspect the entities of a particular Web page by simply clicking a *bookmarklet*[13] and then to semantically explore the properties of the identified entities. Namely, the user can at real-time exploit the aforementioned functionality while browsing.

Figure 12 depicts an indicative screen shot of X-Search in gCube. We notice that for a particular query, the user can see the top results and the metadata of each result (A), the identified entities (B) and the result of textual clustering (C). The user can also inspect semantic resources that match an identified entity (D) and explore their properties (E). Figure 13 depicts a screen shot of an annotated Web page. Specifically, the Wikipedia page of *Thunnus* has been analyzed (using the bookmarklet provided by X-Search), the identified entities have been annotated and the user can start exploring them (A).

X-Search is fully configurable in terms of the supported categories of entities, the underlying KBs and the way the system queries the KBs. Specifically, the user/administrator can add a new category of entities or update an existing one by accessing online semantic KBs (accessible through SPARQL endpoints), and

---

[10] http://www.marinespecies.org/
[11] http://www.ecoscopebc.ird.fr/EcoscopeKB/ShowWelcomePage.action
[12] http://www.fao.org/figis/flod/
[13] A bookmarklet is a bookmark stored in a Web browser that extends the browser's functionality (http://en.wikipedia.org/wiki/Bookmarklet). In X-Search, the bookmarklet sends the current URL (of the Web page the user is viewing) to a server. The server then analyzes the contents of the Web page and presents to the user a new (annotated) Web page.

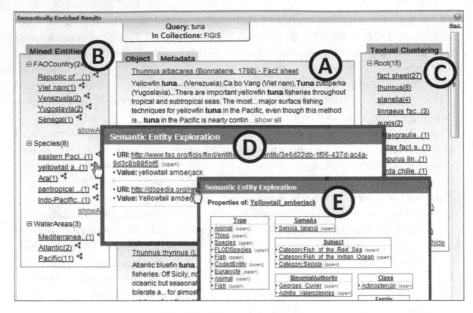

Fig. 12. The X-Search system

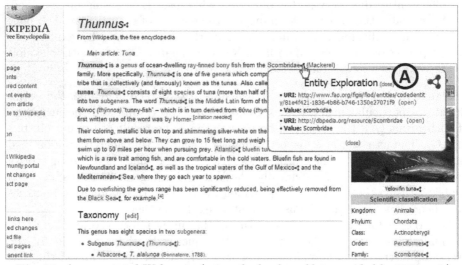

Fig. 13. An annotated Web page (using the bookmarklet provided by X-Search)

specify how to semantically link and enrich the identified entities. This enhanced configurability allows X-Search to be lightly (and dynamically) configured for different contexts, for building domain-specific applications. In the context of iMarine, X-Search has been configured to identify Fish Species, FAO Countries, Water Areas and Regional Fishery Bodies. It links the identified entities with resources from the MarineTLO-based warehouse [53] and enrich them by retrieving their outgoing properties.

5.2   PerFedPat: Pluggable Platform for Personalized Multilingual Patent Search

The PerFedPat[14] project aims to research into a new generation of advanced patent search systems for the patent related industries and the whole spectrum of patent users by designing a framework for integrating multiple patent data sources, patent search tools and UIs.

The iPerFedPat system [51], which is the main result of the project, is based on the ezDL framework [12] and has a pluggable architecture, providing core services and operations being able to integrate multiple patent data sources and patent related data streams, thus providing multiple patent search tools and UIs while hiding complexity from the end user. iPerFedPat currently integrates the results of four patent search systems: Clef-IP 2011 [46], Espacenet[15], Google Patents[16] and WIPO PatentScope[17]. It can post-process the federated results in various ways using pluggable tools, and supports all the functionalities described in Section 2, i.e. *metadata-based grouping*, *entity mining* and *textual clustering*.

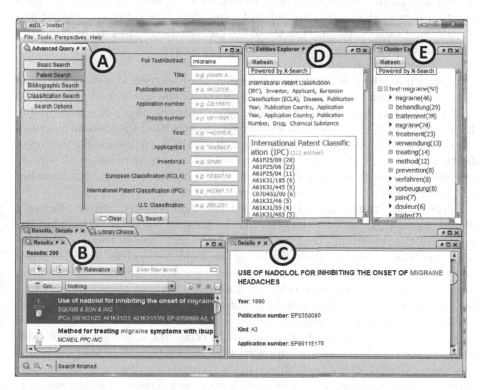

Fig. 14. The iPerFedPat system

14 http://www.perfedpat.eu/
15 http://www.epo.org/searching/free/espacenet.html
16 https://www.google.com/?tbm=pts
17 http://patentscope.wipo.int/search/en/search.jsf

Figure 14 depicts an indicative screen shot of iPerFedPat. We notice that the interface is split in several windows, each corresponding to a different tool. In this example, the user has submitted the query migraine using the "Advanced Query" tool (A) and the top results are shown in the "Results" tool (B). The user can also see the details of a particular result (C) and to inspect the entities and the metadata (grouped in categories) that exist in the search results (D), as well as a clustering of the search space (E). Thereby, the user can narrow the search space by a selecting one or more entities, metadata values or clusters.

6   Conclusion and Future Research

We have presented an exploratory method for professional search that exploits the available metadata plus the results of *textual clustering* and *entity mining* in a *faceted* and *session-based* interaction scheme that allows the users to get an overview of the search space and to restrict their focus gradually. We have seen that *Linked Data* can be exploited for specifying the entities of interest and for providing further information about the identified entities. This functionality essentially offers an *entity-based integration* of search results, metadata and other external (semantic) resources.

In particular, the described approach offers the ability to a) restrict the focus using static metadata values that are important for the searchers, b) restrict the focus using entity values and important topics (clusters) that were discovered in the search results, c) inspect and explore the properties of the identified entities by exploiting KBs that are accessible through SPARQL endpoints. Furthermore, showing values and their count gives an overview (e.g. percentage of patents published in a particular country). Note also that the described functionality can be exploited by any professional search system.

Experimental results have showed that this functionality can be efficiently offered at real-time however the time that we have to pay is proportional to the number of the top results that we want to "explore" (pay-as-you-go). Furthermore, the time for semantically exploring the identified entities highly depends on the efficiency and reliability of the underlying KBs. Ultimately, we should stress that the post-analysis services that we described can considerably reduce the time that a user must devote in a professional search context.

The long term vision is to be able to mine not only correct entities but probably entire *conceptual models* that describe and relate the identified entities (plus other external entities) and are appropriate for the context of the user's information need. After reaching that objective the exploratory process could support the interaction paradigm of faceted search over such (crispy or fuzzy) semantic models, e.g. [30] for plain RDF/S, or [41] for the case Fuzzy RDF.

Acknowledgement. This work was supported by *iMarine* (FP7 Research Infrastructures, 2011-2014) and *MUMIA* COST action (IC1002, 2010-2014).

References

1. Alchemyapi, http://www.alchemyapi.com/
2. Lupedia enrichment service, ontotext, http://lupedia.ontotext.com/
3. Opencalais, thomson reuters, http://www.opencalais.com/
4. Opensearch, http://www.opensearch.org/
5. Sparql 1.1 federated query, w3c recommendation (March 21, 2013), http://www.w3.org/TR/sparql11-federated-query/
6. Sparql query language for rdf, w3c recommendation (January 15, 2008), http://www.w3.org/TR/rdf-sparql-query/
7. Wikimeta, http://www.wikimeta.com/
8. Allocca, C., d'Aquin, M., Motta, E.: Impact of using relationships between ontologies to enhance the ontology search results. In: Simperl, E., Cimiano, P., Polleres, A., Corcho, O., Presutti, V. (eds.) ESWC 2012. LNCS, vol. 7295, pp. 453–468. Springer, Heidelberg (2012)
9. Ambrus, O., Möller, K., Handschuh, S.: Konduit vqb: A visual query builder for sparql on the social semantic desktop. In: Workshop on Visual Interfaces to the Social and Semantic Web (2010)
10. Auer, S., Bizer, C., Kobilarov, G., Lehmann, J., Cyganiak, R., Ives, Z.G.: Dbpedia: A nucleus for a web of open data. In: Aberer, K., et al. (eds.) ISWC/ASWC 2007. LNCS, vol. 4825, pp. 722–735. Springer, Heidelberg (2007)
11. Bast, H., Chitea, A., Suchanek, F., Weber, I.: Ester: Efficient search on text, entities, and relations. In: 30th International ACM SIGIR Conference on Research and Development in Information Retrieval (2007)
12. Beckers, T., Dungs, S., Fuhr, N., Jordan, M., Kriewel, S., Tran, V.T.: ezdl: An interactive search and evaluation system. In: SIGIR 2012 Workshop on Open Source Information Retrieval, pp. 9–16 (2012)
13. Bishop, B., Kiryakov, A., Ognyanov, D., Peikov, I., Tashev, Z., Velkov, R.: Factforge: A fast track to the web of data. Semantic Web 2(2), 157–166 (2011)
14. Bizer, C., Heath, T., Berners-Lee, T.: Linked data-the story so far. International Journal on Semantic Web and Information Systems (IJSWIS) 5(3), 1–22 (2009)
15. Bonino, D., Ciaramella, A., Corno, F.: Review of the state-of-the-art in patent information and forthcoming evolutions in intelligent patent informatics. World Patent Information 32(1) (2010)
16. Bontcheva, K., Tablan, V., Maynard, D., Cunningham, H.: Evolving gate to meet new challenges in language engineering. Natural Language Engineering 10(3-4), 349–373 (2004)
17. Candela, L., Castelli, D., Pagano, P.: gcube: A service-oriented application framework on the grid. ERCIM News 72, 48–49 (2008)
18. Cardellini, V., Colajanni, M., Yu, P.S.: Dynamic load balancing on web-server systems. IEEE Internet Computing 3(3), 28–39 (1999)
19. Carpineto, C., DAmico, M., Romano, G.: Evaluating subtopic retrieval methods: Clustering versus diversification of search results. Information Processing and Management 48(2), 358–373 (2012)
20. Charton, E., Gagnon, M., Ozell, B.: Automatic semantic web annotation of named entities. In: Butz, C., Lingras, P. (eds.) Canadian AI 2011. LNCS, vol. 6657, pp. 74–85. Springer, Heidelberg (2011)
21. Cheng, T., Chang, K.: Beyond pages: supporting efficient, scalable entity search with dual-inversion index. In: 13th International Conference on Extending Database Technology (2010)

22. Cunningham, H., Maynard, D., Bontcheva, K., Tablan, V.: GATE: A Framework and Graphical Development Environment for Robust NLP Tools and Applications. In: Proceedings of the 40th Anniversary Meeting of the Association for Computational Linguistics, ACL 2002 (2002)
23. Dean, J., Ghemawat, S.: Mapreduce: Simplified data processing on large clusters. Communications of the ACM 51(1), 107–113 (2008)
24. Franconi, M.T.E., Guagliardo, P.: Quelo: A nl-based intelligent query interface. In: Procs of the Second Workshop on Controlled Natural Languages (CNL 2010) (2010)
25. Fafalios, P., Kitsos, I., Marketakis, Y., Baldassarre, C., Salampasis, M., Tzitzikas, Y.: Web searching with entity mining at query time. In: Proceedings of the 5th Information Retrieval Facility Conference, Vienna, Austria (July 2012)
26. Fafalios, P., Kitsos, I., Tzitzikas, Y.: Scalable, flexible and generic instant overview search. In: Proceedings of the 21st International Conference Companion on World Wide Web, pp. 333–336. ACM (2012)
27. Fafalios, P., Salampasis, M., Tzitzikas, Y.: Exploratory patent search with faceted search and configurable entity mining. In: 1st International Workshop on Integrating IR Technologies for Professional Search (ECIR 2013 Workshop) (2013)
28. Fafalios, P., Tzitzikas, Y.: Exploiting available memory and disk for scalable instant overview search. In: Bouguettaya, A., Hauswirth, M., Liu, L. (eds.) WISE 2011. LNCS, vol. 6997, pp. 101–115. Springer, Heidelberg (2011)
29. Fafalios, P., Tzitzikas, Y.: Post-analysis of keyword-based search results using entity mining, linked data and link analysis at query time. In: 2014 IEEE Eighth International Conference on Semantic Computing (ICSC 2014), Newport Beach, California, USA, June 16-18. IEEE (2014)
30. Ferré, S., Hermann, A.: Semantic search: reconciling expressive querying and exploratory search. In: Aroyo, L., Welty, C., Alani, H., Taylor, J., Bernstein, A., Kagal, L., Noy, N., Blomqvist, E. (eds.) ISWC 2011, Part I. LNCS, vol. 7031, pp. 177–192. Springer, Heidelberg (2011)
31. Froese, R., Pauly, D.: Fishbase, http://www.fishbase.org/
32. Halevy, A.Y.: Answering queries using views: A survey. The VLDB Journa–The International Journal on Very Large Data Bases 10(4), 270–294 (2001)
33. Jiménez-Ruiz, E., Cuenca Grau, B., Horrocks, I., Berlanga, R.: Ontology integration using mappings: Towards getting the right logical consequences. In: Aroyo, L., et al. (eds.) ESWC 2009. LNCS, vol. 5554, pp. 173–187. Springer, Heidelberg (2009)
34. Joho, H., Azzopardi, L., Vanderbauwhede, W.: A survey of patent users: an analysis of tasks, behavior, search functionality and system requirements. In: Procs of the 3rd Symposium on Information Interaction in Context. ACM (2010)
35. Käki, M.: Findex: search result categories help users when document ranking fails. In: Proceedings of the SIGCHI Conference on Human Factors in Computing Systems. ACM (2005)
36. Käki, M., Aula, A.: Findex: Improving search result use through automatic filtering categories. Interacting with Computers 17(2), 187–206 (2005)
37. Kitsos, I., Magoutis, K., Tzitzikas, Y.: Scalable entity-based summarization of web search results using mapreduce. Distributed and Parallel Databases, 1–42 (2013)
38. Kohn, A., Bry, F., Manta, A., Ifenthaler, D.: Professional Search: Requirements, Prototype and Preliminary Experience Report, 195–202 (2008)
39. Kopidaki, S., Papadakos, P., Tzitzikas, Y.: STC+ and NM-STC: Two novel online results clustering methods for web searching. In: Vossen, G., Long, D.D.E., Yu, J.X. (eds.) WISE 2009. LNCS, vol. 5802, pp. 523–537. Springer, Heidelberg (2009)

40. Kules, B., Capra, R., Banta, M., Sierra, T.: What do exploratory searchers look at in a faceted search interface? In: Proceedings of the 9th ACM/IEEE-CS Joint Conference on Digital Libraries, pp. 313–322. ACM (2009)

41. Manolis, N., Tzitzikas, Y.: Interactive Exploration of Fuzzy RDF Knowledge Bases. In: Antoniou, G., Grobelnik, M., Simperl, E., Parsia, B., Plexousakis, D., De Leenheer, P., Pan, J. (eds.) ESWC 2011, Part I. LNCS, vol. 6643, pp. 1–16. Springer, Heidelberg (2011)

42. Marchionini, G.: Exploratory search: from finding to understanding. Communications of the ACM (2006)

43. Mendes, P.N., Jakob, M., García-Silva, A., Bizer, C.: Dbpedia spotlight: shedding light on the web of documents. In: Proceedings of the 7th International Conference on Semantic Systems, pp. 1–8. ACM (2011)

44. Papadakos, P., Armenatzoglou, N., Kopidaki, S., Tzitzikas, Y.: On exploiting static and dynamically mined metadata for exploratory web searching. Knowledge and Information Systems 30, 493–525 (2012)

45. Papadakos, P., Kopidaki, S., Armenatzoglou, N., Tzitzikas, Y.: Exploratory web searching with dynamic taxonomies and results clustering. In: Agosti, M., Borbinha, J., Kapidakis, S., Papatheodorou, C., Tsakonas, G. (eds.) ECDL 2009. LNCS, vol. 5714, pp. 106–118. Springer, Heidelberg (2009)

46. Piroi, F., Lupu, M., Hanbury, A., Zenz, V.: Clef-ip 2011: Retrieval in the intellectual property domain. In: CLEF (Notebook Papers/Labs/Workshop) (2011)

47. Pratt, W., Fagan, L.: The usefulness of dynamically categorizing search results. Journal of the American Medical Informatics Association 7(6), 605–617 (2000)

48. Russell, A., Smart, P.R., Braines, D., Shadbolt, N.R.: Nitelight: A graphical tool for semantic query construction. In: Semantic Web User Interaction Workshop (SWUI 2008) (April 2008)

49. Sacco, G., Tzitzikas, Y.: Dynamic Taxonomies and Faceted Search: Theory, Practice, and Experience, vol. 25. Springer (2009)

50. Sahami, M., Yusufali, S., Baldonaldo, M.Q.: Sonia: A service for organizing networked information autonomously. In: Proceedings of the Third ACM Conference on Digital Libraries, pp. 200–209. ACM (1998)

51. Salampasis, M., Hanbury, A.: A generalized framework for integrated professional search systems. In: Lupu, M., Kanoulas, E., Loizides, F. (eds.) IRFC 2013. LNCS, vol. 8201, pp. 99–110. Springer, Heidelberg (2013)

52. Suchanek, F., Kasneci, G., Weikum, G.: Yago: A core of semantic knowledge. In: Procs of the 16th World Wide Web Conf., pp. 697–706 (2007)

53. Tzitzikas, Y., et al.: Integrating heterogeneous and distributed information about marine species through a top level ontology. In: Garoufallou, E., Greenberg, J. (eds.) MTSR 2013. CCIS, vol. 390, pp. 289–301. Springer, Heidelberg (2013)

54. Tzitzikas, Y., Meghini, C.: Ostensive automatic schema mapping for taxonomy-based peer-to-peer systems. In: Klusch, M., Omicini, A., Ossowski, S., Laamanen, H. (eds.) CIA 2003. LNCS (LNAI), vol. 2782, pp. 78–92. Springer, Heidelberg (2003)

55. Tzitzikas, Y., Spyratos, N., Constantopoulos, P.: Mediators over taxonomy-based information sources. The VLDB Journal–The International Journal on Very Large Data Bases 14(1), 112–136 (2005)

56. Umbrich, J., Karnstedt, M., Hogan, A., Parreira, J.X.: Hybrid sparql queries: fresh vs. fast results. In: Cudré-Mauroux, P., et al. (eds.) ISWC 2012, Part I. LNCS, vol. 7649, pp. 608–624. Springer, Heidelberg (2012)

57. Weninger, T., Danilevsky, M., Fumarola, F., Hailpern, J., Han, J., Johnston, T., Kallumadi, S., Kim, H., Li, Z., McCloskey, D., et al.: Winacs: Construction and analysis of web-based computer science information networks. In: ACM SIGMOD International Conference on Management of Data (2011)
58. White, R., Kules, B., Drucker, S., Schraefel, M.: Supporting exploratory search. Communications of the ACM 49(4) (2006)
59. Wilson, M., et al.: A longitudinal study of exploratory and keyword search. In: Proceedings of the 8th ACM/IEEE-CS Joint Conference on Digital Libraries, JCDL 2008, pp. 52–56. ACM (2008)
60. Zamir, O., Etzioni, O.: Web document clustering: A feasibility demonstration. In: Proceedings of the 21st Annual International ACM SIGIR Conference on Research and Development in Information Retrieval. ACM (1998)

Opinion Retrieval:
Searching for Opinions in Social Media

Georgios Paltoglou[1] and Anastasia Giachanou[2]

[1] School of Mathematics and Computer Science, Faculty of Science and Engineering
University of Wolverhampton, Wulfruna Street, WV1 1LY, UK
g.paltoglou@wlv.ac.uk
[2] Faculty of Informatics, University of Lugano
via G.Buffi 13, 6900 Lugano, Switzerland
anastasia.giachanou@usi.ch

Abstract. *Opinion retrieval* deals with discovery and retrieval of content, primarily from social media, that is relevant to the user's information needs and contains opinions that pertain to them. It combines methodologies and approaches from two distinct areas of research: information retrieval and sentiment analysis. The former deals with the representation, storage and access to information, while the latter focuses on the detection, extraction and analysis of affective content. In this chapter, we will provide a brief but concise introduction to the area, focusing on the most relevant and influential work that has taken place in both distinct areas of research, as well as discuss how those approaches can be combined effectively and efficiently to fulfill the field's stated goal.

Keywords: Social media, sentiment analysis, opinion mining, opinion retrieval, information retrieval.

1   Introduction

The proliferation of blogs, forums, and, in general, social networking sites has created an online landscape where people are able to publicly express their thoughts, opinions and emotions through a variety of means and applications. For example, Twitter, the prevalent microblog service, reports that every week a billion tweets are being posted[1] while Tumblr, one of the most popular blog services, reports that, as of November 2013, 98.5 million blog posts are being created every day[2].

This increase of user-generated digital content has resulted in an unprecedented wealth of information that can be of significant value to professionals, institutions, governments, corporations, etc. That is because it can provide them with ways to research and analyse their audience's opinions, identify problems, discover different perspectives on prominent issues, manage their reputation and identify new opportunities. Typical examples where public perception is important include companies researching how their products or services are being

---

[1] https://blog.twitter.com/2011/numbers
[2] http://www.tumblr.com/press

G. Paltoglou et al. (Eds.): Professional Search in the Modern World, LNCS 8830, pp. 193–214, 2014.

regarded by their customers or governments debating a new legislation. The standard approaches in both cases for getting an insight on the public's opinion include conducting surveys, focus groups and questionnaires, all lengthy and costly processes. However, with the aforementioned growth of social media content where people publicly communicate their views on issues and products on the web, such information is readily available [1].

In order for this type of online content to be harnessed and utilized two conditions must be met. The available information must be initially filtered so that unrelated and redundant content is removed and only relevant and qualitative information is retained. For example, a government official studying how a new legislation is being perceived by citizens or a marketing professional investigating public perception of a new product, both have specific information needs, that is, they are both searching for data which is relevant to specific topics (e.g., the former is interested in the public's views about the proposed law).

The retrieved information must also be efficiently and effectively analysed so that the opinionated and affective content is identified, extracted and its nature and disposition assessed and characterized. In the aforementioned examples, the official isn't just interested in web pages related to the new legislation, but is particularly interested in the citizens' opinions about it. Similarly, the professional's interest is focused to the first-hand experiences and opinions of people who have already bought the product.

Opinion Retrieval provides an answer to those issues. It deals with the retrieval of documents (i.e., web pages, blog posts, tweets) that are both relevant to the user's information need and also contain opinions in reference to that information need. Technically, it refers to the ranking of documents on both notions of *relevance* and *opinionatedness* [2]. It is a sub-discipline within Information retrieval and Opinion Analysis, bringing together these two otherwise distinct areas of research.

Information Retrieval (IR) [3] deals with the problems of representing, storing, organising and providing access to information (i.e., documents, web pages, phrases, etc.). Its overall aim is to provide the user with quick and easy access to information that is relevant to his/her information needs. Standard IR techniques have as their primary objective to filter out unrelated and non-qualitative content, such as spam pages, and provide relevant information, but make no explicit provision for discriminating between objective (e.g., wikipedia-style documents) and subjective (e.g., typical blog posts) content.

Opinion Analysis (OA)[3] [4,5] is a sub-discipline within natural language processing (NLP), machine learning and computational linguistics and also borrows elements from psychology and sociology. It deals with the computational treatment of expressions of opinion, sentiment, emotion, beliefs and speculations, concisely defined as *private states*, that is, states that are not open to objective observation or verification. More specifically, it addresses the problem of de-

---

[3] The field is also known as sentiment analysis or opinion mining. Refer to chapter 1.5 of [4] for a detailed discussion about the terminology. Here, we will use all the definitions interchangeably.

tecting, extracting, analyzing and quantifying expressions of private states in written text in an automatic, computer-mediated fashion. Particular emphasis should be placed on the term "computer-mediated", as the field has a particular focus on designing, analysing and implementing algorithms that performs the aforementioned analysis in an automatic manner.

In this chapter, we will provide a concise but thorough introduction to the topic, providing an overview of the current state-of-the-art. We will discuss the particular challenges in the field and describe recent research that attempts to address them. Concretely, we will examine the issue of IR within social media, which significantly differs from standard web-based search due to the unique nature of the domain (e.g., ephemerality of content, importance of timeliness). Similarly, we will define and provide solutions to the challenges of conducting sentiment analysis of social media exchanges, such as the extensive use of informal, abbreviated language and unique prose elements, like hashtags. We will also formally define and analyse the constituent parts of "opinions" from a linguistic point of view and discuss their role in the effective analysis of relevant and opinionated content. Importantly we will address the issue of combining the research findings of those two areas of research in successfully ranking documents in response to user's information needs.

The discussed work is very relevant to the aims and objectives of the EU-funded COST action MUMIA and in general, professional search, for a number of reasons. First, opinion retrieval and filtering is a vital component of *online reputation monitoring*, that is, the tracking of an individual's or organisation's reputation over time in social media. This is a fast-growing industry with numerous companies offering such services [6,7,8] throughout the world. Second, opinion retrieval provides a concrete example of successful integration of IR and NLP for professional search. That is because opinion analysis is a field of research that is mainly investigated within the NLP community and the outputs and solutions that are proposed, such as affective dictionaries [9,10], machine-learning solutions [11] or off-the-shelf libraries [12,13] are extensively applied in opinion retrieval research [14,15,16]. In reference to the stated objectives of the MUMIA project, the above phenomenon is a direct implementation of its secondary objectives that relate to the harmonisation and transferability of methods from various disciplines[4]. Lastly, outputs of this research have already been used to a diverse set of real-world environments and applications, such as providing insights to the stock market [17], discovering how the public perceives politicians [18], and predicting movie box office revenues [19].

The rest of the chapter is structured as follows. The next section will describe the particular challenges of information retrieval in social media. Section 3 will provide an introduction to opinion analysis and discuss how the problem has been addressed. Section 4 will discuss how IR and OA can be combined in creating opinion retrieval systems. Lastly, we conclude and summarize in section 5.

---

[4] More concretely, this addresses the 1st secondary objective from the project's "Memorandum of Understanding", page 13.

2   Information Retrieval in Social Media

As previously mentioned, Information Retrieval deals with the issues of storing and retrieving information from semi-structured or unstructured sources, such as documents, web pages, etc. In contrast to standard web-based IR, applying such techniques to social media presents unique challenges [20]. In this section we'll focus on two specific social environments which are dominant nowadays, that is, *blogs* and *microblogs*, but our conclusions can easily be generalised to other settings too, such as forums or question-answering platforms (e.g., Yahoo! Answers).

One of the main differences between social search and general web-based search is the type of language being used. Research [21,22] has shown that a significant part of textual communication in social media contains non-standard language, including misspellings (e.g., "earthquake" vs. "earthquak" vs. "erthqu"), ad hoc abbreviations ("m8" vs. "mate"), phonetic substitutions ("fone" vs. "phone"), emoticons, etc. Those can be problematic for text processing, such as tokenization [22], named-entity extraction [23], part-of-speech tagging [24] and subsequently negatively influence the retrieval process. As a result, significant work has been put into the *normalization* of such content [25], that is, the transformation of out-of-vocabulary tokens into their canonical form. For example, Han et al. [22] use a machine-learning approach to detect non-standard words and locate their canonical form based on their morphophonemic similarity and context. Similarly, Gimpel et al. [24] use conditional random fields (CRFs) [26] incorporating specifically-built features for text normalization, such as hashtags and phonetic normalization in order to train a part-of-speed tagger. Kaufman and Kalita [27] view the normalization problem as a machine-translation one and implement a two-step process. In the first, pre-processing step, easy-to-identify orthographic errors are corrected (such as "wt" vs. "what" and "hellooooo" vs. "hello") and environment-specific prose elements, that is, hashtags and "@" symbols are dealt with according to the syntactic purpose they serve. The output is fed into a machine-translation system (Moses [28] in the particular case), that produces the final normalized text form. Generally, text normalization has significant benefits in analysing social media text, depending on the specific task; for example, Ritter et al. [23] report an increase of more than 50% in entity-extraction and 40% in pos-tagging compared to a standard off-the-shelf toolkit.

Apart from lexical issues, the application of standard information retrieval techniques, such as link structure analysis are also often problematic in this environment, unless specifically modified. Although standard algorithms, like Pagerank [29] and SALSA [30] are still useful in the blogosphere [31], they often need some adaptation [32,33] to better capture the social, dynamic and structural aspects of blogs. For example, BRank [32] explicitly classifies links into four different types: comments, trackbacks, citations, and blogrolls in order to give different weights to the outgoing links (e.g., comment links are weighted less importantly than citations) using a variation of Pagerank. iRank [33] aims at identifying blogs that serve as information sources for the spread of news and is more robust to the dynamic nature of the blogosphere as it considers the propagation of information over time.

In contrast, such approaches are often inapplicable in microblogs, as all posts are part of the same domain name (e.g., Twitter) and post length limitations practically prohibit the inclusion of more than one link per post. In these settings, the focus is rather on individual users and the influence they have over the specific social network (e.g., number of "followers" or number of posts forwarded - retweeted). Research [34] has shown that the number of followers users have is very closely correlated with their Pagerank, where linking is defined as following someone on the service, but re-tweeting isn't, that is, posts of users are often disproportionably shared in the service compared to their number of followers. TwitterRank [35] attempts to quantify the influence of Twitter users by considering both the link structure between them and the topical similarity of their posts. The advantage of the approach over the aforementioned analysis in the fact that it considers the presence of homophily and reciprocity within the service, that is, the phenomenon that many users follow others as a way to reciprocate their act of following, and compensates this by considering the similarity of posts between users. Tunkelang also proposes a Twitter analog to Pagerank [36] focusing on re-tweets, rather than followers or post content as TwitterRank, although no comparison between the approach and standard Pagerank is conducted.

Standard Information Retrieval term weighting approaches, like BM25 [37] and language models [38], also need adaptation for the particular requirements and idiosyncrasies of the microblog environment. Research [39] has shown that significant benefits to retrieval effectiveness can be observed when both term frequency and document length are ignored (i.e., when the k_1 and b parameters of BM25 are near zero). Specifically, improvements up to 22% can be noted in precision at early ranks ($P@30$). The same phenomenon has also been observed for language models [40]. In addition, document length normalization always seems to harm performance, potentially because it tends to favour short posts which are more likely to be of poor quality [39].

Term dependency models [41] are also affected by the microblog environment. Matzler and Cai show that in contrast to standard web-based retrieval where the sequential and the full dependence models perform similarly[5], the latter performs substantially better in this setting, potentially because it is more able to capture longer-distance token dependencies within short and noisy documents [42]. Similarly, query expansion techniques can benefit from the dynamic and time-dependent nature of microposts, in order to provide better expansion terms. Massoudi and Tsagkias [40] give a preference for terms that have occurred temporarily closer to the query time and report a performance gain of more than 100% in mean average precision compared to standard query expansion techniques. Metzler et al. [43] exploit term burstiness within pre-defined timespans and exploit the co-occurence of tokens with query words to extract useful expansion terms.

---

[5] The *sequential* dependence model assumes that only neighboring query terms are dependent, while the *full* model assumes that all query terms are dependant regardless of their order.

It is important at this point to mention the TREC Microblog track which focuses on search tasks in microblog environments [44]. The task was first introduced in 2011 addressing a real-time adhoc search task, according to which a user is interested in retrieving the most recent relevant posts. The track provided users with a mechanism to obtain a 16M tweet crawl of Twitter, spanning a period of 16 days, named the *Tweets11* corpus, for its 2011 and 2012 iterations. Its evaluation metrics were precision at rank 30 ($P@30$) and mean average precision (MAP). It has since moved to a Track-as-a-Service[6] setting, where participating teams do not have direct access to the corpus but are able to conduct basic retrieval of tweets, extract metadata, access corpus-level statistics, etc. through a publicly available, open-source API [7]. For its first iteration in 2011, the task attracted 59 groups with a total of 189 submitted runs, the largest task in the history of the TREC. It is beyond the scope of this work to analyze in detail the approaches employed by the different participating teams, but the interested reader is strongly advised to seek further information at the TREC website[8].

3   Opinion Analysis

Opinion Analysis addresses the problem of detecting, extracting, analyzing and quantifying expressions of affect in written text in an automatic or semi-automatic manner [45]. In essense, it provides an answer to the question: *"Who* thinks (or feels) *how* about *what?"*. There are three main components to this analysis: a) the opinion holder (*"who"*), b) the opinion object (*"what"*), and c) the opinion itself (*"how"*). In the following, we will discuss all three elements.

3.1   The Opinion Holder

The *opinion holder* is the entity that possesses the opinion being expressed or more generally is the owner of the private state[9]. They can be an individual, an organisation, a group, a corporation, etc. Generally, we classify them into two distinct categories: *direct* opinion holders and *indirect*. The former class contains all the instances where the author of the text is the owner of the private state. Reviews are a typical example of such instances, as their author typically reports her own thoughts and opinions about a product or service. Similarly, forum posts or tweets typically report the thoughts of their author. In contrast, a post contains an *indirect* opinion holder when a third party (e.g., a journalist) presents the opinions of other entities. For example, the sentence "In New Zealand, the

---

[6] https://github.com/lintool/twitter-tools/wiki/TREC-2013-Track-Guidelines

[7] The specification for the API is available at: https://github.com/lintool/twitter-tools/wiki/TREC-2013-API-Specifications while the source code can be found at: https://github.com/lintool/twitter-tools.

[8] http://trec.nist.gov/proceedings/proceedings.html

[9] Refer to section 1 for a definition of private states.

parliament exploded into fury against the government when ..." [10] reports the affective reaction of the New Zealand parliament (an organisation), rather than the reporter writing the article.

In practice, most approaches to automatically extract opinion holders, especially in the latter case, are based on a three-step approach [46,47]. Initially, all named entities are extracted from the text. For this, a standard entity extraction toolkit, such as Gate [48] or IdentiFinder[11] are typically used. The pool of potential entities is subsequently filtered and only those that *can* hold opinions are retained (e.g., persons rather than dates or places). Lastly, the text is syntactically parsed to extract relationships between potential holders and opinion segments, that is, text segments that contain opinions, and the most probable entity is identified as the opinion holder. Alternatively, if the domain is particularly noisy (e.g., tweets), the closest entity to the opinion segment is identified as its holder. Maynard and Funk [47] apply the approach in a microblog environment and also make provisions for direct opinion holders, by assuming that the absence of indirect ones implies that the author is the holder (e.g., "Loved the latest Harry Potter movie").

In contrast, Choi et al. [49] view the issue as a machine-learning problem and train a conditional random fields (CRFs) [26] classifier using a combination of syntactic, semantic and orthographic lexical features, such as extracted entities, capitalization, part-of-speech, etc. They report that simple entity extraction approaches have a high recall (up to 77.3% in some settings), but low precision (as low as 28.8%), while the proposed learned solution performs substantially better, especially with additional information extraction features, to a maximum F1 score of 69.4% (compared to a baseline maximum of 61.4%)

3.2   The Opinion Object

The *opinion object* refers to the entity about which the opinion or affect is being expressed, that is, the target of the private state. Often, as in case of the opinion holder, it is also implicit, rather than directly mentioned. That is quite commonly the case in reviews, blog comments or tweet replies, where the general context of the post indicates what the writer is referring to. Also, it is often not a monolithic entity but comprises an hierarchy of components and attributes, typically referred to as *aspects* [50,51]. For example, a phone can comprise the aspects: design, reception, voice quality, features, weight, etc. It is subsequently not always sufficient nor practical to only detect whether a review is overall positive or negative towards the opinion object, but to distill how each such aspect is being discussed (e.g., "good reception, but quite heavy"). This can be particularly challenging, since any given aspect can often be referred to by many synonyms; for example, following the above example, a well-designed phone can be discussed as good-looking, classy, modern, beautiful without explicitly mentioning the "design" keyword.

---

[10] Extract taken from `http://dollarsandsense.org/archives/1998/0798taylor.html`.

[11] `http://bbn.com/technology/speech/identifinder`

Ma and Wan [52] propose a solution to the problem of automatic opinion target extraction focusing on news stories comments. Initially, they parse the text and apply some heuristic syntactic rules to decide whether the target is mentioned or is implicit. In the former case, they detect the entities mentioned in the opinion segment and use Centering Theory [53] to rank them as candidate targets. In the latter case, they extract all the entities mentioned anywhere in the text (e.g., title) and use semantic relatedness [54] to decide which one is most likely to be the implicit target. In contrast, Jakob and Gurevych view the problem as a variation of an information extraction (IE) task [55]. Subsequently, they use CRFs and enrich the feature set with specifically designed features like distance of candidates from opinion segments, their part-of-speech tag, etc. Although their approach is able to correctly detect targets that are mentioned near opinion segments (explicitly or implicitly), it makes no provisions for longer distance relationships, such as when the target is mentioned in a different post or title. It should be pointed out that in microblogs specific prose elements, such as hashtags, can be particularly useful in detecting the opinion targets. For example, the tweet "It's my birthday today #hobbit will be seen with my family in IMAX 3D better than presents" implicitly refers to a movie, although it is only referenced in the text via a hashtag.

Titov and McDonald [56] deal with the problem of aspect extraction, focusing on product reviews. Their solution is based on an extension of topic models (such as LDA), named multi-grain topics (MG-LDA) according to which both global and local topics are extracted from documents. The former refer to topics that are present in the whole document, while the latter correspond to different aspects of the opinion object and are allowed to vary within a document. For example, a review about a hotel may have the global topics "hotel", "resorts" present throughout but at different parts may address different local topics, such as "service", "location", etc. Quantitative and qualitative evaluations showed the advantages of the approach, compared with standard topic models.

3.3   The Opinion

The *opinion* refers to the nature of the private state, that is, the actual affective state that is being expressed. Its automatic extraction has historically been one of the main focal points of sentiment analysis, that is, given a text segment (e.g., review, tweet, blog post) provide an informed estimate of the sentiment it expresses. This estimate can take a different number of forms depending on a number of factors, such as the specific prerequisites of the analysis, the domain of application, the psychological paradigm adopted, etc. Typical examples of analyses can include, but are not limited to:

- A *binary* decision indicating whether the affective content belongs to one of two predefined categories, typically positive or negative. Typical examples include product reviews [11,57], opinions about a new legislation that can either be in favor or against them [58] or points-of-view about current political issues [59]. In some environments, such as online discussions, where not all exchanges necessarily contain affective segments, a *ternary* scheme is more appropriate and adopted [60]: {*objective, positive, negative*}, where the objective category typically signifies the absence of opinionated or affective content, such as encyclopedic-type, mainly informative, content.

- A *real* value providing more fine-grained and detailed information about the nature of the affective content. Typical applications include studies of the level of valence or arousal[12] at a specific scale (e.g., [1,9]) expressed in forums or presidential speeches [62,63,64]. Such types of analyses are most common in social or psychological studies as they tend to better correlate with current psychological theories [62].

- A *categorical* classification where the analysis aims to determine the general psychological state of the author of a message. Typically, the analysis will involve several potential states such as nervousness, anxiety, fear, fatigue and tension [65,66]. In the same manner, basic emotions, such as love, hate, etc. [67] can be detected in written text [68] although there is significant debate within the field of psychology on the human agreement [68] and universality [69] of such states.

This analysis is a non-trivial task, as even people often disagree on the affective content of written text [68,70]. Prosaic elements, such as irony and thwarted expectations (the latter occurring when a change of opinion occurs in the end of a text segment) pose particular challenges [71]. Contextuality is also often vital; a review comprising only of the sentence "go read the book!" would be considered positive in a book review, but negative if referring to a movie (inspired by a book). People also often find unique ways of expressing affect without necessarily using affective words and occasionally communicate ambiguous messages. For example, the sentence "If you are reading this because it is your darling fragrance, please wear it at home exclusively and tape the windows shut" contains no explicit affective words, yet it contains a rather negative opinion about a product.

Generally, the problem has been addressed from two distinct points-of-view: machine-learning and lexicon-based solutions. Below we discuss both approaches.

Machine-learning solutions have been an integral part of sentiment analysis [72,11] as a significant number of solutions are based on them. In typical scenarios, an appropriate labeled dataset[13] (e.g., positive and negative reviews about a product or category of products) is used to train a standard algorithm, such as as Support Vector Machines (SVMs) [73] or Naive Bayes [74] and the acquired knowledge is subsequently applied to new, unlabeled documents in order to predict their affective disposition. Typical features used for training include standard bag-of-words unigrams and bigrams and part-of-speech tags; overall

---

[12] Valence is defined as the dimension of experience that refers to hedonism (i.e., pleasure and displeasure) and arousal refers to the level of excitement or energy of the individual [61].

[13] "Labeled" refers to datasets where documents have had their affective content manually assessed.

they tend to perform adequately well despite their simplicity [11]. Subsequently, there is significant work that focuses on extending those features with additional, sentiment-based elements by taking advantage of the idiosyncrasies of affective communication [57,75,71]. For example, limited human assistance can be employed in annotating specific emotionally definitive phrases [76] or analyzing the syntax of the text in order to extract useful patterns [9]. Currently, the state-of-the-art solution is based on recursive neural tensor networks trained on a sentiment treebank [77], with a reported accuracy of 85.4% for single sentence, binary classification. Pang and Lee [4] provide a thorough introduction to the topic in their seminal book.

One of the main bottlenecks of the approach is the development of appropriate datasets, as the trained classifiers tend to be particularly domain-dependant [78]; a model that is trained on reviews of toys will have substantially deteriorated effectiveness if applied to book reviews. Their development is generally a time-consuming process, as it requires manual effort for the text to be read and its affective content evaluated [70,79]. Nonetheless, there are ways to automate this, for example by extracting the metadata that accompany the text, such as the "number of stars" in product reviews [11] or the ideological stand or final vote in political issues [58]. Implicit signals within the message itself, such as the type of emoticons used [80] can also be used to infer an overall affective state. Lastly, crowdsourcing approaches can provide an alternative solution [81].

Alternatively to producing domain-dependent datasets, there is work that focuses on *adapting* trained classifiers from one domain to another [78,82,83,84]. This can be a viable solution when there is some labeled data from one domain (*source domain*) but there is none from another (*target domain*). Structural correspondence learning [82,83], one of the most effective solutions, relies on words, called *pivots*, which are common and retain their affective denotation in multiple domains. It functions by correlating their co-occurrence with emotionally-ambiguous words in order to extract the latters' affective connotation in other domains. For example, if the pivot word "excellent" often co-occurs often with the word "light" in labeled reviews of mobile devices and with the phrase "accurate steering" in unlabeled car reviews, the algorithm can extract that the latter phrase is also probably utilized as a positive attribute. In settings where pivot words are rare, graph-based solutions [78,84] that rely on document similarity between different domains can be applied. Those exploit the similarity of documents between the source and target domains in order to estimate the probability that unlabeled documents belong to a specific category and then iteratively use this estimation to train a classifier.

Lexicon-based solutions [85,13,86,12] are typically based on estimating the affective content of text segments by utilizing one or more *affective dictionaries*, that is, word lists in which each lemma has been assigned an affective value [87,88,10,89], for example the level of positivity or negativity it typically conveys. We discuss them more in detail below. Usually, such solutions also incorporate various prose and syntactic-based rules to increase their accuracy and coverage.

Typical extensions include capitalization, negation, abbreviation (e.g., "lol") and emoticon detection and incorporation of lists of intensifier/diminisher words that increase or decrease respectively the affective strength of affective words. In addition, they may have provisions for detecting misspelled words [13], which is particularly useful when the misspelling itself provides an indication of affect (e.g., "Microsoft" vs. "Micro$oft" or "loved" vs. "loooooved").

The advantage of lexicon-based solutions is that they can be utilized *off-the-shelf* to a multitude of environments, without requiring training, which is often a significant advantage in occasions where labeled data is difficult or expensive to produce. They have also been shown to perform adequately effectively in a number of diverse social media settings, such as forums, microblogs, blogs, etc. [85,90,12], often reaching human-level accuracy [13]. Nonetheless, anecdotal evidence suggests that compared to in-domain trained machine-learning classifiers they tend to underperform, especially in longer, review-type content.

As expected, their effectiveness is predominately characterised by the coverage and accuracy of the affective dictionary they employ. There is a significant number of such lexicons that have been developed either automatically or semi-automatically [91] by extending WordNet[14] [92] with additional, affective annotations. Examples include WordNet-Affect [89] and SentiWordNet [10], both of which adopt a different annotation scheme. The former contains 4,787 words, mainly nouns and verbs, that directly or indirectly refer to mental states. For example the term "anger" is annotated as referring to "emotion" while "cry" belongs to the "behavior" category. SentiWordNet on the other hand, uses a simpler ternary scheme and gives each lemma three scores based on how positive, negative or objective it is. The three scores sum up to 1, giving the annotations an interesting probabilistic interpretation. For example the noun "love" has a positive value of 0.625 and negative value of 0.0, while "hate" has a negative value of 0.75 and a positive value of 0.0.

An addition to those lexicons, there are dictionaries that were populated manually by human annotators. They include the "Linguistic Inquiry and Word Count" (LIWC) [87] and the "Affective Norms for English words" (ANEW) [88], which also offer different type of annotations. LIWC classifies words in one or several, not necessarily affective, categories, such as social, family, time, positive, anger, etc. while ANEW provides for each word three values of valence, arousal and dominance on a $[1, 9]$ range. Both have been used in a number of large scale studies [63,93,94].

Hybrid solutions [95,96] offer a third alternative to detecting the emotional content of text. They typically employ an iterative, bootstrapping methodology. The text is initially analysed using lexicon-based techniques and the produced output is fed into a machine-learning algorithm as training data. The output of the second phase is subsequently utilized in order to expand the affective dictionary and the whole process is repeated until some stopping criterion is satisfied,

---

[14] WordNet is a lexical database, which in addition to providing the definition of words also provides semantic relations between them, such as antonyms, synonyms, etc.

for example, the accuracy on a small, labeled subset reaches a pre-specified threshold or no more words are added/removed from the affective dictionary. Hybrid solutions can be applied in settings where some limited labeled training data is available and standard lexicon-based solutions perform inadequately.

4   Bringing It All Together

Having discussed in previous sections the issues of informational retrieval in social media and opinion analysis, in this section we present and discuss how they can be combined to retrieve relevant and opinionated social media content. Metrics used to evaluate the effectiveness of proposed solutions include typical IR metrics, such as mean average precision (MAP), binary Preference (bPref) etc., where documents are considered *relevant* only if they contain "an explicit expression of opinion or sentiment" about the target topic [2]. Therefore, relevancy in the context of opinion retrieval is a combination of standard IR topical relevancy[15] and opinionatedness; a document must satisfy both criteria to be considered *relevant*.

A typical approach [2,16,97,98] to solving the problem is by implementing a two-phase strategy; first, a *topical* retrieval algorithm is applied to the environment of interest, such as blogs, microblogs or forums. The algorithm can be a variation of standard IR $tf.idf$ techniques, such as BM25 [37] or language models [38], appropriately modified for the particular medium as discussed in detail in section 2. Second, the top-retrieved results are automatically analysed so that their affective content is assessed and they are subsequently filtered or re-ranked. Filtering typically refers to the complete removal of documents that are found to contain only non-opinionated content while re-ranking refers to the *promoting* of opinionated documents in higher positions in the final ranking. The affective analysis can be done through any of the techniques discussed in section 3, that is, machine-learning, lexicon-based or a combination of both, depending on the application requirements and environment idiosyncrasies. Lastly, the retrieved opinionated content can be further analysed so that its polarity is estimated (e.g., positive vs. negative opinions) or summarised based on the extracted aspects of the discussed entities [99,100].

A typical example of this approach is presented by Yang et al. [97,98]. Their solution employs a standard vector-space model for topical retrieval, enhanced with BM25 term weighting. Subsequently, the top retrieved documents are analysed so that their affective contents are extracted using a multitude of evidence and resources. For example, they use pre-compiled lists of affective terms extracted from labeled, opinionated blog-posts, using information gain [101] as the ranking criterion to filter out tokens that appear equally in negative and positive blog posts. They also attempt to capture rarely occurring affective terms by extracting low frequency, out-of-vocabulary terms from the same labeled dataset and then manually inspecting them. Lastly, they further enhance their affective dictionary with adjectives and verbs through an iterative process, using an initial

---

[15] We use the term "topical" to denote a standard topic-based retrieval.

seed list and exploiting the synonym structure within WordNet [92] in a process similar to Kamps et al. [102]. The gathered evidence is then utilized in order to promote documents that have a high probability of containing affective content. The combination of the above elements results on one of the highest MAP in the relevant TREC Blog Track[16] of 0.2052.

The re-ranking approach is conceptually similar to another solution to opinion retrieval: the combination of independent scores of relevancy and opinionatedness if applied to every retrieved document. According to this approach, the final $score(Q, D)$ of document D given query Q is calculated as:

$$score(Q, D) = a \times relevance\_score(Q, D) + (1 - a) \times opinion\_score(Q, D) \quad (1)$$

where $relevance\_score(Q, D)$ is the topical score of document D given query Q (using a standard $tf.idf$ weighting scheme), $opinion\_score(Q, D)$ is the affective score of document D (e.g., the probability that it contains opinions), and a, where $a \in [0, 1]$, is a parameter the leverages the two scores. Typically, those scores are combined using a linear combination as above [97,103,104] although other combinations have also been presented [16,105,106], but they are less often used in practice.

Following the above formulation, most of the research has focused on calculating $opinion\_score(Q, D)$. Two general solutions have been proposed; the first estimates an opinion score which is *independent* of the query, that is, $opinion\_score(Q, D) = opinion\_score(D)$ for every Q. The second is based on query-*dependent* opinion scores. Each approach has its advantages and disadvantages. Typically, the latter approach is less efficient, since it relies on the creation of query-dependent affective lexicons or the analysis of text during query-time. In contrast, the former is based on pre-compiled lexicons or pre-trained machine-learning models. Although one would expect the latter to be more effective, research [107,103] has shown that both approaches tend to perform similarly, with a mixture solution typically performing best [104]. Below, we discuss the more prevalent and effective solutions.

Query-Dependent solutions aim at estimating the affective content of documents in reference to the user query. Such approaches would optimally be able to distill that the term "unpredictable" is generally used in a positive manner when discussing a movie or a book, but negatively when discussing a car or motorbike. In addition, they would be able to differentiate when a term is being used in an objective manner (e.g., the term "cool" in "cool evening") and when it's been used in an affective manner (e.g., "the new product received a rather cool reception").

A standard way of producing a query-dependent affective lexicon is by exploiting and modifying the standard pseudo-query expansion phase [104,108] during query time. For example, Huang and Croft [104], instead of extracting the most frequent terms from the top-k ranked documents and adding them to

---

[16] We discuss the TREC Blog Track in detail in the end of section 4.

the query, extract the most frequent terms from a set of top-retrieved manually-labelled opinionated documents. Na et al. [108] focus on updating the probability $Prob(subj|w)$ that the affective term w of a domain-independent lexicon (i.e., SentiWordNet) is subjective in real-time, per-query basis. To achieve that, they count the occurrences of affective terms w in the set of top-retrieved documents, normalize them by the total number of tokens in the document and use this estimation to update the original affective weight $Prob(subj|w)$. Lastly, the discovered affective terms are added to the initial query. In both cases, statistical significant improvements over standard query-expansion techniques are reported. When applied to the same dataset, both approaches perform similarly (i.e., MAP of 0.3147 vs 0.3159).

Jijkoun et al. [91] start with a domain-independent affective dictionary [9] and search for specific syntactic patterns within the topically-retrieved documents in which affective terms are used to express opinions, in order to extract potential opinion targets. To identify them they compare their frequency within the extracted patterns to an external corpus, using the chi-square metric. Lastly, they re-visit the initially extracted patterns and keep only the affective terms that co-occur with the extracted targets.

Query-Independent solutions are based on either computing a static *opinion_score(D)* for each document in the collection [105], or using pre-compiled affective dictionaries [103,104] or trained machine-learning classifiers, as discussed in section 3.3. Typically, they identify whether any expressed opinion refers to the query topic by measuring the proximity of the query terms to the discovered subjective text segments.

He et al. [105] start by creating a generic dictionary by filtering out too frequent or too rare collection terms. They subsequently weigh the remaining terms exploiting the difference of their distributions in the sets of manually-labelled objective and opinionated documents, using the Divergence From Randomness framework [109]. Lastly, they create a query from the X top weighted opinionated terms (where X is a parameter in the $[50, 500]$ interval that requires tuning) and calculate an *opinion_score(D)* for each retrieved document using a standard document weighting model (e.g., BM25). During query time they combine the above calculated score with a standard topical score (equation 1). The approach outperformed the best TREC baseline run, attaining a MAP value of 0.3671 on the same dataset.

Other approaches focus on utilizing or modifying pre-compiled affective dictionaries [103,104]. Typically, one of more lexicons are combined and the most frequent affective tokens are selected to expand the original query [104]. Dietz et al. [103] use SentiWordNet in order to limit the query expansion terms during a pseudo-relevance query-expansion step, to only those that appear in the dictionary.

Off-the-shelf sentiment analysis tools, like OpinionFinder [12], have also been successfully used in research [16,15]. Typically, they are used to analyse the top-retrieved documents and provide an informed estimation of their affective content. For example, He et al. [16] estimate it as the normalized *opinion_score(D)*

$= sum\_diff \times \frac{\#subj}{\#sent}$, where the second multiplicand represents the ratio of subjective sentences in a document, while sum_diff is the sum of the confidence scores of subjectivity that OpinionFinder provides for the particular document. Importantly, in an extension of the previous work, Santos et al. [15] also consider the *proximity* of query terms to opinionated sentences in a document. Their idea relies on the intuition that if query terms are near or within subjective text segments then they are more likely to contain opinion about those terms, rather that other, non-relevant topics and should therefore be promoted in the final ranking list. They model this proximity by modifying a standard term-dependency model [41] within the DFR framework [110], where instead of considering the proximity of query terms they consider the proximity of query terms to subjective sentences; documents in which those occur closer get a higher final score.

Zhang et al. [14] approach the problem as a classification one. They train an SVM [73] classifier using as training data subjective documents from reviews sites, like rateitall.com and epinions.com, and objective documents from wikipedia. As features, they use standard unigrams and bigrams, ranked by the Pearson's chi-square test. In a subsequent step, they attempt to detect if any opinions expressed in the document refer to the query topic by looking whether the query terms occur near the opinionated segments. In their subsequent work [111] they also add a *polarity* classification step, trained on positive and negative reviews. They extract the final polarity of the document by applying a decision tree classifier using as features the number of positive and negative sentences in the document, the ratio of positive and negative sentences that occur near query terms, etc.

A third approach to opinion retrieval is offered by Luo et al. [112]. Their solution is based on the application of the learning-to-rank framework [113] applied to Twitter posts. They combine standard IR features (i.e., BM25) with social features (e.g., number of author followers or tweet hasthtags) and opinionatedness features, using a corpus-derived lexicon, to train a ranking function, based on SVMs. Their results indicate that retrieval effectiveness increases when all the above features are considered (i.e., best MAP of 0.4020 compared to a baseline of topical retrieval with BM25 of 0.2509).

In closing this section, special mention should be made to the TREC Blog Track [114,115] and in particular the opinion finding task that ran from 2006 to 2008. The task utilized the Blogs06 corpus [116] that contains an uncompressed 148GB (over 3.2M permalinks from over 100K blogs) crawl of the blogosphere. Participants of the task had to find relevant and opinionated content about a given target entity X; in effect, the task asked the participants to answer the question "What do people think about X?". Between 2007 and 2008, the Track also ran a polarity sub-task, according to which participants where asked to detect the *polarity* of the expressed opinion, using a binary scheme, positive vs. negative. It is beyond the score to discuss in detail the approaches that were adopted for either task, although the most representative and effective solutions have been presented, but the interested reader is encouraged to seek the proceedings from the official TREC site[17].

---

[17] http://trec.nist.gov/

5   Summary and Future Work

In this chapter, we presented a brief but concise introduction to Opinion Retrieval. The field has known particular popularity in recent years, significantly
aided by the wide range of applications that it can be applied to, the financial impact that it can have, as well as by the existence of standard testbeds,
developed by the academic community.

In section 2 we discussed the challenges and solutions to retrieving information
from social media. Although no single solution will be optimal for the diverse set
of social media environments currently in existence (blogs, microblogs, forums,
etc.), a wide variety of solutions was presented that attempt to address the most
prevalent issues, such as the informality of language, the ephemerality of content,
the limited document length, etc.

In section 3, we presented an overview of sentiment analysis. We discussed the
different constituent parts of private states, that is, the owner, the object and
the actual nature of the private state, and discussed methods for addressing the
problem of automatically extracting them from text. Especially, in reference to
the issue of extracting the affective content of texts, we classified solutions into
three categories; machine-learning based, lexicon-based and hybrid solutions. We
presented the most significant approaches from each category and discussed their
advantages and disadvantages.

In section 4, we discussed how those two areas can be combined in order
to retrieve both relevant and opinionated content from social media. Although
opinion retrieval has known significant popularity within the IR community, it
has often used insights and solutions originally developed with the NLP field.
This has resulted in a pragmatic and substantial collaboration within these two,
related but often distinct, areas of research. Proposed solutions use a variety of
techniques and approaches for solving the problem, including machine-learning
and lexicon-based solutions.

Despite the significant work in the field, there are still important challenges.
One of those pertains to that fact that opinion analysis solutions are, as discussed, particularly domain-dependent; a classifier that has been optimised on
a specific type of content will often perform poorly on another. The domain-
sensitivity phenomenon takes place not only within different genres of documents
(e.g., product reviews vs. political forum discussions) but also within different
topics belonging to the same genre (e.g., movie vs. electronics reviews). Although
significant progress has been made in addressing the issue, in the form of domain-
adaptation solutions, one key aspect that has not been thoroughly researched is
genre/topic recognition in the context of opinion analysis. The above has been
researched in terms of standard topical text categorisation, but its potential effect in opinion analysis remains unclear, that is, given a random piece of text
automatically decide its genre and topicality and apply the appropriate model.

In addition, the diversity of genres and topics makes the above analysis particularly difficult. For example, determining whether a forum post is pro or

against gun-control[18] requires a classifer explicitly trained on the specific topic. Often, the acquisition of such training data is either non-trivial or prohibitively expensive. Although crowdsourcing has been successfully used in the past for annotating documents, results tend to be mixed when the tasks become more complex, such as determining the political stand of a forum post. As a result, it remains challenging to train classifiers on fine-grained topics and multiple genres.

Challenges also remain in the context of combining information retrieval and opinion analysis. As discussed, most solutions approach the problem with a two-phase strategy. Although this has generally proved relatively effective, it has been shown that they are bound by the effectiveness of the topical retrieval solution, that is, strong IR baselines will generally perform better. As such, the role of opinion analysis is only to rerank or filter out the retrieved documents. In contrast, one could envision a solution where signals of both opinionatedness and relevancy are combined at the same level to retrieve and rank documents. An initial example of this approach is provided by Luo et al. [112], but more work that addresses the domain-sensitivity issue is required.

In conclusion, despite the important work in both the areas of opinion analysis and opinion retrieval, there is still significant work to be done towards a *universal opinion analysis system* that would be able to retrieve social media content that is relevant to a target topic and make informed decisions about its affectiveness and opinionatedness towards that topic regardless of its genre.

References

1. Zeng, D., Chen, H., Lusch, R., Li, S.H.: Social media analytics and intelligence. IEEE Intelligent Systems 25(6), 13–16 (2010)
2. Macdonald, C., Ounis, I., Soboroff, I.: Overview of the trec-2008 blog track. In: Proc. TREC 2008 (2008)
3. Baeza-Yates, R.A., Ribeiro-Neto, B.: Modern Information Retrieval. Addison-Wesley Longman Publishing Co., Inc., Boston (1999)
4. Pang, B., Lee, L.: Opinion mining and sentiment analysis. Found. Trends Inf. Retr. 2(1-2), 1–135 (2008)
5. Liu, B.: Sentiment Analysis and Opinion Mining. Synthesis Lectures on Human Language Technologies. Morgan & Claypool Publishers (2012)
6. Bilton, N.: The growing business of online reputation management. New York Times (April 4, 2011), http://bits.blogs.nytimes.com/2011/04/04/the-growing-business-of-online-reputation-management/ (last accessed January 23, 2014)
7. Tozzi, J.: Do reputation management services work? Bloomberg Bussiness Week (April 30, 2008), http://www.businessweek.com/stories/2008-04-30/do-reputation-management-services-work-businessweek-business-news-stock-market-and-and-financial-advice (last accessed January 23, 2014)
8. Schawbel, D.: Do reputation management services work? Mashable (December 29, 2008), http://mashable.com/2008/12/29/brand-reputation-monitoring-tools/ (last accessed January 23, 2014)

---

[18] Gun control is a prevalent topic in USA politics.

9. Wilson, T., Wiebe, J., Hoffmann, P.: Recognizing contextual polarity in phrase-level sentiment analysis. In: Proc. EMNLP 2005, pp. 347–354 (2005)
10. Baccianella, S., Esuli, A., Sebastiani, F.: Sentiwordnet 3.0. In: Proc. LREC 2010 (2010)
11. Pang, B., Lee, L., Vaithyanathan, S.: Thumbs up? Sentiment classification using machine learning techniques. In: Proc. EMNLP 2002, pp. 79–86 (2002)
12. Wilson, T., Hoffmann, P., Somasundaran, S., Kessler, J., Wiebe, J., Choi, Y., Cardie, C., Riloff, E., Patwardhan, S.: Opinionfinder: A system for subjectivity analysis. In: Proc. HLT-Demo 2005, pp. 34–35 (2005)
13. Thelwall, M., Buckley, K., Paltoglou, G., Di, C., Kappas, A.: Sentiment strength detection in short informal text. JASIST 61(12), 2544–2558 (2010)
14. Zhang, W., Yu, C., Meng, W.: Opinion retrieval from blogs. In: Proc. CIKM 2007, pp. 831–840 (2007)
15. Santos, R.L.T., He, B., Macdonald, C., Ounis, I.: Integrating proximity to sub-jective sentences for blog opinion retrieval. In: Boughanem, M., Berrut, C., Mothe, J., Soule-Dupuy, C. (eds.) ECIR 2009. LNCS, vol. 5478, pp. 325–336. Springer, Heidelberg (2009)
16. He, B., Macdonald, C., Ounis, I.: Ranking opinionated blog posts using opinion-finder. In: Proc. SIGIR 2008, pp. 727–728 (2008)
17. Bollen, J., Mao, H., Zeng, X.: Twitter mood predicts the stock market. Journal of Computational Science (2011)
18. Lerman, K., Gilder, A., Dredze, M., Pereira, F.: Reading the markets: Forecasting public opinion of political candidates by news analysis. In: Proc. COLING 2008, pp. 473–480 (2008)
19. Asur, S., Huberman, B.A.: Predicting the future with social media. In: Proc. WI-IAT 2010, pp. 492–499 (2010)
20. Boughanem, M.: Information retrieval and social media. In: Amine, A., Mohamed, O.A., Bellatreche, L. (eds.) Modeling Approaches and Algorithms. SCI, vol. 488, p. 7. Springer, Heidelberg (2013)
21. Thelwall, M.: Myspace comments. Online Information Review 33(1), 58–76 (2009)
22. Han, B., Cook, P., Baldwin, T.: Lexical normalization for social media text. ACM Trans. Intell. Syst. Technol. 4(1), 5:1–5:27 (2013)
23. Ritter, A., Clark, S., Mausam, E.O.: Named entity recognition in tweets: An experimental study. In: Proc. EMNLP 2011, pp. 1524–1534 (2011)
24. Gimpel, K., Schneider, N., O'Connor, B., Das, D., Mills, D., Eisenstein, J., Heil-man, M., Yogatama, D., Flanigan, J., Smith, N.A.: Part-of-speech tagging for twitter: Annotation, features, and experiments. In: Proc. HLT 2011, pp. 42–47 (2011)
25. Sproat, R., Black, A.W., Chen, S.F., Kumar, S., Ostendorf, M., Richards, C.: Normalization of non-standard words. Computer Speech and Language 15(3), 287–333 (2001)
26. Lafferty, J.D., McCallum, A., Pereira, F.C.N.: Conditional random fields: Prob-abilistic models for segmenting and labeling sequence data. In: Proc. ICML 2001, pp. 282–289 (2001)
27. Kaufmann, M., Kalita, J.: Syntactic normalization of Twitter messages. In: Proc. ICON 2010, Chennai, India (2010)
28. Koehn, P., Hoang, H., Birch, A., Callison-Burch, C., Federico, M., Bertoldi, N., Cowan, B., Shen, W., Moran, C., Zens, R., Dyer, C., Bojar, O., Constantin, A., Herbst, E.: Moses: Open source toolkit for statistical machine translation. In: Proc. ACL 2007, pp. 177–180 (2007)

29. Page, L., Brin, S., Motwani, R., Winograd, T.: The pagerank citation ranking: Bringing order to the web. In: Proc. WWW 1998, pp. 161–172 (1998)
30. Lempel, R., Moran, S.: Salsa: The stochastic approach for link-structure analysis. ACM Trans. Inf. Syst. 19(2), 131–160 (2001)
31. Kirchhoff, L., Bruns, A., Nicolai, T.: Investigating the impact of the blogosphere: Using pagerank to determine the distribution of attention. In: Association of Internet Researchers (2007)
32. Lin, C.L., Kao, H.Y.: Blog popularity mining using social interconnection analysis. IEEE Internet Computing 14(4), 41–49 (2010)
33. Adar, E., Zhang, L., Adamic, L., Lukose, R.: Implicit structure and the dynamics of blogspace. In: Workshop on the Weblogging Ecosystem, vol. 13 (2004)
34. Kwak, H., Lee, C., Park, H., Moon, S.: What is twitter, a social network or a news media? In: Proc. WWW 2010, pp. 591–600 (2010)
35. Weng, J., Lim, E.P., Jiang, J., He, Q.: Twitterrank: Finding topic-sensitive influential twitterers. In: Proc. WSDM 2010, pp. 261–270 (2010)
36. Tunkelang, D.: A twitter analog to pagerank. The Noisy Channel (2009), http://thenoisychannel.com/2009/01/13/a-twitter-analog-to-pagerank/ (last visited: December 13, 2013)
37. Jones, K.S., Walker, S., Robertson, S.E.: A probabilistic model of information retrieval: Development and comparative experiments. Inf. Process. Manage. 36(6), 779–808 (2000)
38. Lavrenko, V., Croft, W.B.: Relevance-based language models. In: Proc. SIGIR 2001, pp. 120–127 (2001)
39. Ferguson, P., O'Hare, N., Lanagan, J., Phelan, O., McCarthy, K.: An investigation of term weighting approaches for microblog retrieval. In: Baeza-Yates, R., de Vries, A.P., Zaragoza, H., Cambazoglu, B.B., Murdock, V., Lempel, R., Silvestri, F. (eds.) ECIR 2012. LNCS, vol. 7224, pp. 552–555. Springer, Heidelberg (2012)
40. Massoudi, K., Tsagkias, M., de Rijke, M., Weerkamp, W.: Incorporating query expansion and quality indicators in searching microblog posts. In: Clough, P., Foley, C., Gurrin, C., Jones, G.J.F., Kraaij, W., Lee, H., Mudoch, V. (eds.) ECIR 2011. LNCS, vol. 6611, pp. 362–367. Springer, Heidelberg (2011)
41. Metzler, D., Croft, W.B.: A markov random field model for term dependencies. In: Proc. SIGIR 2005, pp. 472–479 (2005)
42. Metzler, D., Cai, C.: Usc/isi at trec 2011: Microblog track. In: Proc. TREC (2011)
43. Metzler, D., Cai, C., Hovy, E.: Structured event retrieval over microblog archives. In: Proc. NAACL HLT 2012, pp. 646–655 (2012)
44. Ounis, I., Macdonald, C., Lin, J., Soboroff, I.: Overview of the trec-2011 microblog track. In: Proc. TREC 2011, pp. 1–13 (2011)
45. Paltoglou, G.: Sentiment analysis in social media. In: Agarwal, N., Lim, M., Wigard, R. (eds.) Online Collective Action: Dynamics of the Crowd in Social Media. Lecture Notes in Social Networks Series. Springer International Publishing (in press)
46. Kim, S.M., Hovy, E.: Determining the sentiment of opinions. In: Proc. COLING 2004 (2004)
47. Maynard, D., Funk, A.: Automatic detection of political opinions in tweets. In: García-Castro, R., Fensel, D., Antoniou, G. (eds.) ESWC 2011. LNCS, vol. 7117, pp. 88–99. Springer, Heidelberg (2012)
48. Cunningham, H., Maynard, D., Bontcheva, K., Tablan, V., Aswani, N., Roberts, I., Gorrell, G., Funk, A., Roberts, A., Damljanovic, D., Heitz, T., Greenwood, M.A., Saggion, H., Petrak, J., Li, Y., Peters, W.: Text Processing with GATE, Version 6 (2011)

49. Choi, Y., Cardie, C., Riloff, E., Patwardhan, S.: Identifying sources of opinions with conditional random fields and extraction patterns. In: Proc. HLT/EMNLP (2005)
50. Titov, I., McDonald, R.: Modeling online reviews with multi-grain topic models. In: Proc. WWW 2008, pp. 111–120 (2008)
51. Kim, S.M., Hovy, E.: Automatic identification of pro and con reasons in online reviews. In: Proc. COLING-ACL 2006, pp. 483–490 (2006)
52. Ma, T., Wan, X.: Opinion target extraction in chinese news comments. In: Proc. COLING 2010, pp. 782–790 (2010)
53. Grosz, B.J., Weinstein, S., Joshi, A.K.: Centering: A framework for modeling the local coherence of discourse. Comput. Linguist. 21, 203–225 (1995)
54. Gabrilovich, E., Markovitch, S.: Computing semantic relatedness using wikipedia-based explicit semantic analysis. In: Proc. IJCAI 2007, pp. 1606–1611 (2007)
55. Jakob, N., Gurevych, I.: Extracting opinion targets in a single- and cross-domain setting with conditional random fields. In: Proc. EMNLP 2010, pp. 1035–1045 (2010)
56. Titov, I., McDonald, R.: Modeling online reviews with multi-grain topic models. In: Proc. WWW 2008, pp. 111–120 (2008)
57. Whitelaw, C., Garg, N., Argamon, S.: Using appraisal groups for sentiment analysis. In: Proc. CIKM 2005, pp. 625–631 (2005)
58. Thomas, M., Pang, B., Lee, L.: Get out the vote: Determining support or opposition from Congressional floor-debate transcripts. In: Proc. EMNLP 2006, pp. 327–335 (2006)
59. Lin, W.H., Wilson, T., Wiebe, J., Hauptmann, A.: Which side are you on? identifying perspectives at the document and sentence levels. In: Proc. CoNLL 2006 (2006)
60. Chmiel, A., Sienkiewicz, J., Thelwall, M., Paltoglou, G., Buckley, K., Kappas, A., Hoyst, J.A.: Collective emotions online and their influence on community life. PLoS ONE 6(7), e22207 (2011)
61. Barrett, L.F., Russell, J.A.: The structure of current affect: Controversies and emerging consensus. Current Directions in Psychological Science 8(1) (1999)
62. Paltoglou, G., Theunis, M., Kappas, A., Thelwall, M.: Predicting emotional responses to long informal text. T. Affective Computing 4(1), 106–115 (2013)
63. Gonzalez-Bailon, S., Banchs, R.E., Kaltenbrunner, A.: Emotional reactions and the pulse of public opinion: Measuring the impact of political events on the sentiment of online discussions. CoRR abs/1009.4019 (2010)
64. Dodds, P., Danforth, C.: Measuring the happiness of Large-Scale written expression: Songs, blogs, and presidents. Journal of Happiness Studies (July 2009)
65. Mishne, G.: Experiments with mood classification in blog posts. In: 1st Workshop on Stylistic Analysis of Text for Information Access (2005)
66. Bollen, J., Mao, H., Pepe, A.: Modeling public mood and emotion: Twitter sentiment and socio-economic phenomena. In: Proc. ICWSM 2011 (2011)
67. Dalgleish, T., Power, M.: Handbook of Cognition and Emotion. John Wiley & Sons (March 1999)
68. Strapparava, C., Mihalcea, R.: Semeval-2007 task 14: Affective text. In: Proc. SemEval 2007, pp. 70–74 (2007)
69. Mauss, I.B., Robinson, M.D.: Measures of emotion: A review. Cognition & Emotion 23(2), 209–237 (2009)
70. Paltoglou, G., Thelwall, M., Buckely, K.: Online textual communication annotated with grades of emotion strength. In: Proc. EMOTION 2010, pp. 25–31 (2010)
71. Paltoglou, G., Thelwall, M.: More than bag-of-words: Sentence-based document representation for sentiment analysis. In: Proc. RANLP 2013, pp. 546–552 (2013)
72. Chen, H., Zimbra, D.: Ai and opinion mining. IEEE Intelligent Systems 25, 74–80 (2010)

73. Platt, J.C.: Fast training of support vector machines using sequential minimal optimization, pp. 185–208 (1999)
74. John, G.H., Langley, P.: Estimating continuous distributions in bayesian classifiers, pp. 338–345 (1995)
75. Agarwal, A., Xie, B., Vovsha, I., Rambow, O., Passonneau, R.: Sentiment analysis of twitter data. In: Proc. LSM 2011, pp. 30–38 (2011)
76. Zaidan, O., Eisner, J., Piatko, C.D.: Using annotator rationales to improve machine learning for text categorization. In: Proc. HLT-NAACL, pp. 260–267 (2007)
77. Socher, R., Perelygin, A., Wu, J., Chuang, J., Manning, C.D., Ng, A.Y., Potts, C.: Recursive deep models for semantic compositionality over a sentiment treebank. In: Proc. EMNLP 2013, pp. 1631–1642 (2013)
78. Ponomareva, N., Thelwall, M.: Biographies or blenders: Which resource is best for cross-domain sentiment analysis? In: Gelbukh, A. (ed.) CICLing 2012, Part I. LNCS, vol. 7181, pp. 488–499. Springer, Heidelberg (2012)
79. Paltoglou, G., Buckley, K.: Subjectivity annotation of the microblog 2011 realtime adhoc relevance judgments. In: Serdyukov, P., Braslavski, P., Kuznetsov, S.O., Kamps, J., Rüger, S., Agichtein, E., Segalovich, I., Yilmaz, E. (eds.) ECIR 2013. LNCS, vol. 7814, pp. 344–355. Springer, Heidelberg (2013)
80. Pak, A., Paroubek, P.: Twitter as a corpus for sentiment analysis and opinion mining. In: Proc. LREC 2010 (2010)
81. Brew, A., Greene, D., Cunningham, P.: Using crowdsourcing and active learning to track sentiment in online media. In: Proc. ECAI 2010, pp. 145–150 (2010)
82. Blitzer, J., Dredze, M., Pereira, F.: Biographies, bollywood, boom-boxes and blenders: Domain adaptation for sentiment classification. In: Proc. ACL 2007, pp. 440–447 (2007)
83. Blitzer, J., McDonald, R., Pereira, F.: Domain adaptation with structural correspondence learning. In: Proc. EMNLP 2006, pp. 120–128 (2006)
84. Ponomareva, N., Thelwall, M.: Do neighbours help? an exploration of graph-based algorithms for cross-domain sentiment classification. In: Proc. EMNLP-CoNLL 2012, pp. 655–665 (2012)
85. Paltoglou, G., Thelwall, M.: Twitter, myspace, digg: Unsupervised sentiment analysis in social media. ACM Trans. Intell. Syst. Technol. 3(4), 66:1–66:19 (2012)
86. Taboada, M., Brooke, J., Tofiloski, M., Voll, K., Stede, M.: Lexicon-based methods for sentiment analysis. Comput. Linguist. 37(2), 267–307 (2011)
87. Pennebaker, J.W., Francis, M.E.: Linguistic Inquiry and Word Count, 1st edn. Lawrence Erlbaum (1999)
88. Bradley, M.M., Lang, P.J.: Affective norms for English words (ANEW): Instruction manual and affective ratings (1999)
89. Strapparava, C., Valitutti, A.: WordNet-Affect: An affective extension of WordNet. In: Proc. LREC 2004, vol. 4, pp. 1083–1086 (2004)
90. Paltoglou, G., Gobron, S., Skowron, M., Thelwall, M., Thalmann, D.: Sentiment analysis of informal textual communication in cyberspace. In: Proc. ENGAGE 2010, pp. 13–25 (2010)
91. Jijkoun, V., de Rijke, M., Weerkamp, W.: Generating focused topic-specific sentiment lexicons. In: Proc. ACL 2008, pp. 585–594 (2010)
92. Miller, G.A.: Wordnet: A lexical database for english. Commun. ACM 38(11), 39–41 (1995)
93. Owsley, S., Sood, S., Hammond, K.J.: Domain specific affective classification of documents. In: Proc. AAAICAAW 2006, pp. 181–183 (2006)
94. Bollen, J., Pepe, A., Mao, H.: Modeling public mood and emotion: Twitter sentiment and socio-economic phenomena. CoRR abs/0911.1583 (2009)

95. Qiu, L., Zhang, W., Hu, C., Zhao, K.: Selc: A self-supervised model for sentiment classification. In: Proc. CIKM 2009, pp. 929–936 (2009)
96. Prabowo, R., Thelwall, M.: Sentiment analysis: A combined approach. Journal of Informetrics 3(2), 143–157 (2009)
97. Yang, K., Yu, N., Valerio, A., Zhang, H.: Widit in trec 2006 blog track. In: Proc. TREC 2006 (2006)
98. Yang, K., Yu, N., Valerio, A., Zhang, H., Ke, W.: Fusion approach to finding opinions in blogosphere. In: Proc. ICWSM (2007)
99. Zhu, J., Wang, H., Zhu, M., Tsou, B.K., Ma, M.: Aspect-based opinion polling from customer reviews. IEEE Trans. Affect. Comput. 2(1) (2011)
100. Zhu, J., Wang, H., Tsou, B.K., Zhu, M.: Multi-aspect opinion polling from textual reviews. In: Proc. CIKM 2009, pp. 1799–1802 (2009)
101. Hunt, E.B., Marin, J., Stone, P.J.: Experiments in induction (1966)
102. Kamps, J., Mokken, R.J., Marx, M., de Rijke, M.: Using WordNet to measure semantic orientation of adjectives. In: Proc. LREC 2004, pp. 1115–1118 (2004)
103. Dietz, L., Wang, Z., Huston, S., Croft, W.B.: Retrieving opinions from discussion forums. In: Proc. CIKM 2013, pp. 1225–1228 (2013)
104. Huang, X., Croft, W.B.: A unified relevance model for opinion retrieval. In: Proc, CIKM 2009, pp. 947–956 (2009)
105. He, B., Macdonald, C., He, J., Ounis, I.: An effective statistical approach to blog post opinion retrieval. In: Proc. CIKM 2008, pp. 1063–1072 (2008)
106. Zhang, M., Ye, X.: A generation model to unify topic relevance and lexicon-based sentiment for opinion retrieval. In: Proc. SIGIR 2008, pp. 411–418 (2008)
107. Jijkoun, V., de Rijke, M., Weerkamp, W.: Generating focused topic-specific sentiment lexicons. In: Proc. ACL 2010, pp. 585–594 (2010)
108. Na, S.-H., Lee, Y., Nam, S.-H., Lee, J.-H.: Improving opinion retrieval based on query-specific sentiment lexicon. In: Boughanem, M., Berrut, C., Mothe, J., Soule-Dupuy, C. (eds.) ECIR 2009. LNCS, vol. 5478, pp. 734–738. Springer, Heidelberg (2009)
109. Amati, G., Van Rijsbergen, C.J.: Probabilistic models of information retrieval based on measuring the divergence from randomness. ACM Trans. Inf. Syst. 20(4), 357–389 (2002)
110. Peng, J., Macdonald, C., He, B., Plachouras, V., Ounis, I.: Incorporating term dependency in the dfr framework. In: Proc. SIGIR 2007, pp 843–844 (2007)
111. Zhang, W., Jia, L., Yu, C., Meng, W.: Improve the effectiveness of the opinion retrieval and opinion polarity classification. In: Proc. CIKM 2008, pp. 1415–1416 (2008)
112. Luo, Z., Osborne, M., Wang, T.: Opinion retrieval in twitter. In: Proc. ICWSM 2012 (2012)
113. Li, H.: Learning to Rank for Information Retrieval and Natural Language Processing. Synthesis Lectures on Human Language Technologies. Morgan and Claypool Publishers (2011)
114. Macdonald, C., Ounis, I., Soboroff, I.: Overview of trec-2009 blog track. In: Proc. TREC 2009 (2009)
115. Macdonald, C., Santos, R.L., Ounis, I., Soboroff, I.: Blog track research at trec. SIGIR Forum 44(1), 58–75 (2010)
116. Macdonald, C., Ounis, I.: The TREC Blogs06 collection: creating and analysing a blog test collection. Technical report, Department of Computer Science, University of Glasgow (2006)

A Survey of Automated Hierarchical Classification of Patents

Juan Carlos Gomez and Marie-Francine Moens

KU Leuven, Department of Computer Science
Celestijnenlaan 200A, 3001 Heverlee, Belgium
{juancarlos.gomez,sien.moens}@cs.kuleuven.be

Abstract. In this era of "big data", hundreds or even thousands of patent applications arrive every day to patent offices around the world. One of the first tasks of the professional analysts in patent offices is to assign classification codes to those patents based on their content. Such classification codes are usually organized in hierarchical structures of concepts. Traditionally the classification task has been done manually by professional experts. However, given the large amount of documents, the patent professionals are becoming overwhelmed. If we add that the hierarchical structures of classification are very complex (containing thousands of categories), reliable, fast and scalable methods and algorithms are needed to help the experts in patent classification tasks. This chapter describes, analyzes and reviews systems that, based on the textual content of patents, automatically classify such patents into a hierarchy of categories. This chapter focuses specially in the patent classification task applied for the International Patent Classification (IPC) hierarchy. The IPC is the most used classification structure to organize patents, it is world-wide recognized, and several other structures use or are based on it to ensure office inter-operability.

Keywords: hierarchical classification, patent classification, IPC, WIPO, patent content, text mining.

1 Introduction

When a new patent application arrives at the office of one of the organizations in charge of issuing patents around the world, one of the first tasks is to assign classification codes to it based on its content. In this way, it is ensured that patents and patent applications with similar characteristics, dealing with similar topics or in specific technological areas are grouped under the same codes. Accurate classification of patent documents (or simply *patents*, referring to granted patents or patent applications) is vital for the inter-operability between different patent offices and for conducting reliable patent search, management and retrieval tasks, during a patent application procedure. These tasks are crucial to companies, inventors, patent-granting authorities, governments, research and development units, and all individuals and organizations involved in the application or development of technology.

G. Paltoglou et al. (Eds.): Professional Search in the Modern World, LNCS 8830, pp. 215–249, 2014.

However, the more patents there are, the more complex the classification process becomes. This is observed mainly in two directions: first, when there are many patents to manage, the classification structure should be very well organized and detailed to allow easy classification, navigation and precise search. Moreover, since patents somehow reflect the technological knowledge of the world and this knowledge changes over time, the classification structure should also be flexible enough to capture such changes. One valuable approach to deal with the previous details is to use hierarchies of concepts, where the more general concepts or subjects are at the top levels and the more specific ones at the lower levels. The most important structures to organize patents, like the International Patent Classification (IPC), follow such an approach. Second, when a great amount of patents arrive to be processed in a patent office, they need to be classified in the hierarchical structure in a short period of time. Traditionally this has been done manually by patent experts. Nevertheless, in this era of "big data", where a large amount of data in many forms are generated every day, hundreds or even thousands of patent applications arrive daily to patent offices around the world, and the professional experts are becoming overwhelmed by these great amounts of documents. For example, the number of patent applications received by the United States Patent and Trademark Office (USPTO) in 2000 amounted to 380,000, reaching approximately 580,000 in 2012 [66]. The European Patent Office (EPO) received approximately 180,000 patent applications in 2004; this number increased to 257,000 in 2012 [18]. If we add that the hierarchical structures of classification are very complex (containing thousands of concepts/categories) and that experts are costly and vary in capabilities, reliable, fast and scalable methods and algorithms are needed in order to help the experts in the patent classification tasks and to automatize part of the classification process.

This chapter is meant to describe, analyze and review the building of systems that, based on the content of patents, automatically classify patents into a hierarchy of categories. We call this task automated hierarchical classification of patents (AHCP).

The content in a patent is well-structured (divided by sections and fields) and composed of text, figures, draws, plots, etc. Every component of a patent provides useful information to conduct the classification. In this chapter we focus only on the textual content, since it is one of the largest components in patents and several other elements in the content are usually explained using phrases, concepts or words. It is then possible to mention that the AHCP is an instance of the more general hierarchical text classification (HTC) task.

This chapter describes the AHCP as a task of HTC applied particularly for the International Patent Classification (IPC) hierarchy (or simply *IPC*). We use the IPC hierarchy since it is the most used classification structure to organize patents in the world. Other classification structures, such as the European CLAssification (ECLA), the Japanese File Index (FI) and the new Cooperative Patent Classification (CPC), were designed taking the IPC as a basis; while the United States Patent Classification (USPC) uses the IPC codes to maintain communication with other offices. Furthermore, most of the systems for AHCP in the IPC could be extended to other hierarchical structures, since the most used hierarchies follow the same structural and organizational principles as the IPC (not the same categories, but the way they are organized).

Patent classification is closely related to patent search, which is a professional search task. Patent classification and search are tasks conducted by experts in patent offices and other patent-related organizations around the world. Patent classification could be seen by itself as a search task, where the goal is to find and assign the most relevant category codes for a given patent. Assigning the most appropriate codes for a patent is a fundamental step in several tasks of patent analysis. For example, in prior art search, the assigned categories could help to narrow the search when looking for relevant patents. Moreover, the category codes assigned to a patent are language independent, which facilitate retrieval tasks in multi-language environments.

This chapter is very relevant to the objectives of the EU-funded COST Action MUMIA. First, it relates with the working group of Semantic Search, Faceted Search and Visualization in terms of the automatic hierarchical classification of patents based on their content. Faceted classification allows the assignment of multiple classifications to an object, enabling the classifications to be ordered in multiple ways. Faceted search could then rely on several hierarchical structures at the same time, where those structures can reflect different properties of the patent content. This relates our chapter with the fourth secondary objective defined in the Memorandum of Understanding (MoU) of the MUMIA COST Action: To critically examine the use of Taxonomies for Faceted search. Second, the contribution of this chapter consists on providing a survey of works devoted to the AHCP in the IPC. The survey offers an overview of existing technologies and pinpoints their shortcomings. This study could provide to other researches with valuable information about the relevant current methods for AHCP and the research questions still open in the subject. This should encourage further research work for the AHCP. This correlates with the main objective of the MUMIA COST Action, defined in its MoU, by fostering research in areas related with multi-lingual information retrieval, given that patent is by nature a multi-lingual domain and that the AHCP is a relevant task for patent search and retrieval in large-scale digital scenarios.

The rest of this chapter is organized as follows: the IPC is described in section 2. The particularities of the AHCP in the IPC are given in section 3, including the constraints in classification for this task, the structure of patents and the distribution of patents in collections. Section 4 presents the formal definition of hierarchical text classification, the several components that could be used in an AHCP system, and review several recent works focused on tackling the AHCP in the IPC. In section 5 we present our conclusions and various possibilities and perspectives in the near future for AHCP.

2 International Patent Classification

There exist several classification structures (proposed by the different patent offices around the world) to organize patents. The most recognized ones are the

European CLAssification (ECLA), used by the European Patent Office (EPO), the United States Patent Classification (USPC), proposed by the United States Patent and Trademark Office (USPTO), the Japanese F-Terms and the Japanese File Index (FI), devised by the Japanese Patent Office (JPO), and the International Patent Classification (IPC), used internationally. In addition, recently the EPO and the USPTO launched a project to create the Cooperative Patent Classification (CPC) in order to harmonise the patent classifications between the two offices [12]. Among the previous structures, the IPC is considered as the most widely spread and globally agreed. Some other structures, such as the ECLA, FI and the new CPC, are based on it, and others (like the USPTO) use it for helping maintaining a communication with other offices.

The IPC was created under the Strasbourg Agreement in 1971 and it is administered and maintained by the World Intellectual Property Organization (WIPO) [73]. The IPC is used in a worldwide context, having 95% of all existing patents classified according to it and used in more than 100 countries. The IPC is updated periodically by groups of experts, and until 2005 this updating was done every five years. Currently the IPC is under continual revision, with new editions coming into force on the 1st of January each year. The current version is IPC2014.01.

Every category in the IPC is indicated by a code and has a title [72][73]. The IPC divides all technological fields into eight sections designated by one of the capital letters A to H. Each section is subdivided into classes, whose codes consist of the section code followed by a two-digit number, such as B64. Each class is divided into several subclasses, whose codes consist of the class code followed by a capital letter, for example B64C. Each subclass is broken down into main groups, whose codes consist of the subclass code followed by a one-to three-digit number, an oblique stroke and the number 00, for example B64C 25/00. Subgroups form subdivisions under the main groups. Each subgroup code includes the main group code, but replaces the last two digits by other than 00, for example B64C 25/02. Subgroups are ordered in the scheme as if their numbers were decimals of the number before the oblique stroke. For example, 3/036 is to be found after 3/03 and before 3/04, and 3/0971 is to be found after 3/097 and before 3/098. The hierarchy after subgroup level is determined solely by the number of dots preceding their titles, i.e. their level of indentation, and not by the numbering of the subgroups.

An example of a sequence of category codes along the different levels of the IPC is shown in table 1 (extracted from [72]). The IPC has then 5 levels in its hierarchy: sections, classes, subclasses, main groups and subgroups. The total number of categories per level of the IPC is shown in table 2.

2.1 Graphical Description of the IPC

The IPC structure could be considered as a rooted tree graph, which in turn is a kind of directed acyclic graph (DAG). In the rooted tree, every category is represented as a vertex or node in the graph. The hierarchy has a root node from where the rest of the nodes depart. The nodes are connected by directed edges

Table 1. Example of a sequence of codes along the different levels of the IPC

IPC	Code	Title
Section	B	Performing operations; Transporting
Class	B64	Aircraft; Aviation; Cosmonautics
Subclass	B64C	Aeroplanes; Helicopters
Main group	B64C 25/00	Alighting gear
Subgroup	B64C 25/02	Undercarriages

Table 2. Number of categories in each level of the IPC

Level	Name	No. of Categories
1	Section	8
2	Class	129
3	Subclass	638
4	Main Group	7391
5	Subgroup	64046

which represent PARENT-OF relationships (with the parent at the beginning of the edge and the child at the end), and every node can only have one parent node, i.e. any node can only have exactly one simple path from the root to it. In the IPC the parent nodes represent more general concepts than the child nodes. The lowest nodes of the tree are named *leaf* nodes. Figure 1 shows a portion of the IPC hierarchy representing the tree graph. As mentioned above, the root node is considered as level 0 of the IPC.

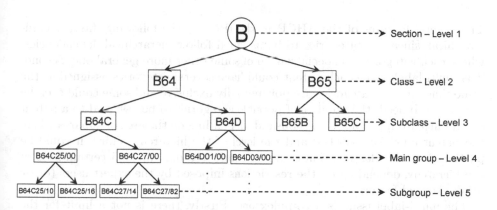

Fig. 1. Example of a portion of the IPC hierarchy starting in level 1, section B. The root node is level 0 (not shown).

Following the definitions of Silla and Freitas [55] and Wu et al. [75], we can say that the IPC is a rooted tree hierarchy Υ defined over a partial order set $(\mathbb{C}, \prec)$, where $\mathbb{C} = \{c_1, c_2, \ldots, c_p\}$ is the previously defined set of possible categories over Υ, and $\prec$ represent the PARENT-OF relationship, which is asymmetric, anti-reflexive and transitive. We then have:

- The origin of the graph is the root of the tree
- $\forall c_i, c_j \in \mathbb{C}$, if $c_i \prec c_j$ then $c_j \nprec c_i$
- $\forall c_i \in \mathbb{C}$, $c_i \nprec c_i$
- $\forall c_i, c_j, c_k \in \mathbb{C}$, if $c_i \prec c_j$ and $c_j \prec c_k$ then $c_i \prec c_k$

Up to the main group level, the IPC category codes indicate by themselves paths in the hierarchy. That is, the codes are aggregations of the codes from the root until a given level (with the exception of the root that is never included in the codes). However, at the subgroup level the IPC uses a different way to assign the codes. It uses a dot indentation system. The number of dots indicate the level of the hierarchy for a given code. At the subgroup level is not possible to look at the code and define directly a path in the hierarchy.

Usually, the codes in the leaf nodes of the IPC are the ones assigned to a patent. This would correspond to the codes of the subgroup level. However, if there exist some restrictions, it is also possible to assign a code only up to a certain level of the IPC. One of such restrictions is given by the WIPO itself, where they specify that industrial property offices that do not have sufficient expertise for classifying to a detailed level have the option to classify in main groups only (level 4 of the IPC) [73].

3   Details of the AHCP in the IPC

The general features of the AHCP in the IPC are the following: first, it is hierarchical, since the categories to be assigned follow hierarchical dependencies, where each category is a specialization of some other more general one. Second, it is multi-label, since each patent could have several categories assigned at the same time, i.e. the categories are not mutually exclusive and some could even be correlated. Indeed, the number of possible categories to be assigned to a patent could range from just a few to thousands depending on the area or subarea where the patent must be classified and the level of the hierarchy. Third, it could be partial, since the classification could be conducted only up to a certain level of the hierarchy, depending on the restrictions imposed by the expert users (or by other external factors).

The multi-label issue is a complex one. Firstly, there is not a limit for the number of categories a patent can be assigned, so in principle a patent could have an unlimited number of categories. During the test phase of any given AHCP system, this is an important issue, since the system could output from one to thousands of categories, influencing its performance. Secondly, since a patent in the training data belongs to more than one category, how to consider to which category it belongs when building a classification model is an important issue that also has influence on the performance of the AHCP system [34]. For example, in the collection of patents from the WIPO-alpha dataset [72][1] the maximum number of assigned categories to a patent is 25 and the average number is 1.88 with a standard deviation of 1.43. In the collection of patents from the CLEF-IP 2011 dataset the maximum number of assigned categories to a patent is 102 and the average is 2.16 with a standard deviation of 1.68.

Because of this multi-label issue, the AHCP in the IPC is considered as well as a task where high recall is preferred. That means that recall is an important aspect to consider when developing a system and when evaluating it. A high recall means that it is usually more important to assign the patent to many categories, rather to miss a relevant category. When conducting patent analysis, missing a relevant category for a patent could produce poor search results and in consequence it could lead to legal and economical complications because of patent infringement.

Nevertheless, high recall usually comes at the expense of low precision (several of the categories assigned by a system to a patent could not be relevant for the patent). Because of that, it is usually an important factor for an AHCP system to consider a confidence level when assigning a category for a patent [35]. Using a level of confidence could help to avoid the hurting in performance regarding precision by only allowing the assigning of categories for which the system is really confident. This would also save time to the expert users when analyzing the output of the system.

In order to better define the AHCP in the IPC, we use and extend here the notation by Silla and Freitas [55]. We can then describe the AHCP in the IPC as a 3-tuple $< T, ML, PD >$, where T specifies that the hierarchy T used in the task (the IPC) is defined as a rooted tree; ML that the task is multi-label (i.e. several categories could be assigned to a patent) and PD (standing for partial depth) that the task could be conducted only up to a certain level of the hierarchy (depending on the restrictions defined by the expert users in charge of the system or other external restrictions).

The AHCP in the IPC is indeed a complex task, given the large number of categories in the IPC, the variable number of possible categories in each subarea and given that there is not a fixed or specific number of categories to be assigned to a patent.

In addition to the characteristics of the AHCP as a general task, there are other issues that have an influence on the task. These issues are described in the following two subsections.

3.1   Patent Structure

Patents are complex documents and present some differences w.r.t other documents that are usually automatically classified (like news, emails or web pages): patents are long documents (up to several pages), their content is governed by legal agreements and is therefore well-structured (divided by sections and usually

---

[1] The WIPO-alpha dataset and the CLEF-IP 2011 dataset will be used in the following sections to illustrate the several issues regarding the AHCP in the IPC, and will be explained with more detail in section 4.6.

with well defined paragraphs) and they use natural language in a formal way, with many technical words and sometimes fuzzy sentences (in order to avoid direct similarities with other patents and to extend the scope of the invention).

The structure of a patent is important because it allows to provide different types of input data to an AHPC system; which directly influences the performance of the system during training and testing. Although there are several ways to represent the structure of a patent (with more or less details and different ways of grouping the information), the content of most patents is organized in the following way [4][40][72].

- **Title:** indicates a descriptive *name* of the patent.
- **Bibliographical data:** contains the ID number of the patent, the names of the inventor and the applicant, and the citations to other patents and documents.
- **Abstract:** includes a brief description of the invention presented in the patent.
- **Description:** contains a detailed description of the invention, including prior work, related technologies and examples.
- **Claims:** explains the legal scope of the invention and which application fields the patent is sought for.

In addition to the previous fields, it is also frequent to find graphics, plots, draws or other types of figures. Every component of a patent provides useful information to conduct the classification. In this chapter we focus only on the textual content, since it is usually one of the largest components in patents and several other elements in the content are often explained using phrases, concepts or words.

The several sections of a patent are usually presented in a XML format. Figure 2 presents an example of the XML structure of a patent extracted from the WIPO-alpha dataset [72].

The sections of a patent vary largely in size, with the title usually being the shortest section and the description the longest. To illustrate this, table 3 presents the number of words appearing in the collections of patents from the WIPO-alpha dataset and the CLEF-IP 2011 dataset. The table shows the minimum, maximum and average number of words per section, counting them in two ways: total words (counts every word in the patent, even if it is a repeated word) and unique words (if a word appears more than once in a patent it only counts as one). The words counted do not include stop words and words composed of less than 3 characters. We observe in this table that the description is by far the longest section, the second is the one containing the claims, the third is the abstract and the shortest one is the title. We also can see that the averages of total and unique words in both datasets are similar.

As mentioned above, the use of the different sections of a patent in the AHCP task is an important issue, since the amount and quality of data processed by a system affects its performance in terms of computing or processing time (efficiency), and in terms of the results it presents to the user (efficacy). Which section, portion,

```
<?xml version="1.0" encoding="iso-8859-1"?>
<!DOCTYPE record SYSTEM "../../../../ipctraining.dtd">
<record cy="WO" an="AU9700792" pn="W0992646519990603" dnum="9926465" kind="A1">
<ipcs ed="6" mc="A01B00116">
<ipc ic="A01M02100"></ipc>
</ipcs>
<pas>
<pa>ANDERSON, Frank, Malcolm</pa>
</pas>
<tis>
<ti xml:lang="EN">HYDRAULIC PROBE FOR PLANT REMOVAL
</ti>
</tis>
<abs>
<ab xml:lang="EN">A movable device to facilitate removal of plants with roots intact
from a soil or growing medium is disclosed. The device comprises a rigid
hollow shaft
[... abridged ...]</ab>
</abs>
<cls>
<cl xml:lang="EN">CLAIMS
The claims defining the invention are as follows:1. A movable device facilitating plant
removal with roots intact from a soil or growing medium, the device comprising a rigid
hollow shaft with one end
[... abridged ...]</cl>
</cls>
<txts>
<txt xml:lang="EN"> HYDRAULIC PROBE FOR PLANT REMOVAL
DESCRIPTION
This invention relates to a device for aiding the removal of individual plants with roots
intact from a soil or growing medium.There are several methods for removing plants from
a soil or growing medium.
[... abridged ...]</txt>
</txts>
</record>
```

Fig. 2. Example of the XML structure of an abridged patent from the WIPO-alpha dataset

Table 3. Statistics on number of words in each section of the WIPO-alpha and CLEF-IP 2011 patent datasets

Section	WIPO-alpha						CLEF-IP 2011					
	Total Words			Unique Words			Total Words			Unique Words		
	Min	Max	Average	Min	Max	Average	Min	Max	Average	Min	Max	Average
Title	1	33	5.4	1	23	5.2	1	111	10.3	1	36	5.6
Abstract	2	277	58.5	2	146	36.1	2	1407	67.4	2	625	37.7
Description	63	354769	3072.8	40	86337	747.3	8	1290673	3107.2	8	302867	656.7
Claims	5	32507	539.5	5	13737	103.8	2	89746	447.8	2	11339	121.2

or combination of sections is the best to provide useful information for the AHCP task is still an open question, as we will discuss in section 4.7.

3.2   Other Issues for the AHCP in the IPC

In addition to the generalities of the AHCP in the IPC and the structured content of the patents, there are other issues that have an influence on the task.

The first issue is related to the distribution of patents along the predefined categories of the IPC. The IPC is an artificially created structure that is defined by human experts. As a consequence it imposes external criteria to classify patents, instead of following a definition of the categories based on the "natural" content of patents. In addition, since the focus of research and technological development changes over time, so do the categories in the IPC. These two previous details affect the categories of the IPC in two ways: some categories receive many patents in a given point of time, and the IPC structure changes over time, including the creation and merging (because of deprecation) of categories. This variability in turn creates a highly imbalanced distribution of patents across the IPC. They tend to follow a Pareto-like distribution, with about 80% of them classified in about 20% of the categories [4][19]. To illustrate this effect, figures 3.a and 3.b show the distribution of patents across the categories present in the WIPO-alpha dataset and the CLEF-IP dataset respectively. The categories extracted correspond to the main group level in the IPC. The plots show the number of categories containing between 1 to 50 patents, 51 to 100, and so on. For the WIPO-alpha dataset, we see in the figure that of a total of 5,907 categories, around 89% (5,260) contain only between 1 to 50 patents, while only around 0.02% (1) contain more than 2,000 patents. For the CLEF-IP 2011 dataset, we see that of a total of 7,069 categories, around 28% (1,991) contain only between 1 to 50 patents, while only around 8% (550) contain more than 2,000 patents.

The second issue is related with the previous mentioned details of the dynamical nature of the IPC [19]. This dynamics implies the creation and deprecation (or merge) of categories over time, which in turn affects the performance of an AHCP system, since the definitions of categories could be modified in a given moment, and part of the system could be outdated to classify some patents.

The third issue is related with the distribution of words inside the patents. As seen in the previous section, a patent can contain up to thousands of words. However, of these words only a small portion corresponds to unique words in each patent; and moreover, most of the words appearing in a collection of patents are used very rarely (they are only mentioned in a couple of patents). Similarly than in collections of other documents [38], the distribution of words in a collection of patents tend to follow approximately Zipf's law [4]. To illustrate this fact, figures 3.c and 3.d show the frequency of words in the collection of patents from the WIPO-alpha dataset and the CLEF-IP 2011 dataset. The figures show how many words appear in only 2, 3, 4 and so on patents. The words extracted form the collection do not include stop words, words composed of less than 3 characters and ignores those that are used in only 1 patent. For the WIPO-alpha dataset we observe that from the total vocabulary of 480,422 words, 189,402 words (corresponding to almost 40% of the total) appear in only 2 patents, while 103,607 words (corresponding to around 22% of the total) appear in more than 10 patents. For the CLEF-IP 2011 dataset we observe that from the total vocabulary of 7,373,151 words, 2,685,340 words (corresponding to around 36% of the total) appear in only 2 patents, while 1,424,050 words (corresponding to around 19% of the total) appear in more than 10 patents.

The two mentioned issues of scarcity (lack of data) in most of the categories and the fact that most of the words in a collection of patents are infrequent, largely affect the performance of an AHCP system. To train robust classification

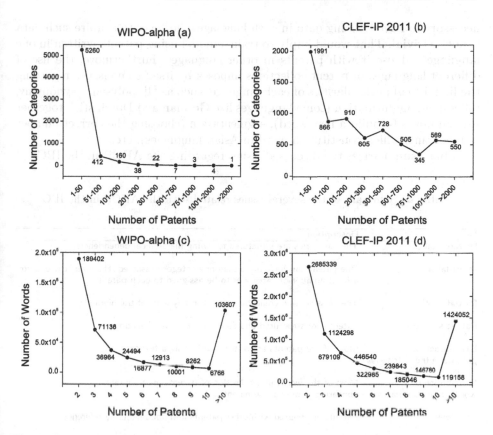

Fig. 3. Statistics in the collections of patents from the WIPO-alpha dataset and the CLEF-IP dataset. (a) and (b) number of patents per category. (c) and (d) frequency of words.

models, a sufficient amount of training data is required [3]. In addition, most of the words are rare, but since most of the categories are rare as well (by the number of patents it contains), it means that some rare words are descriptive of some rare categories and should be kept; imposing the use of a large number of words in the system. This could lead to the so called *curse of dimensionality* [5] for some classification methods.

The fourth issue is related to the citations (or links) inside the patents. Patents are linked to other patents and documents by references to prior art or examples of similar technology. The links could have an effect on the performance of an AHCP system, since usually patents are linked with other patents in the same categories. However, this is still not completely clear, as we will see in section 4.7.

The final issue is related with the language of the patents. By its nature the AHCP in the IPC is a multi-lingual and cross-lingual task. As a matter of generality it should be possible to automatically classify any patent written in (almost) any language by the IPC codes [40]. This is indeed a very complex and hard issue for the AHCP. In order to build models in different languages it is necessary to have training data in such languages; however to acquire such data is not so trivial. That would imply to train a model using patents written in one language and use it with patents in other languages. Furthermore, the use of different languages in patent collections imposes by itself some issues regarding the linguistical particularities of each language, such as [4]: polysemy, synonymy, inflections, agglutination (some languages like German and Dutch stick together several words to build a new word), segmentation (choosing the correct number of ideograms which constitute a word in Asian languages), etc.

Table 4 summarizes the discussed issues regarding the AHCP in the IPC.

Table 4. Summary of the several issues related with the AHCP in the IPC

Issue	Description
Hierarchical	The categories are structured following hierarchical dependencies.
Multi-label	One patent can have more than one category assigned. However, there is not a fixed number of categories to be assigned to each patent.
Partial-depth	The classification could be stopped in any level of the hierarchy.
Patent structure	Patents are structured and composed of several sections.
Distribution of patents in the categories	Most of the patents are distributed in only a few categories.
Distribution of words inside the patents	Most of the words in a collection of patents are very rare, appearing in only a few patents.
Citations	Patents are related with other patents and documents by references.
Language	Patents are written in many languages. Each language needs training patents and imposes linguistical particularities to the task.

4   Recent Models and Advances for the AHCP in the IPC

There are two main points of view for models applied to the AHCP: the first one involves people working with patents and whose main interest is to develop a complete system to assist the experts in the classification of the patents [36][35][56][70]. The second point of view involves the data mining/machine learning communities, where they aim to develop efficient methods to perform the classification task [1][64][50][69]. The first approach uses the methods from the second to accomplish their task, but they put more emphasis on the usability of the final tools and not on the high performance of the methods. The second approach focuses on understanding the structure of the patent data and then tries to derive efficient and effective methods to conduct the classification. Both approaches converge and merge sometimes in the literature; however there still seems to exist a communication gap between the two.

This section presents a revision of several works for the AHCP in the IPC. The works revisited here come from literature in areas related to the two points of view mentioned above. Our goal is to produce a normalized and structured analysis of the works; using for that a defined set of components.

In the direction of structuring our analysis and with the intention of better understanding the AHCP in the IPC, we give first in the next subsection a more formal definition of the general hierarchical text classification (HTC) task, from where the AHCP is derived. Later, we see also the components that could be included in an AHCP system and we describe the possible approaches to reach the goal of AHCP.

4.1 Hierarchical Text Classification

The HTC is divided in two phases: training and testing. For training we have a hierarchical structure Υ that is composed by a set $\mathbb{C} = \{c_1, c_2, \ldots, c_p\}$ of possible categories that follow the restrictions imposed by the hierarchy. We also have a set of n previously classified text documents $\mathbb{X} = \{(\mathbf{d}_1, \zeta_1), \ldots, (\mathbf{d}_n, \zeta_n)\}$; where $\mathbf{D} = \{\mathbf{d}_1, \mathbf{d}_2, \ldots, \mathbf{d}_m\}$ is the training document matrix, with $\mathbf{d}_i \in \mathbb{R}^m$ as the i-th document represented by a m dimensional column vector; and $\mathbf{L} = \{\zeta_1, \zeta_2, \ldots, \zeta_n\}$ is the category matrix, with $\zeta_i \subset \mathbb{C}$ as the set of categories assigned to document $\mathbf{d}_i$. The objective of the training phase is to build a classification model Ω over the hierarchical structure Υ using the previously classified documents $\mathbb{X}$.

In this definition, the model Ω is understood as a black box. Inside it there could be several components, phases or steps, such as base classifiers, meta classifiers, hierarchical management processes, etc. There are many ways of building Ω, using different components, as we will see later.

For testing we have the hierarchical trained model Ω and a set of k unclassified documents $\mathbf{U} = \{\mathbf{u}_1, \mathbf{u}_2, \ldots, \mathbf{u}_k\}$, with $\mathbf{u}_i \in \mathbb{R}^m$. The objective in this phase is then to use the model Ω to predict or assign a set $\mathbf{V} = \{\nu_1, \nu_2, \ldots, \nu_k\}$ of valid categories to each document $\mathbf{u}_i$. $\mathbf{V}$ is the resulting category matrix for the test documents, with $\nu_i \subset \mathbb{C}$ as the set of assigned categories to $\mathbf{u}_i$. The model Ω and the assigned categories $\mathbf{V}$ implicitly follow the restrictions imposed by the hierarchy Υ.

The AHCP in the IPC is indeed an instance of the HTC task. The goal of the ACHP in the IPC is to assign a set of category codes to a given patent, considering the particularities of the IPC hierarchy and the issues of the patent data and the task itself, as seen in sections 2 and 3. The classification model Ω from the above definition represents any AHCP system.

4.2 Steps and Components of an AHCP system

Figure 4 shows a general schema of a system performing the AHCP in the IPC [63][19]. The schema is divided in several stages. The process starts with a collection of patents assuming they are in an electronic readable format. The first stage consists of cleaning the collection by eliminating noisy patents (patents that are not electronically readable) and standardizing them to a given format (for example using XML to define the sections). The second stage is the preprocessing of the

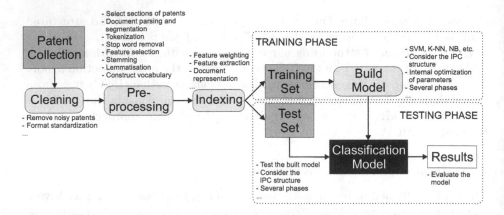

Fig. 4. General steps in the AHCP

patents. This stage could consist of several steps such as: selection of patent sections, tokenization (breaking the text into words, n-grams, phrases, paragraphs, etc. which are called *features*) [71], stop word removal, feature selection (removing the features that are less relevant for the classification task) [78][23], stemming or lemmatisation (grouping together the different inflected forms of a word) [32], vocabulary construction (indexing the features), etc. The third stage is indexing the patent. This stage also could include several steps, such as: feature weighting (how important is each feature for a patent/category), feature extraction (constructing new features using combinations of the original ones) [24], document representation (representing the patents in a format that an algorithm can understand, like vectors, matrices, lists, maps, etc.), among others. Once the patents are processed and expressed in a format that is understandable for a computer, they are divided in a training set and a test set. The training set is used to build the AHCP system, while the test set is held out apart to test the performance of the system. Then, there are two later phases in the process, the training and the testing. During training, as specified in subsection 4.1, the objective is to build a model Ω (understood as the AHCP system) using the already classified set of training patents. The training phase could be done in several steps depending on what base classification algorithms are used (like the optimization of the meta parameters of some of them), how the IPC is used to build the model or if the training is done in several phases, among others. The testing phase consists of providing a set of unclassified patents to the system and obtain a set of categories for each of them. This phase could also be composed of several steps depending on how the model was built, it may need performing the testing in several phases or considering the IPC structure in some specific manner. Once the model is tested, its results are evaluated. How the evaluation is conducted largely depends on the final objectives of the user, as we will see later.

In the next subsection we present the overview of the methods found in the literature to perform the ACHP in the IPC. As mentioned above, the creation of a classification model implies the use of several components, phases or steps. In order to normalize and structure the presentation of the methods used to build classification models to tackle the AHCP in the IPC we use the following components:

- **Classification method**
- **Features**
- **Hierarchy**
- **Evaluation**

We explain each component in more detail in the next sections, and then in section 4.7 we present the schematized overview of works in the literature for the AHCP in the IPC.

4.3   Classification Method

The field of text classification (TC) has been greatly developed during the past decades, because of that a variety of algorithms has been created. We present and describe here in a general way the main classification methods used in the literature for tackling the AHCP in the IPC. The formal and deep mathematical details of each of them can be found in the literature of machine learning and data mining [5][29][33][43][51][74].

Naïve Bayes. The naïve Bayes (NB) classifier is a simple probabilistic classifier based on applying Bayes' theorem with strong ("naive") independence assumptions. In simple terms, the NB classifier assumes that the presence (or absence) of a particular feature in a category is unrelated to the presence (or absence) of any other feature [37]. When training the classifier, the probabilities of each feature belonging to every category are estimated. When testing the classifier, the previously estimated probabilities are used to determine the probabilities that a document belongs to various categories. There are in essence two ways of estimating such probabilities [42]: the multi-variate Bernoulli model (where the features are considered in a document only as present or not present), and the multinomial model (where the features considered are the number of times they appear). The NB is easy to implement and despite its independence assumptions, it performs generally well in TC tasks.

k-Nearest Neighbors. The k-nearest neighbors (kNN) classifier is a type of instance-based method. It encapsulates all the training data in order to use them later in the test phase. When a test document is to be classified, the kNN looks in the stored training data for the k most similar documents (neighbors) to it. Commonly, similarity is computed using a distance metric based on the feature distributions of the documents. The suggested category of the test document can then be estimated from the neighboring documents by weighting their contributions according to their distance [77]. Even if the kNN classifier relies on the whole training data to perform classification, it can be trained to find the optimal number of neighbors k as well as the best similarity metric. This method is very popular in TC tasks, where it performs generally well. There are many versions of this algorithm, depending on how the similarities and weights are computed.

Support Vector Machines. A support vector machine (SVM) [11] performs classification by constructing a hyperplane that optimally separates the training documents into two categories. The hyperplane is defined over the feature space of the documents, where they are represented as vectors. During training the classifier identifies the hyperplane with longest margin that separates the training documents into two categories. During testing, the classifier uses that hyperplane to decide which category a new document belongs to. SVMs are powerful algorithms to perform TC. They can handle a large number of features without loosing generality, and can easily be extended to the multi-label classification scenario.

Artificial Neural Networks. An artificial neural network (ANN) [30] consists of a network of many simple processing units interconnected between them with varying connection weights. The units are usually positioned in successive layers. Used for classification, a network layer receives an input in the form of features representing a document, processes it and gives an output to the next layer, and so on, until the final layer outputs the category(ies) of the document. During training, the method assigns and updates the weights to each unit by using the categorized trained data trying to minimize the categorization error. During testing, the network processes the features of the test document across the units and layers and outputs the categories. There exists a large number of versions of this method.

A particular version of ANN is the Universal Feature Extractor (UFEX) [60] algorithm. This method is a kind of one-layer ANN, which receives as an input a vector of features representing a document, and then outputs a set of categories for it. The training phase is done by a greedy update of the weights in each unit of the network, where each unit represents a category expressed as a vector of features (or category descriptor). When a document from the training set is assigned incorrectly to a category, the algorithm updates both category descriptors: the one of the true category (to force a correct classification) and the one of the wrong category (to avoid that similar documents reach that category).

Another version of ANN is the Winnow [39] algorithm. Winnow is a perceptron-like algorithm that uses a multiplicative scheme for updating the weights in the network units. This method could be extended to a multi-label scenario by learning a set of several hyperplanes at the same time.

Decision Trees. Decision tree (DT) algorithms [49] classify a document by following a set of classification rules. The rules indicate when a feature, a set of features or the absence of a feature are good indicators that a document belongs to a certain category. During training the algorithm learns such rules from the training data, where the rules are ordered in a tree-like structure, from more general to more specific rules. During testing the algorithms apply the rules to conduct the classification.

Logistic Regression. The logistic regression (LR) model performs classification by determining the impact of multiple independent variables (features) presented simultaneously to predict one of two categories (binary classification, similarly than with SVM). The probabilities describing the possible category are modeled as a function of the features using a logistic function. During training, logistic regression forms a best fitting equation or function using the maximum likelihood method, which maximizes the probability of classifying the training documents into the appropriate category by updating a set of regression coefficients. During testing, a test document, expressed as a vector of features, is multiplied by the regression coefficients and the model outputs the probability of the document belonging to one of the two categories. This method is very powerful for TC tasks, it can handle a large number of features without loosing generality, and can easily be extended to the multi-label classification scenario.

Minimizer of the Reconstruction Error. The Minimizer of the Reconstruction Error (mRE) [26][27] performs classification using the reconstruction errors provided by a set of projection matrices. In the training phase, it first builds a term-document matrix per category. Then, it performs a principal component analysis for each category matrix and obtain a projection matrix per category. During testing, a new test document is first projected using the reconstruction matrices, then it is reconstructed used the same matrices and the error between the reconstructed document and the original one is measured. The projection matrix that minimizes the error of reconstruction assigns the category. This model could be directly extended to a multi-label scenario by using thresholds to define the confidence of assigning a category to a document.

There are other classifiers that could be used inside a AHCP system. We do not intend to mention all the alternatives here, rather we mention only the most common, well-known or studied methods. When a different classification method is used in a specific system we will mention it and refer to the corresponding work for further details.

4.4   Features

There are many kinds of possible features to extract from the textual content of a patent. Among the most commonly used for TC tasks are: words, context words, word n-grams, phrases, character n-grams, and links. Except for the character n-grams, words are the basic block of construction (they are built of words). Words could be simply defined as sequences of characters (strings) separated by blanks. Context words for a given word w, are the words that co-occur in a patent together with w. Word n-grams are ordered sequences of words. Phrases are sequences of words following a syntactic scheme. Character n-grams are ordered sequences of characters. Links are words or sequences of words that make a reference to other patents or documents. The previous features are used to build a representation of the patent except for the links, which are used to extract information from related patents.

Patents, as we have seen in section 3.1, are structured and divided into a number of sections: the bibliographical data, the title, the abstract, the claims and the description. Then, the above described features (except for the links that could be extracted only from the bibliographical data) could be extracted from one, a portion of one, several or all the sections.

Once the features are extracted from the textual content, there are several preprocessing steps that could be conducted, as explained in the first part of this section: stop word removal (SWR), stemming, lemmatization, feature selection and vocabulary construction. The first three options are language dependant, and there exist several ways of performing these tasks. Stop word removal could be done by comparing a word with a list of already known stop words in a given language. Stemming [48] and lemmatization are related tasks; they try to reduce inflected (or sometimes derived) words to their root form in a given language. Lemmatization is more complex since it involves subtasks such as understanding the context and determining the part of speech for a word. Feature selection is usually independent of the language, and there is a collection of methods such as [78][23]: document frequency (DF), information gain (IG), mutual information gain, χ^2, etc.

After preprocessing, the resulting features are used to represent the patent in a format that the classification method can understand. That is done usually by expressing the patent as a vector of feature weights (named *vector space model* or VSM) that reflects the importance of each feature regarding the patent. There are several weighting schemes, the most common are: binary, term frequency (TF), term frequency inverse document frequency (TF-IDF), entropy and BM25 [41]. In the binary weighting each feature is expressed only as 1 or 0, if it is present or not in the patent. In the TF weighting each feature is counted the number of times it appears in the patent. In the TF-IDF weighting, the TF weighting is multiplied by the inverse of the number of times the feature appears in the whole patent collection (IDF). Entropy is based on information theory ideas and is a most sophisticated weighting scheme. Entropy gives higher weight for features that appear fewer times in a small number of patents, while it gives lower weight for features that appear many times along the collection of patents. BM25 indeed refers to a family of weighting schemas using different components and parameters. It is usually estimated using a logarithmic version of the IDF multiplied by the frequency of the feature which is normalized by the length of the patent and the average length of patents along the collection.

With the document representation done, there is still a last step of feature extraction, where several of the original features are combined to create a new set of reduced combined features. There is a collection of methods to perform this [43]: latent semantic indexing (LSI) [13], principal component analysis (PCA)

[5], linear discriminant analysis (LiDA) [61], non-negative matrix factorization (NMF) [53], latent Dirichlet allocation (LDA) [6], etc.

During training there are also a number of possibilities when considering several categories of each patent in the training data (the multi-label issue). Following the definition by Tsoumakas et al. [65] there are two ways to do it: problem transformation (PT), and algorithm adaptation (AA).

The methods following the PT approach are algorithm independent. They transform the multi-label task into one or more single-label classification tasks. As an example consider the following set of patents with their corresponding sets of categories: $\{(\mathbf{d}_1, \{c_1, c_2\}), (\mathbf{d}_2, \{c_1\}), (\mathbf{d}_3, \{c_1, c_2, c_3\})\}$. One way to transform this set into a single-label set is by copying each patent in each one of the categories it has assigned, this would produce a new set as follows: $\{(\mathbf{d}_{1a}, \{c_1\}), (\mathbf{d}_{1b}, \{c_2\}), (\mathbf{d}_2, \{c_1\}), (\mathbf{d}_{3a}, \{c_1\}), (\mathbf{d}_{3b}, \{c_2\}), (\mathbf{d}_{3c}, \{c_3\})\}$. A second possibility is to select at random only one category for the patents with more than one category assigned, this would produce a new set of patents as follows: $\{(\mathbf{d}_1, \{c_2\}), (\mathbf{d}_2, \{c_1\}), (\mathbf{d}_3, \{c_1\})\}$. Another alternative is to simple ignore the examples with multiple categories, as follows: $\{(\mathbf{d}_2, \{c_1\})\}$.

The methods following the AA approach extend specific learning algorithms in order to handle multi-label data directly. These methods usually learn at once the complete set of labels for all the patents. Following this approach, several well known methods have been adapted to handle multi-label data, such as SVM [17], decision trees [10] and k-NN [80].

4.5 Hierarchy

The AHCP task in section 4.1 was defined to classify patents over the hierarchy structure Υ, in our case the IPC. In general there are two approaches to use the structure when building the classification model: flat and hierarchical. The flat approach ignores completely the IPC. It simply trains a classification model in the desired level of the IPC and the predictions always concern that level.

The hierarchical approach could indeed be implemented in several ways using the IPC structure. Following the definitions by Silla and Freitas [55], the possibilities are: local classifier per node (LCN), local classifier per level (LCL), local classifier per parent node (LCPN) and global classifier (GC). In the LCN, a base binary classification method is trained for each category (node) of the IPC, and it decides if a test patent belongs or not to that category (and the classification is conducted only on the children nodes of the category assigned). In the LCL, a multi-class classification method is trained in each level of the IPC, and it decides to which categories in a given level a test patent belongs to (restricting the classification to the children nodes of the categories assigned in the previous level). In the LCPN, a multi-class classifier is trained in each node that is not a leaf, and it decides to which of its children categories belongs a test patent. In the GC, a single classifier considering all the IPC structure at once is created, and it predicts all the possible categories for a test patent at once.

In both cases, flat and hierarchical, the output could be single-label or multi-label, i.e. only assigning one category to the patent or several. As we have seen in section 3, the AHCP task is by nature multi-label. However, some systems restrict their output only to the most probable category to simplify the task.

Using the previous alternatives to include the hierarchy, the training and testing of the model could be also done in a single phase (SP) or in multiple phases (MP). In the single-phase approach, both the training and test phases are done only by using the training or test data only once, respectively. In the multi-phase approach, during the training phase the training patents are read several times to refine the classification model [3]. During the test phase, the predictions for each test patent are also refined based on ranking methods or combinations of several outputs [76].

Finally, it is important to determine the level of classification in the IPC for an AHCP system. The different levels impose different complexities, the lower the level the more difficult the task is. The levels are specified in section 2.

4.6 Evaluation

The output of an AHCP system is the category matrix $\mathbf{V} = \nu_1, \nu_2, \ldots, \nu_k$. That is, the collection of assigned categories for the patent test set. Once the system has provided all the categories for the test set, these results are then evaluated to measure the performance of the system. There are several performance measures, among the most used are: accuracy (Acc), precision (P), recall (R), F1-measure, mean average precision (MAP) and Hamming loss (H-loss). Accuracy is the percentage of correctly classified documents. There is a version of this measure called parent accuracy (PAcc). The PAcc is the Acc measured for each category node that has children in a hierarchy, and then the Acc is assigned to the corresponding children of such categories. Precision is the number of correctly classified positive documents divided by the number of documents classified by the system as positive. Recall is the number of correctly classified positive documents divided by the number of positive documents in the test data. In this case, the positive class is considered as the specific category that is being evaluated and the negative class includes all the other categories. F1-measure is the harmonic mean of precision and recall. P, R and F1-measure can be computed per individual patent and then averaged, i.e. micro-averaged (Mi-P, Mi-R, Mi-F1); or per complete category and then averaged, i.e. macro-averaged (Ma-P, Ma-R, Ma-F1). They could also be computed depending on the order of the categories returned by a system. These measures are defined as P@N, R@N and F1@N, where N indicates the number of sorted categories (from 1 to N) to consider when computing the measure. Finally, they could be also computed in a hierarchical way (hP, hR, hF1), to consider the classification in the different levels of a hierarchy, and in that way discount wrong assignments to categories lower in the hierarchy. MAP is the mean of the average precision over the test set, understood as the correct categories for a patent ranked by order. H-loss is the mean of the percentages of the wrong assigned categories to the total number of true categories for each patent in the test set. This loss could also be computed in a hierarchical way (Δ-loss), considering the loss along the hierarchy. We refer to Silla and Freitas [55], Sokolova and Lapalme [57], and Tsoumakas et al. [65] for a review of these measures applied in multi-class, multi-label and hierarchical scenarios.

The previous measures take into account the output of the AHCP system to compare with the true categories of the test patent. In this sense they measure the efficacy or correctness of the system. However, it is also expected that any AHCP system performs its task efficiently, i.e. it does not take a very long time to execute the training phase and/or the testing phase. This is usually done by estimating the computational complexity of the methods involved in the two phases (how many single operations the system needs to do its job), or by estimating the real time the system takes to perform the training and testing phases under a specific computer architecture.

Any evaluation measure should be checked for statistical significance, in order to ensure that a given performance is not produced by chance. There are several statistical tests, such as: t-test, Friedman test, McNemar test, Wilcoxon signed-ranks test, etc. We refer to the work of Demšar [14] for the use of statistical tests in classification tasks.

To conduct training, testing and evaluation, a collection of patents is needed. There are some datasets used to evaluate an AHCP system, such as: the WIPO-alpha dataset, the WIPO-de dataset and the CLEF-IP 2010 and 2011 datasets.

The WIPO-alpha collection [72] consists of patent applications submitted to WIPO under the Patent Cooperation Treaty (PCT). Each of these patents includes a title, a set of bibliographical data (except references), an abstract, a claims section, and a long description. The patents are in XML format (as seen in section 3.1), in English, and were published between 1998 and 2002. The collection is composed of 75,250 patents (46,324 for training and 28,926 for testing). These patents are distributed over 5,000 categories in the top four IPC levels: 8 sections, 114 classes, 451 subclasses, and 4,427 main groups.

The documents in the WIPO-de collection [72] were extracted from the DE-PAROM source and were published between 1987 and 2002. The patents are written in German and also presented in XML format with the same structure as the ones in the WIPO-alpha dataset. The collection is composed of 117,246 patents. The collection is divided in training and test sets differently for the two top levels of the IPC hierarchy. At the class level there are 50,555 patents for training and 21,271 for testing. At the subclass level there are 84,822 patents for training and 26,006 for testing. These patents are distributed over 120 classes and 598 subclasses of the IPC.

The CLEF-IP 2010 [47] collection consists of patents in XML format in three languages: English, German and French. Each patent in this collection includes a title, a set of bibliographical data, an abstract, a claims section and a long description. These patents are mostly patents submitted to EPO. The collection is divided in about 1.3 millions of patents for training (with the proportions of 68% in English, 24% in German and 8% in French), and 2,000 patents for testing (1,468 in English, 409 in German and 123 in French). The patents are distributed across the complete IPC.

The CLEF-IP 2011 [46] collection is based on the CLEF-IP 2010 dataset. This dataset contains the patents of the CLEF-IP 2010 collection and 200,000 additional patents submitted to WIPO in its training set. The patents in this collection have the same XML format and structure as the ones in the CLEF-IP 2010 dataset, and there are about the same proportions of patents for English, German and French. The test set is composed of 3,000 patents (1,000 in each language). The patents are distributed across the complete IPC.

One last thing to consider when evaluating an AHCP system is the language it could process: mono-lingual (MoL), multi-lingual (MuL) or cross-lingual (CoL).

4.7   Comparison Between Different Systems for the AHCP in the IPC

Table 5 summarizes the components described in the previous sections and some of the alternatives for each one of them.

Table 5. Summary of the several components that could be used in the AHCP in the IPC. For explanation of the acronyms we refer to the corresponding section. In case a component is not completely defined in this chapter, we refer to the corresponding work for further details.

Component	Alternatives
Classification Method (CM)	NB, kNN, SVM, ANN, UFEX, Winnow, DT, LR, mRE, others
Features	**Features:** Words, context words, words n-grams, phrases, links, others **Sections of patents:** Title, abstract, description, claims, bibliographical data **Preprocessing:** SWR, stemming, lemmatization, other **Feature selection:** DF, IG, χ^2, others **Feature weighting:** Binary, TF, TF-IDF, entropy, BM25, others **Feature extraction:** LSI, PCA, LiDA, NMF, LDA, others **Multi-label consideration:** PT, AA
Hierarchy	**Hierarchy use:** Flat, hierarchical (LCN, LCL, LCPN or GC) **Output:** SL, ML **Level of classification in IPC:** class, subclass, main group, subgroup **Phases of classification:** SP, MP
Evaluation	**Dataset:** WIPO-alpha, WIPO-de, CLEF-IP 2010, CLEF-IP 2011, others **Language capability:** MoL, MuL, CoL **Evaluation measure:** Acc, PAcc, (Mi-, Ma- or h)P, (Mi-, Ma- or h)R, (Mi-, Ma- or h)F1-measure, MAP, H-loss, Δ-loss, others **Efficiency:** Complexity, computing time **Statistical test:** t-test, Friedman test, Wilcoxon signed-ranks test, others

Using the components summarized in table 5, in tables 6, 7, 8 and 9 we present a schematized summary of the several works found in the literature for the AHCP in the IPC.

In addition to the works described in the tables below, there are a set of overview papers regarding the AHCP in the IPC. Firstly there are two overview papers related with the classification tasks in the CLEF-IP 2010 and CLEF-IP 2011 workshops. These tasks used the corresponding datasets mentioned in section 4.6. The goal of each task was to classify the corresponding test sets, which consist of patents written in three languages: English, German and French (see section 4.6 for details). The overviews of the tasks are presented in [47] for CLEF-IP 2010 and in [46] for CLEF-IP 2011.

For the CLEF-IP 2010 classification task, the goal was to classify the test patents up to the subclass level of the IPC. There were seven participants submitting a total of 27 runs. The runs were variations of their corresponding systems (using different internal parameters). The organizers evaluated the performance of the submitted runs using the following measures: P@1, P@5, P@10, P@25, P@50, R@5, R@25, R@50, F1@5, F1@25, F1@50 and MAP. The results of the evaluation are presented per language (English, German and French) and as an average over the three languages. The organizers of this task sorted the performances using the P@5, R@5 and F1@5 measures.

Table 6. Overview of existing literature for the AHCP in the IPC. We try to detail as much as possible each component. If one of them is not listed for a given work is because it is not used, mentioned or considered in the corresponding work.

Work	Details
Aiolli et al. [1]	**Classification Method**: GPLM (generalized preference learning model) **Features**: Words **Sections of patents**: Title, abstract and first 300 words of description (all combined) **Preprocessing**: SWR and Porter stemming **Feature weighting**: Cosine normalized TF-IDF **Hierarchy use**: LCN **Output**: ML (variable) **Level of classification in IPC**: Subclass **Phases of classification**: SP **Dataset**: WIPO-alpha **Language capability**: MoL (English) **Evaluation measure**: 3-Layered Mi-F1. Best performance 0.5298 **Efficiency**: Linear on training **Statistical test**: Standard deviation
Beney [2]	**Classification Method**: Balanced Winnow **Features**: Words or linguistic triplets **Sections of patents**: Title or abstract or names or description (each section separated) **Output**: ML **Level of classification in IPC**: Class and Subclass **Phases of classification**: SP **Dataset**: CLEF-IP 2010 **Language capability**: MuL (English, German, French) **Evaluation measure**: Mi-F1. Best performance (using words+triplets in combination with title+abstract+names) 0.77 at the class level and (using words+title+abstract+names) 0.68 at the subclass level **Efficiency**: about 9 hours for training **Statistical test**: Standard deviation

Table 6. *Continued*

Work	Details
Cai & Hofmann [7]	**Classification Method**: hSVM (hierarchical SVM) **Features:** Words **Sections of patents:** Title and claims (combined) **Feature weighting:** Term normalization **Hierarchy use:** GC **Output:** SL (only the main category) **Level of classification in IPC:** Main group **Phases of classification:** SP **Dataset:** WIPO-alpha using 3-fold cross validation over the whole dataset **Language capability:** MoL (English) **Evaluation measure:** Acc, P, taxonomy-based loss (Δ-loss), parent accuracy (PAcc) Best performance Acc=0.38, P=0.49, Δ-loss=1.23, PAcc=0.65 **Efficiency:** 2,200 seconds for training
Chen & Chang [9]	**Classification Method**: SVM and kNN **Features:** Words **Sections of patents:** Title and claims (combined) **Preprocessing:** SWR and Porter stemming **Feature selection:** Inverse category frequency (TF-ICF) to select 1,040 features **Feature weighting:** TF-IDF **Hierarchy use:** LCL **Output:** ML in the first two phases (11 and 37 respectively), SL in the final decision (only the main category) **Level of classification in IPC:** Subgroup **Phases of classification:** MP. Three phases for training and testing Two initial phases with SVM and one final with kNN **Dataset:** A subset of WIPO-alpha (21,104 patents, 12,042 for training and 9,062 for testing) **Language capability:** MoL (English) **Evaluation measure:** Acc Top (main category). Best performance 0.36
Derieux et al. [15]	**Classification Method**: SVM **Features:** Words and phrases **Sections of patents:** Title, abstract, description and claims (all combined) **Preprocessing:** SWR, Part-Of-Spech tagging, lemmatization and polysemy filtering **Feature weighting:** Based on the section of the patent **Hierarchy use:** Flat **Output:** ML (20 categories) **Level of classification in IPC:** Subclass **Phases of classification:** MP. Two phases for training and testing **Dataset:** CLEF-IP 2010. Subset of training set (670,000 patents in English, 240,000 patents in German and 75,000 in French). The complete test set. **Language capability:** MuL (English, German, French) **Evaluation measure:** P@N. Best performance P@5=0.97 in English, P@5=0.96 in German and P@5=0.94 in French

Table 7. Continuation of table 6

Work	Details
Fall et al. [20]	**Classification Method**: SVM or NB or kNN or SNoW **Features**: Words **Sections of patents**: (a) Title or (b) claims (separate) (c) 300 first words of titles, inventors, applicants, abstracts and descriptions (combined) (d) titles, inventors, applicants, and abstracts (combined) **Preprocessing**: SWR and stemming **Feature selection**: IG **Feature weighting**: Binary **Multi-label consideration**: PT. Each patent is considered in each category where it is assigned, or it is considered in its main category. **Hierarchy use**: Flat **Output**: ML (3 categories) **Level of classification in IPC**: Class and subclass **Phases of classification**: SP **Dataset**: WIPO-alpha **Language capability**: MoL (English) **Evaluation measure**: Acc Top, Acc Three and Acc All Best performance at class level, Acc Top=0.55 (SVM, set of features (c)), Acc Three=0.79 (NB, 300 words), Acc All=0.63(NB, set of features (c)) Best performance at subclass level, Acc top=0.41 (SVM, set of features (c)), Acc Three=0.62 (kNN, 300 words), Acc All=0.48(SVM, set of features (c))
Fall et al. [21]	**Classification Method**: NB or kNN or SVM or LLSF (Linear Least Squares Fit) **Features**: Words **Sections of patents**: Two sets (a) the first 300 different words of the titles, inventors, applicants and claims sections. (b) the first 300 different words of the titles, inventors, companies and descriptions **Preprocessing**: SWR and stemming **Feature weighting**: Binary (kNN) and TF (NB and SVM) **Hierarchy use**: Flat **Output**: ML **Level of classification in IPC**: Class and cubclass **Phases of classification**: SP **Dataset**: WIPO-de **Language capability**: MoL (German) **Evaluation measure**: Acc Top, Acc Three and Acc All. Best performance Acc Top—0.65 (LLSF, set (b) of features) at class level Acc Three=0.86 (LLSF, set (b) of features) at class level Acc All=0.76 (LLSF, set (b) of features) at class level Acc Top=0.56 (LLSF, set (b) of features) at subclass level Acc Three=0.78 (LLSF, set (b) of features) at subclass level Acc All=0.71 (LLSF, set (b) of features) at subclass level
Gomez & Moens [27]	**Classification Method**: mRE (Minimizer of the Reconstruction Error) **Features**: Words **Sections of patents**: Title, abstract and 30 first lines of description (all combined) **Preprocessing**: SWR **Feature weighting**: Normalized TF-IDF **Multi-label consideration**: PT. Each patent is considered in each category where it is assigned **Hierarchy use**: Flat **Output**: SL (only the main category) **Level of classification in IPC**: Section **Phases of classification**: SP **Dataset**: WIPO-alpha, WIPO-de **Language capability**: MuL (English, German) **Evaluation measure**: Acc, Ma-F1. Best performance Acc=0.74, Ma-F1=0.72 for WIPO-alpha Best performance Acc=0.69, Ma-F1=0.68 for WIPO-de **Efficiency**: Quasi-linear on training
Guyot et al. [28]	**Classification Method**: Winnow **Features**: Words and context words (collocations) **Sections of patents**: Inventor, applicant, title, abstract, claims, first 4,000 characters of description (all combined) **Preprocessing**: SWR **Feature selection**: TF (remove words that appear less than 4 times), and keep collocations that appear more than 16 times **Hierarchy use**: Flat **Output**: ML **Level of classification in IPC**: Subclass **Phases of classification**: SP **Dataset**: CLEF-IP 2010 **Language capability**: MuL (English, German, French) **Evaluation measure**: MAP and P@N Best performance MAP=0.79, P@1=.83 (average over the three languages) **Efficiency**: About 3 hours for training and 3 minutes for testing (common PC)

Table 8. Continuation of table 6

Work	Details
Hofmann & Cai [31]	**Classification Method**: SVM **Features:** Words **Sections of patents:** Title and claims (combined) **Feature weighting:** Normalization **Hierarchy use:** GC **Output:** SL (only the main category) **Level of classification in IPC:** Main group **Phases of classification:** SP **Dataset:** Section D of WIPO-alpha (1,710 patents) using 3-fold cross validation **Language capability:** MoL (English) **Evaluation measure:** Acc, Δ-loss. Best performance Acc=0.30, Δ-loss=1.21
Rousu et al. [50]	**Classification Method**: H-M^3 (Maximum Margin Hierarchical Multilabel Classifier) **Features:** Words **Feature weighting:** TF-IDF **Multi-label consideration:** AA **Hierarchy use:** GC **Output:** ML **Level of classification in IPC:** Main group **Phases of classification:** SP **Dataset:** Section D of WIPO-alpha (1,372 patents for training and 358 for testing) **Language capability:** MoL (English) **Evaluation measure:** Mi-F1, Δ-loss. Best performance Mi-F1 = 0.76, Δ-loss=1.67 **Efficiency:** Linear
Seeger 2006 [52]	**Classification Method**: Kernel classification model **Features:** Words **Sections of patents:** Title and claims (combined) **Preprocessing:** SWR and Porter stemming **Feature weighting:** Normalization **Multi-label consideration:** AA **Hierarchy use:** GC **Output:** ML **Level of classification in IPC:** Main group **Phases of classification:** SP **Dataset:** WIPO-alpha (experiments per section A to H) with 3 different splits **Language capability:** MoL (English) **Evaluation measure:** Acc, P, taxo-loss Best performance Acc=0.37, P=0.49, taxo-loss=1.25 **Efficiency:** Linear for training
Teodoro et al. [59]	**Classification Method**: kNN **Features:** Words **Sections of patents:** Title, abstract, claims and links (combined) **Feature weighting:** Normalized BM25 **Hierarchy use:** Flat **Output:** ML **Level of classification in IPC:** Subgroup **Phases of classification:** MP. No training phase. Two phases for testing **Dataset:** PAJ (2,382,595 patents in Japanese) and USPTO (889,116 patents in English) for training. 633 abstracts in English and 639 in Japanese for testing **Language capability:** MoL (English), CoL (Classify papers written in Japanese, using patents written in English) **Evaluation measure:** MAP. Best performance 0.68 at subclass level, 0.5 at main group level and 0.3 at subgroup level

Table 9. Continuation of table 6

Work	Details
Tikk et al. [60]	Classification Method: UFEX Features: Words or phrases Sections of patents: Title, inventor, applicant, abstract, claims (combined) Feature selection: DF (disregard words appearing in less 2 patents and in more than 25% of the training set) Feature weighting: Entropy Multi-label consideration: AA Hierarchy use: LCN Output: ML (3 categories) Level of classification in IPC: Class, subclass and main group Phases of classification: SP Dataset: WIPO-alpha, WIPO-de Language capability: MuL (English, German) Evaluation measure: Acc Top, Acc Three and Acc All. Best performance Acc Top=0.66, Acc Three=0.89, Acc All=0.76 for WIPO-alpha at class level Acc Top=0.55, Acc Three=0.79, Acc All=0.66 for WIPO-alpha at subclass level Acc Top=0.38, Acc Three=0.60, Acc All=0.51 for WIPO-alpha at main group level Acc Top=0.65, Acc Three=0.87, Acc All=0.75 for WIPO-de at class level Acc Top=0.55, Acc Three=0.78, Acc All=0.67 for WIPO-de at subclass level Acc Top=0.38, Acc Three=0.57, Acc All=0.51 for WIPO-de at main group level Efficiency: 2 hours 40 minutes for training on a PC (2Ghz, 1GB in RAM)
Trappey et al. [62]	Classification Method: NN Features: Phrases (made of correlated words) Preprocessing: SWR Feature selection: DF (the 67 most frequent words are selected) Hierarchy use: Flat Output: SL (only the main category) Level of classification in IPC: Main group and subgroup Phases of classification: SP Dataset: Class B25 from WIPO-alpha (124 patents for testing) Language capability: MoL (English) Evaluation measure: P Best performance 0.92 at main group level, 0.9 at subgroup level
Verbene et al. [68]	Classification Method: Winnow Features: Words and dependency triplets (two words and their dependency) Sections of patents: Abstract Feature weighting: Binary Multi-label consideration: AA Hierarchy use: Flat Output: ML Level of classification in IPC: Subclass Phases of classification: SP Dataset: CLEF-IP 2010. Only the English part for training and the whole test set Language capability: CoL (Classify patents written in English, German or French, using patents written in English) Evaluation measure: P, R, F1, MAP Best performance (using words+triplets) P=0.62, R=0.52, F1=0.56, MAP=0.69 (average over the three languages) Efficiency: 2 hours for training
Verbene et al.[67]	Classification Method: Winnow Features: Words, dependency triplets, links Sections of patents: Abstract, metadata, description and first 400 words of description (combined) Feature weighting: Binary Multi-label consideration: MP. Two phases for testing (voting scheme using categories from linked patents) Hierarchy use: Flat Output: ML Level of classification in IPC: Subclass Phases of classification: SP Dataset: CLEF-IP 2011 Language capability: MoL (English) Evaluation measure: P, R, F1 Best performance (words+abstract+description) P=0.74 (words+triplets+abstract+400 words of description) R=0.86 (words+abstract+description) F1=0.71

For the CLEF-IP 2010 classification task [47], the participant group from Simple Shift (described as Guyot et al. [28] in the tables above) obtained the best performance. However, as a matter of fact, the general performance of the systems for this task varies depending on which measure to consider. The other published works related with this task and described in the tables are the ones of Beney [2], Derieux et al. [15] and Verberne et al. [68].

In the CLEF-IP 2011 [46], there were two classification tasks: the first was to classify the test patents in the subclass level of the IPC, the second was to classify the test patents in the subgroup level of the IPC provided the real subclass of each patent (i.e. to refine the classification). There were only two participants with a total 25 runs for both tasks. The organizers evaluated the performance of the submitted runs using the following measures: P@1, P@5, R@1, R@5, F1@1 and F1@5. For the subclass level the best results were from the group of the Information Foraging Lab of the Radboud Universiteit Nijmegen (described as Verberne et al. [67] in the tables above). For the subgroup level the best results reported in the overview paper were from the group WISEnut Inc with P@5≈0.32 for English, P@5≈0.29 for German and P@5≈0.27 for French. However, we were unable to access the published work of this group.

There exist also two overview papers regarding the classification task in the NTCIR-7 [44] and NTCIR-8 [45] workshops. The task was the same in both workshops: to classify research papers (not patents) using the IPC, but the AHCP systems had to be trained using patents. In NTCIR-7 the classification was done in the subgroup level, while in NTCIR-8 the classification was done in the subclass, main group and subgroup levels. The task was multi-lingual and cross-lingual, using patents and papers written in Japanese and English. There were four subtasks: classification of research papers written in English using a system trained with patents written in English; classification of research papers written in Japanese using a system trained with patents written in Japanese; classification of research papers written in Japanese using a system trained with patents written in English (J2E subtask); and classification of research papers written in English using a system trained with patents written in Japanese (E2J). The organizers provided the participants with a dataset for training of about 8 million patents. 7 millions of those patents were written in Japanese and from there 3.5 million of patents were automatically translated, the remaining 1 million of patents were written in English. For testing they provided 644 research papers in English and Japanese. For the NTCIR-7 workshop there were twelve participants submitting a total of 50 runs for the first three subtasks (no submissions for the E2J subtask). The best performances were obtained for the Japanese subtask with a MAP=0.44, for the English subtask with a MAP=0.49, and for the J2E subtask with a MAP=0.44.

In the case of the NTCIR-8 workshop there were six participants submitting a total of 101 runs for the first three subtasks (no submissions for the E2J subtask). The best performances at the subclass level were obtained for the Japanese subtask with a MAP=0.8, for the English subtask with a MAP=0.72, and for the J2E subtask with a MAP=0.71; at the main group level for the Japanese subtask a MAP=0.64, for the English subtask a MAP=0.55, and for the J2E subtask a MAP=0.5 were cited; and at the subgroup level for the Japanese subtask a MAP=0.45, for the English subtask a MAP=0.37, and for the J2E subtask a MAP=0.30 were obtained.

We could observe that the CLEF-IP and NTCIR classification tasks have a predominant natural language processing (NLP) background and follow an information retrieval (IR) approach for the AHCP in the IPC. The IR approach sees the problem as retrieving the most relevant categories for a given test patent, rather than classifying the patent in a set of categories.

From all the tables above and the description of the overview papers, we can observe the diversity of methodologies used to perform the AHCP in the IPC. One interesting point to highlight is that most of the authors agree that the use of more data for training is always beneficial to improve the performance of any AHCP system. They also agree that the deeper the level of classification in the IPC structure, the more complex the problem is and the worse the results are. As a matter of fact it is noticeable that there is still not a clear solution to the general problem of AHCP in the IPC. The descriptions of works show a large variety of results using different classification methods, features, sections of the patents, datasets, levels of classification and evaluation measures. Each group of authors claims to obtain better results based on their proposed framework. It is easily observable that there are still several aspects of the AHCP in the IPC that present a lack of agreement between researchers. What classifier method, features, preprocessing and section(s) of the patents are the best for the classification task and what is the best way of using the IPC structure are still open questions that are not completely nor clearly answered by any methodology. The results largely vary depending on the components used to implement a system and the evaluation measures used to estimate its performance. In this direction, there is a lack of a standard framework to evaluate the AHCP systems. We observe from the presented works in the above tables that most of the researchers use ad-hoc datasets and evaluation measures. There are few exceptions: the evaluation under the CLEF-IP 2010 and CLEF-IP 2011 tasks, which used the corresponding CLEF-IP datasets and used the same evaluation standard; and the works by Fall et al. (2003) [20], Fall et al. (2004) [21], Tikk et al. [60] and Chen&Chang [9], where the authors use the complete WIPO-alpha and WIPO-de datasets as they were originally defined, and use the same evaluation measures. In those cases it is possible to compare systems. Besides these, the comparison is rather complicated. We conclude that a standard framework of evaluation is required. In addition, deeper studies and experiments regarding the alternatives of the aforementioned components of an AHCP system are necessary, in order to better understand the effects of each one of them in the performance of the systems. Moreover, a better description of the complexity or computing times of the methods employed in a given AHCP system is desirable. This task is a large-scale task, and scalability of the methods should be considered, since the system would need to deal with thousands of patents per day.

5   Conclusions and Perspectives for the AHCP in the IPC

In this chapter we have surveyed and presented a revision of several works found in the literature for the automated hierarchical classification of patents (AHCP) in the International Patent Classification (IPC) hierarchy. This task, as we have seen throughout the sections of the chapter, is a very hard problem. It involves issues regarding the complex structure of the IPC, concerning its imbalanced distribution of categories, and its dynamical nature, together with particularities from the patents as written documents, from distributions of words to issues with the language used.

We have presented as well a series of components that can be included in an AHCP system. We then used these components to describe the works presented in the literature that deal with the task. We could observe from those works that there are still holes and lacks in the definition, scope and evaluation of the task. The works in the literature vary largely in their methodologies but also in their results, where the absence of a standard of evaluation (both in data and measures) is noticeable. It is also common that the works do not present the details used for the implementation of their methods, such as complexity, which would help to understand the scalability and usability of the algorithms.

This is one of the main concerns here. The definition of a standard framework adopted generally to evaluate AHCP systems. This framerwork should include standard datasets and evaluation measures, defined under the agreement of users and designer of the systems and considering both efficacy and efficiency.

Furthermore, most of the works devoted to the AHCP in the IPC are based on classical and traditional methods and use straightforward methodologies. There are several alternatives for the components described in section 4 that are not yet (well) explored for the ACHP in the IPC. Some authors claim in their works that SVMs are slow to train, but efficient implementations of the linear version of this classifier already exist [8][22][54]. There also exist other methods that consider the complex dependencies in a hierarchy and the multi-label nature of some problems which could be applied here [16][58][79][80]. The refinement of the final prediction of the categories to be assigned to a patent or the inclusion of several phases during training is also not well studied [3]. However, our guess is that given the large-scale nature of the AHCP in the IPC, some methods that impose dependencies or refinement during training or testing could have issues with efficiency. In that sense, more research is expected to fully exploit all the knowledge at hand when dealing with a complex hierarchy such as the IPC.

Additionally, the effects of the alternatives for feature selection and feature extraction are not yet clearly understood for the AHCP in the IPC. Some works apply basic statistics for feature selection, like DF or TF, but the use and scope of these methods in the task are still unclear. Feature extraction is even less explored, we have not found the application of methods like LiDA, NMF or LDA. In both cases of feature selection and extraction, it would be interesting to investigate how to use those methods along the hierarchy [25] in order to find features, topics or components describing the categories (and possibly the relations among them).

Acknowledgments. This research was supported partially by the KU Leuven project RADICAL (GOA 12/003).

References

1. Aiolli, F., Cardin, R., Sebastiani, F., Sperduti, A.: Preferential text classification: Learning algorithms and evaluation measures. Information Retrieval 12(5), 559–580 (2009)
2. Beney, J.: LCI-INSA linguistic experiment for CLEF-IP classification track. In: CLEF (Notebook Papers/LABs/Workshops) (2010)
3. Bennett, P.N., Nguyen, N.: Refined experts: Improving classification in large taxonomies. In: Proceedings of the 32nd International ACM SIGIR Conference on Research and Development in Information Retrieval, pp. 11–18. ACM (2009)
4. Benzineb, K., Guyot, J.: Automated patent classification. In: Lupu, M., Mayer, K., Tait, J., Trippe, A.J. (eds.) Current Challenges in Patent Information Retrieval. The Information Retrieval Series, vol. 29, pp. 239–261. Springer (2011)
5. Bishop, C.M., Nasrabadi, N.M.: Pattern Recognition and Machine Learning. Springer (2006)
6. Blei, D.M., Ng, A.Y., Jordan, M.I.: Latent Dirichlet allocation. Journal of Machine Learning Research 3, 993–1022 (2003)
7. Cai, L., Hofmann, T.: Hierarchical document categorization with support vector machines. In: Proceedings of the 13th ACM International Conference on Information and Knowledge Management, pp. 78–87. ACM (2004)
8. Chang, C.C., Lin, C.J.: LIBSVM: A library for support vector machines. ACM Transactions on Intelligent Systems and Technology 2(3), 27:1–27:27 (2011)
9. Chen, Y.L., Chang, Y.C.: A three-phase method for patent classification. Information Processing and Management 48(6), 1017–1030 (2012)
10. Clare, A.J., King, R.D.: Knowledge discovery in multi-label phenotype data. In: Siebes, A., De Raedt, L. (eds.) PKDD 2001. LNCS (LNAI), vol. 2168, pp. 42–53. Springer, Heidelberg (2001)
11. Cortes, C., Vapnik, V.: Support-vector networks. Machine Learning 20(3), 273–297 (1995)
12. CPC: Website of the Cooperative Patent Classification, http://www.cooperativepatentclassification.org/index.html (2013) (accessed: January 01, 2014)
13. Deerwester, S.C., Dumais, S.T., Landauer, T.K., Furnas, G.W., Harshman, R.A.: Indexing by latent semantic analysis. Journal of the American Society for Information Science 41(6), 391–407 (1990)
14. Demšar, J.: Statistical comparisons of classifiers over multiple data sets. Journal of Machine Learning Research 7, 1–30 (2006)
15. Derieux, F., Bobeica, M., Pois, D., Raysz, J.P.: Combining semantics and statistics for patent classification. In: CLEF (Notebook Papers/LABs/Workshops) (2010)
16. Deschacht, K., Moens, M.F.: Efficient hierarchical entity classifier using conditional random fields. In: Proceedings of the 2nd Workshop on Ontology Learning and Population, pp. 33–40 (2006)
17. Elisseeff, A., Weston, J.: A kernel method for multi-labelled classification. In: Dietterich, T.G., Becker, S., Ghahramani, Z. (eds.) Advances in Neural Information Processing Systems, vol. 14, pp. 681–687. MIT (2002)

18. EPO: Website of the European Patent Office, http://www.epo.org/ (accessed: January 1, 2014)
19. Fall, C.J., Benzineb, K.: Literature survey: Issues to be considered in the automatic classification of patents. Tech. rep., World Intellectual Property Organization (October 2002)
20. Fall, C.J., Törcsvári, A., Benzineb, K., Karetka, G.: Automated categorization in the international patent classification. SIGIR Forum 37(1), 10–25 (2003)
21. Fall, C., Törcsvári, A., Fiévet, P., Karetka, G.: Automated categorization of German-language patent documents. Expert Systems with Applications 26(2), 269–277 (2004)
22. Fan, R.E., Chang, K.W., Hsieh, C.J., Wang, X.R., Lin, C.J.: LIBLINEAR: A library for large linear classification. Journal of Machine Learning Research 9, 1871–1874 (2008)
23. Forman, G.: An extensive empirical study of feature selection metrics for text classification. Journal of Machine Learning Research 3, 1289–1305 (2003)
24. Gomez, J.C., Boiy, E., Moens, M.F.: Highly discriminative statistical features for email classification. Knowledge and Information Systems 31(1), 23–53 (2012)
25. Gomez, J.C., Moens, M.-F.: Hierarchical classification of web documents by stratified discriminant analysis. In: Salampasis, M., Larsen, B. (eds.) IRFC 2012. LNCS, vol. 7356, pp. 94–108. Springer, Heidelberg (2012)
26. Gomez, J.C., Moens, M.-F.: PCA document reconstruction for email classification. Computational Statistics & Data Analysis 56(3), 741–751 (2012)
27. Gomez, J.C., Moens, M.-F.: Minimizer of the reconstruction error for multi-class document categorization. Expert Systems with Applications 41(3), 861–868 (2014)
28. Guyot, J., Benzineb, K., Falquet, G., Shift, S.: myclass: A mature tool for patent classification. In: CLEF (Notebook Papers/LABs/Workshops) (2010)
29. Han, J., Kamber, M., Pei, J.: Data Mining: Concepts and Techniques. Morgan Kaufmann (2006)
30. Haykin, S.: Neural Networks: A Comprehensive Foundation. Prentice Hall (1994)
31. Hofmann, T., Cai, L., Ciaramita, M.: Learning with taxonomies: Classifying documents and words. In: NIPS Workshop on Syntax, Semantics, and Statistics (2003)
32. Hull, D.A.: Stemming algorithms: A case study for detailed evaluation. Journal of the American Society for Information Science 47(1), 70–84 (1996)
33. Kantardzic, M.: Data Mining: Concepts, Models, Methods, and Algorithms. John Wiley & Sons (2011)
34. Seutter, C.H.A.K.M., Beney, J.G.: Multi-classification of patent applications with Winnow. In: Broy, M., Zamulin, A.V. (eds.) PSI 2003. LNCS, vol. 2890, pp. 546–555. Springer, Heidelberg (2004)
35. Krier, M., Zaccà, F.: Automatic categorisation applications at the European patent office. World Patent Information 24(3), 187–196 (2002)
36. Larkey, L.S.: A patent search and classification system. In: Proceedings of the 4th ACM Conference on Digital Libraries, pp. 179–187. ACM (1999)
37. Lewis, D.D.: Naive (Bayes) at forty: The independence assumption in information retrieval. In: Nédellec, C., Rouveirol, C. (eds.) ECML 1998. LNCS (LNAI), vol. 1398, pp. 4–15. Springer, Heidelberg (1998)
38. Li, W.: Random texts exhibit Zipf's-law-like word frequency distribution. IEEE Transactions on Information Theory 38(6), 1842–1845 (1992)
39. Littlestone, N.: Learning quickly when irrelevant attributes abound: A new linear-threshold algorithm. Machine Learning 2(4), 285–318 (1988)
40. Lupu, M., Hanbury, A.: Patent retrieval. Foundations and Trends in Information Retrieval 7(1), 1–97 (2013)

41. Manning, C.D., Raghavan, P., Schütze, H.: Introduction to Information Retrieval. Cambridge University Press (2008)
42. McCallum, A., Nigam, K.: A comparison of event models for naive Bayes text classification. In: AAAI 1998 Workshop on Learning for Text Categorization, vol. 752, pp. 41–48. AAAI Press (1998)
43. Murphy, K.P.: Machine Learning: A Probabilistic Perspective. The MIT Press (2012)
44. Nanba, H., Fujii, A., Iwayama, M., Hashimoto, T.: Overview of the patent mining task at the NTCIR-7 workshop. In: Proceedings of the NII Test Collection for IR Systems-7. NTCIR (2008)
45. Nanba, H., Fujii, A., Iwayama, M., Hashimoto, T.: Overview of the patent mining task at the NTCIR-8 workshop. In: Proceedings of the NII Test Collection for IR Systems-8. NTCIR (2010)
46. Piroi, F., Lupu, M., Hanbury, A., Zenz, V.: CLEF-IP 2011: Retrieval in the intellectual property domain. In: Petras, V., Forner, P., Clough, P.D. (eds.) Proceedings of CLEF 2011 (Notebook Papers/Labs/Workshop) (2011)
47. Piroi, F.: CLEF-IP 2010: Classification task evaluation summary. Tech. Rep. IRF-TR-2010-00005, Information Retrieval Facility (August 2010)
48. Porter, M.F.: An algorithm for suffix stripping. Program: Electronic Library and Information Systems 14(3), 130–137 (1980)
49. Quinlan, J.R.: Induction of decision trees. Machine Learning 1(1), 81–106 (1986)
50. Rousu, J., Saunders, C., Szedmak, S., Shawe-Taylor, J.: Kernel-based learning of hierarchical multilabel classification models. Journal of Machine Learning Research 7, 1601–1626 (2006)
51. Sebastiani, F.: Machine learning in automated text categorization. ACM Computing Surveys 34(1), 1–47 (2002)
52. Seeger, M.: Cross-validation optimization for large scale hierarchical classification kernel methods. In: Advances in Neural Information Processing Systems, pp. 1233–1240 (2006)
53. Seung, D., Lee, L.: Algorithms for non-negative matrix factorization. Advances in Neural Information Processing Systems 13, 556–562 (2001)
54. Shalev-Shwartz, S., Singer, Y., Srebro, N.: Pegasos: Primal estimated sub-gradient solver for svm. In: Proceedings of the 24th International Conference on Machine Learning, pp. 807–814. ACM (2007)
55. Silla Jr., C.N., Freitas, A.A.: A survey of hierarchical classification across different application domains. Data Mining and Knowledge Discovery 22(1-2), 31–72 (2011)
56. Smith, H.: Automation of patent classification. World Patent Information 24(4), 269–271 (2002)
57. Sokolova, M., Lapalme, G.: A systematic analysis of performance measures for classification tasks. Information Processing and Management 45(4), 427–437 (2009)
58. Tang, L., Rajan, S., Narayanan, V.K.: Large scale multi-label classification via metalabeler. In: Proceedings of the 18th International Conference on World Wide Web, pp. 211–220. ACM (2009)
59. Teodoro, D., Gobeill, J., Pasche, E., Ruch, P., Vishnyakova, D., Lovis, C.: Automatic IPC encoding and novelty tracking for effective patent mining. In: Proceedings of the 8th NTCIR Workshop Meeting, pp. 309–317. National Institute of Informatics Japan (2010)
60. Tikk, D., Biró, G., Yang, J.: Experiment with a hierarchical text categorization method on WIPO patent collections. In: Attoh-Okine, N., Ayyub, B. (eds.) Applied Research in Uncertainty Modeling and Analysis. International Series in Intelligent Technologies, vol. 20, pp. 283–302. Springer (2005)

61. Torkkola, K.: Linear discriminant analysis in document classification. In: IEEE ICDM Workshop on Text Mining, pp. 800–806. IEEE (2001)
62. Trappey, A.J.C., Hsu, F.C., Trappey, C.V., Lin, C.I.: Development of a patent document classification and search platform using a back-propagation network. Expert Systems with Applications 31(4), 755–765 (2006)
63. Tseng, Y.H., Lin, C.J., Lin, Y.I.: Text mining techniques for patent analysis. Information Processing and Management 43(5), 1216–1247 (2007)
64. Tsochantaridis, I., Joachims, T., Hofmann, T., Altun, Y.: Large margin methods for structured and interdependent output variables. Journal of Machine Learning Research 6, 1453–1484 (2005)
65. Tsoumakas, G., Katakis, I., Vlahavas, I.: Mining multi-label data. In: Data Mining and Knowledge Discovery Handbook, pp. 667–685. Springer (2010)
66. USPTO: Website of the United States Patent and Trademark Office (2014), http://www.uspto.gov/ (accessed January 01, 2014)
67. Verberne, S., D'hondt, E.: Patent classification experiments with the Linguistic Classification System LCS in CLEF-IP 2011. In: Proceedings of CLEF 2011 (Notebook Papers/Labs/Workshop) (2011)
68. Verberne, S., Vogel, M., D'hondt, E.: Patent classification experiments with the linguistic classification system LCS. In: CLEF (Notebook Papers/LABs/Workshops) (2010)
69. Vishwanathan, S.V., Schraudolph, N.N., Smola, A.J.: Step size adaptation in reproducing kernel hilbert space. Journal of Machine Learning Research 7, 1107–1133 (2006)
70. Wanner, L., Baeza-Yates, R., Brügmann, S., Codina, J., Diallo, B., Escorsa, E., Giereth, M., Kompatsiaris, Y., Papadopoulos, S., Pianta, E., Piella, G., Puhlmann, I., Rao, G., Rotard, M., Schoester, P., Serafini, L., Zervaki, V.: Towards content-oriented patent document processing. World Patent Information 30(1), 21–33 (2008)
71. Webster, J.J., Kit, C.: Tokenization as the initial phase in NLP. In: Proceedings of the 14th Conference on Computational Linguistics, pp. 1106–1110. ACL (1992)
72. WIPO: WIPO-alpha readme (2009), http://www.wipo.int/classifications/ipc/en/ITsupport/Categorization/dataset/wipo-alpha-readme.html (accessed: January 01, 2014)
73. WIPO: Website of the World Intellectual Property Organization (2014), http://www.wipo.int/export/sites/www/classifications/ipc/en/guide/guide_ipc.pdf (accessed: January 01, 2014)
74. Witten, I.H., Frank, E., Hall, M.A.: Data Mining: Practical Machine Learning Tools and Techniques. Elsevier (2011)
75. Wu, F., Zhang, J., Honavar, V.: Learning classifiers using hierarchically structured class taxonomies. In: Zucker, J.-D., Saitta, L. (eds.) SARA 2005. LNCS (LNAI), vol. 3607, pp. 313–320. Springer, Heidelberg (2005)
76. Xiao, T., Cao, F., Li, T., Song, G., Zhou, K., Zhu, J., Wang, H.: kNN and re-ranking models for English patent mining at NTICR-7. In: Proceedings of the 7th NTCIR Workshop Meeting. National Institute of Informatics Japan (2008)
77. Yang, Y.: An evaluation of statistical approaches to text categorization. Information Retrieval 1(1-2), 69–90 (1999)
78. Yang, Y., Pedersen, J.O.: A comparative study on feature selection in text categorization. In: Proceedings of the 14th International Conference on Machine Learning, pp. 412–420. Morgan Kaufmann (1997)

79. Zhang, M.L., Zhou, Z.H.: Multilabel neural networks with applications to functional genomics and text categorization. IEEE Transactions on Knowledge and Data Engineering 18(10), 1338–1351 (2006)
80. Zhang, M.L., Zhou, Z.H.: ML-kNN: A lazy learning approach to multi-label learning. Pattern Recognition 40(7), 2038–2048 (2007)

Enhancing Patent Search with Content-Based Image Retrieval

Stefanos Vrochidis, Anastasia Moumtzidou, and Ioannis Kompatsiaris

Centre for Research & Technology Hellas - Information Technologies Institute, Thessaloniki, Greece
{stefanos,moumtzid,ikom}@iti.gr

Abstract. Nowadays most of the patent search systems still rely upon text to provide retrieval functionalities. Recently, the intellectual property and information retrieval communities have shown great interest in patent image retrieval, which could augment the current practices of patent search. In this chapter, we present a patent image extraction and retrieval framework, which deals with patent image extraction and multimodal (textual and visual) metadata generation from patent images with a view to provide content-based search and concept-based retrieval functionalities. Patent image extraction builds upon page orientation detection and segmentation, while metadata extraction from images is based on the generation of low level visual and textual features. The content-based retrieval functionality is based on visual low level features, which have been devised to deal with complex black and white drawings. Extraction of concepts builds upon on a supervised machine learning framework realised with Support Vector Machines and a combination of visual and textual features. We evaluate the different retrieval parts of the framework by using a dataset from the footwear and the lithography domain.

Keywords: patents, images, retrieval, concepts, classification, hybrid, visual.

1 Introduction

Nowadays, the growing number of patent applications submitted in patent offices worldwide requires the development of advanced patent search technologies, which would be able to deal with the complexity and the unique characteristics of patents. Although patent documents describe an invention by using multimodal information encoded in textual, tabular and figure format, most of the patent retrieval techniques and patent search engines to date, still consider mainly text-based retrieval functionalities. To a certain extent, indeed textual data can be considered as a very reliable source of information, since the ideas and the innovations to be patented are almost always described in such a format in the claims and the disclosure parts of the patent. However, many patents contain figures, drawings and diagrams, which are essential for describing innovative artifacts, processes, algorithms and other inventions and thus their importance cannot be ignored [1], [2]. Despite this fact, the majority of the patent search systems to date focus on text, metadata and boolean-based search, while there is not much published work in the field of image-based patent search.

G. Paltoglou et al. (Eds.): Professional Search in the Modern World, LNCS 8830, pp. 250–273, 2014.

Recently, both the Intellectual Property and the Information Retrieval communities have shown great interest in patent image search expressed with research activities and works in the area (e.g. [3], [4]), as well as with prototype systems and demos (e.g. [5], [6]). In addition, dedicated sessions and talks have been organised in relevant symposiums, workshops and conferences (e.g. IRFS[1], CLEF[2], etc.) and several patent search and classification systems are developed.

Image examination is considered very important to patent searchers in their task to understand the patent contents and retrieve relevant patents. During this procedure there are several cases, in which patent searchers are browsing thousands of patents looking only on the images contained in the drawings section. Such tasks could be certainly speeded up with the aid of patent image search engines, which would be capable of retrieving and ranking images based on their visual content. An additional reason that patent image search could be of great importance, is the fact that images by nature are independent of the applicant's language and remain intact despite the evolvement of the scientific terminology (i.e. some terms can become obsolete) over the years and thus creating misunderstanding across the readers. This means that patent searchers could be able to retrieve relevant prior art consisting of multilingual patents without requiring a translation, which in many cases is difficult to be automatically generated (e.g. in Asian patents). Image-based patent search also allows for retrieving patents ranging in time, which could have been written using different terminologies. Motivated by the above, recent works in patent search [5] are directed towards the development of systems, which could automatically extract and retrieve patent images based on visual similarity

It is interesting to notice that the first image retrieval works in the area of intellectual property are dedicated to the field of trademark search [7], [8], [9], [10], [11], [12]; however, as discussed in [13], these efforts had limited success in satisfying the user requirements. On the other hand, in the patent domain, until 2007 no systematic efforts have been conducted with the aim of developing a patent image retrieval system [1]. Only in the recent years, the research in patent image search has started to deal with semantic concept extraction from patent images and figure classification based on visual characteristics. PATSEEK [6] is one of the first attempts dealing with patent image content-based search. PATSEEK is an image-based retrieval system for the US patent database. It consists of two subsystems: one for the image feature extraction and one for query-by-example image retrieval. The image feature representation is achieved through a shape-based image retrieval method called the Edge Orientation Autocorrelogram. The PATSEEK search system interacts with the user through a simple interface that, given a certain query image, returns a set of visually similar images. ImageSeeker is another tool in the field of patent image-based search developed by LTU Technologies [14]. This tool has been used by the French patent office (INPI) to build an image-based patent retrieval system and was also applied in a European project called eMARKS [15] that aims at the development of services for access to trademark and image databases. The performance of the system is claimed to be better compared to existing image classification systems. Apart from

---

[1] Information Retrieval Facility Symposium (IRFS).
[2] Conference on Multilingual and Multimodal Information Access Evaluation (CLEF).

the aforementioned systems, retrieval algorithms that focus on patent image search, have been published in [16] and [17], however they were never tested extensively in large scale databases and were not applied in an integrated patent retrieval framework, where patent images have to be extracted from documents and other metadata need to be taken into account. More recently, the PatMedia image search engine was developed during the PATExpert project [18]. PatMedia is capable of retrieving patent images based on visual similarity using the Adaptive Hierarchical Density Histograms (AHDH) [19] and constitutes the retrieval engine of an integrated patent image extraction and retrieval framework [5].

Although the functionality of retrieving similar images is considered very useful by professional patent searchers [20], there are many situations, in which the actual need is to identify images with common characteristics that that fall into a specific semantic category, as well as images that depict a specific object or concept. For instance, in many cases a patent searcher is submitting textual queries looking for figures that depict specific schemas or objects (e.g. high heel shoes, ski boots, etc.). In order to fully address this requirement we need to understand what exactly a certain figure depicts, not only based on the associated caption (if it is available) but also based on its content. In this context, and following the trend of modern image retrieval approaches, which are moving towards concept-based image search [21], patent image search works have started addressing problems such as content-based classification and concept extraction of patent images by applying image analysis and machine learning algorithms. In this context, the authors in [22] employed a semi-supervised classification approach based on support vector machines and extracted many different image features including Local binary patterns, MPEG-7 Edge histograms, binary image features and image characteristics retrieved with Optical Character Recognition (OCR). In another approach [23], the authors extract SIFT-like local orientation histograms and they build visual vocabularies specific to patent images using Gaussian mixture model (GMM). Then, the images are represented by Fisher features and linear classifiers are employed for the categorisation. Finally, the most recent works in patent image search dealt with semantic concept extraction from patent images. Specifically, in [24] the authors propose a supervised machine learning framework to extract semantic concepts from patent images by combining visual and textual information.

In this chapter, we present a patent image extraction and retrieval framework, which deals with patent image extraction and multimodal (textual and visual) metadata generation with a view to providing content-based search and concept-based retrieval functionalities for patent images. Patent image extraction builds upon page orientation detection and segmentation, metadata extraction considers the generation of low level visual and textual features. Then, the content-based retrieval functionality is based on comparison of visual low level features, while extraction of concepts builds upon a combination of features and a supervised machine learning framework realised with Support Vector Machines (SVM).

2   Use Cases and Requirements

In this section, we briefly discuss the current patent search practices to investigate how patent image retrieval could serve the needs of patent searchers. To this end, we present use cases of patent search, which could benefit from content- and concept-based image retrieval and analyse the requirements that arise.

2.1   Patent Search Use Cases

Patent searchers are experts at searching but not always regarding all the technologies and the areas in which they work. In this context the patent searchers need to learn the gist of an invention, the new and the old terminology and the multiple classifications, which constitutes a really hard task. Let's present an example of a mechanical search as this is described by a professional patent searcher [25]. We assume that we have a disclosure:

"A dancing shoe with a rotatable heel to allow rapid pivoting about your heel. In a preferred embodiment, the heel should have ball bearings."

A patent searcher has to distil the gist for this disclosure, which could be the basis of the upcoming search. In this case the gist could be expressed by the following concepts:
Concept1: Dancing shoe
Concept2: Rotating heel
Refined Concept 2: Rotating heel with ball bearings.

Then, the patent searcher proceeds by defining specific keywords based on the aforementioned concepts and classification areas to search. In many cases, including this example, the important information (and the gist) are usually illustrated and described with the aid of figures. It is evident that if the patent searcher could directly retrieve patents, which include figures depicting these concepts (i.e. dancing shoe and rotating heel for this example), would be of great help.

In addition, there are several use cases, in which the patent searchers need to browse thousands of figures and compare them with a figure from the patent of interest, in order to judge the novelty of a proposed invention. Having the figures sorted by means of visual similarity will certainly help the patent searcher to limit the time required for inspection. Retrieving images based on visual information is also important, when considering that due to the swiftly changing and often inconsistent terminology in emerging technical domains (e.g. electronic devices, digital media), keyword-based and boolean search may frequently return only a subset of the documents that are related to an input document. Visual similarity can overcome the limitation of language inconsistency, especially in the technical areas, since technical drawings of the same domains typically share style and semantics regardless of the time period. In addition, by ordering visually similar images on publication date the patent searcher could analyse how this image evolves over time and find out when a specific feature is introduced for the first time.

2.2   Requirements

In order to support the aforementioned use cases dealing with the retrieval of "dancing shoes" with "rotating heels", we need to identify specific requirements that a patent image search system should satisfy. Given the fact that patents include information encoded both in textual and visual format it would be important to combine this multimodal information in order to retrieve quality results. This involves both the visual content of the image itself, as well as the figure description. Although one could argue that the image description would be adequate for concept extraction and image similarity tasks, this is not always the case due to several reasons. First, many figures can be associated with misleading or incomplete descriptions (e.g. references to other figures or parts of the patent). In addition, there are cases, in which it is not trivial to automatically map the figure caption to the corresponding image due to handwritten figure labels that cannot be automatically recognised. In such cases we need to rely solely on image information. However, when the figure caption is available we can still process it to gain additional information about the image.

From the functional point of view, a set of requirements with regards to the system performance has to be defined. First, the system should be scalable as it has to cope with vast amounts of content (in the order of millions of patent images). This means that the processing techniques have to be fast and efficient and therefore large feature representation vectors and computationally expensive fusion algorithms should be avoided. However, the representations of the patent images should be adequate so that the concept detectors can demonstrate a minimum accuracy of 85-90% (depending also on the concept characteristics). In addition, a vast number of concepts that are characteristic for the patent images of each IPC class and subclass have to be defined by patent experts, while relevant examples have to be annotated to drive the machine learning algorithms. Finally, the framework needs to build upon open technologies and standards, in order to be easily adaptable to the established patent search platforms.

3   Patent Image Extraction and Retrieval Framework

In order to meet the aforementioned requirements, we propose a patent image extraction and retrieval framework that combines advanced techniques from text and document image analysis, as well as content-based image retrieval methodologies and supervised machine learning. The proposed architecture is illustrated in Figure 1.

The framework consists of five main parts:
  a)   Patent document processing in order to extract the patent figures
  b)   Visual and textual metadata extraction
  c)   Image retrieval by visual similarity
  d)   Concept-based image search

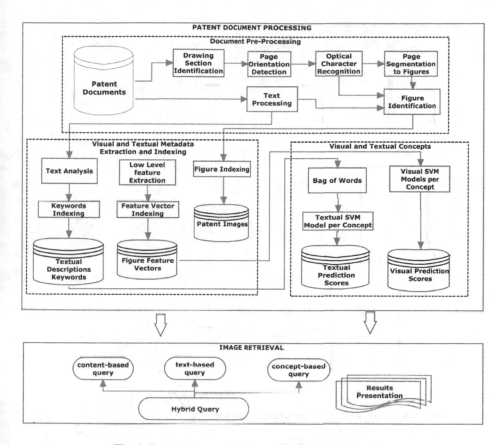

Fig. 1. Patent image extraction and retrieval framework

First, the patents are processed by the document pre-processing module so the patent figures are extracted and mapped to the corresponding textual descriptions. The second step includes visual and textual metadata extraction and figure indexing in order to support content-based search by query example and text-based image retrieval. An additional step is required to extract concepts by exploiting the visual and textual features in a supervised machine learning framework.

Subsequently, these three main parts will be described in detail.

4   Patent Figure Extraction

In the proposed framework, a patent document is considered as the system input. This is processed in order to identify its figures and the related textual descriptions. A detailed example of the whole process is described in Figure 2.

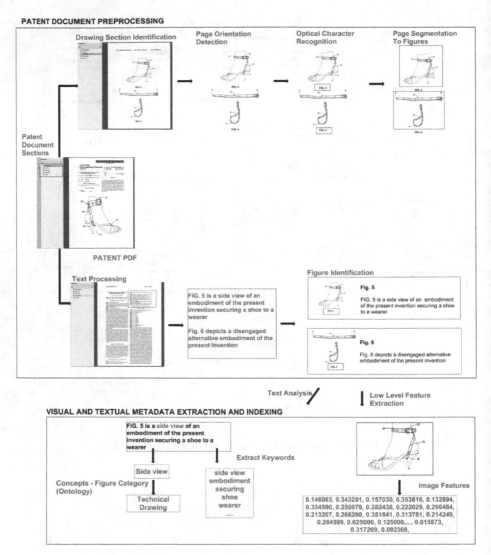

Fig. 2. Schematic example of patent processing procedure

This component consists of several modules: (a) drawings section identification, (b) page orientation detection, (c) optical character recognition (OCR), (e) figure segmentation, (d) text processing, and (f) figure identification.

The first module is required due to the fact that the patent documents that include figures are usually available in PDF format. The drawing page selection from the raw PDF documents is based on section information encoded within the document files. In most cases, a section denoted "Drawings" contains all the drawing-holding pages of a given patent document. Once this section is identified, all pages contained in it are extracted.

After the patent drawing pages have been extracted, it is necessary to detect their orientation and compensate for the cases, in which the true orientation of the image is not the correct one. The orientation detection process is carried out in three steps. First, connected-components regions are extracted. In the second step, regions are classified as "text'" and "non-text'" based on their spatial alignment, their spatial relations and their size. The algorithm used to carry out this step is based on [26]. Finally, the page orientation is estimated by the use of the "text'" regions. If the majority of the text regions are aligned along the horizontal orientation, then the page orientation is classified as "horizontal", otherwise it is classified as "vertical".

In many cases, a patent drawing page contains more than one figure. Thus, it is necessary to employ techniques to identify the number and the position of the figures on the page, in order to isolate them. The employed technique assumes that each separate figure in patents is accompanied by a label of the form "Figure x" or "Fig x". Therefore, we first count the number of occurrences of such a label on a page in order to identify how many figures are contained in that page. The figure label detection can be based on existing OCR tools. The output of this subcomponent includes the figure label (e.g. "FIG. 5"), as well as the relative location of the label on the page.

Subsequently, a segmentation step is required to isolate the images. The segmentation is based on the connected components technique, which identifies the parts in the page that can be considered as separate objects. Overlapping objects are merged in a repetitive process until the main concrete objects that can be considered as separate drawings are identified. The performance of this component can be significantly improved by the introduction of heuristic axioms derived from the observation of a large patent document set (e.g. relatively small objects should be merged with neighbouring objects even in the case they do not overlap).

At the same time, a text processing step is applied to take advantage of the references to the image throughout the patent text. In most patent documents, there is a separate paragraph under the title "BRIEF DESCRIPTION OF DRAWINGS", which contains descriptive text for each of the figures. References to the patent figures and their components are also made in other parts of the patent text. The description of the invention refers to different drawings by specifying the figure number and to the different parts of a drawing by reference letters or numerals.

Although the aforementioned modules employ sophisticated analysis techniques, it is possible that errors are introduced into the results for a variety of reasons. Specifically, handwritten or low quality scanned labels will possibly lead to failure of the OCR tools, while complicated textual descriptions or lack of figure references in the text could introduce errors in the output of the text extraction module. In addition, the segmentation process could fail in certain cases, especially when a single figure consists of spatially disjoint elements or multiple figures are adjacent.

In order to minimise these errors, another step is employed, where the results of the above procedures are combined, in order to produce a reliable output. This is performed in the figure identification module. First, the two sets of labels, extracted by the OCR and text processing subcomponents, are merged and a new updated set of labels is defined. Subsequently, a correction procedure takes place, assuming that the figures labels are appearing, in most cases, sequentially. For instance if we come up with a sequence of labels: "Fig 3, Fig 4, Fig Unknown, Fig 6...", it is very likely, that the unknown label is "Fig 5". Subsequently this information and the coordinates of the labels extracted by the OCR are compared with the extracted figures from the segmentation component. In that way it is possible to correct also cases, in which the segmentation has failed. For example, when label "Fig 1" is recognised by the OCR in page 1, label "Fig 2" in page 2 and segmentation process has outputted two figures in page 1, we are able to merge these images and associate them with the label "Fig 1".

5   Metadata Extraction

This component deals with extraction of visual and textual features from patent images.

5.1   Visual Features

In this approach we are interested in representing each patent image as a whole (i.e. not focus on separate parts of the image) in order to compare it with other images and extract global concepts. Such a global representation requires the employment of global image features, which can deal with the complexity and the special characteristics of patent images. The main characteristic of patent figures is that they are black and white and they depict technical information in diagrammatic form. Given the fact that general case image representation features are based on colour and texture, which are absent in patent images, we need to apply an algorithm which takes into account the geometry and the pixel distribution of these images. In this work we propose the application of the Adaptive Hierarchical Density Histograms (AHDH) as visual feature vectors, which have shown discriminative power between binary complex drawings [19].

The Adaptive Hierarchical Density Histograms (ADHD) are devised specifically to deal with such binary and complex images. The feature vector is generated based on the following steps. First, the algorithm involves a pre-processing phase for noise reduction, coordinate calculation and normalisation. After the pre-processing has taken place, the first geometric centroid of the image plane is calculated and the image area is split into four regions based on the position of this centroid. Then, the feature vector is initialised by estimating the distribution of the black points in each region. This procedure is repeated in a recursive way (Figure 3) for a manually specified number of iterations, and after each iteration, the feature vector is updated. This non-segmentation point-density orientated technique combines high accuracy at low computational cost as it represents the image with a low dimension feature vector (i.e. around 100 features). Based on experiments conducted with patent datasets, the ADHD outperformed the other state of the art methods [19].

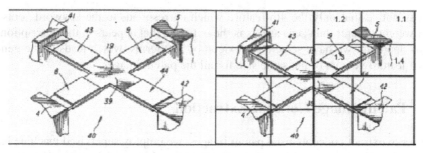

Fig. 3. Extraction of ADHD. Geometric centroids are utilised to iteratively split the image to new regions.

5.2   Textual Features

With a view to exploiting the textual descriptions provided for each figure in the patent document, we process the captions and extract textual features for the patent images. Specifically, we apply a bag of words approach to model each figure with a vector. The bag of words model is a simplifying assumption used in natural language processing and information retrieval. In this model, a text (such as a sentence or a document) is represented as an unordered collection of words, disregarding grammar and even word order.

To generate such a vector we need to define a lexicon, which includes the most frequently used words of this dataset. Then for each figure and based on the associated description we calculate a weight for each word included in the lexicon. The textual annotations are processed with the aid of Porter stemmer [27] and the frequent stop words (e.g. and, so, etc.) are removed. The indexing of the remaining keywords is performed using Lemur [28]. The weight of each term is calculated with the well-established metric *tf-idf* (term frequency multiplied with the inverse document frequency).

Assuming that the lexicon has the following format:

<boot snowboard illustr outsole footwear heel...>

then the corresponding feature vector for the patent image illustrated in Figure 4 would be:

[0 0 0 0.0909091 0 0...]

Example: Patent EP2446767

Figure 1 represent a perspective view of transparency and a lower shell and an insert accommodated in the outsole of the shell according to the first embodiment

Fig. 4. Patent figure with the associated description

We can notice that only the 4th feature which corresponds to the keyword "outsole" has a weight greater than zero as this is the only one that appears in the description. In this approach we have selected a lexicon of 100 terms, which leads to the generation of feature vectors of the same size for all the patent images.

6   Patent Image Concept Extraction

In order to extract concepts from patent images, we employ supervised machine learning-based method that combines well established and state of the art techniques from text and image analysis. The proposed architecture is illustrated in Figure 5.

The initial step of the pipeline is based on the metadata extraction component, where the visual and textual based features are generated (sections 5.1 and 5.2). Subsequently, the dataset is manually annotated and separated into training and test set. Finally, we train a classifier for each concept using the train data and we evaluate its performance using the test data.

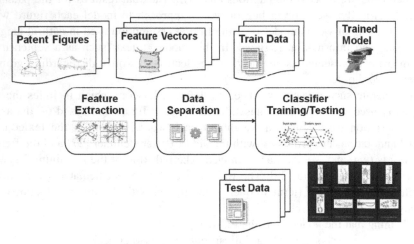

Fig. 5. Patent concept extraction framework

In the following we discuss in more detail the classifier employed and the different combinations of visual and textual features used.

6.1   Supervised Classifier Based on Support Vector Machines

Support Vector Machines (SVMs) constitute a set of supervised learning methods, which are employed to solve classification and regression problems, which involves analysing data and recognizing patterns. SVMs are based on the concept of decision planes that define decision boundaries. A decision plane separates between a set of objects having different class memberships, that is, it divides the feature space into two regions and through the model the objects are assigned to one of the regions/ classes (Figure 6). Support Vector Machine (SVM) performs classification tasks by constructing hyperplanes in a multidimensional space that separates cases of different class labels [29].

A schematic example is shown in Figure 5. In this example, the objects belong either to class GREEN stars or RED circles. The separating line defines a boundary on the right side of which all objects are GREEN and to the left of which all objects are RED. Any new object falling to the right is labelled, i.e., classified, as GREEN (or classified as RED should it fall to the left of the separating line) [29].

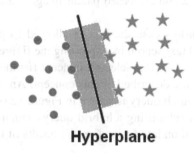

Hyperplane

Fig. 6. Decision plane which separates the RED circles class from the GREEN star class

In this implementation, we make use of the LIBSVM library [30].

6.2 Training Cases and Features

In this approach we train one classifier for each concept. With a view to evaluating the performance of the textual and visual features in the concept extraction process, we have experimented with 3 different training approaches to build the concept detectors.

    a) Visual Case: the classifier was trained only with visual features (section 5.1)
    b) Textual Case: the classifier was trained only with textual features (section 5.2)
    c) Hybrid case: the classifier was trained with a hybrid feature vector which was produced by concatenating the textual and visual feature vectors.

In order to optimise the training process and to select the appropriate parameters that could maximise the performance of the concept detectors, we have conducted a cross-validation process using the training set. In detail, the training set was divided into five subsets of equal size and sequentially each subset is tested using the classifier trained on the remaining (i.e. 4) subsets. Then, the parameters that reported the best performance were selected for training.

7   Patent Image Retrieval

During the retrieval process, the user can perform the following queries by using a dedicated user interface:

a) Content-based query: This query instantiates a patent image similarity search by using the query by visual example paradigm (i.e. by selecting an image and expecting visually similar results) [31]. This involves direct comparison of the generated feature vectors. Such comparison is usually implemented by means of a certain type of distance (e.g. L1 distance) between the vector of the example image and the corresponding vectors for the rest of the figures. Then, the images are sorted according to this distance and presented to the user. An example of a content-based patent image search query is shown in Figure 7 (section 8).

b) Text-based query: In this case the user is allowed to provide a set of keywords to perform full text search by exploiting the figure descriptions.

c) Concept-based query: The user selects a concept (from a predefined set) and retrieves images that are described by this concept. An example of a content-based patent image search query is shown in Figure 12 (section 8).

Finally, the user is capable of submitting a hybrid query, which combines the aforementioned functionalities based on late fusion (i.e. the results of the modules involved are merged)

8   Experiments and Evaluation

This section includes the description of experiments, in order to provide a qualitative and quantitative evaluation of the proposed framework. First we provide a qualitative evaluation of patent image retrieval by assuming real patent search scenarios in a large database. Then, we present a quantitative evaluation and a comparison of content-based and concept-based retrieval functionalities.

8.1   Qualitative Evaluation

With a view to providing a qualitative evaluation of the patent retrieval engine, we have uploaded around 320.000 images from about 15.000 patents from IPC G03F007/20 (relevant to lithography) extracted from MAREC database and performed specific patent search cases. Specifically we demonstrate two interaction modes by considering two patent search scenarios [32].

In the first scenario we have searched for similar images with an image included in the US 6,917,412B2. The results (Figure 7) include relevant prior art (marked with red) that would have been cited on the search report.

In the second patent search scenario we have executed an image similarity search with an image that is commonly used. The results in Figure 8 show many very similar images. By ordering these images on publication date we could analyse how this image evolves over time and answer questions such as: when a specific feature is introduced for the first time.

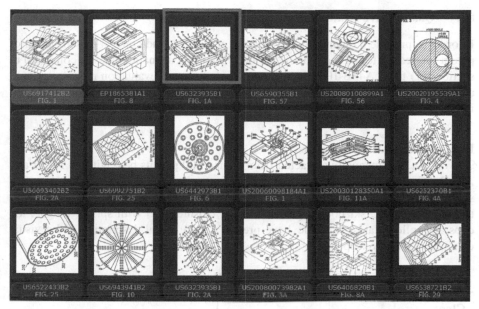

Fig. 7. Image similarity results for Figure 1A in US 6,323,935B1 patent

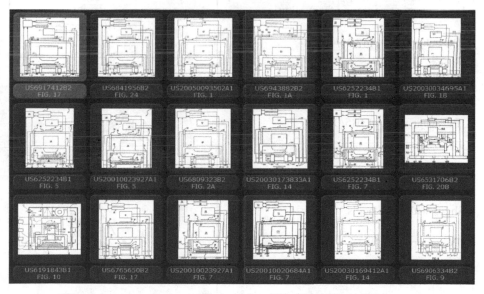

Fig. 8. Image similarity results for Figure 17 in US 6,917,412B2 patent

These and other similar tasks and results during the qualitative evaluation show that patent image retrieval is very useful in patent invalidation, patent valuation and competitive intelligence research.

8.2   Quantitative Evaluation

In order to provide a quantitative evaluation of content- and concept–based search of patent images we tested the proposed framework using a smaller dataset (compared to section 8.1) from A43B IPC class. Since the quantitative evaluation requires manual annotation of the dataset it was not possible to perform it using the dataset described in section 8.1.

Dataset and Selected Concepts.

The dataset was manually extracted from around 300 patents belonging to A43B and A63C IPC subclasses, which contain parts of footwear. Based on the advice of professional patent searchers in this domain we have selected the following 8 concepts for this domain: cleat, ski boot, high heel, lacing closure, heel with spring, tongue, toe caps and roller skates. In Table 1 we present a more detail description and a visual example of each concept.

Table 1. Concepts Description

Cleat A short piece of rubber, metal etc. attached to the bottom of a sports shoe used mainly for preventing someone from slipping IPC subgroup: A43B5/18S	
Ski boot A specially made boot that fastens onto a ski IPC subgroup: A43B5/04	
High Heel Shoes with high heels IPC group: A43B21	

Lacing closure A cord that is drawn through eyelets or around hooks in order to draw together the two edges of a shoe IPC subgroup: A43B5/04	
Spring Heel Heels with metal springs IPC subgroup: A43B21/30	
Tongue The part of a shoe that lies on top of your foot, under the part where you tie it IPC subgroup: A43B23/26	
Toe caps A reinforced covering of leather or metal for the toe of a shoe or boot IPC groups: A43B23 and A43B7	
Roller skate A shoe or boot with two or four wheels or casters attached to its sole for skating on hard surfaces IPC groups: A43B5 and A63C17	

The segmentation of patent images and the association with the figure descriptions in the text have been done manually in order to have quality data to draw safer conclusions on the concept extraction method. Then, the images were manually annotated with the support and advice of professional patent searchers. In case a figure can be described by two or more concepts (e.g. a figure that depicts the "lacing" system on a "ski boot"), the assignment is given with respect to the purpose that the specific figure serves (e.g. whether the aim to describe the "lacing" system or the "ski-boot"). The numerical statistics of the dataset3 can be found in the table 2.

---

3 The dataset can be downloaded at: http://mklab.iti.gr/files/concepts-patent_images.rar

Table 2. Dataset statistics

Concepts	Total figures	Train figures	Test figures
Cleat	148	89	59
Ski boot	123	74	49
High heel	148	89	59
Lacing	117	71	46
Spring	106	64	42
Tongue	124	75	49
Toe caps	108	65	43
Roller	168	101	67
Total	**1042**	**628**	**414**

Evaluation metrics.

To evaluate the performance of the proposed approach, we analyse the results by presenting the accuracy of the concept detectors, the precision and recall of the results and the F-Score. The accuracy of the concept detectors is calculated as:

$$A = \frac{TP + TN}{TP + TN + FP + FN}$$

where:

TP= True Positives, i.e. the relevant images that have been classified as relevant.

TN= True Negatives, i.e. the non-relevant images that have been classified as non-relevant.

FP= False Positives, i.e. the non-relevant images that have been classified as relevant.

FN= False Positives, i.e. the relevant images that have been classified as non-relevant.

In addition, we calculate F-score, precision and recall as follows:

$$F = \frac{2}{\frac{1}{Precision} + \frac{1}{Recall}}$$

in which, precision and recall are defined as follows:

$$Precision = \frac{TP}{TP + FP} \qquad Recall = \frac{TP}{TP + FN}$$

Results.

Table 3 reports the accuracy for each concept detector and training case (section 8.2).

Taking a first look on the results it seems that the accuracy of the three involved approaches is very high for all concepts. In most of the cases the best performance is demonstrated by the hybrid approach, while in general the textual features seem to outperform the visual ones.

Table 3. Accuracy of results

Concepts	Visual	Textual	Hybrid
cleat	91.06%	94.44%	94.93%
ski boot	94.69%	95.17%	97.10%
high_heel	93.96%	93.00%	96.86%
lacing closure	92.27%	91.06%	93.72%
heel with spring	93%	95.65%	94.44%
tongue	92.75%	98.07%	97.10%
toe caps	91.55%	94.20%	94.20%
roller skates	90.10%	95.17%	96.86%
Average	92.42%	94.60%	95.65%

Table 4. Precision, Recall and F-score for the concept detectors

Concepts	Visual			Textual			Hybrid		
	Prec.	Recall	F-score	Prec.	Recall	F-score	Prec.	Recall	F-score
cleat	84.4%	45.8%	59.3%	89.1%	69.5%	78.1%	89.6%	72.9%	80.4%
ski boot	84.6%	67.4%	75.0%	87.2%	69.4%	77.3%	93.0%	81.6%	86.9%
high_heel	82.7%	72.9%	77.5%	76.8%	72.9%	74.8%	92.6%	84.8%	88.5%
lacing closure	79.2%	41.3%	54.3%	63.6%	45.7%	53.2%	88.5%	50.0%	63.9%
heel with spring	69.7%	54.8%	61.3%	96.2%	59.5%	73.5%	100%	45.2%	62.3%
Tongue	75.7%	57.1%	65.1%	100%	83.7%	91.1%	95.1%	79.6%	86.7%
toe caps	60.5%	53.5%	56.8%	75.7%	65.1%	70.0%	70.2%	76.7%	73.3%
roller skates	82.5%	49.3%	61.7%	86.2%	83.6%	84.9%	96.6%	83.6%	89.6%
Average	77.4%	55.2%	63.9%	84.3%	68.7%	75.4%	90.7%	71.8%	78.9%

In this evaluation we consider the F-score as the most important metric to represent the performance as it depends both on precision and recall and it captures the overall performance. In addition, during the training procedure and by an appropriate selection of the parameters it would be possible to tune the system by focusing either on a high performance or recall. However, we agree that it would be important to include also the precision and the recall for our experiments. In Figure 9 we present a graph view of the F-score performance for each concept detector. It is clear that in most cases (six of the eight) the hybrid approach performs better compared to the other two. However, the textual features outperform the hybrid training for the concepts "lacing closure" and "tongue". On the other hand, textual-based results outperform the visual ones with only "high heels" and "lacing closure" being the exceptions.

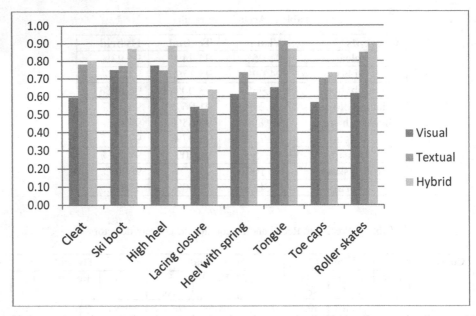

Fig. 9. F-score achieved by the employed concept-detectors

Moreover, in order to have a better insight of the results from the information retrieval perspective we also report the precision, recall and F-score metrics (Table 4).

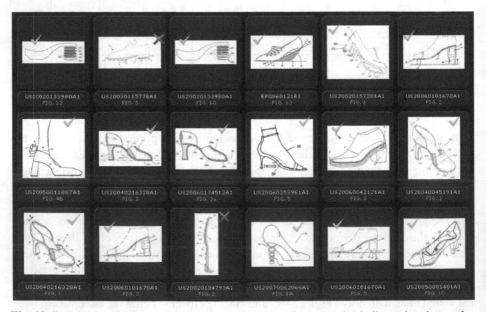

Fig. 10. Results for "high heels" using textual features. The green tics indicate that the results retrieved are correct while the red X indicate the wrong results.

Presentation of Visual Results.
In order to provide insights regarding the performance of the proposed framework, we illustrate visual results of the image retrieval and concept detection and report the precision in the first 18 results (P@18).

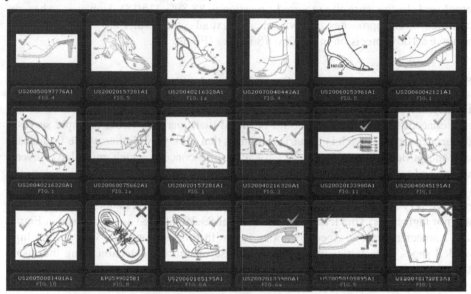

Fig. 11. Results for "high heels" using visual features. The green tics indicate that the results retrieved are correct while the red X indicate the wrong results.

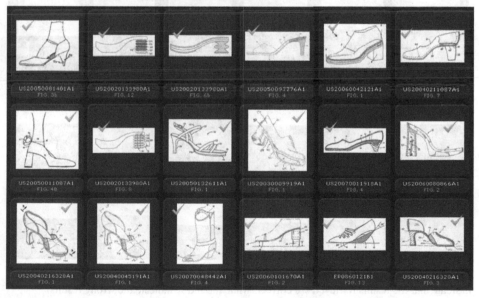

Fig. 12. Results for "high heels" using the hybrid approach. The green tics indicate that the results retrieved are correct.

In the first scenario we assume that the user is interested in retrieving figures depicting "high heels". In Figure 10 we present the first 18 results of the "high heel" concept detector using only textual features. In this case the P@18 achieved is 88.89% (16/18). In Figure 11, we present the first 18 results, when only visual features are employed. In this case the reported precision is 88.89% (16/18). However, when we combine both approaches (i.e. visual and textual), the results are improved as we achieve a 100% precision in the first 18 images (Figure 12).

8.3   Comparison of Concept-Based Retrieval with Image Similarity Search

Finally, we present a comparison between the query by visual example functionality and concept-based search. It should be noted that query by visual example serves a different purpose, which is to retrieve images that look very similar; while in the case of concept detection the user looks for a specific concept, which could have several visual and textual representations with common characteristics. Taking a look at the results after submitting a query by having a high heel as visual example, we indeed retrieve very similar images. However, the system still retrieves another 3 images that are not high-heels. This leads to a precision of 83.3% (15/18) as we can see in Figure 13. Another important aspect to notice is that in this case only the very similar high heeled shoes were retrieved, while in the case of concept detection using the visual features, a variance of high-heels with different orientations, perspectives etc. were retrieved due to the training with several high heels examples.

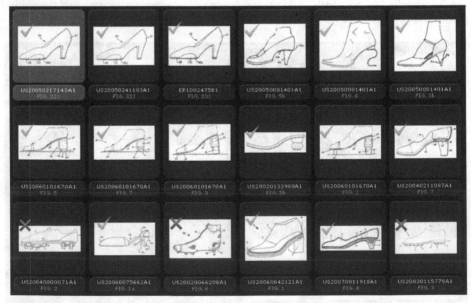

Fig. 13. Results for query by visual example when the query is a "high heel". The green tics indicate that the results retrieved are correct, while the red X indicate the wrong results.

9   Conclusions

This chapter describes an attempt to enhance patent search with content-based and concept-based image retrieval.

In the case of concept extraction, the experiments revealed that the combination of visual and textual information performs better, when compared to each single modality. Although most of the time the text-based classification provides very good results, the visual classification is also very satisfactory and in several cases necessary in order to correct and complete unavoidable text processing limitations. Specifically, it seems that on the one hand, the text-based classification could fail, when the textual description is not clear or it is incomplete, while on the other hand, visual based classification could fail when two visually similar images are described with different concepts. For instance, there are many patent documents, where the textual descriptions cannot automatically been assigned to the correct figures or they cannot be automatically translated, when they are written in certain foreign languages. With respect to scalability, the proposed method for concept detection is not expected to be very efficient in distinguishing among very large number of different concepts. This is because the performance (i.e. precision, recall) of the system is expected to decrease significantly due to visual similarity of conceptually different but visually similar concepts (e.g. concepts "wheel" and "disk"). However, the method can be scalable if we limit the concept detection/classification task within patents of the same IPC class, or group.

On the other hand, the employment of image search by visual similarity further speeds up the figure browsing tasks of patent searchers and in addition improves the recall (i.e. the number of returned results that are relevant to the input query) in patent search. Improving the recall of patent searches in emerging domains is crucial for avoiding cumbersome infringement-related litigations caused by inefficiencies in the patent search process.

It should be noted that all the patent image processing approaches (including this one) require prior segmentation of the drawing section pages to figures. Therefore, either automatic segmentation techniques could be applied, introducing, however, an error of around 20%, or manual segmentation, which is expensive in terms of time and human effort, could be performed. Another requirement of this method is that it requires training set and for each new concept introduced there is a need to have manually annotated images by experts.

Acknowledgements. This work was supported by PATExpert and MULTISENSOR projects, partially funded by the European Commission, under the contract numbers FP6-028116 and FP7-610411 respectively. The authors would also like to acknowledge the contribution of the COST Action IC1002 MUMIA (http://www.mumia-network.eu/).

References

1. List, J.: How Drawings Could Enhance Retrieval in Mechanical and Device Patent Searching. World Patent Information 29, 210–218 (2007)
2. Adams, S.: Electronic non-text material in patent applications—some questions for patent offices, applicants and searchers. World Patent Information 27(2), 99–103 (2005)
3. Zeng, Z., Zhao, J., Xu, B.: An Outward-Appearance Patent-Image Retrieval Approach Based on the Contour-Description Matrix. In: Proceedings of the 2007 Japan-China Joint Workshop on Frontier of Computer Science and Technology, pp. 86–99 (2007)
4. Codina, J., Pianta, E., Vrochidis, S., Papadopoulos, S.: Integration of Semantic, Metadata and Image Search Engines with a Text Search Engine for Patent Retrieval. In: Semantic Search 2008 Workshop, Tenerife, Spain (2008)
5. Vrochidis, S., Papadopoulos, S., Moumtzidou, A., Sidiropoulos, P., Pianta, E., Kompatsiaris, I.: Towards Content-based Patent Image Retrieval; A Framework Perspective. World Patent Information Journal 32(2), 94–106 (2010)
6. Tiwari, A., Bansal, V.: PATSEEK: Content Based Image Retrieval System for Patent Database. In: Proceedings of the International Conference on Electronic Business 2004, Tsinghua University, Beijing, China (2004)
7. Eakins, J.P.: Trademark Image Retrieval. In: Springer-Verlag Principles of Visual Information Retrieval. Berlin (2001)
8. Jain, A.K., Vailaya, A.: Shape-based Retrieval: A case study with trademark image databases. Pattern Recognition 31, 1369–1390 (1998)
9. Kim, Y.S., Kim, W.Y.: Content-based Trademark Retrieval System Using a Visually Salient Feature. Image and Vision Computing 16, 931–939 (1998)
10. Wu, J.K., Lam, C.P., Mehtre, B.M., Gao, Y.J., Desai Narasimhalu, A.: Content-based Retrieval for Trademark Registration. Multimedia Tools and Applications 3, 245–267 (1996)
11. Eakins, J.P., Boardman, J.M., Graham, M.E.: Similarity Retrieval of Trademark Images. IEEE Multimedia 5, 53–63 (1998)
12. Alwis, S., Austin, J.: Trademark Image Retrieval Using Multiple Features. In: Proceedings of the 1999 International Conference on Challenge of Image Retrieval (IM 1999), Newcastle-upon-Tyne, U.K. (1999)
13. Schietse, J., Eakins, J.P., Veltkamp, R.C.: Practice and Challenges in Trademark Image Retrieval. In: Proceedings of the 6th ACM International Conference on Image and Video Retrieval (CIVR), pp. 518–524 (2007)
14. LTU Technologies, http://www.ltutech.com/en/
15. eMARKS Project, http://emarks.iisa-innov.com/
16. Huet, B., Kern, N.J., Guarascio, G., Merialdo, B.: Relational Skeletons for Retrieval In Patent Drawings. In: ICIP 2001, vol. 2, pp. 737–740 (2001)
17. Zeng, Z., Zhao, J., Xu, B.: An Outward-Appearance Patent-Image Retrieval Approach Based on the Contour-Description Matrix. In: Proceedings of the 2007 Japan-China Joint Workshop on Frontier of Computer Science and Technology, pp. 86-89 (2007)
18. PATExpert (FP6-028116), http://www.patexpert.org/
19. Sidiropoulos, P., Vrochidis, S., Kompatsiaris, I.: Content-Based Binary Image Retrieval Using the Adaptive Hierarchical Density Histogram. Pattern Recognition Journal 44(4), 739–750 (2011)
20. Ypma, G.: Evaluation of Patent Image Retrieval. In: Information Retrieval Facility Symposium 2010 (IRFS 2010), Vienna, Austria (2010)

21. Yan, R., Hsu, W.: Recent Developments in Content-based and Concept-based Image/Video Retrieval. In: Proceedings of the 16th ACM International Conference on Multimedia (MM 2008), New York, USA (2008)
22. Mörzinger, R., Horti, A., Thallinger, G., Bhatti, N., Hanbury, A.: Classifying Patent Images. In: Proceedings of CLEF 2011, Amsterdam (2011)
23. Csurka, G., Renders, J., Jacquet, G.: XRCE's Participation at Patent Image Classification and Image-based Patent Retrieval Tasks of the Clef-IP 2011. In: Proceedings of CLEF 2011, Amsterdam (2011)
24. Vrochidis, S., Moumtzidou, A., Kompatsiaris, I.: Concept-based Patent Image Retrieval. World Patent Information Journal 34(4), 292–303 (2012)
25. De Marco, D.: Mechanical Patent Searching: A Moving Target. In: Patent Information Users Group (PIUG), Baltimore, USA (2010)
26. Hoenes, F., Lichter, J.: Layout Extraction of Mixed Mode Documents. Mach. Vision Appl. 7, 237–246 (1994)
27. Porter, M.F.: An Algorithm for Suffix Stripping. Program 14(3), 130–137 (1980)
28. The Lemur Toolkit lemur, http://www.cs.cmu.edu/
29. Boser, B.E., Guyon, I.M., Va, V.N.: A Training Algorithm for Optimal Margin Classifiers. In: Proceedings of the 5th Annual Workshop on Computational Learning Theory (COLT 1992), pp. 144–152. ACM Press, New York (1992)
30. Chang, C., Lin, C.: LIBSVM: A Library for Support Vector Machines. Software available at: http://www.csie.ntu.edu.tw/~cjlin/libsvm
31. Izquierdo, E., Casas, J., Leonardi, R., Migliorati, P., O'Connor, N., Kompatsiaris, I., Strintzis, M.G.: Advanced Content-Based Semantic Scene Analysis and Information Retrieval: The Schema Project. In: Proceedings Workshop on Image Analysis for Multimedia Interactive Services, London, UK, pp. 519–528 (2003)
32. Vrochidis, S., Moumtzidou, A., Ypma, G., Kompatsiaris, I.: PatMedia: Augmenting Patent Search with Content-based Image Retrieval. In: Proceedings of the 5th IRF Conference, Austria, Vienna (2012)

Author Index